Unforgettable

A Love and Spiritual Growth Story

Michael Skowronski

© Copyright 2007 Michael Skowronski
All rights reserved. No part of this publication may be reproduced, stored in a retrieval system, or transmitted, in any form or by any means, electronic, mechanical, photocopying, recording, or otherwise, without the written prior permission of the author.

Note for Librarians: A cataloguing record for this book is available from Library and Archives Canada at www.collectionscanada.ca/amicus/index-e.html
ISBN 1-4120-9273-6

Printed in Victoria, BC, Canada. Printed on paper with minimum 30% recycled fibre.
Trafford's print shop runs on "green energy" from solar, wind and other environmentally-friendly power sources.

TRAFFORD
PUBLISHING

Offices in Canada, USA, Ireland and UK

Book sales for North America and international:
Trafford Publishing, 6E–2333 Government St.,
Victoria, BC V8T 4P4 CANADA
phone 250 383 6864 (toll-free 1 888 232 4444)
fax 250 383 6804; email to orders@trafford.com

Book sales in Europe:
Trafford Publishing (UK) Limited, 9 Park End Street, 2nd Floor
Oxford, UK OX1 1HH UNITED KINGDOM
phone +44 (0)1865 722 113 (local rate 0845 230 9601)
facsimile +44 (0)1865 722 868; info.uk@trafford.com

Order online at:
trafford.com/06-1027

10 9 8 7 6 5 4 3 2

Table of Contents

An Invitation... 1
Preface 2
Dance 7
First Date 12
Fireworks 22
Second Date 31
A Policed Affair 35
Nearly Living Together 40
A Long Distance Relationship 43
Lives Merge 53
Isaiah Our First Master 60
Psychic Answers to Health Issues 67
Our First Reiki Experiences 70
Trouble in Paradise 72
Past Life Regressions 78
A Birthday Gift from Spirit 80
An Amazing Healing 82
A Christmas Gift to Remember 85
Spontaneous Past Life Memories 89
Many Changes 94
Be Careful What You Ask For 124
A New Chapter Begins 138
Amoram Our Second Master 144
A Unique Wedding 152
The Invisible Woman 155
Releasing Our Sharp Corners 161
Ali the Psychic Dog 175
Massage School 179
Temptation Rears Her Lovely Head 182
A Shocking Turn of Events 185

Surgery	196
Chemotherapy	205
Women's Apprenticeship Group Acquires a Man	213
Memories	222
Healing Separation between Healers	227
Radiating and Reflecting	230
Facing Rejection	238
Coming to Acceptance	244
Back Pains, Again!?!	251
Hawaii	264
What Do I Feel?	270
Community	282
Christmas 1997	289
Super Pooper	291
Nausea Returns	295
Lessons in Energy	303
Dead Dogs Don't Lie	305
The End of Summer	311
Farwell Dear Friend	317
The End	319
Opportunities for Further Studies	320

An Invitation...

"Have you ever seen a child who has separated himself from his friends, because of some perceived offence or slight injury that occurred during play? With the injured one pouting, or crying, or in some way trying to drag the others down. The others simply say, 'Come on, let's play.' And when the injured one does not respond do the others not run off and continue on with their fun and games? There is not a grand discussion. There is no begging and coaxing, 'Let's all sit down and fix this problem. What can we do to make you feel better?'

"No, there is only an open invitation, 'You can join us when you are ready.' It is spontaneous, it is playful and it is light. They simply go off to play. Adults can learn much from this natural way of being. Life is a game. It is meant to be fun. Pain and injury happen. But you don't have to sit in it any longer than you choose. And choose you may, how long you wish to sulk and pout, and when it is you wish to join your friends to play."
\- Amoram

I used to want to change the world...I would talk to it, manipulate it, shame it, and even force it if necessary. I thought the world needed to change; it was obvious, and everyone else seemed to agree.

Today, I have come to understand the perfection of the world just as it is. I have experienced that this world eventually delivers whatever I truly desire. I am not unique; I am not special, and I know this is true for you too. Thus, I am inviting you to come and discover how we create our world, our reality, our experience. For this world is not meant to contain only one experience; it is meant to contain and offer all possibilities of experiences.

This is an invitation to come and play in the playground of possibilities. This is an invitation to put aside your beliefs and ideas about life for a little while and to open up to playing with new ideas and new possibilities...why not, what do you have to lose?

This book is based on a true story, an era of my life, time spent with masterful people. It transformed me in ways for which I will forever be grateful.

This is a love story. This is not only a love story between a man and a woman, but a love story between creation and Creator, between humanity and God. I hope that you fall in love while reading this story...fall in love with Life, fall in love with All That Is, fall in love with Yourself!

Come, play with us....

Preface

One thing that Amoram and Isaiah taught us was that time is not linear. At the time they taught us this, I did not understand what they meant nor can I regurgitate the actual words they spoke; however, I am coming to understand what they meant from experience.

This book is based on a "true story." How true can a story be? Most people would think a video of the live event would be the true story, but if you had a video of the events that occurred during the period of time this book covers, my story and the video's story would not exactly match. While reviewing Kathryn's and my journals and trying to make this story as accurate as possible, I found discrepancies between what I remembered and what was written down. A couple of times the order of events, as I remembered them, was different from the journals and transcripts. Is this what Amoram meant when he said time is not linear?

In my mind, the events fell into order in certain ways. I heard what I heard, regardless of what was said. Thus, my reality is my reality, and at times it is different than the external events that actually occurred. My point is there is much more going on in life than meets the eye, or our other senses. Masters tell us we create our own reality, but the average person does not understand what that means, and they stay firmly entrenched in their physical perception of life. People need to soften their ideas and beliefs about what is real and what is possible for there to be expansion. If you begin with admitting that there is much more to learn about life, something that right now seems mystical and magical, and that there are some things that you just don't understand, this will create the opening that is necessary within you. You will learn so much more about "truth" if you will only do this.

So, this story is true for me. It is my experience. Kathryn had a different one. Some of the other people mentioned in this book had their own unique experiences. At one point I had the book finished and was ready for publication until I sought out permission from these people to use their true names and the actual transcripts from the teachings we received. But I encountered great resistance, "You think this is accurate? You think this is a true story?" This as well as other unmentionable things were said in response to my truth. One of my teachers also had her own plans for publishing her own transcripts and chose to retain her copyright as well as wanting her name left out of the book. I was surprised because I figured she would get good publicity for whatever works she did publish due to the popularity of this book.

Because of this I decided to change everyone's name, except my own. I also changed some locations, settings, and names of organizations

Preface

such as the churches to further protect the identities of those individuals who wished to remain anonymous. And because I had to go back and rewrite the transcripts from one teacher I also rewrote the transcripts of the other as well. In rewriting the transcripts I kept the basic themes, but came up with my own wording and different metaphors that fit the theme. In most cases I left the precise wording of questions and responses that Kathryn and I spoke, but the answers from the teachers were reworded. I feel that the true meaning and impact was not lost in these changes, indeed I feel that I was able to clarify the message, however the changes were significant enough to prevent this book from offending those involved and to protect myself from lawsuits.

As you will soon discover, this book is quite revealing, especially of my own personality and state of mind at the time. I do not mind that it made my past personality look bad. As one person said, "I did not always like your character." As the story will show I did not always like myself either. Too many people believe they are stuck with their personality and often say, "That is just how I am." Yet I felt the truth needed to be presented as accurately as possible so that I could demonstrate how much change a person can undergo. So at first I was deeply disappointed that I had to make these changes to the book. But once I got into it, I realized that I had the chance to clarify the parts of the transcripts that were unclear or confusing. I also had the chance to expand them and fill in the gaps with teachings that I did not have in transcript form but that had settled into my being as a result of time and practice.

Although I had to make some minor changes to the parts of those who are still living, the events that occurred between Kathryn and me were not changed. While reading through journals, I had to face the differences between my experience and what was recorded in our journals. In this book, there is only one small case that I knowingly left the events ordered as they occurred in my mind rather than as the journals lead me to believe. In this case, I did not have enough notes to be conclusive about the actual timing of events, but I suspect that my memory was incorrect due to the notes I do have. Still, the events had a big impact on me, and they came together in my mind in the way I tell it in this book, and real learning occurred as a result. Time is not linear.

As a result of the experiences related in this book, and of those that occurred over the four years that followed, I have achieved a level of enlightenment that I, as I was in this unforgettable era of my life, could have only hoped for yet not fully believed I would achieve in this lifetime. Now, however, I have discovered new goals, a higher level of enlightenment I wish to achieve, goals that most people would say are unachievable, but I know they are within my grasp. I am not saying this to make myself important or special in some way. I am a leader, an example, a fellow human being who has unmistakably discovered the

Divinity within by following the teachings of the Masters who have gone before us. I honor those Masters as well as the Master that lives in you. It is my greatest hope that in some way I can help to awaken you to this same awareness, to lead you back to knowing who you really are.

I want to stress this point because so many people get caught up in religion and rituals and then move on with their life without doing anything real to take control of it and become aware. No one is going to do it for you. All of us can and will become enlightened beings at some point in time. All of us...this means you too! You can run, but you cannot hide. One day you will become tired and bored chasing approval from others and having every desire in your life fulfilled. Then you will have much work to undo all of the silliness that you allowed to be programmed into your mind and personality between now and then. You have a lot of nonsense programmed in your subconscious already. Why add more? Why not get on with it and begin to become aware now. Start with this book if you will. Read it carefully, especially when you get to the transcripts, and take the time to contemplate what you read and ask yourself, "How does this apply to my life?"

This is a love story as well as a spiritual growth story. Kathryn and I had a powerful and loving relationship. Many people looked at us and admired and wanted what we had. We evolved over time. In the end I fell in love with myself. This is a big key to becoming enlightened; you must love yourself before it will occur. We let other people take away our self esteem and teach us how little and unimportant we are. Kathryn helped me to understand that I was loveable, even though my actions were not always loveable. In many ways, I respected her as a Master of Love; she was definitely my teacher. She knew me well, including all of my faults, and this Master still loved me. That is something big—very big. I know you will find that love for yourself too, I know you will find it.

Although it was my intention to make this book entertaining, my primary intention is to show you what is possible. The spiritual teachings contained in this book are the most valuable thing I have learned in my life, far more valuable than any other life skill. As a software engineer, I earned a huge income. I have learned many healing arts. I am also a skilled and qualified professional photographer. I have learned to use my body with great dexterity; surfing, skating, skiing, dancing, and much more. I have lived in four different countries, experiencing these cultures, and traveled to many others. With all that I have learned and experienced, I still claim that there is no other study that a person can participate in that will have greater value and impact than studying one's self and true spiritual principals. These principals govern our everyday life and form our reality. By becoming aware, by learning how life works, we no longer stumble around in the dark frustrated and angry that life is not giving us what we need. Life is always giving us what we need, we just don't understand because we are not paying attention. Pay attention.

It is time for people to move past their beliefs. To say, "I believe," is the same as saying, "I do **not** know from personal experience, but I have chosen some arbitrary story or explanation." Unfortunately most people stop there and solidify their beliefs in their mind. They stick with their beliefs and defend them and close their mind to other possibilities. But Masters insist that we can "know." I have studied the life and teachings of many enlightened Masters. Although their paths and techniques differ, there is a common theme in their teachings and the ultimate outcome is the same. The Masters tell us if we watch our minds, consciously choose our thoughts, evaluate the results and the feelings we are left with after thinking our thoughts, that we will come to know and eventually become enlightened and fully self-realized Masters ourselves. They tell us ultimately we will discover that we are one with all of life and that we too are God.

People want proof. I know that I do. I was not satisfied with the beliefs, superstitions and dogma of religions. Often people see a miracle and then go about worshiping the person whom the miracle occurred through. These people have TOTALLY missed the point!!! This is a lazy and immature personality trait that many people have adopted. People do insane and harmful things; mostly they do not realize it. These people deserve compassion and love because they are walking through life deaf, dumb and blind. Sadly, this describes most of humanity. When someone claims to be enlightened, we want them to prove it. So what if someone else can perform miracles; if you can't do it, what is the use? The proof is not in them, it is in you. You must prove their claims by trying out new ways of thinking and practicing the exercises they have given.

The wisdom given in this book can lead you to enlightenment; however, you must try these things and experience them for yourself. This is the nature of life; knowledge comes from experience. Even the failures and living with false beliefs give you experience, because ultimately, truth prevails and illusions unravel. The knowledge that comes from books and other people must be applied in your own life before it becomes real knowledge in you. If you have enough life experience it is possible to take the knowledge of others and use it to reevaluate your life experience and improve your own personal wisdom, but still life will present you the chance to practice and prove to yourself your new knowledge. Before this occurs, it is only theory.

I expose many personal things in this book that most people would not, such as my private thoughts and activities that occurred between my wife and myself. I do this so that you can understand how insidious the mind is. My hope is that when you read about the mistakes we made and how they were ultimately corrected, and you relate them to your own life, you will come to understand life more clearly and advance in your own enlightenment.

Earlier in my experience of life, I wanted to change the world so that I could feel safe living in it. But with enlightenment, comes the awareness that we are totally safe. Now I want to change the world because I love It, because I love You. I am telling you these things in hopes you take me, and all of the other Masters who have walked this planet, seriously. Surely there will be those who crucify me for such statements; I am taking this risk of being ridiculed and scorned in hopes that you the reader will be motivated to take control of your mind and energies. Stop watching so much TV; stop reading the news so often; you are only studying with ignorant teachers when you do so. You become hypnotized by their emotionally charged movements of energy and blind to that which is real. Start following the advice of the Masters. You have much better than TV inside of your own mind! You can create far better things than that sitcom or violent show that so many are watching. Exercise your creativity. Learn to take control of your mind and emotions, and ultimately even the external world in which you live.

There is a lot of pain in this story. But if that is all you see, then you are missing the point. No matter how much pain and suffering was occurring in our lives due to outer circumstances, Kathryn and I found our way through the pain and grew as a result. When awareness finally occurs, one realizes that the pain it took to get there was worth it. When total awareness occurs, one realizes that he himself is the one who caused his own pain.

It is with love for You, who are a part of Me, that I dedicate this book. It is because of my love for God that I love You because I know that You are God. Please enjoy this "Unforgettable" story and discover the Love that is inside of you.

Dance

June 1991—I was thirty-two years old.

As I walked through the doors of the classroom I was pleasantly surprised to see what looked like eighty people, perhaps more, for the East-Coast Swing class. I looked around the room and took it all in, then I thought, *There are a lot of women here; maybe I'll meet someone special. Julie will be pleased with this turn out. Julie will be pleased with me.*

I introduced Julie to the singles group coordinator at the Spiritual Life Center (SLC). They had a huge number of single people that attended the church and various workshops. I told Julie that this would be a good move for her and her business. Yet neither Julie nor I was expecting this many people, so her income turned out to be larger than she expected. I knew that she could use the money, and I bet she even picked up a few serious students from the class. At this point I had been taking private dance lessons from Julie for nearly six months. I was surprised and happy when she asked me to be her assistant for the class...I wanted to attend, but the class was too easy for me. Helping her out was the perfect way for me to participate.

As I looked around the room, I noticed a number of cute women and two that I was particularly attracted to. Since there were more ladies in the class than men, which was usually the case, I got to dance with the ladies. East-Coast Swing is one of the dances that I had learned well, and I had a lot of fun with it. I felt this gave me an advantage in catching the attention of an attractive lady.

I wanted to meet a woman who was just as interested in her spiritual growth as I was...she had to be sincerely trying to become aware. One who was not caught up and stuck with dogmatic religious beliefs. I wanted my life partner to understand that growth and awareness required that her beliefs change with time as Life[1] reveals more of Itself to her. This class seemed like it would be a perfect opportunity for me. I had been looking forward to it ever since Julie received approval for the class from the church. At the time, I thought that meeting the right woman was a matter of numbers, the more women I could meet, the better my chances for meeting that one special person.[2] There were lots of dance classes in the Portland area; however, given the nature of this particular church, I believed that these women were more

---

[1] I use capitalization like this to indicate that "Life" is another way of referring to God.

[2] This is what I believed at that time in my life. As I continued to experience life and grow in awareness I realized that attracting a mate, or creating anything for that matter, was more about desire and being clearly open to receiving, and being in sync with our Source.

interested in spiritual truth and were less likely to be stuck in religious dogma.

There was a group of people from SLC that met up once or twice each weekend at the dances. There was usually more than one dance venue to choose from on any given night. When it was left up to chance, our group would get scattered, thus I was left to dance with old ladies or women who I had no connection with except for dance. So I decided to organize the group, collecting phone numbers and calling people, so that we all made it to the same dance. Even though I had not yet met "Miss Right" from this small group, I was having a lot of fun and had high hopes. There were plenty of nice, attractive women to dance with; we had more things in common for conversation and it gave me the chance to flirt and polish my dance skills.

My wife Maria left me ten months earlier. I missed having a woman in my life, in my bed, as a friend and partner. Like most things I go after in life, I pursued finding another relationship with determination and passion. I hate it when people say, "Aren't you just a little bit desperate? Shouldn't you be giving it some time before you get yourself into another relationship?" In my mind I would scream, *Shouldn't you mind your own business?!?*

One of the downsides of our info age is all the junior therapists running around. They think they have this psychology thing down pat from what they have read, yet what do they really know about life from their personal experience? Funny thing is…I was a bit like that myself.

A few months after Maria left me, my friend Joanne introduced me to her girlfriend Sarah who also had just become single. Joanne warned us both not to get involved, as if she was the expert in relationships. Come on; what else was she introducing us for? Sarah and I had a short relationship, lasting only about a month. It was nice to have someone to cuddle with and make love to. We both enjoyed it for what it was, and there were no head trips later. Since that time, I kept myself busy exploring the variety of things there were to do in this city. Powel's bookstore was one of my favorite places to hang out; I liked to read in their coffee shop. I wanted social contact, opportunities to both enjoy an activity and have a chance to meet women.

Many months earlier, shortly before I began dance lessons, I tried placing personal ads in the Willamette Week, Portland's weekly alternate newspaper. I had tried running personal ads years earlier; that was about a year after my first wife, Kat, left me. Although my prior personal ad experience did not result in a long term relationship,[1] I did meet a few women, had a few dates, and even some hot sex. Even though I was half

---

[1] I met my second wife Maria at a dance, not through a personal ad.

expecting similar results, I had high hopes, and it beat being alone so much of the time. So I gave the personal ads another try. Because of the intensity of my search and the resulting experiences, I was learning just how many different kinds of women were out there.

Ever since Maria left me, I attended Wednesday and Sunday services at SLC and went to a few weekend workshops. I was devouring all I could about spirituality and trying to be more awake and aware. This was a very sincere desire within me; at the time I had no idea just how powerful this desire was. But now I give that desire credit for the story that is about to unfold for you…do continue to read on. There is much to discover here about the mysteries and majesty of Life.

In October 1990, I started attending "A Course in Miracles" (ACIM) a couple of times a week. I was reading the text book and doing the daily lessons in the work book. ACIM is a bit difficult to read and understand for many people. With intense focus, I was able to understand a lot of it;[1] at that time ACIM was a powerful influence in my understanding of life. Many things the book taught, I intuitively knew; it fit. Many things the book taught I did not know, so I took it in as a concept to be explored and proven. It was a delight for me to be able to answer the questions of those who were struggling with the material. Most people seemed to enjoy what I had to offer; some did not. My ego enjoyed being special. I enjoyed engaging in spiritual debates and trying to convert people to seeing the light. It is funny how I did not realize that this kind of separation is just what ACIM was trying to wake us up to seeing.

It was in January, 1991, that I decided to start taking dance lessons. I first went to a West-Coast Swing class: group lessons. I then moved on to taking a private lesson with Julie each week. It was not long before I was taking four to twelve hours of group lessons and one to three hours of privates per week. One weekend I went to a dance workshop that was held on the Oregon Coast. Eating, sleeping, working, studying and dancing that was all I was doing with my time. This was not unusual behavior for me, being a Scorpio I become intensely involved in everything I do.

I found that learning to dance was a bit difficult at first. There was so much to remember, and I had to put all of my focus into each step. Flowing with the music and paying attention to my partner was the last thing on my mind. I believe that many people who think they are poor learners don't realize that repetition is the key. When we were babies learning to walk, we did not do it right the first time. We all fell down many times, but we got up and kept on trying. We had no judgments

---

[1] I understood with my mind, but in many ways direct experience was missing.

about being stupid for falling down. It is the same with anything, including dance. Each exposure to a new dance became less of a struggle because of other dances I had already learned, but still, each one had its challenging moments. Each new style I learned had a ripple effect across all of the other styles I had already learned; each lesson helped me improve all that I had learned. I would practice my steps at home, counting and walking through each of them many times until my body had learned the movements. It takes repetition for things to become automatic. It took only a few months before I could pay attention to my partner and begin to piece each move together in a nice flowing dance. Julie helped me to polish the rough edges off of my posture and improve my style and ability to lead.

As the lessons at SLC continued on, some of the students, including me, started to go out to one of the local bars after class to practice. The bar had a tiny dance floor, yet it was large enough for our small group. This was when I got to really talk with Kathryn; she was one those two women that I found attractive. I talked to the other cute woman from the class too, but we didn't click at all. However with Kathryn…I was enjoying every single encounter. When I would organize the group for the weekend dances, I would make a special point to invite Kathryn personally.

Once Kathryn showed up at a dance, I spent most of my time dancing with her, mostly ignoring the other women there. Kathryn was just a beginner and she limited the things I could do and experience on the dance floor. I had the desire to mingle; I wanted to practice some of the more advanced moves I knew with the other women who could dance well. But I could not walk away from Kathryn. It felt too good to be with her. The feeling was magical and whimsical. One Sunday evening, I met Kathryn at a tavern. This tavern had a live band every other Sunday; the band was well liked by the dancers for swing and ballroom dancing.

I was a recovering drug addict so I did not drink alcohol. I was nearly four years clean and sober. On that evening I was drinking sweet Italian sodas. Each time I would order a drink, Kathryn would order a glass of wine, we each had four that night. After some time had passed I noticed that Kathryn was getting a bit drunk. I thought it was funny because she did not seem like that kind of gal. It was not until many months later that she told me that she thought I was ordering alcoholic drinks and she was trying to keep up with me. We both got a good laugh out of it, by then I knew her well enough to know how out of character it was for her to drink like that.

Kathryn and I were both being silly and playful. I lavished Kathryn with attention, fanning her to keep her cool and popping freshly peeled grapes into her mouth. We had a wonderful time; I did not want that evening to end.

A few days later, after one of the SLC dance classes, while we were out dancing, I gathered up my courage to ask Kathryn out on a date. By that point in my life I was not so nervous to ask a woman out. With Kathryn, I even felt pretty confident that she would say yes, but I liked her so much that I had some fear that she might say no. When I asked, "Kathryn, I'm going to go hiking up to the top of Multnomah Falls on the Fourth of July...I...I was wondering if you would like to go with me?"

Kathryn's response was immediate. She did not hesitate to think about it at all; she simply said, "Yes."

The next part was a bit awkward. I explained to Kathryn, "On the way to dance class tonight, one of the cylinders in my car just stopped working...just tonight! I was so upset when it happened because I was planning on asking you out. I worried about taking you out in a lame car. The car is still working but I am not sure what will happen with it. Would you mind driving? I can make a picnic lunch for us." Again without hesitation, Kathryn agreed.

As I drove home, I was so excited and happy; I was bursting at the seams. I got very little sleep and fantasized all night long about how nice this date was going to be. I loved getting such an enthusiastic response from Kathryn. My mind was filled with fantasies of being with her, kissing her all over, and making love to her. I replayed many scenes of that evening over again in my mind...Kathryn accepting my invitation to go hiking...slow dancing on the dance floor...laughing and joking...holding her in my arms. I dreamed of how a future with this woman might be; the very thought of it filled me with joy. Was it possible that I had found the love I had been looking for?

First Date

On Thursday the Fourth of July, 1991, Kathryn and I had our first date. Even though she accepted my invitation to meet me out dancing, those were group functions that I invited all of the dancers to. This was our first official date.

It was a warm and beautiful summer day. Kathryn found the door to my unit wide open when she arrived to pick me up. I was in the kitchen dancing while I was preparing our picnic lunch; I had the music turned way up. I felt so good that I could not keep my feet still. My Blue-Front Amazon parrot was on top of his cage. He was dancing and acting silly too. I could tell that Kathryn was unaccustomed to the circumstances and what she discovered when she arrived. After all, men were supposed to pick up women, and the women were supposed to prepare the meals. She did not know what to make of my parrot, who tried to bite her when I introduced him to her.

With our lunch packed, we headed out the door. I was taken by surprise when I saw her car, it was a BMW. I couldn't say no when Kathryn asked me to drive it to the falls. She explained to me, "This is not my choice of car. My ex-husband just brought this home one day and told me it was my new car. I will be trading it in on a Honda Accord soon." I knew very little about BMW, except that they were expensive. I knew much more about the Honda Accord, and I liked it. I was impressed with her style and apparent financial abundance.

In the half-hour it took to drive to Multnomah Falls, I told Kathryn about my past struggles with drug abuse and my recovery program. "I started smoking pot when I was eighteen years old. When I reached age twenty-one, I tried LSD, speed, cocaine, and a few other drugs. I married my first wife, Kat, in August of 1982. I was nearly twenty-four. Kat was very much into cocaine, and though I preferred marijuana, I also enjoyed cocaine. Kat wanted it much more often than I did."

Kathryn asked, "Didn't that cost a lot of money?"

I replied, "Yes. I tried to keep up with her cocaine consumption, mostly because it did cost a lot of money, and I did not think it was fair for her to spend so much without me having the same treat too. By that time I had my own business selling my software to precious metal brokerage firms and customizing it. I was making very good money and could afford cocaine...so I thought."

"This marriage was doomed to failure. We were both immature. Kat was four years younger than me and had a lot of emotional problems.

The cocaine, marijuana, and alcohol just made everything worse. Kat and I started selling cocaine to help support our habit, and Kat would often pinch a little...actually a lot of our stash, and consume it herself when I was not around. We fought about this and other things often. Sometimes our fighting would get a little bit violent. I would get so angry...I knew I needed to leave the house for a while to calm down or soon I would end up hitting her. When I tried to drive off, Kat would get into the car or sit on the hood. If I tried to walk away, she would follow me in the car. This prompted me to buy a motorcycle, since we did not have the money for a second car.

"One time I was trying to escape on my motorcycle and Kat followed me in the car. I drove down a narrow road knowing that she could not easily turn the car around. I planned on making a U-turn and losing her. Once I had gotten a fair way down the road I turned my motorbike around and started to drive off. Kat got out of the car and jumped right into my way, causing me to spill my bike. That was it...that was all I could take. I punched her a few times in the stomach and chest before she backed off and told me to leave...not too hard, but enough to let her know I meant business."

"Had you ever hit her before?" Kathryn asked with noticeable concern in her voice.

"Yes, under similar circumstances," I replied, "but this one was the most extreme. That was the last time I saw Kat for nearly three months. I went and stayed the night with a friend, when I returned home I found a message on our answering machine telling me that she flew off to Orange County California. We originally met in Southern California...Kat and I moved to Oregon in June of '83. At least she was nice enough to leave me a message telling me where I could find the car."

I continued with my story, "Before Kat left, we had just started smoking freebase cocaine on a regular basis."

"What is freebase cocaine?" Kathryn inquired.

"You've heard of crack, right?"

"Yes, but what is that?"

"Freebase and crack are really the same thing. There is a process to change the cocaine from a water soluble form into an oily form that won't dissolve in water. It is a better experience...it's cleaner to smoke that way. Snorting it had become too hard on my nasal passages, but in the form of freebase, I became much more addicted to it. I had become just like Kat[1]...just as desperate for base as she was for cocaine. I finally understood her selfish desire to take more than her share.[2] One evening, this was after Kat left me, I had loaded my pipe with a super big hit of the freebase. The pipe was still hot from my last hit, and so it would begin draining down the stem and escaping as smoke very soon. That translates to an expensive loss so I needed to begin taking my hit quickly. After dropping the rocks into the pipe I noticed that my small torch had run low on butane. I grabbed the large torch that I rarely used because it was too dangerous. I was sitting on the floor with a bean bag chair to lean up against. There was a small round exercise trampoline just to the right and a little bit in front of me." I motioned and pointed with my hands to indicate where all of these things were as I drove and described all of this to Kathryn. "I lit the large torch and set it down at the far end of the trampoline, just barely within reach. Then I lit the small torch and consumed that large hit of cocaine with a shallow toke, which I quickly exhaled, and a then I took second longer and deeper toke...essentially I quickly put a lot of drug into my system. After those intense hits I lay back on the bean bag to relax and enjoy."

"When I opened my eyes and sat back up, I found that the back of my right leg, from just above the ankle to three inches below my knee, had been burnt."

I tried to show Kathryn the scar on the back of my right leg, but I was driving. There was panic in her voice when she said, "Please, just drive. I can see it later."

"The scar is quite noticeable." I continued, "You won't be able to miss it. Anyway, the large torch was lying on the ground about a foot further away than I could reach. There was a large burn streak on the carpet that ran from the torch in the direction toward my burnt leg, but it did not go all the way to my leg. The back of my leg looked like a burnt marshmallow with a large black bubble where my skin used to be. I couldn't feel it...it didn't hurt because I was so wasted from the cocaine I had been smoking.

"I sat in amazement...wondering, 'How did this happen? Did I spaz out, kick the trampoline, and send the torch tumbling toward my leg burning the carpet and my leg as it blew itself out?' That did not seem possible; the distance was too great with no burn marks in between where the torch would have started tumbling and where it stopped. 'Was

---

[1] If you pay attention, you will often find yourself expressing the very same energies as someone you judge. It may take time, but sooner or later it you may find yourself doing the same thing you judged another person for doing.

[2] This is often the way we develop compassion, by living a difficult situation ourselves. Once we have recovered from our errors, we have valuable experiences and awareness that empower us in many ways.

there someone else in the house who attacked me with the torch?' I took another hit, checked the house over to make sure no one was watching me, and then I washed my leg with cold water and put some disinfectant on it."

"Is that when you finally stopped doing drugs?" Kathryn inquired.

"No, it was nearly a year longer before I got myself straightened out. From that point on, I would always get major paranoia when smoking freebase cocaine. With each hit came about thirty seconds of ecstasy and five or ten minutes of paranoid searching of my house. I would look in the most ridiculous places, behind doors, under the sofa and bed, out the window. There were times that I would take such a big hit that the floor and walls would move. No matter where I sat or stood, it would be falling out from underneath me. When I sat on the sofa, I felt like I was sinking into it, like it was swallowing me whole. This was absolutely terrifying.

"At one point I had just purchased a major quantity of cocaine. After smoking a fair amount, I decided that I was tired of all of the people who were spying on me so I packed up my computer, some clothes, and of course my drugs and headed for Orange County. I had many clients down there, one in particular owed me about $2,000...but first I had to complete their project, which had been running late due to a slight distraction. I had never driven though the eastern part of Oregon so I decided to take that route. I stopped at a Native American Indian resort to stay the night and get high in peace. This did not work so well because the spies followed me there, I could not understand why they were being so persistent. After a few too many hits of cocaine, I began getting paranoid again and started making a lot of noise and calling for help. I thought that would scare away the people who were watching me.

"It did not take long for security to show up at my door to see what the problem was. When they did, I quickly flushed about $700 worth of cocaine down the toilet and broke my glass pipes and tried to flush them too. The security officers were very suspicious; they even noticed the glass in the toilet. They did not do anything however, just asked me to keep it quiet. After a couple of hours of torture, wanting more, I got the first good night of sleep I had gotten in many days."

A bit worried, Kathryn interrupted my story with a question, "You were quite a mess! How long have you been off of the drugs?"

"I have been totally clean and sober for nearly four years, four years in November. I have not had an urge to have drugs or alcohol for nearly three years now, with the exception of the night that Maria told me she was leaving me but I will get to that later.

"So after that night at the Indian resort, my drive down to Orange County was uneventful and a really nice change of pace. I felt I was free of the spies...I could see no one following me in my rear view mirror. It was the most clear-headed I had been in months. I made it to the office of my client and finished the work in just a few days. I got paid $1,000 with the rest due in a week to give them the chance to test the system out. I then went down to San Diego to visit my mom and dad. I also paid a visit to my younger brother Joe who I knew could get me some cocaine. Before getting high I called my client and found out that there were a few problems with the new software system I wrote so I headed back to Orange County to fix them. I tried to smoke a little in the car on the way. I can't believe how stupid I was...I should have known that I could not smoke base and keep it together enough to drive. I had to pull into a motel and take a room for the night. That one night turned into two days and nights of extreme drug consumption, and more paranoia. At one point I thought my bathroom mirror was a two way mirror and the people in the next room were watching me. I knocked on their door at 3:00 AM to tell them to leave me alone; lucky for me no one answered.

"After I ran out of cocaine, I continued on to my client's office to clean up the last few bugs. I received my remaining funds and went back down to San Diego to spend a few days with my parents before returning to Oregon. I had been telling my brother Joe about all of the trouble I had with spies and he wanted to help me. So I brought him back home with me to Sandy, Oregon, a small suburb out in the sticks,[1] half way between Portland and Mt. Hood. Once I was back home in Oregon, I scored some more coke and went on another binge with my brother. At one point I saw some of the spies in the bushes. I pointed to the place where I saw them and Joe took the gun to go out and round them up. I kept an eye on them. Once he got to where they were and shook the bush they disappeared. He came back to report that there was no one out there. This was the first time I had to admit that my spies were only in my head.

"This continued on for a few months. My computer software business was floundering; the bills were getting out of control. Instead of Kat, now I had Joe ripping off my cocaine. Eventually I put him on a plane back to San Diego. I finally saw the need to stop doing drugs and made an attempt to do so. I went to a minister who offered free counseling and got some help. I attended his Christian church and some of the bible study groups. This was helpful, and I started to feel better. Late in November of 1985, I called my wife Kat and asked her to come back. I told her I had stopped selling and using drugs and everything would be different if she would come back. She decided to let me come

---

[1] For my Australian friends that would be out in "whoop whoop".

and get her so I drove down to Southern California and brought her back to Oregon.

"We did well for about a month. Then Kat decided we deserved a treat for being so good. She did not have a difficult time convincing me. We continued to do okay for the next two months, giving ourselves this cocaine treat only occasionally. But then the inevitable happened, we got back into dealing and began to consume cocaine as often as possible. It was not long before Kat and I began having fights again. When one of them turned physical, she left me for the last time, but this time she moved just a few blocks away.

"Eventually I got tired of the routine of taking a hit, experiencing bliss for few moments, and then returning to full on paranoia. I started interviewing recovery programs and found one that I felt comfortable with. I called my mother and asked her if they would lend me the money so I could check in; both my parents were happy to do so. I made sure to smoke a little bit of cocaine the last night and also some pot the morning before leaving for the treatment center...I still remember the date, July 31st, 1986.

"The 'New Day' treatment center was run by the Seventh Day Adventist church. Someone took me on a tour of the center and then left me with the other inmates to become involved in the routine. At the first break, I met with my counselor. I was to be in for thirty days. I was not allowed any drugs or alcohol, which included sugar and caffeine. I was only allowed immediate family for visitors and only on Sunday afternoon for a few hours. I was supposed to read the 'Big Book' of Alcoholics Anonymous and attend two AA meetings per week.

"I objected to this approach. I was not an Alcoholic. I rarely drank. I just had problems with cocaine. That was all I wanted to quit. My counselor convinced me to give it a real try for thirty days, and by the end of that time, she said that I would understand why the program was arranged the way it was."

Kathryn remained silent but I could tell that she was listening; I continued to tell my story.

"At the end of the program, I felt much better. The burn on my leg had also finished its healing process, more than a year after it happened. I returned home and attended a twelve-step meeting every day...you know...AA or CA?"

Kathryn responded, "No, what is that?"

"Alcoholics Anonymous and Cocaine Anonymous. I enjoyed the meetings and was doing reasonably well. I made a lot of friends, reached out for help, and attended events sponsored by the twelve-step groups. Even though I had come to realize that marijuana had also been a problem, I still did not fully believe that alcohol was a problem for me as well. I tried drinking a few times, just a little, all I got out of it was a little bit of guilt.

"One evening I was buying groceries. I was planning on making a cake for a CA sponsored Thanksgiving potluck dinner. I decided that I wanted a glass or two of wine so I bought a bottle. After consuming two glasses of wine, I found that I did not want to stop, so I ended up drinking the entire bottle. Once I finished that bottle, I wanted more. Actually, I just wanted to fly higher, and I knew more wine would only make me sick so I began considering getting some cocaine. I made two phone calls and found someone who was able to get it for me. Not much had changed in those four months since I had last consumed it. I took a hit, enjoyed it for a short time, and then went through the house checking for spies. Kat even showed up unexpectedly, I had not seen her in at least a month, and of course she wanted some. Lucky for me my options for scoring were severely limited after my absence from the drug scene. I finally ran out of coke, and I ran out of people to call, and after a few painful hours, I got to sleep around 6:00 AM.

"I missed the CA Thanksgiving potluck dinner, but got myself off to an AA meeting later that evening. I confessed my final binge and took a new sobriety date. I continued to attend twelve-step meetings everyday, without fail, for the next two years. That was the last time I drank or smoked dope, and I now have more than three and a half years of continuous sobriety."

I finished my stories of the bad old days just as we were arriving at Multnomah Falls. Kathryn was a good listener. She said, "It is amazing that you could sink so low and then improve your life to such a great extent. You have improved your life, haven't you?" Kathryn chuckled, "I can see that you have...you should be proud of yourself."

"I have...I am," I replied.

Kathryn's words, "I like how open you are," was music to my ears. I was a bit concerned Kathryn would not like me anymore after those stories. I had to let her know the truth about my life and how willing to grow and change I was.

As we began our steep hike up to the top of the Falls, Kathryn said, "I understand how addicting drugs can be because I was addicted to pain killers for a while. They were prescription...I had been in a world of pain for nearly ten years due to fibromyalgia. I could not even make the beds. For years the doctors did not know what disease I had. With all of the different drugs and pain killers being prescribed, I became addicted to them. At first I was sleepy all of the time. Then I tried to do things anyway, and I was too messed up to function. I did not like how I felt, I just wasn't me anymore. Then I sought help to get off of them and onto something else that would work. This is when I found the pain treatment center at Emanuel Hospital, I spent six weeks there; except for the weekends I was living there. They were so good to me...they treated me with respect and helped me to get it together. I learned a lot about who I am and what was important to me, and I learned how to make the pain manageable."

"This was the beginning of the end of my relationship with my second husband James." Kathryn continued, telling me some of the horror stories of her last marriage.

"How did you finally end that nightmare?" I asked.

Kathryn replied, "You won't believe what I had to do to get away from him. After many unsuccessful attempts, I systematically located all of his spare keys to the house and took them. Then one morning I removed the last few keys from his key chain as he was showering for work. I nearly got caught. My heart was racing so fast, I actually stuttered when he asked what I was doing. I thought he might suspect something was up. But once he drove out of the garage and closed the door I pulled the plug to the garage door opener. The rest of the house was locked up tight. I had tried many times to kick him out before but he always managed to find a key somewhere and make his way back into the house. All I could do was hope that I had gotten all of the keys this time. I called him at work to tell him that his things were waiting on the front porch and to find a new place to live.

"James was furious. He came home and banged on the door and demanded to be let in. 'This is my house,' he yelled! He tried all of the windows and doors. I was worried that he would break a window or find a way in. After an exhausting forty minutes, he tried talking to me to convince me that things would change. I did not give in; I had heard that story too many times before. Eventually, he drove off in a fury...with wheels squealing and his personal effects in his car, he tore away from the house. Two hours later, my pain disappeared and I could again use my body."[1]

"That was not very long ago...it has only been two months. Actually I am amazed that it is going so easy for me. I would have never dreamed of making such a strenuous hike to the top of Multnomah Falls. I could not believe it was me signing up for that dance class. I mean a dance class...in the condition I was in...I have always loved dancing, I wanted to learn but not with James...lately, I never thought of it because I was not in good enough health to actually do it. After being in so much pain for all of those years how could I possibly take a dance class?" Kathryn giggled. No matter the age, women are very cute when they

---

[1] Consider the implications of this. It really was a huge miracle for Kathryn.

giggle. "I met a nice woman named Pat…she talked me into signing up for it…it did not even feel like it was me that was filling out the form. Pat was so excited about the class, her enthusiasm was contagious."

"Pat!?!" I interrupted, "That's another of life's amazing coincidences. She is the same one that got me started taking dance classes. Blonde hair, medium height and build…mid forties?"

"Yes, that's her." Kathryn said, "It felt like someone else was moving my hand as I filled out the form for the dance class." Kathryn and I both got goosebumps and could feel that there was a higher power involved in bringing us together in this way.

Once we reached the top of the falls, we stopped at a lookout point to watch the waterfall from the top. It was a long way down. Kathryn broke the silence, "I like watching an individual bit of the water as it falls; I follow it as far as I can."

I tried her viewing technique. It was a whole new experience for me, I liked it. After a short while at the lookout point we began walking. We followed the stream of water that led to the falls until we got to a nice spot to sit; this gave us time to recover from the long hike up the cliff.

The hike up the hill made me hot and sweaty so I removed my shirt and was now wearing nothing but shorts. I hoped she enjoyed how I looked. Kathryn removed her blouse and was now wearing a one-piece bathing suit and shorts. Her large and shapely breasts were much more visible now; I was certainly enjoying the view.

"This reminds me of a place I love to visit called 'Head of Jack Creek' in Central Oregon." Kathryn went on to describe the incredible beauty and uniqueness of this place and then she said, "I have some very dear friends, Rodger and Joan; they used to live at a place called Camp Sherman not too far from Bend Oregon and this creek. Joan has been a mentor for me for many years. She supported me through some very tough times with James." As Kathryn continued to speak about Rodger and Joan with glowing detail, especially Joan, I could tell she deeply loved and admired those two people. After a brief pause Kathryn added, "I would like to take you to see Head of Jack Creek and to meet my friends sometime. They would like you."

Kathryn's declaration did not go unnoticed. *She must be interested in me,* I thought, *otherwise she would not be making future plans with me in them.* My heart leaped for joy as I tried to control the expression on my face and the tone of my voice. I calmly replied, "I would love to go there with you sometime." We sat there, silent for a while; both feeling connected and very comfortable with each other. It was a beautiful summer day.

We continued to walk along the creek until we came to a nice place for our picnic lunch. While eating we talked about dancing. I told her about how I got started, "You know Pat? The woman who signed you up for the class? I was at a SLC singles dance one evening, and saw her dancing with someone else; it looked like she was showing him how to dance. When she finished I asked her to show me how. So she danced a swing dance with me and she led. I had so much fun, and I found it easy to follow her; I knew I could learn too." I continued on and gave Kathryn much of the details of how intensely I had been taking classes. I told her about how much I liked the waltz and foxtrot and then demonstrated to her how they had many moves in common. It was a great excuse to touch her and hold her in my arms. It felt so good; it was more than just a sexual feeling...more like a reconnection of two souls who were happy to meet again. It felt like this was meant to be.

The day was passing far too quickly, and I did not want it to end. But the time came to start heading back down the trail. For a while we walked in comfortable silence. I was enjoying the way it felt to be with Kathryn and out in nature. As we came close to the end of the trail I asked Kathryn "What do you want in your next relationship?" Kathryn stopped in her tracks, looked at me with surprise, thought for just a moment, and replied, "Someone I can talk to. Someone I can be friends with."

I knew that I could be her friend and that I would enjoy talking with her for many years. "That is very important to me too," I said. We continued on in silence. I felt content, whole, and on top of the world.

The beck and call of ice cream awaited us at the bottom. As we sat and ate our frozen delight, I started to realize that the logical end of our date was near, yet there was so much more left to this day, it was only four PM. I did not want this date to end so soon. "Are you busy tonight? Ah...I mean...." I stuttered trying to get the words out, "Would you like to do something...maybe go watch the fireworks or something...like that?" I was feeling nervous. After a brief hesitation Kathryn replied, "I would like that, but I have a dog at home...he needs to be let out...fed. I would have to go home first. I have a frozen pizza, would you like that? We could heat it up. We should have some dinner first."

I wanted to yell, "Yahoo!" as loud as I could, but instead I replied, "Yes, that would be nice."

Fireworks

Driving to Kathryn's home I asked, "Do you have any children?" She replied, "No, my dogs have been the closest I have come to having children. I love children; I always wanted to be a mother. When I was twenty-six, I was diagnosed with cervical cancer and had a hysterectomy; this prevented me from having any kids of my own. James and I talked about adopting, but he was not real interested and there was always some reason why we didn't. Now I'm glad that we did not have any children together. I would not want that tie with him. He is so manipulative." She shuddered just from talking about him.

"I have had many dogs; they have been my children, especially Barney. Oh Barney was quite a character. He would eat everything…and I do mean everything, food, panty hose, everything. Barney had quite a strong will and would force his way into other people's meals. He was so bad that whenever we had people over for dinner, I had to lock him in the car, while it was parked in the garage."

"Noooh…no way!" I said in shock, "You actually locked him in the car to keep him away from the table?"

Kathryn continued, "Not just to keep him away from the table, but to keep him from climbing up on our guests' laps and pulling their plates from the table. Every time we had guests for a meal, we had to lock him up. One time, Barney actually ate a pair of my nylon stockings. Of course they passed all the way through his bowels undigested, but only a little bit came through at a time so he had this piece of stocking hanging out of his rear end for a few hours. Once it became too long and noticeable, I decided to pull it out. Well you can only imagine what a difficult and messy job that turned out to be.

"No matter how challenging Barney was, I loved him dearly. Barney had gotten very sick and needed prescription medications. James and I drove out to Camp Sherman for the weekend. Once we got there, I realized that I had left Barney's medication at home. Well…there was no way that James was going to drive all the way back home to get it, so I had to."

I couldn't believe it, *I wouldn't have driven all the way home for it either,* I thought. In disbelief I said, "You drove all that way home and then back to Camp Sherman again in the same night for a dog?"

"Yes," she replied, "wouldn't you?"

I felt put on the spot but I replied honestly anyways, "I doubt it; it would have to be pretty much life and death for me to do that. Wasn't that about a three-hour drive one way?" I said.

Kathryn had the sound of conviction in her response, "Yes, it took over six hours. By the time I got back to Camp Sherman it was very late in the evening, actually early morning. And it was a life and death situation. Barney would have died without his medication."

"I did not mean to trivialize the situation...." I hoped I had not said the wrong thing.

"That's okay; I did not take it that way. I have six nephews and a great niece. My family is large, typically Italian. My mom is Italian and my dad's Irish. But my mom is the head of the family. I got to have my nephews for sleepovers and to take to special events and shows. This really was the best deal for me...I did not have to handle the day-to-day challenges of raising the boys. I got the good times, and then they went home." As she continued to tell me about each of her nephews, I could tell that she gave them a lot of love and would have made a great mother.

"Do you have any children?" Kathryn asked me.

"No," I replied, "but I have been a stepfather for the last four years. I lived with Maria and her two boys for three years and have been separated from her for nearly a year now. I still have the boys every other weekend...losing them was the hardest part of breaking up with Maria. I even asked her if she would let me adopt and keep them; I was serious. Of course she said no, but I did not think that she cared all that much about spending time with them. She loved them, of this I am sure. But she just did not spend the kind of time with them that I did. I thought that maybe she wouldn't mind leaving them with me. Anyway...she didn't have a job...how was she going to care for the two boys?"

"Why did she leave?" Kathryn asked.

"Well..." it was humiliating to say, "about five months before she left, she told me that she was not in love with me any more. In fact, she said that she did not think she was ever in love with me. She said that I did not appreciate her and that I was always putting her down and acting as if she were not capable. At the time I did not think what she was telling me was true. I told her that the put downs were just my way of being playful, but I did not mean them. But Maria did not accept that. She also said I had a problem with rage, that I was always angry and was taking it out on her and the boys. And that I was not fun anymore.

"This all started at the same time that Maria had begun going to college to get a degree to become a music teacher. This put extra stress on our relationship. She was not working but school was keeping her very busy. I had a full time job, and I was doing most of the cooking and cleaning that went with it. I was also the one who spent most of the time with the boys and kept them entertained. Once Maria started school, I rarely saw her. She was at school mostly in the evenings. By the time she got home, I was in bed or too tired to spend any quality time with her. I had been experiencing severe back pains for quite some time which kept me out of her bed and sleeping on the floor. I asked Maria if all of these things might be contributing to her sense of dissatisfaction, that maybe the contrast of something new and fun, such as college, against the mundane tasks of life at home was the real problem. Maria did not agree.

"I told her I would go to counseling to deal with my anger and she agreed to stay with me a while longer to see if we could work it out. I did go to counseling, and I got better at dealing with my anger. I tried harder to be nice and to treat Maria as if she were competent. But nothing changed; she remained distant and dissatisfied. Due to her academic efforts, she earned a special scholarship to go to a six-week intensive summer program at an expensive nearby college. The intensive part meant that she would have to live on campus the entire time and that the boys and I would be able to visit her only a few times while she was there. This also meant that I would have to find a way to take care of the boys while she was gone. Of course this was summer vacation so they were not in school. To help me out, my mother came up from San Diego, just a few weeks after she had a mastectomy of one breast. She stayed for three of those weeks; it was a major help! Still, it was pretty rough those remaining three weeks...trying to keep a job, pay for a sitter...I had to care for the boys all by myself when I got home. I sure got a taste of what single moms go through.

"On the weekend that Maria was to return home from school, I went on a spiritual retreat at Crystal Mountain, a Resort in Washington. It was fantastic...I found some joy for myself once again! Boy I needed that. When I returned home, Maria was waiting for me...she had cut her long, beautiful hair. I knew it was a sign; it was over between us. She knew how much I liked her hair long.

"Maria began by telling me that our relationship was over. She wanted me to move out immediately but to pay the bills until she could figure out how to take care of herself and the boys. I said, 'No way, can't we work this out?' I told her that we were just in a difficult place and that we needed to stick together so we could get through it, otherwise we both would have to face these issues in another relationship. Then she told me she had been sexually involved with another man. We had a long discussion; I told Maria how I thought we could work it out, and she told me how her priorities in life had changed and that I was not a part of it.

"We ended by Maria agreeing to leave with the boys; she did not know where. I called the home of my friend Steven, the one with whom I had gone to the retreat, and got a hold of John, his roommate. This was the first time I felt like getting drunk or high in nearly two years. I knew I needed support so I asked John if I could come over. He said yes, so I drove over. I made it through that night without getting wasted and started going to twelve-step meetings much more often for a while after that."

Kathryn was listening intently; she said, "I'm sorry, I know how difficult it can be to have someone cheat on you. My first husband did that to me."

I responded, "It was not such a big deal to me that she had sex with someone else...not really...I was just furious that she had time for dating someone else but not for me and the boys. I worked hard all of those months, I made some big inner and outer changes...when I was trying so hard to change and make it work she did nothing to bring us back together."

I realized I had been talking too much, "Please...tell me more about your relationship with your first husband?"

Kathryn said, "Ronny and I dated in High School. He was a good friend...we had fun together. I didn't know what I was doing...getting married to Ronny was just a good way for me to move away from home. He enlisted with the army, and we were sent to Germany. At first I was excited about going to live in a foreign country...I went with him. But he was away at work most of the time, including weekends. He came home to our apartment occasionally...it was rare. I did not know anyone...most people did not speak English, so my social life was nonexistent. There was no heat and no hot water in our apartment; it took nearly a year for me to feel warm again once I returned to Portland. I had very little money to work with so my diet was mostly beans and rice. Life was not much fun. My apartment was part of a house; the family who owned it was horrible. The owner was a butcher. He would get drunk and beat the cattle to death with a club. It was a horrifying experience to hear that going on outside of my window. One day I accidentally locked myself out of my apartment. The door slammed shut behind me when I was going out for just a short moment. I was in a shear negligee and had to go and ask the owners to let me in. They made me sit in their living room, nearly naked, for over an hour while they pretended not to understand me. They did not even give me something to cover up with. They were horrible people."

I couldn't believe she would put up with this. "Couldn't you move somewhere else?" I asked.

Kathryn replied, "I did not know how to stand up for myself at that time. I always tried to make do. This was only one of many lessons in endurance for me. In about a year, we returned to Portland, and eventually time we bought a house together. During the time I was gone, the United States had gone fully into the hippie era. When I returned, I was shocked to see how different people were dressing; all of the tie dye and paisley bell bottoms were not to be seen before I had left. Ronny and

I remained together for a few more years. We slowly drifted apart, and the relationship ended when Ronny had an affair with a good friend of mine."

When Kathryn and I arrived at her house, I was impressed with the quality of her neighborhood, her nice home, and her lovely, landscaped yard. Kathryn said, "Please excuse the mess inside, I had not anticipated bringing you home."

As she took me on a tour inside her beautiful home, I could not find a mess to excuse. It was 2,000 square feet; all of the rooms were papered. I commented on it, "I really like your wallpaper. You don't see this so much anymore...I love it...when it is done well...I mean...this is done well."

"Thank you, I did it myself." Kathryn responded. Everything was matching; even the bed spread matched the wallpaper.

I commented further, "It looks like a professional job...I am impressed. Have you ever considered papering professionally? You are very good at this. You could be an interior decorator."

Kathryn responded, "Yes, I have done a couple of professional jobs, but my health has kept me from doing this kind of work, or any work for that matter. I did teach my twin sister Bridget how to wallpaper, and she does it for a living. She also does house painting."

All of the furnishings were in the best of shape and quite stylish; they had an early colonial look to them. "I love your furniture, they're lovely pieces. Are they antiques? They don't look old enough to be...but it has that antique style to it." I said.

"Thank you. No, they are not antiques; they are about ten years old. They are just designed to look that way."

I never had furniture that looked that good after ten years. The entire home was a couple levels of quality and comfort above what I had become accustomed to. I liked it very much. I thought, *I could enjoy living here.* But out loud I said, "You take very good care of your things; your entire home is beautiful."

Kathryn started to look uncomfortable with all of the attention and changed the subject. "Lets go and get Gus out of his kennel and you can meet him, then I will start heating the pizza." She turned to walk away and I followed her.

While Kathryn prepared our dinner, I played with Gus, a beautiful, large Golden Retriever. We had a great time. Kathryn was pleased to see how well Gus and I took to each other.

During dinner, Kathryn told me more about her family. "It was tough for Judy, my oldest sister, because Bridget and I would always hang around together. We did not pay much attention to her and since we were twins, we always got the attention from other people. My Uncle Ernie used to take Bridget and me out pretty regularly, but not Judy. The youngest, my brother Davey, also had it a bit rough. Bridget and I would tease and pick on him, I feel real bad about it now. I have a big Italian family. My mom is Italian and my dad's Irish. But it is really the relatives on my mom's side that are considered part of the family. They are the ones who get invited to family gatherings; my dad's family seems to get left out.

"I was always trying to be the peacemaker of the family...I wasn't very successful. There was a lot of turmoil in my childhood, my mom and dad fought a lot. For as long as I can remember, Mom slept on the sofa so she would not have to sleep with Dad. I would do things like make sure my mother had enough cigarettes on the end table so that she would wake up in a good mood. I would even light her first cigarette for her. It did not work though. My mother used a wire hanger to beat me and the others kids. When my sisters and I grew old enough to have visits from boys, Mom would terrorize them and scare them away, which sometimes included beating us with the wire hanger right in front of them.

"And then there was Bridget...she was always getting me into trouble. She would use the fact that we were identical to confuse people. She would intentionally do something offensive and then blame it on me. As an example...there was this girl in our school who was a big bully. Everyone was afraid of her. One time Bridget said something really nasty to this bully when her back was turned. When the girl turned around, Bridget shrugged her shoulders and pointed at me. Well I ran as fast as I could but the bully still caught me and beat me up."

Kathryn continued on for a little while longer telling me story after story of the tricks that Bridget pulled as a child and even ones she continued to pull into recent adult years.

I said to Kathryn, "It is quite interesting to me that two people born so close together can be so different. It just goes to show that it is primarily the soul that is responsible for the personality and that astrology, or the planets, are only an influence on the personality. When is your birthday?"

Kathryn replied, "It was just last week, June 28th."

With enthusiasm I said, "You are a Cancerian! Fantastic...I do really well with Cancer. I am a Scorpio. My birthday is November 7th, 1958. What year were you born?"

Looking a bit uncomfortable, Kathryn asked, "How old do you think I am?"

I hate it when women ask that, "I would guess somewhere between thirty-six and forty." Kathryn smiled and replied, "I was born in 1948, I'm forty-three." Kathryn was ten years older than I was.

I was surprised, yet just fine. I replied, "I like older women. You are not the first one I have gone out with who was ten years older than me."

"That's good." Kathryn replied, "Tell me about your family."

"I am the oldest. My brother Joe is nearly three years younger; my sister Sherry is seven years younger; and my other brother Pat is twelve years younger. My mom and dad are still together; they get along pretty well, but they have had their differences. They do work together well. I feel lucky to have grown up in a family without too many problems. I began to hear a lot of stories of abusive families once I got involved in the twelve-step programs. This really surprised me; I was very sheltered from all of that. The worst that happened in my family was that my father expected too much from me. A few times he called me stupid then knocked me on the top of the head with his knuckles, just because I did not meet his expectations. It hurt a little, but more from the humiliation of it. My mother went through a period of being a real bitch when I was a young teenager; it seemed that I always displeased her. We got spanked, sometimes too hard and for too long; often I did not even understand why. Other than that, we were well cared for, well fed, got to be on bowling leagues and fun things like that. My parents raised us to be responsible and reliable…Oh…and they took us to fun places on weekends, especially when we lived in Japan…that was really cool. From children to young teens, in the summer, every summer, my mother took us to the beach or pool nearly every day. Mostly I had a happy and carefree childhood."

We finished our pizza and then left to go to a park on the Willamette River to watch the fireworks. I continued to tell Kathryn about my family, "Joe and I were the closest of the siblings. My sister Sherry was too young for me to play with and I never had much to do with her. Then Pat came along after I turned twelve; I was more of a baby sitter than a brother to him. Sherry and Pat would do things together. Sherry was always watching over Pat and bossing him around. Poor Pat, he had two bitching moms. Joe and I did a lot together as kids but we fought a lot too. As I became a teenager, I found other friends to hang out with and left him behind. As he got older, he got into a lot of trouble at home and at school. He got caught stealing and breaking into people's homes. He was also doing drugs. He ended up in Juvenile hall and spending time in group homes for kids in trouble."

Fourth of July celebrations are usually something I like to miss due to the crowds. With Kathryn's company to distract me, I did not notice the crowd much. We found a nice spot on a grassy hill and placed our blanket there. At first we just sat and watched the crowd. Talking and watching...after a bit of time passed, we heard a roaring fire behind us. Someone had accidentally started a medium sized tree on fire. There was a building right behind the tree and from our vantage point it looked like the building was on fire. Once the fire consumed the leaves and small branches it died down and revealed that it was only the tree that caught fire. We walked over to inspect the damage. On the way back to our blanket, I bought Kathryn and me a glowing necklace, one of those plastic tubes with a green glowing chemical inside. I'd wanted one since the first time I saw them, but I was an adult; adults don't buy themselves things like that. This presented a good excuse to buy one. Little did I realize how much Kathryn would appreciate this gift.

We sat back down on the blanket and engaged in small talk; I found myself lost looking intensely into Kathryn's eyes. I was filled with the hopeful feeling that she was the one that I could fall in love with; I had visions of living happily ever after.

Kathryn started to become uncomfortable. "Please stop." She asked.

"What...looking into your eyes?" I replied.

"Yes," she said, "it is making me feel self conscious."

"Okay," I said. After a slight hesitation and a deep breath, I asked "Can I hold your hand?"

"Yes," Shyly looking down, Kathryn replied sweetly, "I'd like that."

Oh, the exhilarating feeling of that touch as we held each other's hands. We remained silent for what seemed like a very long time. We watched the people as they found patches of bare grass to plant their blankets upon. Children were running around, getting all excited and high on sugar. The summer evening was warm. The anticipated show was soon to begin.

I thought about what holding Kathryn's hand meant. I thought about how fond of her I had already become. I thought about how lucky and grateful I was to be with her and what a contrast this was to the weeks that followed Maria's departure nearly a year prior. Knowing then what I know now, would I have accepted that outcome with more grace and less pain? At the time I did the best I could, I did tell myself that this too would pass and that there must be someone better coming into my life. Was Kathryn that person? I hoped so!

As the fireworks began, I moved to sit behind Kathryn and cuddled close. I reached around her waste with my right hand and held on to her left forearm which had been crossed across her lap. I put my left hand on her left leg. It felt magical to sit this close to her. We watched the fireworks as we cuddled. I could feel Kathryn relax and let go into my arms. I could feel my heart beating fast and strong. I took long, slow breaths to soak up all of sweetness that was flowing between us. With every exploding firework my heart burst with an explosion of love.

The fireworks seemed to go on forever; it was simply magical. But they did end, which meant our date was soon to end…I did not want that to happen, but I also knew that pressing forward could be a bit awkward. We walked back to Kathryn's car and I drove us to my duplex apartment. I parked her car in the driveway, right behind mine. I looked over at Kathryn, with that look that says I want to kiss you. She looked back at me the same way. We kissed. One long, sweet, juicy, delicious kiss. A Scorpio's motto is, "If a little is good, more is better." I wanted to spend a lot more time with Kathryn, starting now. I asked, "Would you like to come in for a while?"

Kathryn replied with a laugh, "Noooh! I am going to go home now." She was emphatic.

"Can I see you tomorrow? There is a dance over at the Red Llyon…the one in downtown Portland. A buffet dinner is part of the cover charge."

"Yes," she said, "I hoped you would ask me to go to that with you. I'll see you there, about 6:30?" I replied, "Great, I'll see you then."

I got out of the car and was intending to open Kathryn's door for her, but she beat me to it. I gave her a big hug good night and snuck in another juicy kiss. I hoped she would change her mind and come in but she did not…she walked around to the driver's side and just before she got in I said, "Hey you! I sure enjoyed our day together."

"Me too." She replied as she dropped into the car and closed the door.

I went up to my room got undressed; my underwear was soaking wet. I fondled myself as I thought of the day I spent with Kathryn. I fantasized about making love to her, as I loved myself into orgasmic ecstasy. I had a fitful night of sleep…on and off I slept a little and then woke up in delightful fantasy…then it was back to sleep again.

Second Date

Nearly an hour before I was supposed to get up, I found myself wide awake. I lay in bed and thought about Kathryn's bedroom and how nice it looked. I wondered what she would think of my thin piece of foam for a mattress on the floor.[1] No matter I'll just have to spend most of my time at her house. I knew it was useless to try to go back to sleep so I got up out of bed and did my usual morning workout, push-ups, sit-ups, ten minutes up and down the stairs, arm and chest work with rubber surgical tubing, all things I could easily and cheaply do at home.

I walked to work early. It was great to live so close to my office. The company I worked for was a small company in Lake Oswego, just a five-minute walk from home. The office was located on the lake, which made it even nicer. I really liked my job...well I used to...actually I was beginning to get a little tired of the work. I had been writing software since I was eighteen years old and professionally since the age of twenty. So after thirteen years, I longed to do something else with my time. I still enjoyed it, but not with the same enthusiasm. One of the nicest parts about this work was the flexibility. Once I had been given an assignment, I could pretty much work on my own until it was done. That can be a matter of days, weeks, or months. But it did mean that I could come and go as I pleased, as long as I put in the time and got the work done.

As the day went by, I often found myself reliving the highlights of the prior day I spent with Kathryn. The work day crept by slowly in anticipation of my date with her that evening. Would I get to spend the night with Kathryn? Getting into work an hour early turned out to be a big help. My work day was over early, it felt like summer vacation, a half day of school and then I was off to play for a long weekend. I went home early, took a short nap, took my time getting ready to go to the dance, and had plenty of time for my commute. My car limped along on three cylinders but it made it. In fact I continued to drive it that way for more than a year before I got a new one.

When I arrived, Kathryn was already there, sitting at a table with a group of other dancers; friends that we both knew. Unfortunately, that table was full so I had to find another table to sit at. Kathryn was seated against a wall and between other people so I could not easily speak to her or give her a hug like I wanted to. I wondered if she positioned herself that way on purpose so that it would be harder for me

---

[1] I was basically sleeping on the floor because of my back pains. The thin piece of foam was to soften the floor just a little. I hadn't yet discovered the firm mattresses that were available.

to get close to her. Was she backing off? I quickly put those thoughts out of my mind and tried to enjoy the company of the people at my table, but my mind and attention kept migrating to the other table, where Kathryn was.

After we had all finished our meals, we were informed that it would be another hour before the band would start playing. One by one, in search of other amusements, people left the tables. I was happy because I could not hold my focus on a conversation with anyone, my attention was elsewhere. I was listening, waiting, watching for my opportunity...as soon as I could, I took my first chance to talk with Kathryn, "Hi, how are you?"

"Good...and you?" Kathryn replied with a big smile that raised my confidence level.

I replied, "I'm doing well. Would you like to go for a walk before the music starts?"

"Yes, I would." Kathryn and I left the hotel and set off walking in downtown Portland. Soon we came to a beautiful fountain; we stopped and sat down. While listening to the water and watching it do its dance, we engaged in idle chit chat...until I got up the courage to kiss Kathryn again. She passionately returned my kiss and my heart soared to new heights. We must have spent at least half an hour kissing each other with long silent breaks to look into each other's eyes and catch our breaths. Even though we were in a public place in the middle of downtown Portland, we were oblivious to the rest of the world; we cared not who might be around.

We took our time walking back to the Red Llyon. I could feel all of my enthusiasm for dancing disappear. It was replaced by an enthusiastic desire to get to know Kathryn better. Normally I would dance at least one or two dances with other women, to have the variety and to improve. But not tonight. Tonight it was just the two of us...we danced with each other exclusively for about two hours. I was being as sexy as I knew how to be. When we slow danced with our bodies pressing closely together I could not hide my excitement from Kathryn, I knew she could feel it pressing against her thigh. Kathryn knees went weak many times, I thought she was going to faint. Quiet, but audible gasps of pleasure and surprise came from her sweet mouth as we continued our seductive dance. It was like no one else was in the room, until a song was over, then we both became very aware that we were not alone. Finally I asked Kathryn if she wanted to go home, and she agreed that it would be best.

We took my car and drove back to her car which she left at the Spiritual Life Center. She had driven to the center and then carpooled to the hotel with some of the other women from the church. I followed Kathryn home which was only another seven minutes drive. I was pleased that Kathryn did not want to waste much time downstairs, instead we headed straight up to her bedroom. Kathryn was a little bit uneasy, but at the same time it was clear that she wanted the same thing as I did.

We kissed each other while standing at the foot of her bed. I began to unzip her dress. Smoothly at first, but then the zipper stuck just enough to require my full attention. Wouldn't it be nice if it were to work like in the movies, one smooth zip while I passionately kiss her? But not this time, the kiss had to be interrupted to work that zipper. With my full attention the zipper gave up without much of a fight; I helped the dress slide from her body to the floor. Before continuing to remove her clothes I stepped back to admire the view and Kathryn moved to turn off the lights. Wow, her bedroom got very dark when the lights were out. I convinced her to turn on a night light in the adjoining bathroom which allowed the minimal of light to enter the room. I quickly removed most of my clothes, down to my underwear, and then met Kathryn just as she was turning down the bed. I removed her bra and panties. Kathryn removed my underwear. Naked at last, I could hardly believe this was happening.

Touching, holding, loving each other came very natural for us both; at first...then she got a bit uneasy when I went down on her...at first, but she came to relax and enjoyed it. I could sense her distress when I would try to look at her body, even though it was way too dark to see anything. In some ways, this was not the most fluid start I had had with a woman, yet emotionally, it felt like the yummiest experience of my entire life. I felt at home with Kathryn, like we were meant to be together. We held each other all night long, made love many times, and got very little sleep.

In the morning light I couldn't stop studying Kathryn's pretty face. She was so beautiful, with lovely big brown eyes, dimples on her cheeks, and lips that were just a little out of symmetry. She had peach fuzz on her face that is only noticeable close up; I called her my Peach Face Lovebird. I felt at home in Kathryn's arms and I knew I could pass away many hours just looking at her angelic face. I knew that I was already in love with this woman.

"Did you sleep well?" Kathryn asked.

"Yes, but I remember having this really hot dream in the middle of the night." I replied. "I was making love to this incredibly sexy woman...hey! Wait a minute that wasn't a dream. That was you." We both giggled.

"I'm getting up now, but you can sleep in if you want." Kathryn said.

"What time is it? Wow, its only 6:10 AM," I said answering my own question. "Yes, I would like to sleep…perhaps a few hours more," I kissed Kathryn on the lips, then her forehead, down to her sternum, each breast…when I got to her tummy she said "You are not going to get much sleep that way."

I replied, "I wasn't trying to start something, you're just irresistible. Go on, I'll leave you alone now." With that Kathryn left the room and I went back to sleep.

A few hours later Kathryn came and sat on the bed. "Would you like to sleep some more?" she asked.

"No, I think I will get up now." I replied as I grabbed her around the waist.

"Would you like some breakfast? I can make eggs, bacon, and pancakes?" Kathryn inquired.

"Thank you, that would be nice." I replied, "But first I would like to have a shower and meditate, my morning routine usually takes about an hour. Would that be okay with you?"

"Yes." Kathryn said with a slight hesitation. Then after a moments pause to think she added, "In that case, I will take Gus for a walk. Lately I have not been taking him out as much as I should; he could really use a good walk."

With a goodbye kiss, Kathryn attempted to get up out of the bed. I playfully reached out and grabbed her once again pulling her into my arms. She squealed and I kissed her passionately. With that Kathryn got up from the bed, straightened herself out, and then ran for the protection of her dog Gus before my further attempts to grab her were once again successful.

A Policed Affair

I got myself out of bed and headed for the bathroom sink. Kathryn had left me a brand new toothbrush, and I used it to clean away the morning breath. I wondered how we never notice it in a new relationship, but as time goes on, it becomes quite noticeable. Kathryn kept a neat and tidy home. I searched for a trash can to throw out my toothbrush packaging but could find none. I left the bedroom, went into the hallway bathroom and found one. It was heart shaped and matched the décor of the bathroom. As I dumped the packaging into it I noticed that the waste basket was empty, clean; it had no liner nor was there an indication that trash had ever been thrown in it.

After my shower I headed downstairs in search of an appropriate meditation location. As I soon as I stepped into the living room a loud sound filled the room, "Whoop...whoop...whoop...."

What is this? I thought, *Oh Kathryn...you set the alarm before you left!* I went out the patio door hoping it would be quieter outside but it was even louder. I decided to try going back upstairs. At first I tried the bear room; a bedroom dedicated to teddy bears. The double bed was totally covered, chairs, tables, dressers all covered with teddy bears. There was a real bear skin rug on the floor. There was also a counted cross-stitch picture of five bears dressed up like classy 1935 college students with a caption "Bearsevelt High School Reunion" hung up on the wall.

Since the bears occupied all of the chairs in that room, I tried the room next door. This was Kathryn's sewing and craft room. It was in keeping with the rest of the house, cute and well decorated, with a craft theme. There was another counted cross-stitch picture hanging in this room too, this one, including the frame was in the shape of a heart. Inside the heart it said "Memories are Souvenirs of the Heart." I found my spot, shut the door and sat down to try meditating.

I had not been sitting there for very long when the phone began to ring. I quickly debated whether I should answer or not as I walked toward the phone...given the circumstances I thought I should. I picked up the phone, "Hello."

"Who is this?" said the man on the other end.

"This is Mike, Mike Skowronski, who is this?"

"This is Jerry at Brinks Home Security. Is James or Kathryn there?"

"No," I replied, James does not live here anymore. I am...an overnight guest. Kathryn went to go walk her dog while I was taking a shower and when I went downstairs the alarm started ringing. I'm sure she will be home soon."

Jerry said, "Oh...can you turn it off? Do you know the code?"

"No," I replied out loud, then I thought, *He must think I am stupid. If I knew the code I would have turned it off by now.*

"Do you know the password?" Jerry continued to inquire.

"No, this is the first time I spent the night here. She did not give me the password. I am sure she armed the alarm by mistake." I replied.

"Well tell Kathryn to give us a call when she gets home." Jerry said.

"Okay bye," and I hung up. I thought to myself, *Wow, that was too easy. Was that all there was too it? Did he believe me?*

I went back into the sewing room and closed the door. The alarm was still ringing, but I thought I would again try to meditate. Within five minutes the phone rang again. I went back to the master bedroom and answered, "Hello."

"Hello, is Kathryn there?" it was an older woman at the other end.

"No," I replied, "can I tell Kathryn who called?"

"This is her mother!" She said sharply, "Where is Kathryn? What are you doing there? Who are you?"

I thought, *Oh no, what do I tell her?* Then I replied, "My name is Mike. I was visiting Kathryn and she went to walk her dog. She must have turned on the alarm out of habit."

"Well tell Kat to call her mother when she comes home." And with that she hung up the phone.

Again I returned to the sewing room to meditate, as I sat down the alarm stopped ringing. Peace at last. I wondered when Kathryn would come back and if it was Brinks that shut the alarm off. I listened for a bit, but I did not hear anything downstairs; so I figured it was not Kathryn who turned it off.

After ten minutes passed the damn alarm started ringing again, I thought, *What the...what is wrong with that stupid thing?* Then I heard some noise. I listened for a little bit...silence...silence...and then I heard some more noise. *It can't be a real burglar this time, could it? No...that would be way too weird.* I continued to sit and listen. For a long while all I could hear was the alarm, then I heard a sound at the bottom of the stairs. This time I kept hearing the sound and it was coming up the stairs.

This is so weird; what the hell could that be? I was getting pissed off. I opened the door and walked out into the hallway to look down the stairs.

"Freeze!" a police officer shouted while pointing a gun at me. My hands shot up into the air. A second police officer slipped by the armed cop and took my hands behind my back and cuffed me. "You have the right to remain silent...." the police officer read me my rights. It was difficult to keep from laughing; they were taking everything way too seriously.

The two police men took me downstairs and sat me down in the living room. "Who are you and what are you doing here?" asked one of the police men. From my seat I could now see that there were three police cars sitting outside. There was a police officer in the front yard and I could hear another around the corner in the next room.

"My name is Mike Skowronski. I am Kathryn's boyfriend. I just spend the night for the first time last night and she went to walk her dog while I got cleaned up. When she left, she must have turned the alarm on by mistake...out of habit. I'm surprised she has not returned yet."

One of the police officers replied, "We can stay and wait a little while for her to return, but if she does not come back soon we'll have to take you in."

So we waited. A few minutes later I could see Kathryn walking calmly toward the house with Gus on his leash. I thought, *What is wrong with her!?! Doesn't she see three police cars in front of her house? Oh...there she goes, now she's awake.* Kathryn suddenly began running toward the house. She dropped the leash and her arms were flailing in the air. Kathryn burst through the front door and asked, "Officer what is going on? What did he do?"

"Please turn off the alarm Ma'am," replied the officer. We had all gotten tired of hearing that noisy alarm blaring away.

"Oh my God!" I could almost see the lights going on in Kathryn's head. It was as if she had not heard the alarm blaring away, and now she just became aware of it; she ran to turn it off. When she returned she said, "Did I turn that on when I left? Is that what this is about?"

"Yes, apparently you did, at least that is what this man says. Do you know him?" asked the police officer.

"Yes, I am so sorry." Kathryn replied. Then she looked at me and said, "Mike, I'm sorry are you okay?"

"I'm all right. Don't worry." I replied with a laugh. The police officer then gave Kathryn a lecture about being more careful with her alarm system. That after two false alerts she would be sent a bill for any more that required the police to come out. I interrupted his lecture by clearing my throat loudly, and I growled, "Hey, take the cuffs off."

After a brief apology, the police left, and the house was quiet again.

Kathryn and I laughed and sat down. "I can't believe I did that. You must have been very worried. Have the police been here long?" Kathryn said.

"Maybe ten minutes, but you were sure gone for a long time." I replied.

"I thought you would need the time so I took an extra long walk with Gus. I would have been mortified if the police handcuffed me. Are you really okay?" She said.

"Yes," I laughed, "at least I have a great story I can tell my friends."

"No way, you can't tell them about this..." Kathryn implored, paused and then added, "I am so embarrassed."

"Well that's not the end of it. Your mom called while the alarm was going off. Did Brinks have her number? I think they told her the alarm had been triggered?"

"Yes, they were supposed to call her in an emergency. Oh shit, what am I going to tell her? I haven't even told her I was dating you. She'll disown me. Did you tell her anything?" She said.

"Not really, I tried to tell her as little as possible. But she did not sound happy...I think she was putting it together...just tell her the truth."

"She is way too proper for that. I can't tell my mom that I had someone sleep over; she really will disown me. She has done it before. She does not even sleep with my dad so that she doesn't have to have sex with him." Kathryn spoke with great concern in her voice. "I'll have to give her a call before I make breakfast; do you mind?"

"No, go right ahead." I replied, "I never did get to meditate. You go on and call her then get breakfast together. I'll be outside meditating. I'm sure I'll be done before you."

When I finished my meditation Kathryn was nearly done making breakfast. "How did your conversation with your mother go?" I asked.

Kathryn replied, "Fine, I had to tell her I have been seeing you for a while. Which...in a way, I have been. She could tell that you spent the night...so I had to fess up."

"Did she disown you or make a fuss?" I asked.

Kathryn replied, "No, she just changed the subject."

We had breakfast on Kathryn's patio. After we finished, and cleaned up the dishes, I taught Kathryn how to follow some of my favorite Waltz and Foxtrot dance steps. We caught her next door neighbor peeking through the fence. She was pretending to weed her garden but every so often she would watch us through the cracks in the fence.

Kathryn and I planned a late afternoon outing at Washington Park near downtown Portland; I was also invited to spend the night with her. I went home to get fresh clothes and let Kathryn take care of some errands. When I returned later that day Kathryn told me that Brinks had also called Molly, a close friend of hers who lived a few houses down and across the street. My poor Kathryn...she was very uncomfortable that the whole world knew she had a man sleeping over. Life has a way of making us face our discomfort...and Kathryn had a lot of discomfort around her sexuality.

That evening I noticed that the toothbrush packaging was no longer in the trash can. I thought, *The bin must be for decoration only,* which made me laugh. I have never known someone who kept things so perfect. I liked Kathryn's style, but this seemed a bit much. Some things just need to be practical.

Nearly Living Together

Over the course of the next few weeks I was nearly living with Kathryn. During the week I would go to work and stop at home only to exchange dirty clothes for clean ones. Once a week I would make myself stay home at night, just because I thought it would be best, but I did not want to. On those evenings, Kathryn and I would spend an hour or more talking to each other on the phone.

We were enjoying each other's company very much. Cuddling with Kathryn, holding her in my arms...that was an amazing feeling. I honestly had never felt anything so nice. Sexually, Kathryn was a bit cautious; it was frustrating at times...but there was something special in the feeling between us. As much as I loved my prior two wives, it never felt this good. It would not be until many years later that I would understand energy and that these feelings were due to the power of true love from someone who really knew what it means to love. It was also much later that I realized how numb I had been to life and love in my past relationships.

I spent a lot of time just looking into Kathryn's beautiful face and being grateful that she was in my life. The feeling of love was so strong I thought I would burst into a million pieces. It was not long, only a few days after our first night, that I told Kathryn, "I love you." She smiled but did not say anything. I did not need her to, I could feel her love and had no doubt that she loved me too.

I continued to take dance lessons, but not quite so many group classes. I kept my private lessons at the same level though, and soon Kathryn started taking privates from Julie as well. There were a few weekends that we went to dance workshops together. We continued to go to dances, but not quite as much as I had before we started seeing each other. Kathryn's dancing improved, yet she was never as good as some of the women I had gotten to know and enjoyed dancing with. I made an arrangement to practice with another woman and when I told Kathryn about it she was furious. "Why do you want to do this? Do you need to have other women approve of you?" She demanded to know.

I could not understand her reaction. "No, I just want to improve my dancing. I might want to teach someday." I responded in defense.

"Well I don't like it. Either you are with me or you are not." Kathryn said like a woman scorned.

We argued back and forth for a little while about this, and then I went outside to calm myself down. I did not understand Kathryn's reaction. I didn't have sex or romance with this other lady in mind...however I did like the attention. I was a bit alarmed that we would be having such an intense fight so soon into our relationship. I have never had this happen before. Maria and I hardly ever fought about anything. However, it did remind me of fights I had with my first wife Kat, but not until we had been living together for a long time. Both Kathryns had the star sign of Cancer, which I thought might have something to do with it. I didn't like this at all. I thought, *What is it going to be like when we have known each other for a long time, constant fighting?* After a while I calmed down and decided that I did not need to push this issue yet. I went in and told Kathryn that although I did not agree with her, I would cancel my arrangements to practice with the other woman.

Kathryn and I were both devoted to our spiritual path. Because I had been actively studying and going to church for many years, and because Kathryn had just recently found SLC and started attending services, I saw Kathryn as someone who was just getting started on her spiritual path. Months before I met Kathryn, I had written up a list of attributes that I wanted the next woman in my life to have. Kathryn had most of these qualities and I was in awe of the Universe's ability to deliver. Yet, one of the things that I was looking for was someone who could teach me something about spirituality. I believed that I was the teacher in my relationship with Maria, and I now wanted a teacher in my life. I was a little disappointed that I would again have to be the teacher with Kathryn. Such was my arrogance at the time...little did I know just how much Kathryn would teach me over the next few years to come.

Kathryn started coming to the ACIM[1] meetings with me. She liked it enough that she got her own book. Many evenings before going to sleep, we would sit in bed and read a few pages to each other and discuss it. Sometimes we would stay up for hours talking about what we read; how we had used these principles in our lives; or how we could have used them in some situation and how the outcome would have been different.

I was amazed at how easily Kathryn understood the material. I was also impressed with how caring and considerate of others she was. ACIM talks about how the basis of the illusionary experience we have here on the Earth plane is our belief that we are separate from each other and from God. Considering the needs of others was something that I needed to improve. Kathryn was at the opposite end of the spectrum; she placed the needs of others before her own. Both actions were based on our belief in separation and ACIM was helping us to see this. But Kathryn had a deep compassion for others that came from an inner awareness of oneness. Although I did understand that oneness on a mental level, my

---

[1] "A Course In Miracles"

belief was firmly in separation and my actions were based on this belief and what others could do for me.

A Long Distance Relationship

One day at work, about four weeks after Kathryn and I had begun our relationship, the woman who took care of payroll came into my office, handed me my paycheck, and said, "I have some bad news for you. The IRS sent me this letter of garnishment. I just got off the phone with them and they said since I had already written out your check you could have it, but from the next one onward they will be taking a big piece of it."

I had my own Software business for six years during my early twenties. I had never gotten into the routine of deducting tax money from my pay and saving it. I kept putting it off thinking that because my income continued to go up, one day it would be easy to catch up and then stay current. This went on for four years until my income started to decline, and for two more years after that. I declared bankruptcy right before going into drug rehab but it did not free me from my debt to the States of California and Oregon or to the IRS. My attorney told me that I could not clear these debts through bankruptcy.

About a year after getting clean and sober, I got a Software Engineering job in Salem, Oregon, and of course they deducted for my taxes. But I still had those six years of unpaid taxes. I had read the book "A Bridge Across Forever" by Richard Bach where he talked about his experience with unpaid taxes, the IRS, and bankruptcy.[1] So I went to a different attorney to find out what I could do. I was told that the debt had to be three years old and the tax forms filed in order to bankrupt them. Damn! I had not even filed the forms! Back then I thought, *What was the use if I could not pay the debt*? The attorney advised me to first file the tax forms. Then I was to either work out a deal with the IRS or to try to stay out of their reach for three years…after which time I could bankrupt the debt.

I had tried to bargain with the IRS once before, so that option seemed hopeless to me. The wait and file bankruptcy option sounded like a long wait, but it was the best option I could see. I filed the tax forms and hoped that I could avoid the IRS. No such luck, within about six months' time, the IRS had garnished my wages at the company I worked for in Salem. Then I filled a bogus Chapter 13 bankruptcy in hopes that it would buy me some time. The Chapter 13 protected me from garnishment for the few months that it took for the court to evaluate my plan.

---

[1] "A Bridge Across Forever" is an excellent book! I highly recommend it. http://gr8Wisdom.com/Books/Bridge (proper capitalization is important when locating this website)

Unfortunately it also delayed the three year period of time before I could file a Chapter 7 bankruptcy. But I did NOT miss a paycheck! Within a few months the courts dismissed my Chapter 13 plan as unworkable, and it was. Once the clock began to run again, the IRS had forgotten about me.

It was just a few weeks after I filed my Chapter 13 that I got the current job in Lake Oswego. The State of Oregon was more on the ball than the IRS and had caught up with me eighteen months earlier and was already taking twenty-five percent of my pay. I could live with that and I had the ability to pay that off eventually...but with the IRS catching up to me again and wanting seventy-five percent of my pay I did not know what I was going to do. I went home to Kathryn that evening and told her about what had happened.

"What are you going to do?" she asked.

"I don't know," I said, "but I am sure it will all work out. Still, I am a little bit worried."

The next morning while I was at work I got a phone call from Bill, the VP of Raima Corporation in Bellevue Washington, a suburb of Seattle. This was a database company whose software I had recommended to both my current employer and the previous one in Salem. I had been using their software for a few years by that time.

Bill said, "Do you remember applying for a management job with us last year? Actually I am the one who got that job, but I do need more software engineers. Would you be interested in coming up for an interview?"

"Yes, I would. When would you like to see me?" I replied calmly, trying to conceal my excitement.

"The sooner the better. I have a few openings and a lot of work that needs to get done now. How about tomorrow?" Bill said.

"How about this afternoon?" I replied.

"Yes, I can see you at 3:30 today."

"Good, I'll be there."

I left work, went home to get a few things, and then drove three hours to Bellevue. The interview went well, and I was offered a job on the spot with a small pay increase to boot. I accepted the job and agreed to start work on Monday. As I drove home, I was high on life and how it always works out. I have believed this for many years, and once again I had proof. But, what about Kathryn and me? What would happen with us?

When I got back from Bellevue, I told Kathryn all about the interview. She was surprised at the synchronicity; however, she was less than enthusiastic and did not see how this was part of a divine plan. "What will happen to us?" she asked.

"I don't know. Maybe you could come to Bellevue and live with me."

"I can't leave my home," Kathryn said, "what would I do about Gus? I can't abandon him."

I replied, "I'm not sure what we will do but I know that I'm not really interested in a long distance relationship. I'd be willing to try for a while but if we continue to feel the same about each other, I would want to live with you."

Kathryn said, "But couldn't you find another job here in Portland?" I responded, "I'm sure I could, given enough time, but the synchronicity of this offer coming at the same time as the IRS garnishment seems like God is trying to move me...perhaps us...in that direction. This job is in Bellevue, I always said if I had to live and work in the Seattle area it would have to be Bellevue. Also, I'll shake off the State of Oregon's garnishment by moving to Washington. This job has the benefit that I will get to do development work in Microsoft Windows. Recently it has been taking off like a rocket, and I know it will be the way of the future. I've wanted to work with Windows for nearly a year now. It is all coming together perfectly. Except for our relationship, of course, but somehow, someway, it must be perfect for it too. We just don't see it right now."

We decided to take it a day at a time and let the next few weeks unfold. I called the Unity of Bellevue church in hopes that they might know someone who had a room for rent. They gave me the phone number of a man who had a mother-in-law apartment, he needed a tenant. It turned out that his place was only minutes from my new office and I took it sight-unseen. I felt that God was leading me to just the right place, and it did work out perfectly for the few months that I would be there. It was truly amazing how smoothly things were going; I am certain I would have encountered one road block after another had I attempted to stay in Portland.[1]

I began organizing and sorting out my belongings. I decided not to keep much. I figured Kathryn and I would end up living together at some point and didn't want to haul all of my stuff to Bellevue. If we didn't it

---

[1] Dear reader, life really is that simple. Sit back and relax and take it as it comes and give thanks for it, all of it. Because Life really is going perfectly, when you get in harmony with this FACT then you too will have the smoothness of transitions that I testify to in this book. My life is still like this, but many levels more fantastic still.

would not be much of a loss, most of my stuff was junk. Some of it went to Goodwill and the rest got thrown out.

Kathryn's sister Bridget got married on the following Saturday. We had a romantic time at the ceremony. I thought to myself, *One day I will marry Kathryn.* After the wedding, Kathryn came over to my house to help me pack the things that I would store in her garage. We stopped for ice-cream on the way and got it to go. It was particularly memorable because we were being so silly and playful. I made a comment about how stale the ice-cream cone was and bent the bottom up a little like a comma to show her. Kathryn had a great laugh; I loved to hear her laugh. Once she got started, it was hard to stop her, she could keep going for a long time. This was one of those times and it was contagious. I got to laughing so hard that I was making a mess with my ice-cream and the tears were making if difficult to see the road, so I had to pull over until we both settled down.

Late Sunday afternoon, I left for Bellevue with a fully loaded car. The last few days with Kathryn had been bittersweet. Emotionally we kept getting closer and closer yet the physical distance that would be between us frightened us both. When I got to my new home, I was delighted to see how nice it was. I had a lot of private space for myself. My new housemate was nice…so were the people at my new job…the work was fun. It all fell into place very easily.

Kathryn and I talked on the phone every day for an hour or more. I went back to Portland on Friday to be with her and to pick up more of my stuff. I was so excited when I turned the corner into her neighborhood. Kathryn was happy to see me when I arrived; we held each other for a very long time.

Kathryn took me by the hand, sat me down in the living room, and said to me, "I have a surprise for you." Then she put on a tape of Natalie Cole and her deceased father Nat King Cole singing "Unforgettable"[1] and said "I dedicate this song to you, my unforgettable lover." After the song finished, we made love on the living room floor while the rest of the tape played in the background. We lay there and cuddled, talking some and sleeping some, for at least an hour before we went out for dinner.

We did our usual things, dancing, taking Gus for walks, and attending church services at the Spiritual Life Center. At night before

---

[1] The words to Irving Gordon's song "Unforgettable" "That's why darling it's incredible, that someone so unforgettable, would think that I was, unforgettable too," expressed the way that Kathryn and I felt about each other and how we could hardly believe that we had found each other. I still think of Kathryn whenever I hear this song.

going to sleep we read to each other from "A Course In Miracles." We talked for hours and continued to get to know each other better.

"I have a friend named Steven who I'd love for you to meet." I said to Kathryn.

"Who is Steven, why do you want me to meet him?" She replied.

I began to tell Kathryn the story, "I met Steven at the Unity Church in Gresham; I was with Maria at the time. Maria and I were sitting in church waiting for the service to start; the boys were in Sunday school. I noticed Steven walk in with another man named John, they sat in the row of pews right in front of us. When I saw Steven, I knew that we would become friends, it was just a feeling I had. After the service was over and we were all socializing, I saw John and Steven and introduced Maria and myself. We discovered that they were a gay couple, which was no surprise to me. Steven and I did become good friends. Steven and John came to our house on a few occasions."

"Do you remember? I told you I went with Steven on that weekend retreat at Crystal Mountain. When I returned from the retreat Maria dropped the news about her affair and announced that she was leaving me. I called Steven for support, he was not home, but John was. John invited me over and then later Steven showed up. They both helped me make it through a very rough night, and I remained clean and sober. My relationship with Steven grew much closer as a result of that weekend and the next year. Steven and John had gone through a kind of a split as well. John had a serious problem with drinking, and Steven gave the ultimatum to stop or split up. John tried but was not quite ready to stop.[1] They continued to live in the same apartment for awhile but no longer as a couple. Steven eventually bought a house and moved out leaving John on his own."

"As this last year unfolded, Steven met a new man, Drew. They had a very close connection from the start. It was not long before Drew moved in with Steven. In the beginning I received a couple of phone calls about a few of their dramas; each time Steven thought their relationship was over. Then they seemed to settle into a rhythm, and were able to cope with whatever difference that came up...at least well enough to stay together. I gave Steven and Drew private dance lessons, East-Coast Swing and Waltz. The last report I had from them was that they were using what they had learned at a gay club and was enjoying some group lessons they found in the gay community. The reason I want you to meet

---

[1] Over the years John continued to be good friends with Steven and Steven helped John attempt to get sober many times. It was near the conclusion of this story that Steven's help was fully received by John and John is now many years clean and sober and working as a well respected drug and alcohol counselor.

Steven is that he is a dear friend of mine and I just know you will like him too. He is a very nice man."

With a questioning tone Kathryn said, "Okay...I don't know what to say...I don't really know any gay people. I can keep an open mind. Did you have a time in mind for meeting up with Steven?"

"Have you ever had Dim-Sum?"

"Dim-Sum? No, what is that?"

"Dim-Sum is a type of Chinese lunch. They come around with a cart containing lots of different dishes. Each dish contains two to four of the same small items in it...they are like Chinese appetizers that you make a meal out of. They are tasty, filling, and reasonable in price. You like Chinese food so I know you will like this. This is one of Steven and my favorite ways to meet and catch up. Shall I invite him this Sunday?"

"Sure, I'll meet your friend Steven and try Dim-Sum."

When Kathryn met Steven, there was an immediate connection with the two of them as I suspected there would be. She was not as keen about the Dim-Sum as Steven and I were, but she did not mind it. Little did we know what dear friends the three of us would become. When Steven left, Kathryn told me, "He was nice. I've never had a gay man for a friend before so this seems very strange to me, but I do like Steven."

On the way back to Kathryn's house she one again suggested that I try to find work in Portland. I had missed her so much while I was working up in Bellevue, that I gave it another try. I looked in the Sunday Oregonian but found nothing that was appropriate. I even called a couple of people I knew in the industry, but they had nothing. It seemed like all the road blocks were up in Portland for me, which contrasted with how everything was clear and easy in Seattle.

On Sunday afternoon we loaded up my car with most of my remaining possessions. I cried as I was getting into my car to return to Bellevue. It was a long and lonely ride home. I thought about how nice it would be if Kathryn would move up to Bellevue to live with me. I went dancing that evening but it wasn't the same. I didn't know anyone, and I was not that interested in getting to know anyone else...it was Kathryn I wanted to be with.

Thank God we could afford the phone calls. When we were away from each other, there was not a day that went by that I did not talk to Kathryn on the phone.

On the following Friday, Kathryn came up to stay with me. I was inside my house looking out the window when I saw her pull into the driveway. I was so excited I was actually jumping up and down. I didn't realize that she could see me, but she did, and over the years she commented repeatedly about how much that touched her heart.

I had spent some of my free time exploring the Seattle area and was happy to take Kathryn to the best spots I had found. One of our favorites was Pike Place Market. Later that evening we went to a dance together. She too commented about it not being as much fun. "They are all so serious here." She said.

"But they are very good dancers, better on the whole than those in Portland." I replied.

Kathryn wasn't swayed by logic, reason, or a good dance performance, she said, "I miss our group, our church friends that we usually go dancing with."

"Yeah, me too." I replied, "Maybe we can find a similar group here in Seattle."[1]

On Sunday we tried the local "New Thought" church in Bellevue, but it did not have the same wonderful feeling that we got from SLC…actually it was depressing. Because the church was so close, and to give the minister the benefit of the doubt, we decided to give it another try the next time Kathryn came to Bellevue. Who knows the minister might have been having an off day. The next time we went to the early service so that we could attend a late service at another church, such was our determination to find a spiritual home. Again we were not impressed with the first service at the Bellevue church; however, the late service at a Seattle new thought church was a better experience. This church was a much longer drive from home, but it turned out to be worth the extra commute.

Right away we knew that this was going to be more to our liking. Upon our arrival we noticed that the people from the last service, those who were heading to their cars, were much more joyful and enthusiastic. The greeters at the door also had a light and joyful energy about them. We sat in the front row and waited for the service to begin. A few people sat near us and introduced themselves. There was more life to the service. The music was more uplifting, and one of the songs was a favorite of ours from SLC. The minister was funny and animated, much more so than the minister from SLC, but she was not as deep and inspiring. At times she could be, but not so often. We found it easy to meet and talk to people when the service was over.

---

[1] It is a common trait when humans change environments to try to recreate in the new environment something that gave them joy in the old environment. I have found it is often easier to discover what new delights exist in the new environment, than it is to attempt to try to recreate the old.

On our way back to my place, we talked about the experience. Fishing for Kathryn's approval I said, "I enjoyed that...very much. Finally we found a church...do you agree?"

"Oh yes, it was much better than the other church, but still it was not SLC."

"Yeah, but it will do." I replied trying to break her attachment to SLC, "There are still a few more churches that we can check out. We can give them a try next time. Who knows maybe one of them will be as good as SLC. But if not, this one will do." I wanted Kathryn to like it enough for her to come and live here with me. I knew finding a good church was an important factor.

The following Sunday after we had been to an SLC service just as we got into our car to leave Kathryn said, "Mike, I've been giving it a lot of thought..." With just enough pause for me to wonder if this was going to be good news or bad, she continued, "I've decided to come to Bellevue to live with you. I love you Mike, and I want to be with you."

Wow, finally she made the decision; I was overwhelmed with happiness. Love's tears trickled down my face, I reached over to hold her and whispered in her ear, "You dear sweet woman, you have made me so happy...thank you...I love you."

One of our favorite swing dance groups was holding their monthly dance that evening. Last month, someone announced that there was a dress code and that shorts would no longer be permitted at the dances. That pissed me off. I liked wearing shorts...even in shorts I was soaking wet from sweat, long pants were only going to make my discomfort worse. So that evening I asked Kathryn if she had a dress I could wear, I wanted to make a statement. She found a skirt which fit me. I also brought along a pair of pants just in case they would not let me in. The organizers took the joke quite well, and I got a lot of comments from the other dancers. After a few hours, I changed into my pants, feeling that I had already made my statement.

Kathryn came up to Bellevue the following weekend. She had been rethinking her decision to move in with me and told me she was not sure again. It was very upsetting to me but I decided to just give her a little more time; I was confident that she would come around. Later that week, on Wednesday evening when I tried calling Kathryn, I got her machine. It wasn't until I was settling into bed that she returned my call.

"Hello Mike," she said, "did I wake you?"

"No," I replied, "I was just getting ready for bed."

"Well I've come to a decision." She said with a solemn tone in her voice.

"Ohhh...." I said as my heart started to beat much faster and fear over came me in a cold flush. I could barely ask, "What decision is that?"

"James came over tonight and we had a long talk. He was very sorry and it sounds like he really wants to change and to give our relationship another try...I've been giving it a lot of thought and...I...I decided that I need to try to work it out with him."

My heart felt heavy; depression rushed through me like a bad drug. "Are you sure?" I asked, "Why do you think it is going to be different this time?"

She did not reply. After a long pause I added, "Well if that is what you have decided I wish you all the best. Look I better go now, I guess there is not much more to talk about."

"I love you Mike" she said, "I just can't let go of fourteen years without giving it one more try. I hope you understand."

"I don't like it, but I understand." I replied choking back the tears, "I've got to go, I love you too." I hung up the phone.

I began to cry uncontrollably. I thought, *How could she? Wasn't I better for her than he was? In a few weeks or months she is going to regret this and then I may have already moved on. I'll be all right by then, but will she?* I tried to sleep but my mind would not turn off. I tossed and turned and cried all night long. In the end I got maybe two hours of broken sleep.

I went into work a total mess. It was tough going, trying to focus on my job. I went and talked to a work mate who listened attentively and was sympathetic. Still not able to focus on work, I called up my private dance instructor and asked if she was free for a lesson...she was. So I left work hoping that an hour of something I enjoyed would help me get my mind off of Kathryn. My instructor, Joyce, was an attractive woman; when I first met her, I thought that if I was not with Kathryn, I would like to date her. Given the change in relationship, I decided to ask Joyce out that weekend. She politely declined. I felt very weird asking her, like I was cheating on Kathryn.

I went back to work feeling as bad as I had before I left. When I got to my desk, the message light on my phone was blinking. I listened to my voice message, and it was Kathryn. She said with tears in her voice, "Oh Mike, I've made such a big mistake. How could I have thought I could make it work with James. I am so sorry. Please call, I am not going to get back together with him."

My heart leapt for joy. I called Kathryn immediately, "Hi Kathryn it's me, I got your message."

"Oh Mike, can you forgive me?" Kathryn's voice was soft and sincere. "I was awake all night. It was not long after I talked to you that I knew I had made a big mistake. I would have called but I did not want to wake you."

"Wake me! Are you kidding?" I said nearly shouting, "I couldn't sleep at all…you kept me up all night long." I ended with a pout.

"You handled it so well on the phone last night that I thought I did not mean that much to you after all. Why didn't you try to make me change my mind?"

"Because you do mean that much to me," I replied, "I don't want to manipulate you; I want you to want to be with me. It seemed as if you wanted to be with him."

"Oh, no," Kathryn said, "James is such a manipulator; he spent hours wearing me down. Prior to that, my friend Molly worked on me while we waited for James to come over. Between the two of them, I was convinced it was the right thing to do…temporarily that is…but I don't love him; it is you that I love. I never want to be without you."

I loved hearing those words. "I love you, Kathryn. I am so glad you changed your mind." I thought about how I almost made a very bad mistake asking Joyce out on a date.

Kathryn said, "I do want to come and live in Bellevue with you. I really do love you…I can see now that I need to get out of Portland. It is toxic for me here—Poison people, poisoned relationships. I know it is your weekend to come down here, but how about if I come up there and we look for a place to live together."

Yes, YES, **YES!** I shouted in the privacy of my own mind. With a calm and steady voice I said, "That would be wonderful."

Lives Merge

I left work after we hung up. I could not concentrate anyway. I got an apartment guide and went looking at the various places that sounded good. I was very happy to see Kathryn when she drove up on Friday evening. I held her tight and whispered in her ear, "I never want to let you go." On Saturday, we went around and looked at the best apartments I had seen on Thursday. Kathryn and I both liked the same apartment, but the cost was more than we wanted to spend. In the end we took it, because the others just could not compare; for the few extra dollars, it was a much better value.

"How can we afford this?" Kathryn asked.

"I know it will work out. The other places just won't do. Somehow God will provide what we need. Look at how perfectly things have worked out already. It is even starting to look like this move to Seattle is perfect for you too. Between James, Molly, and your family, you have a lot of negative influences in Oregon. Moving here will take you away from them, and you can have a fresh start to your life."

"Yes, I believe you are right. It looks that way to me, too."

We signed the necessary paperwork and agreed to take possession in two weeks. Kathryn and I went to my apartment and made love; our connection kept growing stronger and deeper. The whole weekend was so good, that late Sunday afternoon, Kathryn decided she would rather stay another night with me. That meant she had to drive to her job in Portland in the morning.

Kathryn had only been at the office for a few hours before she decided to quit her job right then and there. She had planned on waiting another week, but then she figured her life in Portland was over anyway so why wait. She went home and started packing up her things to move in with me. I started organizing things like utilities and a bed. Kathryn had a water bed which was not good for my back so we needed a new bed. It's funny how we limit ourselves. The money to do all of this seemed overwhelming and yet the expenses were necessary. I went looking for a good quality used bed but found nothing but junk. After a while, I realized I was spending more time on this search than it was worth. I decided my time was valuable and bought a new bed. The funny thing is we survived that purchase and many others like it. We put ourselves through much drama over such financial issues, and in the end the only real drama was the one we created in our mind.

I went down to Portland the following weekend and helped Kathryn pack up her things. I brought a car load of her stuff up with me.

It had to stay in my apartment for five more days, that's when we got possession of the new apartment. The following weekend, Kathryn came to me with a carload of her stuff as well. Between those two car loads of stuff and what I already had, we were ready to live there. It was a little bit like camping out but it was our first home together. This was a very nice two bed room apartment that even had a washer and dryer in a hall closet. It was a little over 1,200 sq ft and had a lovely view of Lake Sammamish. We were close to two good shopping centers. The freeway was near, yet we did not get much noise from it. Both Kathryn and I were delighted to be there.

We went to a nearby bank and opened a joint checking and savings account. I had a good job and was making good money. Kathryn no longer had a job but was receiving support payments from her ex-husband. Kathryn had more possessions of value, a home, a little jewelry, and very nice furnishings. But I had a much larger cash flow. I felt that it was important for us to have a joint bank account because I considered Kathryn to be my partner.

In my last two marriages, it did not feel like a partnership. I earned the income yet Kat and Maria mostly stayed at home doing as they pleased. Unfortunately, neither one of them was much of a housewife. A lot went undone and there were conflicts around who did what and who should do what. I felt that if I earned the money, then they should take care of the home, but it did not work that way with them, at least not to my level of satisfaction.

With Kathryn this was very different. Even though she never worked a real job during the entire time we were together, she always did her share. Actually she worked harder than me; I had to work hard to get her to slow down and play.

Kathryn stayed in our apartment until Tuesday afternoon when she dropped me off at SeaTac airport. She continued driving down to Portland…I flew to Central California to visit a client of Raima[1] to write some custom software for them. On Friday, I flew back into Portland. We organized the weekend to place some of her things in storage and bring the rest up to Bellevue in a U-Haul truck. The timings and orchestrations were perfect. Since I did not have a car sitting in Portland, I drove the truck home and Kathryn drove her car. Everything we did to make this move and to integrate our lives flowed as smoothly as can be. Every time we resisted or tried to hang on to the old, things got difficult.

In the next few weeks, Kathryn found an agency to manage the rental of her home. By the beginning of December, 1991, the agency had found a responsible couple for tenants. It was only five months after our

---

[1] My employer.

first date...I had a new job; we had moved to a new city; we were all settled into our first apartment; and Kathryn had her home rented out. If you had told us then how much our lives would change in five months, I would not have believed you. If we had tried to plan a better beginning we could not have done so. Things were going very well.

My dear friend Steven topped off our good fortune when he called me at work one afternoon. He called to let us know that he and Drew were moving up to Seattle and they would love to get together with Kathryn and me once they had settled in. I told him that we would like that too. It became a regular thing for us to meet up with them once every couple of months.

I enjoyed living with Kathryn. Our conversations were stimulating and we loved playing together. Our love life was awesome; Kathryn had loosened up a great deal. We loved exploring this new city and the countryside together. One time, Kathryn came and picked me up at work; we drove over to a park on Lake Washington in a very affluent part of Bellevue. We sat in the car and watched the rain fall; the wind was blowing the last of the fall colors off of the trees. It was nice to have such a sweet loving woman make me lunch and take me out for a picnic in the car.

We were quite content...until we weren't.

We found that our relationship was beginning to become stressed by our heavy dependence upon each other for company. Because this was a new city for us both, we were lacking in close friends...we spent a lot of time together. We did not balance it with taking time for ourselves or with other people. In our social outreach efforts, we continued trying out different churches. In the end we settled for the Seattle new thought church. We had been going to ACIM meetings held at the local Unity church. We met people in both of these places, but we still had not really met anyone we wanted to call friends.

One day when the need for the company of other people got the better of us, we both decided to go out and have lunch with a friend...but who? Kathryn knew a woman who used to be her neighbor in Portland, the last Kathryn heard was that her friend was living in Bellevue. So Kathryn called her, they had a long chat on the phone; and then Kathryn arranged a lunch date. I called a man named Joe who I had met at an ACIM meeting. We also arranged to have lunch.

Kathryn and I both went our separate ways for our respective lunch dates. I met Joe at his office. He knew this town much better than I did so he drove us to one of his favorite restaurants. I was shocked when the hostess seated us at the table right next to Kathryn and her friend. There must be hundreds of restaurants in the area. How did we pick the same one? Empty tables everywhere, we were the only two sets of patrons in the entire restaurant, and the hostess seated us right next to the woman I was trying to get away from. I was so stunned that I did not have the presence of mind to ask to be seated elsewhere. When I got home...let me tell you...I got an earful about that mistake. Kathryn imagined that I had overheard where she was going, and I followed her there. It was something that James might have done, but not me. It was easy to make her understand it was a "coincidence." All in all, it was quite a funny experience. I am sure we were both drawn to that place together because we were such a close vibrational match to each other.

Kathryn and I continued our ballroom dancing...for a time. We went to some of the dances, and we both took private lessons. But after many months, we felt dissatisfied with the experience. It was just not the same for us as it had been in Portland. Also, Kathryn and I were beginning to experience a fair bit of conflict around the topic of dance.

Kathryn was only a fair dancer, as far as technique goes. I was definitely infatuated with her and enjoyed dancing with her. But as style and technique goes, she was very limiting to dance with. I enjoyed dancing with other women because it gave me the chance to use all that I had learned. I enjoyed it. I also enjoyed the attention I got, both from the other women, and from the men who watched me dance as well. Kathryn addressed this issue with me often and the dancing became more stressful for us. Kathryn had the ability to feel and know my true inner intention, often before I was even consciously aware of it. She did not like it that I sought attention from other women, or even at all. She wanted to be invisible. And she certainly did not want me getting too close to another woman. I had a difficult time owning my part in the separation this was creating between us, but I eventually did see it through her eyes. If I was dancing with other women out of friendship or because I felt compassion for them and how they had to sit so many songs out, I know Kathryn would not have had a problem with it. But because I was seeking attention, and usually from the attractive women, my actions had a completely different feel to her, and she did not like it. It wasn't long before dancing became something we only did at home...with the exception of a few special social occasions each year.

When the new year rolled around, we both volunteered as ushers at our church and took our first class there as well. We enjoyed both of these activities, and we started to make friends. I went into the class with the attitude that I was only there to make friends, that I already had this stuff down pat. I spoke up often and shared my "wealth of experience and knowledge" with the class. It wasn't until years later that I finally understood how arrogant I was, how much attention I was seeking, and how much approval from others I needed so that I could feel good about myself. Although I understood the spiritual topics presented in the class with my mind, I had not fully integrated them on an experiential level, and thus did not really understand at all. I was doing well with manifesting events and things I needed, but my people and relationship skills were still lacking. My self-worth was tenuous at best, and my peace and joy were heavily dependent upon outside circumstances.

Kathryn and I enjoyed doing our homework together. I liked how she was able to understand the material with such ease. We would read our assigned chapters out loud while sitting up in bed. Often this would evolve into lively discussions, a close cuddle, and very sweet lovemaking.

One Saturday afternoon, after completing a workshop at our church, a few of us decided to have a small party at the home of Bonnie, a woman in her 60s, who lived near the church. Julie, a very funny woman in her early 50s, was there; her life was a total mess. There was also Phylis, a nurse who was transitioning into a new career as a chef; she was a large woman with a large heart and a jolly personality. Kathryn and I made it a dinner party of five.

Julie was the funniest and most interesting of all. She told us stories of some of her past misadventures. It had been a long time since I had laughed so much. She told us a story about a time when she needed money, so she advertised in the paper as a painter. She got a job to do a bathroom. She wound up putting a hole in the wall and as she tried to repair it she just kept making it bigger and bigger. She went to great lengths to hide her mistake and not get caught while the owners kept needing to use the bathroom while she was trying to work. Julie reminded me of Lucile Ball and the *I Love Lucy* show when I listened to her story.

As the months moved on, Julie, Kathryn, and I came to spend a lot of time together. I thought we could help Julie see life a little more clearly, and I enjoyed her stories. They did, however, make me wonder, *Would we become one of Julie's stories? There were a lot of assholes in her life. How long would it be before I would become one of them?*[1] Kathryn and I included Julie in some of our outings and even paid her way a few times.[2] Kathryn met Julie at work, a job from hell, and they shared meals and conversation. Well not quite conversation...it was really an energy draining monologue that went on for hours on end. Julie would call

---

[1] If you want a quick way to sort someone out, this is it. Listen to them tell you about three to five people in their life...let them pick the people to talk about. What kind of things do they say about these people? Ask yourself is this the role I want to play in their life? Is this how I want them talking about me a few months from now? Then listen to yourself talk about others and turn these questions on yourself.

[2] By this point in my life I realized I had much more fun if I just paid their way when it came to outings with certain people. If I let their financial limitation be mine, then there were many activities I could not participate in. But when I paid for us all, we could do anything. I did not count up what was owed to me, I just wanted to enjoy.

Kathryn on the phone and talk non-stop. Kathryn did not have the necessary skills to get out of it...she was however in the process of developing them. Julie was Kathryn's current teacher.

This was our first experience with recognizing an energy vampire. I had been operating under the false assumption that everyone wanted to grow. We all have some area in our lives where we are not very skilled at getting what we say we want out of life. I have since learned that even if someone says they want something, like being treated with respect for example, they are not always ready to make the necessary changes to achieve that desire. There are other unspoken desires and learned behaviors that conflict with the spoken desire. They are not ready to let go of the conflicting desires; this is the reason they don't have what they want already. This conflict is the real source of pain and suffering in people's lives.

Julie did not really want the problems solved. They were giving her something she needed...attention and energy. In her mind, the problems gave her the right to call up her friends and talk non-stop about how difficult life was or how no one respected her or treated her right. Eventually, those friends she was calling would dump her, and then she would tell us all about how unfair they were. In time we too were in that category. After a while, Kathryn realized that Julie was sucking her dry energetically. At first Kathryn tried getting out of conversations with Julie quickly, screening phone calls, and making up excuses of why she could not talk long. But Julie was persistent; she demanded that we did not abandon her.

Finally Kathryn had to write Julie a letter to end the friendship. She kept it simple and kind. At the time, I thought she was being too kind; however I grew to respect that quality in her. Kathryn was always sensitive to the feelings of others and bent over backwards to try to make things comfortable for them. Kathryn's letter simply stated that she was complete with the friendship and wished Julie the best. She did not go into the reasons or blame of any sort. Julie however, was not so kind. She wrote a scathing letter in response; fair-weathered-friends were one of the nicer ways she referred to Kathryn and me. Julie even left a few nasty messages on our answering machine.

This is when I stepped in. I wrote Julie a letter too, but this one was not as nice as Kathryn's. I detailed her problems and told her how angry I felt every time she held Kathryn captive on the phone. This just added more fuel to the fire, and showed that I had not really learned the spiritual lessons that I thought I had. In the end, we learned to ignore her phone calls and letters, and even hung up on her the few times she got one of us on the phone. This method proved to be the most effective. Now that I really do understand the true nature of life, it is the only solution that makes any sense at all. Pushing against or resisting a problem only supports it. Ignoring it and focusing in the opposite direction allows the energy to dissipate. Certainly, one needs to deal with whatever drops in one's lap. But the emotional ego energy we apply toward resisting a problem does not help; it only diminishes ones own energy and fuels the fire.

Jesus told us to turn the other cheek. What he meant by this was to change our focus, to look and think in another direction. To fight back or to resist the problem, only perpetuates the erroneous thinking that brought on the problem in the first place. Resist not evil, because it is by your resistance that you feed it. By turning the other cheek and focusing elsewhere, all energy is withdrawn from the evil and movement is created in the direction of your focus.

Spiritual lessons such as this deserve contemplation and to be programmed into your subconscious by repetition. It is so important to understand, that these are not just concepts, because they are the keys to getting you what you are truly seeking in life. These spiritual axioms are the guide posts that lead us down the correct path to our chosen destination. They are the light houses that prevent us from running into the rocky shores of trouble.

Resistance gives power to the thing you are resisting. Focus your mind, your thoughts, your energy on what you do want, not on what you don't want. Stop reading, stop doing…sit and contemplate this.

Isaiah Our First Master

It was at a workshop in June of 1992 that Lin approached me to invite Kathryn and me to become members of a group that she was forming. By this time, we were enrolled in the second level class at our church…this is where we met Lin and her husband Dan. A few weeks earlier at one of the classes, Lin and I had paired up for an exercise, and this is when I first found out that Lin was a psychic. I was fascinated and asked a lot of questions, but I was skeptical. I wondered why she was telling me this. Later, Kathryn and Lin pared up and hit it off. After that, we chatted with Lin and Dan whenever we saw them at church.

Lin explained to me that she would be channeling an entity named Isaiah, and the group would be getting lessons and the chance to ask questions. I was very excited that Lin sought us out to invite us to be a part of this group. Lin had invited others from the class, and our friend Bonnie offered to hold the group meetings in her apartment. Including Lin and her husband Dan, there were seven of us at that first meeting. When the group started, Lin announced that she would not accept any money as payment for doing the group; this was a gift of love she was offering to us and to the world. We got Lin to agree to accept money to pay the baby sitter who watched her little boy.

Lin started out by telling us her history with Isaiah and what to expect. It seems that Isaiah, a disincarnate entity, had approached her many years ago. The first few encounters were very traumatic for her and caused her to have severe headaches. She then went a few years without much contact from Isaiah until just recently when he asked her to start this group. Lin was reluctant to do so and had her own issues of disbelief and privacy regarding it.

As Lin prepared to start channeling, she sat in a cross-legged posture on the floor. She warned us that nothing might happen; she was not sure. It took a few minutes for Isaiah to come through, but then it happened. Lin's body began to move and twitch just a little, and she tried to make it comfortable.

> Greetings, dear ones. We are here. We are pleased to see that you have accepted our invitation to join this group of healers. You are to be healers…you are to be teachers of teachers. You will learn much about energy and how it works in your lives. One of you here is also capable of channeling and will do so in the near future. There are those of you who mistakenly think that it is you. There will be jealousy and surprise when you discover it is not you but another.

Isaiah went on with the lesson which was primarily about energy. We all got to ask questions of Isaiah after he finished his lecture.

When the group was over, both Kathryn and I were impressed enough to make appointments for a private counseling session with Lin and Isaiah. Feeling high as a kite from the meeting, we wondered if this was the energy that Isaiah had been talking about. I had never really understood that life could be broken down into movements of energy, or how we each emit an energy that can be felt by others. Maybe I had, but it had not been emphasized like it had this evening...okay, for the first time I was ready to hear it. This was the first time I realized it was actually an important topic.

Even though I was not so sure I was feeling energy from Isaiah, I did feel like I needed grounding before making the forty-minute drive home, so Kathryn and I stopped for a cup of tea and desert at a nearby restaurant. It was one of those magical evenings that happen this far north; at 9:00 PM there was still ample daylight and it was warm outside. We were truly in a state of bliss.

As I was listening to Isaiah, I thought it would be me who would also channel, after all, I have been studying this stuff for many years longer than the rest of the group. For years I had prayed and asked to do this kind of work.

Later at home, while reading in bed, Kathryn said to me "I know who it is that will be channeling. I could feel Isaiah's words before he even said them...there were many times I knew exactly, word for word, what he was going to say next. I know it is me."

When Kathryn said that, I knew she was right, and I knew it was me that Isaiah was talking about when he said "there are those of you that think it is you." This was when I first began to realize that all of my study and practice of spiritual principals had made it into my mind but had yet to become integrated into who I was. I realized how much power Kathryn really had; she already knew all of this stuff on an experiential level from previous lifetimes; she just did not have all of the clever words and phrases. Yet, in so many ways, she already lived it.

I had my first private session with Lin a few days later. Lin wanted Kathryn and me to come on different days so she would not have to deal with two energies in the room. The session was fantastic. I learned a lot about myself that I had not been aware of. I was told of past lives; I was very intrigued. I was told to be careful about becoming sexually involved with another woman. Lin saw this in my energy and told me that Kathryn would not tolerate it, that she would leave me if that happened. As Lin was talking about my past wives, she said that it was me who left them.

"No no...." I corrected her by saying, "No...they left me. I didn't leave them. They left me."

Lin's response blew me away, "Emotionally...you left them emotionally long before they left you physically. Do you understand what we mean?" This was the first time I had looked at it this way, but I knew it was true. I also began to realize just how ignorant I was about my own intentions and energies.

Although I told Lin nothing about my family she knew them well and told me many things which totally amazed me. She described some of my past lives with them. She told me a lot about myself that I liked to hear. She also told me about traits I was nearly blind to; they were not pleasant to hear. Deep inside, I knew what she was telling me was true, both the good and the bad. I felt very fortunate, like I had just had a conversation with God. I was determined to grow and become all that I could be, so I took her wisdom and words of advice to heart.

Kathryn was very keen to listen to the tape of my session when I got home. We both took notes and it served to bond us even closer. My love for Kathryn and her love for me was growing with each day we spent together. Holding her in my arms, even just sitting next to her was like magic. The energy that moved between us was sweet and powerful, like two souls dancing to a divine melody. We had finally settled into the Seattle area and made friends. Our lives had become more balanced, which served to strengthen our relationship. This was a moment in time when we thought all was right with the world.

We both had been changing due to our choice to be aware and responsible. Kathryn was a doormat when I first met her, very meek, mild, and soft-spoken. But now, after nearly a year together, she was standing up for herself; I encouraged her and supported her in doing this, even when it was me she was standing up to. While listening to the tape, Kathryn heard Lin tell me that I liked to "needle," that it was harmful, and that it came from un-clarified energy from my past. I did not know what needling was; Lin explained, "Needling is when you say something unkind about Kathryn in the pretense of humor, but it really masks your own disturbed emotional state. You tell yourself that you are doing it in humor. Yet, it is an attack and felt as such."

Lately Kathryn had been calling me on this with ever increasing frequency. I would tell her "It's just a joke."

Then Kathryn would respond with, "Yes, but at whose expense?"

In defense I would say, "But everyone else does it, especially the guys at work. It's a hard habit to break."

Kathryn just got angrier and would respond with, "I don't like being treated that way, even if you think it is a joke."[1]

Kathryn derived great joy at hearing Lin confirm what Kathryn had been telling me all along. Kathryn loved seeing that I was finally listening, that I was beginning to recognize how destructive needling was. Over the next few weeks and months I took a look at how I was feeling and the energy that was moving through me when I would needle Kathryn. Lin and Kathryn were right; I did have a nasty streak running through me at the time. It was like all of my pent up anger and frustration would come up inside of me and I was dressing it up as a joke to hide my insane mental condition. Sometimes on my own, I would recognize when I was needling and apologize, but in the beginning Kathryn had to call it to my attention. Eventually I changed and came to find it equally distasteful when I witnessed others needling.

Kathryn had her session with Lin the following day. When she got home with the tape I was very excited, I could hardly wait to listen to it. What an angelic picture she painted of Kathryn. Of course areas in which Kathryn could grow were enumerated as well. But the difference between Kathryn and me was dramatic. Kathryn's issues were around caring for others too much and not taking enough care of herself. And my issues created harm or disharmony for others. I felt humbled. I finally began to realize that Kathryn was to be an incredible teacher for me. It's even funnier because before I met Kathryn, I wrote out a list of the qualities I wanted in a woman. I felt that I was the teacher for my previous two wives and that in my next relationship I wanted someone who could teach me. Once I met Kathryn, I thought I had gotten everything I wanted from my list except a teacher. I thought again I would be my wife's teacher. Now I saw the humor in my perspective on myself and others. I wondered what learning opportunities I missed in my previous marriages.

Lin confirmed that it was Kathryn who would also be a channeler. She talked of Kathryn's love of animals and their love for her, and that she mothered everything and everybody. Lin accurately tuned into Kathryn's family as was evidenced by her comments about them. She also tuned into Kathryn's dear friend, Joan that lived in Eastern Oregon; she was Kathryn's mother in a past life. Lin told Kathryn, "This one is loving, very loving...I wish I had a mother like that." As much as I believed that this psychic stuff was possible, it was astonishing to think

---

[1] You can still point out the obvious and humorous imperfections of others when you are clear and loving...then it will come across as humor to most people. It is the intention that matters, all words and actions are born from our intentions; this is why clarity of energy, focus and purpose in life is so important.

that we were actually working with someone who was as in tune as Lin was. It was a truly mind blowing experience.

We learned that Kathryn and I had over sixty-three lifetimes together. She said that I was very protective of Kathryn and told about the lifetime where I took that protective energy on. It was at a time when Kathryn and I were married and lived in Russia; we had the same genders as we do now. I had gone out to gather firewood and when I returned Kathryn and our baby had been mauled and partially eaten by a wolf. The wolf got into the house because I had neglected to fix the door.

As I listened to this story a feeling of intense guilt along with grief and loss overwhelmed me; I wailed deeply due to the pain I was feeling. It was not like I was hearing of a sad story that happened to someone else. It was as if I was transported back to the feeling I had at the time it happened. I felt the pain of discovering the corpse of my wife and little girl. Although I did not get visual pictures of the event, the feelings were as real as if I was experiencing them right then and there.

As we continued to listen to the tape, Lin went on to tell us about a lifetime that followed. One where I was a pickpocket in England and Kathryn was my younger brother. I had been caught and shipped to Australia and since I was the caretaker of Kathryn, she had to come with me as well. I was only sixteen at the time, yet I was very protective of my little brother. On the ship to Australia I caught a man attempting to sodomize my brother. I rescued my brother by stabbing the would-be rapist in the arm. He was much bigger than me…after that I always had to watch my back and was lucky to have made it alive. My brother (Kathryn) and I lived a good life in Australia…after I served my time in the penal colony. We lived near each other, both got married and our families were very close. Funny thing is that in this lifetime I have always wanted to go to Australia[1]; I am certain this is one of the reasons.

Sixty-three life times together! No wonder Kathryn and I had such a close bond. These sessions were deepening that bond between Kathryn and me. It led to a romantic experience that was perfect in its timing. For two days we basked in the intensity of these spiritual and romantic energies. It was because of our openness and readiness for these energies that this love and information could come to us through Lin. The next day was the Fourth of July. It was our first anniversary. We decided to take the day and drive up to Paradise, a resort hotel on Mount Rainer.

It was a typical Seattle day; cool and gray with a little rain, more like a mist. We took our time and drove the most scenic route to Mt Rainer. We stopped for lunch along the way. The whole time we were talking about all of the new information and energy we had received. We

---

[1] Shortly after the conclusion of this story I lived in Australia for five years. I loved it!

talked about our feelings for each other and how deeply grateful we were to be having such a wonderful life together. Once we got to the national forest, the scenery changed dramatically. It was so lush and green that the beauty of it all helped us to appreciate the abundance of rain that we got. Along the winding road to the Paradise Hotel, we stopped to enjoy the waterfalls and scenic outlooks.

When the rain stopped, we took a walk, hip to hip down a lovely path in the woods. We focused on the feeling of the energy that was moving through us. We listened to the sounds of the birds and of the water as it rushed by on its well carved path down the mountain. That was a moment, like many others we had experienced, yet each one seemed more intense and powerful than the last.

We found a perfect log alongside the creek to stop and sit. For a few minutes we just sat there taking in the sweet smells and the fresh air. Then at the exact same moment we turned and looked into each other's eyes.[1] The impulse to kiss was irresistible. I turned and straddled the log to make it easier to reach Kathryn's waiting mouth and to pull her closer. Our lips met, eyes closed, our tongues exploring and expressing the love and passion we had for each other. After a while Kathryn turned her back to me, straddled the log too and settled back into my open arms. I wrapped my arms around her and placed one of my hands on her breast…I gently fondled her for a time…I held her tight. I was consciously breathing and becoming aware of the life force energy that had intensified as a result of the love we were sharing. We stayed there for quite sometime enjoying the bliss and sexual energy that was present. Kathryn could feel how firm I had become and said to me, "Let's go and check into our hotel room; I want you inside of me."

I squeezed her again, took another deep breath of that sweet energy, and said, "Mmmm, there is nothing I would enjoy more. I love you, my dearest friend." With that we headed off.

It took another twenty minutes of driving before we reached Paradise; we rode in silence broken only by a few ooohs and aaahs as we took in the spectacular views. Our passions cooled and we became temporarily distracted by the details of checking in and the beautiful art work on display in a shop. When we got to our room, we each took a few minutes to freshen up and settle in.

I would not let Kathryn go too far in organizing our new love nest; I interrupted her before she could finish putting everything where she thought it belonged. I took Kathryn by the hand and led her over to the

---

[1] We were so in tune with each other that we often did such things or thought the same thing at the same time. Even though this is quite common in relationships it is not to be trivialized. There is definitely some unseen force at work that causes such "coincidences".

bed, stopping at the foot, we embraced sweetly. We stood there and slowly undressed each other while we touched and kissed. Kathryn made a move for the bed but I pulled her back, I kept her standing there, making love, I wouldn't let Kathryn into the bed until we were both wobbly in knees. After that we both fell onto the bed and made love intensely...passionately. When we were finished we lay there in silence, Kathryn's head on my chest, a leg wrapped between my legs, her naked body pressed against mine. I loved it all, but cuddling always seemed like the best part. I could feel her love for me and mine for her, there was no hurry to do anything else; we just lay there, soaking in all of this wonderful energy.

Psychic Answers to Health Issues

One evening, soon after Lin began channeling for our healer's apprenticeship group, everyone asked about their aches and pains. Isaiah told many amazing stories of past lives. One woman who had problems with her esophagus in this life was told of a past life where her tribe poured hot molten gold down her throat as part of a sacred ritual. As she was seeking to be more spiritually aware in this life her subconscious fears of superstitious religious idiots, due to past lives, was in her energy and manifesting physically in her body now. She was given some advice that was personal and appropriate for her, eventually her throat problem cleared up.

Kathryn had by far the most interesting medical history of everyone in the group. She had a twenty-five-page report detailing all of her surgeries, x-rays, medications and doctors. She maintained this document herself so she would not have to write it out for the next new doctor that she had to see.

She already had an amazing healing experience when years of fibromyalgia induced pain went away two hours after her ex-husband had been kicked out of the house. She also had two other unusual, even bizarre, outstanding conditions.

When Kathryn was nineteen years old, she was thrown from a car during an automobile accident. She spent two weeks in a coma. When she awoke she felt her prickly head and thought she had curlers in her hair. Then she asked the nurse, "What is going on? Why am I in the hospital?" The nurse brought her a mirror and had a good laugh. Kathryn could not understand the nurse's cruelty. Kathryn's head had been shaven and she had undergone brain surgery; she now had a steel plate in her head.

Kathryn lost her sense of smell as a result of the accident or the operation. I knew this was true because there was a long period of time where I had a problem with flatulence. Kathryn never noticed, except when the farts were audible. And believe me, they were noticeable. Now she was forty four years old and asking Isaiah if she could get her sense of smell back. Isaiah told her that the parts of the brain that dealt with sense of smell were next to the memory portion of the brain. If she did some work on remembering her childhood and worked through her rage issues, it would come back.

Kathryn adamantly denied that she had any rage but told Isaiah that she would do the memory work and see what came up. Isaiah went on to tell Kathryn to write letters to her family telling them how their actions had affected her. She did not need to send the letters to them, but she did need to write them. She was supposed to let all the rage that was in her come out in those letters.

Kathryn understood the instructions and went to work on it. She expected to spend half a day writing, instead she ended up spending five full days. Kathryn was quite surprised to discover all the memories that came back and the amount and intensity of the rage she was holding inside. Within a few weeks she began complaining about the farts; her sense of smell had returned.

For over ten years, Kathryn had also lived with a bizarre skin condition on her hands; I don't even think they have a name for it. She could not put her hands in water for very long or the skin would crack and peal. It was painful and unsightly. She wore rubber gloves when she took a shower or washed anything. If she had to wash her hands she would do it as quickly as possible, in cold water, and dry them straight away.

When she asked Isaiah about this condition he said, "In a past life you were a healer who used her hands to give healing energy to people. You were so effective at it that it frightened many of the other villagers; they thought you were a witch and in league with the devil. So they captured you and put you in a cage in the town square. In a public ceremony they declared you to be a witch. They burned your hands and then placed them in a bucket of water and your skin sloughed off. Then they chopped your hands off and left you to die."

"Your issues of wanting to be invisible are related to this incident. In order to heal this, we recommend that you take Reiki classes and become more visible with your healing work. Dear one, you will not be harmed for your healing abilities this time. There is no one waiting to burn you at the stake. We know it is frightening to you, to become visible, but this is what you have chosen for yourself this lifetime."

It was quite a shock to hear this but it felt very real as Isaiah described this event to us. Kathryn had been a healer all of her life, but she had done so empathically. She took others' pain and suffering away and took it into her own body. She had been ill with one disease or another much of her life. She believed in the nobility of this and that it was good to be a martyr. Isaiah (and later Amoram too) told her that she needed to heal this martyr issue. That she could do her healing work without taking it on herself.

Kathryn definitely wanted to be invisible. She worked hard to keep her light under a basket. Physically she was a beautiful woman but she purposely carried extra weight so that she would not attract the unwanted attention of men.

When my turn came to ask a question, I asked about my nightly back pains. For the five years prior I had suffered with back pains every single night. I would wake up in excruciating pain after about four hours of sleep. I already tried two different doctors, two chiropractors, two physical therapists and many massage therapists; none of them could offer me any relief or explanation.

When I asked about my back pains, Isaiah told me that I would have to get that information myself. That seemed a bit rough to me, and definitely unfair! When I asked him why, Isaiah replied, "You are too much in your head. You need to balance yourself by moving more into your heart. These others have a greater ability to feel these things and can benefit from the information we shared with them. But you need proof, and you will not heal unless you get this information for yourself. We know you can do this."

Our First Reiki Experiences

The first thing we did after Isaiah suggested Reiki to help Kathryn heal her hands was to look for a Reiki teacher in the *New Times*, a monthly spiritual publication that advertised alternative healers. Kathryn found a teacher she liked, and we began taking Reiki classes. Over the next few months, we practiced on each other and on friends. Occasionally Kathryn would try a little water on her hands and still she had her skin problem.

I did not feel much when I gave a Reiki treatment. Occasionally I would pick up information about the people I was working on, but my head kept questioning the validity of what I was feeling. One time when Kathryn was having back pains she asked me for some help. I was happy to be able to help and almost surprised that she believed that I could. She sat in a dining room chair, leaned forward and asked me to do Reiki on her back. In my mind I prayed, *Please Holy Spirit move through me to help Kathryn in the best way possible.*

After a short while she said, "Oh Mike, that feels great; it's just what I needed. You have such good healing energy."

I believed Kathryn could really feel the energy so I was excited to hear that coming from her. Without saying anything, I did not move a muscle; I only thought to myself, *Wow, I am doing this. It is actually working. I might just turn out to be a healer after all.* I felt thrilled and excited; I was even more enthusiastic to continue treating Kathryn, until....

At the very same moment I was having those thoughts, Kathryn responded, "That's not it, it's changed. The energy feels bad now."

I immediately recognized how I let my ego get in the way. I prayed quietly, *Okay Holy Spirit, I'm sorry, I'll get out of the way and allow you to move the energy as you see fit. I am only an instrument of your healing.*

Once again, at the very same moment I began having those new thoughts, Kathryn responded with, "That's better...It's back." Not only was I amazed that I was actually changing my energy with each thought, but that Kathryn really could pick it up. This experience made a profound impression on my mind.

Although I was clearly doing something with my energy, I still did not feel it nor did I understand what it was or how to use it or even how to begin to perceive it. I was not all that impressed with the woman who taught us Reiki; it seemed too simple and superstitious to me. I found a man named Jerry who was advertising in the Seattle area as an energy healer and teacher. I called him up and he had much to say about his many talents and skills. I decided to take a treatment from him to see if I could feel anything.

I did feel more relaxed and a bit light headed after Jerry worked on me. He filled my head with stories of the things he had done, and I was very interested in learning how to move energy like he did and what that actually meant. Jerry had a weekend class that I talked Kathryn into attending with me. Halfway through the first day, Kathryn talked me into leaving the class early. She did not like Jerry's energy because it was too much about his own ego and he was projecting sexual energy toward the women of the class, including her. I had no idea of what she meant but I knew enough not to try and argue with her about this. I was disappointed that we could not continue the classes because I expected to learn some cool stuff in it. Later Isaiah confirmed Kathryn's knowing and told us it was a great lesson in what we did not want to become.

Trouble in Paradise

With all of this intensive study, practice, and introspection we were becoming quite aware that we each had a lot to heal. At times we found it difficult to focus on our own healing. It was easier to see the faults in the other one. It seemed natural that we should point these things out and tell the other exactly where they went wrong in their thinking. It seemed obvious; to one of us at least, that the problem we brought to the other's attention needed an immediate remedy. Such is the level of blindness suffered by most of humanity. In our relationship, as in all relationships, this kind of thinking only created a bigger mess. It was difficult for us to understand that we were doing exactly the opposite of what we needed to be doing. We should have been looking for the best in our partner; we should have been focusing on how much we appreciated those qualities and actions. What we focus on increases, thus we want to give more energy to our partner when their behavior feels good and less energy to those things they do that irritate us.

On many occasions, Kathryn took offense at something I said. She would try to convince me that my intention was harmful and that hurtful things kept coming out of me. I would try to convince Kathryn that I did not mean to offend her with what I said. As I would proceed to explain, our conversations just turned into frustrating, angry arguments.

Most of the time I would leave the room or even the apartment to get away from Kathryn to clear my head. I knew I loved her but nothing was coming out right. I felt such rage, I wanted to hit, kick and hurt something; I did not want it to be Kathryn. I don't wish to share the full details of my thoughts because they were so horrible and violent. Doing so would only create that energy in you the reader; this is not my goal. Rest assured that I do understand the depths of despair and frustration that can bring a man to rageful insanity.

One time, after running out on a fight, I went to my office and wrote Kathryn a letter. This was a technique that I used a lot of the time because I felt it was the best way to sort through my thoughts and accurately convey what I meant to say. In the heat of an argument I found myself too caught up in attacking or defending to accurately state my true thoughts and feelings. Over time I found problems with this technique. One of them was that no matter how much I tried, those letters were a manipulation. I was trying to get her to change. The problem I was having was with me not her. But I did not understand this; even though so many books I read were telling me this, I could not see it...not very often. I was just taking my views and trying to present them in a pretty package so she would finally accept what she did not want to accept. My problem was that I needed her to change, and she did not want to.

There were other problems with those letters, the biggest was that I did not really understand the perspective of my sweetheart, or whoever it was I was in conflict with, and I wasted a great deal of time and energy attacking an agenda that I erroneously imagined they had. I was defending myself against an attack that was never made. For my own sanity I needed to listen to what Kathryn had to say and come to understand her. Instead I was in a panic as I tried to squash the kind of thinking that created her attacks on me before those ideas solidified in her mind and became facts.

I did the best I could at the time with the skills I had. The time I spent writing did help me settle down and get some clarity of mind back. Even though the answers had been in front of me for a long time, I could not see them. I tried; I really did, but it never seemed to be enough. Fear of losing my dearest friend, fear of being a failure, fear of being the bad guy all scrambled my mind and left me desperately reaching for something that would end these horrible fights once and for all. Unfortunately, fear does not make a good guide. It brought me to defend my words and actions in those letters and to blame Kathryn for the problems. At the time I attributed no power to the unspoken thoughts I held in my mind during these ego battles I had with Kathryn. No, it was the spoken words and the actions that I focused on. I believed my letters would have won my case in a court of law; the letters were clear, honest (according to the outer circumstances), and concisely stated. They got me nowhere with Kathryn who saw through the writing, the words and the actions, and saw straight into the very energy of my thoughts.

Kathryn was no better than I in this department. She had all sorts of ideas of how I should be. Her judgments on how I missed the mark were a sad and frightening awareness for me to hold. After a round of fighting, I would go to my corner to settle down and contemplate what had just happened. I would realize the errors[1] in my own thoughts and actions. I would apologize and tell Kathryn what I had learned about myself and how I would do it differently the next time. Yet, she rarely reciprocated; thus I assumed she was doing no introspection at all, just blaming me. It frightened me to think that I might grow and heal myself and that she would remain the same. I assumed the day would come that

---

[1] I assumed I had realized all of my errors, and that I had realized correctly. For years I stumbled through these fights with Kathryn. If I look back honestly I said a lot of stupid things and came to many wrong conclusions. If I could just go back to that person I was and say, "Shut up...just stop talking and thinking. Just listen and try to understand her." If I would have followed that advice, I would have said fewer stupid things, I would have embarrassed myself less, I would have hurt Kathryn less...I'd have been further ahead; instead I kept putting myself behind.

I might have to leave her due to the unfairness and imbalance of it all. It did not even cross my mind that these things she did would cease to affect me so strongly when I became whole and complete in and of myself.

Kathryn had some furniture in storage in Portland. One day she decided she wanted to bring home one of the beds she had for the spare bedroom. I put up a bit of a fight because this included me driving six hours and doing a bunch of work on my day off. I wanted to play on my days off, not work. It was experiences like this that taught Kathryn and me that if one of us did not want to do something, it should not prevent the other from having what they wanted. Kathryn had a lot of good ideas that I did not want to participate in…that bed came in handy when we had overnight guests.

One time Kathryn and I were talking to Lin and I said, "Let me tell you how I surprised Kathryn on her birthday." Kathryn interrupted, "Embarrassed is more like it." Lin inquired, "Oh, what happened?"

"I took Kathryn out to a live performance…a play, on her birthday. Before the show began, I abruptly left my seat, without telling Kathryn what I was doing. I walked down to the stage and stepped up onto it. I asked the audience if I could have their attention. Everyone got quiet and listened.[1] They probably assumed I had something to do with the play or the theater management."

"Today is my sweetheart's birthday. Would you all join me in singing happy birthday to her? I began to sing…the audience joined in…when we got to the 'Happy birthday dear <u>name</u>' part they all sang 'sweetheart'…'Happy birthday dear sweetheart'…I had not told the audience her name."

"It was so difficult to get up the courage to do this. I'd tell myself I was going to do it on the count of five…then when I counted to five I did not get up. Finally I knew my time was running short and it was now or never and I found myself walking down the aisle to do the deed. Kathryn pretended to be embarrassed, but I knew she loved it."

"Are you sure?" asked Lin in a strong tone of voice.

"Noooh! I DID NOT love it!" replied Kathryn, "I was mortified."

Lin scolded, "Are you listening Mike? It is important for you to listen to Kathryn and not interpret what she is saying. Do you have any idea of how much you do that? What she has to communicate won't always fit into your experience of life because Kathryn is not like you. You would have loved it, but she did not. Kathryn likes to be invisible. In

---

[1] This actually surprised me that the audience got so quite and paid attention to me.

all of this time you have been together...haven't you realized this yet? Kathryn likes to be invisible."

"You need to feel what Kathryn is saying. I know that is difficult for you as you tend to be in your thoughts or get mixed up in your own feelings. Mike, it is important for you to move into the feelings of others as you communicate with them. This does require that you become aware of your own feelings and to remain peaceful and centered. Then you will feel what others are experiencing."

Now that Kathryn had an ally on this issue she piped in, "That is just like last Christmas. Remember, when we took your step sons to Chucky Cheese's? Those colored balls...you wanted me to come in and play in the pit with you and the boys. You kept insisting that I come in and join you. You thought I was just too shy or embarrassed to get in and play, and that I secretly wanted to. No, I did not want to. Mike that is not my thing, I don't want to go crawling around in a children's playground. You were loving it and I was enjoying watching you and the boys play. I did not need to go in there like you did."

It took embarrassing myself in front of Lin to hear Kathryn and comprehend what she was saying. But I finally got it, and Kathryn was pleased. It also felt to me like there was a "put upon" woman inside of Lin that was enjoying watching a man squirm under the realization of how he has ignored and misunderstood his woman.

Often during a meal Kathryn would criticize me about how noisy I was while eating, she especially hated how I sipped tea or soup. For me it was a matter of cooling it down so it did not burn me. I also found that the added oxygen seemed to increase its flavor. She would also criticize me for eating with my fingers[1] and hovering over my food like a starved dog. In all fairness I needed to hear about the hovering because in the back of my mind it was a bit like I had to protect my food; it helped me to notice that energy and transform it. Really it was the judgment in her and how she said it that felt horrible to me.[2]

---

[1] As I am proof reading this section, I am laughing because I am currently in India where it is normal to eat with your fingers. Isn't it great that our past suffering can bring us laughter today? Remember that the next time you are suffering!

[2] One of the most common things that happen with people is that when they are under any sort of stress they become hyper-critical and judgmental. Any little unexpected behavior, or words they don't like to hear, can be one too many straws to place on the already stressed camel's back. Too many people live under constant stress and don't even realize how severe the level is until that one extra straw is added. It is that straw that takes the brunt of the blame for the painful back breaking experience. Understanding this can help us to realize that this person who is judging us is under stress. If it is someone else, have compassion for their stressed situation and assist in easing it if you can. If it is yourself, the same wisdom applies, yes have compassion for yourself and do <u>anything</u> you can to ease the stress. Meditation, contemplation these are best.

On one occasion I blew up about this. My rage was pretty intense but short lived. Once I had let it out, I felt like I could move on. But Kathryn would not. She would hold onto a perceived offence and remain cold and distant for days.[1] My most frequent response to this was a constant reaching and seeking of affection and confirmation that she still loved me…it did not come. Energetically it was like I was attempting to reach into her heart and pull her love out against her will. At the time I did not understand this was what I was doing, I only knew that I felt frightened and inadequate. Trying to win Kathryn's love back took up too much of my time and energy, so I was also frustrated that I was not getting the things done[2] that I believed I needed to do. Between the two of us we kept this negative cycle going far longer than was necessary.

In one of Kathryn's own automatic writings[3] her guides told her "It is freeing for you to now realize that you don't have to save [fix] everyone and everything. Your focus will be much more effective this way and your sense of inner peace will be felt on a stronger level. Congratulations. This is an empowering lesson for you. As you reclaim your power, you are also realizing what is worth standing up for and what doesn't deserve your energy being placed on it." I was a witness to her transformation in this area. At this time she was just getting started, but it only took her about a year to significantly shift this; she realized a lot of power as a result.

Kathryn frequently made trips to Portland…to visit a doctor, her hair dresser, or to deal with various business issues and to attend family gatherings. Sometimes she went on her own. Those trips usually wiped her out because she still had such a difficult time with her energy draining relatives. She would take an energy depleting hit just by crossing the bridge from Washington State to Oregon.

---

[1] This is how I saw it at the time. Now, February 2005, I am aware that it was the intensity that was short lived. Although I would go through the outward motions of being loving faster than Kathryn, I was keeping track of offenses in the back of my mind. When something of a similar nature came up, the past offense was the fuel that created the next intense outburst. If there was no outburst the judgment or hurt that lived in my mind pushed out the love, even though I was going through the outward motions of being loving. Kathryn definitely felt this, just as I could feel how distant she would be from me for many days on end.

[2] Now I understand it was far more important for me to sort through these difficulties and come to understand my mind and its illusions. It is not a waste of time. All of the other things we do, that have to get done, those things are meaningless, they eventually lose their value and meaning. The only thing of value is clarity of mind and understanding, with that all of life becomes a fantastic game. Being able to find clarity of mind under any circumstance is a permanent and eternal achievement, not subject to rotting or rust. Your physical actions will eventually die, but lessons learned through experience and effort will always serve you.

[3] August 12th, 1992

I wanted Kathryn to cut most of her ties with Portland, especially with her family. It seemed like the sanest thing for her to do.[1] She ignored my opinion, and I often left her to make those trips on her own. It was what I needed to do to take care of myself. On one occasion, Kathryn asked me to go with her, and I resisted. She then presented to me her automatic writing which said, "Mike is allowing you to not have to be so strong and to ask for help and allow yourself to feel weak. We know this does not feel good to you, but it is part of surrendering. Your trip to Portland will go much smoother and can even be fun if Mike goes with you. We suggest that you let him know how important this is for you so that he understands. You and he have much support for each other's comfort and growth. So communicate with him. He will understand and can make the necessary arrangements at work. Let the trip be fun and nurturing—for you."

Even though our differences often resulted in clashes between us, they always created great opportunities to love and nurture each other. It really was a matter of how often we took the sweet opportunity that was on offer. I wasn't sure if that writing came from Kathryn or her Guides, but it opened my heart enough to make this trip with her.

"Love takes time."[2] The six hours of traveling together plus running the necessary errands gave us plenty of time to relax into being loving with each other. We loved listening to SLC tapes and spiritual music as we drove. We spent hours in conversation and simply held a very sweet loving energy. My mere presence on this journey with Kathryn was what was needed. I pitched in physically of course, with the driving and lifting heavy things and all such, but it was my presence and love for Kathryn that was the real support.

---

[1] From my limited perspective I thought that Kathryn needed to take care of herself first, I thought Kathryn needed to cut the ties. But time proves there are other perspectives. It is a true Master who can move past the limited perspective of the now moment and maintain Her course even though it may seem harmful to self at the time. Kathryn's continued connection with her family resulted in very big shifts for them; as a result they became much more loving people. Somewhere deep inside she knew she had the strength to do it and that she needed to keep the connection with her family.

[2] This is a quote from Bartholomew. You cannot be in a hurry and have love present. Hurry is action induced by fear or limitations; this is the opposite of love. We seemed to have the most trouble when we were in a hurry, and the best loving exchanges of energy when we had hours of time to spend together. http://gr8Wisdom.com/Books/Bart (proper capitalization is important when locating this website)

Past Life Regressions

One evening, during our apprenticeship group meeting, the entire group did a past life regression. The intention was for each of us to go back into another lifetime where we wanted to be a healer and find out what we could learn about our experience. As a group we were talked into a relaxed trance state, then we were directed to look down at our feet and observe what we saw. I saw the hairy legs of a man much larger than myself, wearing sandals with two leather straps that crossed over each other many times as they wrapped around my calves. Then we were directed to observe what we were wearing and then what was going on directly in front of us. I was dressed as I imagined a Roman or Trojan solder would have been dressed. I was caring a shield and a knife and that was all. Before me were my fallen country men. Further on up ahead the battle raged on. I found myself slashing the throats of our wounded; many of them were even my friends. It was my job to determine who could survive and who to put out of their misery. The man I was in that time wanted to be a healer and was in shock to find this as his assignment. This experience gave me great emotional and physical pain for the rest of my life. I died a lonely old man in his fifties, under the care of a not so caring person.

When the regression was over, we all talked about our experiences. I had never heard of such a thing. I asked others if they knew whether it was a common practice to slash the throats of the mortally wounded in ancient times. Both Lin and another man replied affirmatively. It seemed very real to me, not that the images were all that vivid; it was not like a movie, but the feelings were strong, and it felt like an experience I had at one point in a distant past. Still I had my doubts, how could I be remembering such things? Was this valid; did it really happen to me?

There was so much I did not understand and so many things that I did not feel. Because of the intense spiritual growth work I was doing I kept finding more about myself that was lacking. During one of our group sessions we did a kinesiology exercise. We all paired up with a partner from the group, Kathryn and I usually chose someone else to do these exercises with. Isaiah asked us questions that could be answered with either "yes" or "no." The subjects would hold their arm out straight to the side; the question was directed at them. The other person was there to push down on their arm. If the answer was "yes" the arm would remain strong and difficult to push down. If the answer was "no" the arm would be easy to push down. Over time I have found that not everyone responds well to this system, but I did.

Isaiah asked, "Do you love yourself?" If you had asked me this question even six months earlier, I would have said "yes," but not this time. I knew the answer was "no" even before my arm was pushed down. For years I had heard that arrogance was tied to low self-esteem. At the time many teachers stated that while looking in the mirror if you could not look yourself in the eyes and say "I love you" then you knew you had low self-esteem. For years I kept trying this…I could say, "I love you," to myself. This was my primary defense when people, my ex-wife for example, told me I was arrogant. I would say, "I am not arrogant, I am confident and naturally better than most people at many things. People consistently show me how they don't think or don't understand so why shouldn't I just ignore what they think and stick to my own clear understanding of things."

Isaiah continued, "Are you loveable?" I answered, "No."

"Do you deserve love?" Again I answered, "No."

"Do you deserve to be happy?" And yet again I answered, "No."

I was so embarrassed. I always present myself with such confidence and now it is coming out in front of the whole group. I could have broken down and cried a room full of tears but it felt like I would only embarrass myself even more. My God, Maria, Kathryn and others were right. I was arrogant! This was just another crushing blow to my ego. But one that was timely and necessary.

On another evening, we did another past life regression. This was the second one we had done as a group. In it, I found myself being wrongfully accused of helping to rob a stage coach and being hung for it. I asked Isaiah if this was accurate and he confirmed that it was without going into any great detail. I still had my doubts. Little did I know this was all leading up to a very profound experience, one that would change my life forever.

One weekend in September I wanted to go to a herbal studies retreat at Brietenbush Hot Springs Retreat Center, near Detroit, Oregon. Kathryn did not want to go, nor did she want me to go on my own. She used money as a primary concern, but she also knew there were hot springs and nude bathing involved; something I liked very much and that she was too shy to participate in. Of course we had a bit of a fight about this too. We brought this issue to Isaiah who neither encouraged nor discouraged it, but helped us realize it was not a big deal either way and diffused our bickering about it. When I returned from the retreat, we were both rejuvenated and happy to see each other. It was amazing how taking some space to do our own thing and getting away from each other for a few days could make a lot of our problems go away. As we all know, "Absence makes the heart grow fonder." We had a few weeks of peace as a result.

A Birthday Gift from Spirit

In the early morning of my birthday, November 7th, 1992, I had a dream about rainsticks and how they were designed inside so as to create the sound effect they make. When I awoke I was really surprised to have had that dream. I knew it was a sign that a rainstick was one of the gifts that Kathryn had bought me for my birthday. I already suspected that I was receiving a kaleidoscope that I had admired at the East West Bookstore in Seattle. A few nights prior Kathryn stopped me from looking at the check book after I casually noticed an entry for that shop. I knew she had no evil secrets, so I got it in my head that the check was for my birthday gift. The kaleidoscope was at the top of my list. So after having the dream I was left with the impression that there were two gifts the second being the rainstick.

When Kathryn noticed me waking from my dream, she said, "Happy birthday Michael." She smothered me with kisses, affectionately at first and then with too much playfulness she began to tickle me. "I've been waiting for you to wake up. Wait here I want to bring you your presents…close your eyes." Then she got up, returned shortly with my gifts, and placing them on the bed in front of me said, "Happy birthday! Now you can open your eyes." However, before I did, and even before I touched the gifts, I said to her, "One of them is a kaleidoscope and the other is a rainstick."

"How did you know? Did you go snooping? Did you peek in the check book?" Kathryn asked with a shocked tone in her voice.

I then proceeded to explain to her how I figured out. She was just as impressed with the dream as I was. Having the confirmation was pretty cool.

Kathryn loved giving gifts and using her creative energy to wrap them so beautifully that everyone had to comment on it. This time was no exception. However I was not going to let that keep me from my new toys. I was excited and furiously tore the wrapping paper from them.

The rainstick was first; I wanted to see if it really was made how I dreamt it was made. I had casually wondered about this a few times in the past yet I had not put any real effort into thinking it through or inspecting a rain stick carefully, I did not think the outside of the stick would offer any clues. After the dream I knew…I knew that I knew, and I knew the signs would be visible from the outside. Just by thinking it through, the design I dreamt about made sense. No other way I could think of would do. It wasn't like it took a genius to figure it out, but then I had never really tried. To me the amazing part was that I got it in a dream, and that at one point I had wondered about it…ask and you shall receive. Upon close examination of the rainstick I could see that it was made exactly as I saw in my dream.

For a few months, since August, I had been doing automatic writing. This morning I got the following...

> Your dream last night was our gift to you. We know how much you wish to break through the barriers. We wanted you to know that significant holes are showing through and more insight, wisdom, love, and blessings are making their way through from the spirit, your Essence, to you and to those that you touch.
>
> Please continue to be aware. Notice your mind, notice when your ego takes control and plays with your life. Reassure your ego that you are not out to kill or harm it, but that you are growing in order to benefit yourself and all of those around you. Your ego will benefit as you will be safe, and full of joy. The ego's life will not end until the body has completed its purpose and that is inevitable. There is nothing that can be done to change this nor would you want to.
>
> You have been catching yourself before saying things that would hurt Kathryn's feelings. Cheap shots, on the surface intended in humor yet they are not really funny at all; they come from an unconscious pain. They are really an attack. Keep this up [catching myself that is]. Do not let them slip out as you did this morning. You knew before you said them how they might be taken, but you had to try them out once again. Let them go and do not say them any more, great growth is coming through with this insight.

In those days when I did that writing I had expectations from the writing that were not met. Yet as I read those writings today, mostly they are clear with good information. The information was not all that new to me; other people and books were telling me similar things to what I was getting in my automatic writing. But it came to me as more of a summary and clarification of what I was learning from my outer world. It was relevant. More than anything, doing that writing stretched me and exercised my mind in a new way; I began experiencing that I actually did have inner guidance that I could access.

An Amazing Healing

A few months had gone by since I asked Isaiah about my back pains. In my morning meditations, I made a few futile attempts at getting the information I needed to heal this myself, but I gave up too easily. Eventually I got the courage to ask Isaiah again and he told me, "The reason we want you to get this information yourself is because you are too much in your mind. We are trying to teach you to balance yourself and move into your heart as well. You wish to be a healer and a teacher...how will you teach if you do not know? How will you know if you do not experience it? These others are in touch with their hearts. They can feel what you cannot."

This was encouraging in the sense that Isaiah believed that I could do it, because I wasn't so sure. Still it was quite upsetting to me as these pains plagued me every single night and they seemed to be getting worse! Finally I got fed up with them and I became determined that I was going to get the answers I needed.

On the Monday evening after my birthday, I had Fred from our apprenticeship group come over. He had some experience with Kinesiology and I hoped that he could help me get the information I needed to heal my back. We got some insight into my early childhood years, but it was not what I needed to solve this problem.

On Tuesday, I had a massage appointment scheduled for the afternoon so I decided to take the entire day off from work and sit in meditation until I got what I was looking for...this pain had to end. Sitting in meditation like this felt to me more like a punishment than an adventure. Meditation did not seem to yield the results I was expecting. Sure it relaxed me, but I was looking for more. Overall, I found it boring and wondered if it really was worth the effort. So the commitment to meditate for hours was a serious, if not drastic, step for me to take.[1]

On Tuesday morning, I had my breakfast and shower as usual, then I sat down to meditate. It was not long before I had a vague image of a man stabbing me in the back, right behind my shoulder blade where my nightly pains were. In this lifetime this man is my brother, Joe. I died.

Something did not feel right about this so I shook it out of my mind and began again. Another vague image came to me. This time I was

---

[1] Meditation is a much better experience for me these days, one I would not do with out. In the past I had unrealistic expectations. I did not understand the real purpose or the techniques. No one who was explaining it to me really seemed to understand either. If you find yourself in that situation please visit http://gr8Wisdom.com/Meditate (proper capitalization is important when locating this website)

struck in the back with a long pole. Again the man who did this was my brother in this lifetime. The blow left me with a limited range of motion in my left arm, and pain for the rest of my life. I could also feel that he was someone who was a part of my life and that he was angry with me for acting like I was so much better than him. Again the issue of my arrogance reared its ugly head.

That image felt right to me in some way, and the first image felt wrong...I figured the first one was a mistake. Within half an hour I truly believed that I had the results I was seeking; I stopped my meditation and went on with my day. I enjoyed my massage that afternoon and later that evening went to a lecture at the Seattle Church of Religious Science. Half way through the lecture I had to ask Kathryn to drive me home. I felt wasted, like I was on drugs...bad drugs. I assure you that I was clean and sober.

During that night of sleep, I had no back pains; none at all! This was the first time in five years! I could hardly believe it. Before I got too excited I waited to see if the next night would be the same, and it was; again no pain! This kept on for a couple of weeks. Then one night I had a mild case of the same kind of pain just under my shoulder blade. Many more pain free weeks passed, followed by another night of mild pain. This freedom from pain interspersed with occasional reminders continued on for many more months, until I took the next step.

About a week after having the memory and my first night of peaceful sleep, I went back to the apprenticeship group and asked Isaiah about it. The only thing I said was, "I had a memory come up in my meditation and now my back pain is gone. Can you tell me more about it?" I was deliberately vague with my question. I wanted independent validation for my experience and did not want to give Lin any clue to what I had remembered.

I was overwhelmed and amazed when Isaiah told me, "There were two life times. In the first one it was war. The one who is your brother this time was the enemy. He stabbed you in the back, where you carry your pain...you died. Because it was war and this was the expected outcome it did not have a very strong impact on you."

"There was another lifetime however, that had a far greater impact. Your brother and you were cousins. You were much older and wealthy, you were also quite arrogant. He was a gondola driver, you were his employer. One day he took all the abuse that he could from you, and when you turned your back to walk away, he struck you with his pole. Physically you never had the same mobility. There was pain."

That was really something special to hear! I did not realize that I had remembered two past lives...I thought the first memory I had was a mistake. If ever I needed proof that we had past lives, for me this was it. I had both a physical healing as a result of the experience and also independent confirmation of the memories from another person. Years later while seeing an aware chiropractor about other back problems that I was having he touched that very spot on my back where I was stabbed and said, "This has something to do with your brother."

A Christmas Gift to Remember

Monday morning, December 7th, 1992, I was getting ready for work. I felt tired and exhausted and I thought, *There are only a few weeks left before Christmas and I haven't even done my shopping yet. When am I going to find the time for that? I'm too busy at work to take time off, and weekends at the malls are pure hell. Okay God, help me out here, please!*

Later at work...I had only been at my desk a few hours when Bill, my boss, came in and closed the door behind him. Bill said, "Mike, I have some bad news for you. The company needs to cut costs so I am going to have to let you go. Right now you are the only one, but if our financial picture doesn't change you won't be the last.[1] We are letting you go because you have the highest wage of the engineers and you are the least willing to put in long hours or travel."

I was shocked. This was the first time I had ever been laid off. I was a little bit hurt that I was the only one, but I understood the reason why I was the first. Then Bill said, "We are letting you go today. You will be getting two weeks severance pay, all of your accrued vacation pay and pay for all of your unused sick days. I'd go straight down to the unemployment office and sign up for benefits today if I were you. You should also be eligible for benefits for this same time period even though you are being paid for it...so don't wait, go today."

When Bill left my office, I took a deep breath and thought, *Well, I did ask God for some time off. That was a pretty fast answer to a prayer! Now I will have plenty of time to enjoy my Christmas shopping.* I only felt the slightest bit of fear. Mostly I was amazed and excited. Somehow I knew all was going to be well.

Kathryn was not as confident as I was when I tried to reassure her that all of this was going to work out fine. I worried a little too, but not so much about the finances. Being a gainfully-employed software engineer supported my fragile self-esteem, so now my self-worth had nothing to rest on. At the time, I was not consciously aware of this relationship even though it had been mentioned to me many times by Isaiah. Even with these minor negatives, I enjoyed my freedom and was happy to have the time off. I got to slow down a bit and take care of myself. I was happy to have time to spend with Kathryn.

All in all, to have this time off during the Christmas season was perfect! This was Kathryn's favorite time of the year. She went all out in decorating the house with her handmade decorations. They filled every

---

[1] Within six months everyone was gone, the company folded.

available flat surface, wall space and doorknob. For the nearly ten years that Kathryn suffered from fibromyalgia, she was confined to a chair or bed. She kept herself busy by making handicrafts; counted cross stitch wall hangings, personalized miniature teddy bears, and a lot of cute hand made Christmas ornaments.

We went down to Portland for Christmas Eve, and I got to spend time with my stepsons. Kathryn dropped us off at the Discovery Zone, a shopping mall version of an indoor children's playground, while she visited some of her friends. The boys and I had a nice time; we connected better than we did the last few times we had gotten together. It was getting to the point that when the boys and I talked on the phone or when I would come to see them, I could tell they would rather be somewhere else. But not this time, this time it was like old times and we had fun.

The early evening of Christmas Eve was the traditional time for Kathryn's family to gather together; all twenty-four of them. Although I could not relate well to anyone in her family, save one or two of them for a brief period, I was content to bide my time and observe. I was there to support Kathryn, yet I could not understand why she kept returning to a group of people who she had so much trouble with. Today, as I write this book, I understand its purposefulness; this Master Mistress of mine brought much healing into the hearts of a family who very much needed it. And she still had a bit of her own karma to clean up as was exemplified by the exchange of nasty words and gestures she had with her eldest sister Judy, in whose home we were meeting. This was a feisty Italian family to say the least.

Back at our hotel, Kathryn and I lay down for a short nap before going to SLC[1] for a midnight candlelight service. I set the alarm clock to the wrong time and we ended up sleeping too long. We both woke up from a very deep sleep and could barley function enough to get ourselves out the door to the service. In the end we were glad we went, the service was inspiring and it felt like home. We loved this church and loved seeing that it was still thriving.

On Christmas day, we made our three hour drive back and spent a quiet evening at home. I got to speak to my whole family on the phone; even my Sister Sherry was visiting Mom and Dad in San Diego all the way from the East Coast. I really missed seeing them. I know my mom missed me too; not so sure about my dad, brothers, and sister though. My mother was really the only one I was close with.

Two days later, Kathryn and I drove up to Canada and stayed at a classic bed and breakfast in Vancouver for a few days. We got snow just as we entered the city limits of Vancouver; it helped slow our normally

---

[1] Spiritual Living Center, the church we met at.

hectic pace. We did not really feel like driving around too much with the snow. So we stayed inside, we laughed, played, made love, and conversed with each other for hours on end. The B&B was in a lovely restored home that was ninety five years old with all of the necessary modern touches. It was a beautiful place to hang out and unwind. How nice to have time off from work, the company of my best friend, and the financial resources to do such things. Thank you, God!

After a few days, we came home just in time to find a message that had been left for me half an hour earlier. A recruiter wanted me to go to a job interview at Microsoft that very same afternoon. I was excited...working for Microsoft sounded like a great opportunity. My excitement was short lived though; a few days later I found out I did not get the job. My energy and feelings soon took a nose dive into depression and despair.[1] Like attracts like and thus Kathryn began nagging, criticizing, and yelling at me as well. She kept trying to explain what she wanted from me, I kept trying to give it to her, yet she kept changing her story about what it was she wanted. I was really confused and things were not nice at home. Today I know that in this past situation, I was too focused on what I was doing, on my outer world actions, while I was holding quite a bit of rage and judgment in my mind. It wasn't my actions that was lacking, it was my thinking. The nicest actions done with a mean heart are never well received; this was especially true for Kathryn.

In church on Sunday, I heard the Minister say to stop focusing on the problem and to focus on the solution. In regards to work, I had realized that I was thinking, *They probably won't want me because I only have seven months of Windows experience.* I changed my thinking to *There is some one out there who wants me for exactly the experience that I do have.* On Monday I called on a job I saw advertised in the paper. On Tuesday I had an interview. On Wednesday, January 13th, 1993, I started working at a small company in Bothell.

I got what I asked for...I had just over five weeks off during the Christmas season and received the pay equivalent of seven weeks. During this time I worried less about getting a job than I did about Kathryn's reaction to it. Somehow the first worry was easy to avoid, and the second was difficult. I felt I needed to change her which did not help the situation any. My pay at this new job was a little bit more than my last one, but the best part was that it got me working in C++ and with

---

[1] This is the source of all of our troubles...we let outside circumstances dictate our feelings. When I thought I was getting what I wanted, I felt good...when I thought was not getting what I wanted, I felt bad. No person can ever feel safe in this world if the outside circumstances have to line up in some specific and perfect order for there to be happiness, because circumstances will not always do that, not even for the most advanced deliberate creator.

Windows. Both were skills I wanted to develop further; up to this point I had only minimum exposure.

Can you see how I kept getting just what I needed and often what I wanted? Actually everyone does, this is how life works. It's just that when seemingly bad things are happening, most people lock up and resist, thus they push what they want away from them. When I got laid off from my job at Raima, mostly I was able to relax and go with the flow, thus I was open to receive. Even "bad experiences" like those have been some of the sweetest experiences of my life. Never have I regretted going with the flow, yet often I regretted not doing so.

Spontaneous Past Life Memories

One evening Kathryn and I watched a movie, *Thunderheart*, which is about conflicts on an Indian reservation. During the movie, I had many strong feelings come up. Instead of resisting them or pushing them away, I felt them and kept silently asking for insight into what I was experiencing. When the movie was over I asked again and closed my eyes. A past life memory came to me and I nearly shut it down with the thought that I was probably making it up. But then, I just let that resistance go and let the memory happen and be what it was.

I had a vision of a group of men coming out to line up as a firing squad in front of me...they raised their guns, then shot me dead. I had tried to desert their group. It no longer fit in with who I was, and I tried to get away. It felt like they were the US Army "protecting" the frontier. These were at one time my friends, and they killed me.

When I asked Lin and Isaiah about it they told me I had actually written an article and published it exposing some of the activities of this group. This was treason and the firing squad was the punishment. It is interesting with these things because they are not really visions as much as they are feelings and ideas about those feelings. It takes practice and clarity of mind to interpret them correctly.

This past life memory seemed to fit with the current events because at that point in my life I was trying to change dramatically. My changes did not fit in with the consciousness of the material world. I was moving away from seeing the external world and calling it the cause, and moving into the consciousness of seeing my inner world and calling it the cause. I felt that I might be abandoning the skills that supported me and gave me life. Those skills had been used for my survival. I had lost my life by trying to turn to and live by my ideals in past lives, thus there was some resistance in me that was coming up to be seen at this time.

A few weeks later, I had another vision. In the vision, I had just finished having sex with a woman. We were both naked, and I was sitting on the bed, she was lying down with her legs around my waist, I was still inside of her. All I could see was her torso. All of a sudden I stabbed her below the left breast and killed her. When I wondered who the woman was, I got that it was my mom but I had doubts. Then I wondered if it were I who was stabbed. Then a different scenario appeared, it was not very clear, but I was a man being stabbed, by another man. Then the image went back to me stabbing the woman. Later that day, I had pains that I used to get from time to time in my left chest, just below the breast. I knew the pain was connected to those visions.

When I asked Lin and Isaiah about this they confirmed that they were related to two past life memories that were bleeding into this one. In one I was stabbing a prostitute due to my religious judgments of her; they did not say if it was my mother or not. In the other memory I had been at a pub drinking, and I took a bag of money from the man who in this lifetime is my father. In that situation, he was smaller than me, and I was just being a bully. I was only playing around intending to give it back, but he was serious. So he stabbed and killed me. There was karmic balance achieved by these two events.

In a past life my judgments made me kill. I must have evolved some since then...now these judgments only play havoc with my thoughts, feelings...my experience of life. Whether I kill someone or not, my judgments were having a negative affect on my experience of life. They kept me from thinking and communicating clearly. They left me confused and not knowing who to blame or how to fix problems when conflicts arose in my relationship with Kathryn or others. My judgments left me powerless. On one hand this was the usual state of mind and behavior of a thirty four year old man, but I had many teachers that were assuring me there was a better way; that I could improve my current state of mind and thus my life.

The feelings I had when Isaiah told me about my past lives and the feelings I had during my own past life recollections accurately reflected the feeling of confusion and despair I often felt at this stage in my life. Let the following story serve as a prime example of how judgments and inner confusion caused suffering in my life....

It was a Sunday afternoon, Kathryn and I had been to church and had just finished having lunch at a restaurant. We were driving and looking for parking so we could shop at the University Bookstore. I was in a good mood...until I had a difficult time finding a spot. Finally I found a good spot, only two and a half blocks away, when Kathryn told me that she did not want to walk a long ways to the bookstore because she was wearing high heels. That irritated me. I believed we were under a time stress because we had company coming for dinner. I knew that Kathryn would rush me if we got home too close to dinner, and I hated to be rushed. I wanted to have as much time as possible to get home. These thoughts were making me feel worse not better. I was using my mind to create problems before they even became problems. I was not in touch with my ability to create love and gentleness no matter what the situation. I could have focused my mind differently, if only I understood how. This essential skill, which I was so lacking in at this time in my life, could have saved me and Kathryn from the suffering that was to follow. Why is it that this skill is not taught to us in grade school? Humanity has been around for millions of years,[1] Masters have been teaching this for probably just as long, and we call ourselves civilized. Ha! Such is the arrogance of our current society; we can create computers and send men to the moon, but still as a whole, our society is unaware of the benefit of controlling one's own mind. It is a skill that is far more valuable than mathematics, language, or history. If we first learned to focus our minds correctly, then everything else would fall into place so much more easily.

While looking for parking, anger and frustration grew in me. I blew up and was cursing the other idiots on the road who were thwarting my efforts and causing me to miss out on prime parking spots. Even though my anger was not directed at Kathryn, she could feel it, and it did affect her. Kathryn made a few comments about how negative my energy was; this did not help my state of mind one little bit. Now I was focused on her, judging her, blaming her for this. We had a spot, many spots, we could have parked anywhere if only she would wear sensible shoes.

Once I parked, we then had to spend valuable time working this negativity out. ARRRG!!! I did not want to waste valuable time talking, "Just let it go. Let's move on!" I snapped at Kathryn. Then Kathryn told me that I was not communicating with her. Although she was right, I had no idea what I should have communicated as I was not clear in my own mind what was causing me such difficulties. Somehow we made it through that and got back into a loving space with each other. Yet in my mind, she was being difficult and was the one to blame.

When we got home, we had to talk about it a bit more. I was exhausted and just wanted to take a nap. Then she asked me to take Andy Pandy, a full sized toy Panda Bear that was taking up chair space in our living room, out to my car to make room for our company to sit. I told her that I would and continued on about my business. She then asked me to do it now! When Kathryn asked such things it was more like an order, if I did not jump right to it, there were problems. I got angry and started to defend my right to do it in my own time. This was when Kathryn finally lost her cool with me. From the past, I knew that she would stay in that state for many hours or even days. *Why does everything have to be so difficult?* I thought, *Kathryn is certainly to blame for these difficulties. After all my anger is only due to the way she is treating me.*[2]

---

[1] If you doubt that humans have walked the planet for more than a million years then just do a little research on the internet. You will find plenty of good solid evidence to substantiate this fact.

[2] I did not have a clue that my anger was due to how I slowly let my mind and energies get away from me all day long. Yet I blamed everyone and everything each time a little irritation came my way.

When the Hudson's came over for their visit, we had a very nice time. Kathryn was as pleasant and loving as could be, even toward me. I was relieved and thought, *Finally all is well with us again.* But as soon as they left, Kathryn's whole attitude changed. Again Kathryn was snapping at me, and cold toward me. I took this as a sure sign that she was to blame; after all I was in a good mood. I was in a loving and peaceful place while they were here and even after they left...until Kathryn started snapping.[1]

We had our words. I pushed blame upon her as she tried to blame me and how my energy was affecting her.[2] In my mind, I kept hearing her tell me why our relationship would not make it; I felt abandoned. I kept hearing her blame me for starting the problem; I felt unworthy and frightened. All I wanted was to be in a loving space, to move on from those earlier issues, and to relax in front of an episode of *Star Trek the Next Generation*.

A feeling of hopelessness moved through me...I was afraid to communicate because I felt that what I had to say would be invalidated. I did not have the confidence to present my point of view clearly, how will this ever be resolved if I cannot do so? If my point of view does not stand up under scrutiny or is not understood in its proper light, I will appear unworthy of love and respect.

I desperately felt the need for resolution. Mulling over all that had transpired in my mind, I soon I began to think that I was the one who started it all. My rationalization was, "It was me who got angry first. Kathryn remained calm for a while and helped us though my initial problem. After a while, she could not do it any longer and she stopped trying and stood up for herself." This made me feel like such a fool and so sorry. I loved her so much and did not want to hurt her.

I went to Kathryn with this new perspective and yet even this did not resolve the issue nor did it bring Kathryn around to loving me again. With this frustration I realized I had just tried to take more of the blame than I was due. And so around in circles my mind and emotions went.

Today, when I look back on these and similar events, I know that I could have chosen to think differently at many stages in this adventure. This would have changed how I felt in the moment; this would have

---

[1] Do you see how I had given my power away to Kathryn? She had the power to take away my peaceful loving mood.

[2] My anger was like a bucket that was nearly full of water. As soon as a little water was added, it overflowed. It was only then that I noticed a problem, when my bucket of anger overflowed. Mostly I ignored the hateful thoughts I held and only noticed when angry words spewed from my mouth. But Kathryn felt the full weight of that bucket full of anger, even before it overflowed.

changed my energy; it would have changed how Kathryn reacted to me. I did not love myself so I was desperate for the approval of others, especially Kathryn's. If she was in judgment of me or being distant for any reason, I pulled on her with a desperate energy, and she could feel it. This only made her more distant as she tried to stabilize her tenuous grip on clarity and balance. Today, I readily pardon myself or others for a failure to be loving or aware and quickly move back into an aware, loving space no matter what the other person is thinking, doing, or saying. Today I look to no one for approval and no one controls my inner peace but me. I am stable in my own being; this creates a conducive energy for the other person to return to stability in.[1]

That was the last of the past life memories I have had, they no longer come up spontaneously for me. These memories came up at a time when I was very interested in learning about my past lives, when I came to believe that it was possible for me to remember, when I was ready to make profound changes, and when I had the support of wise teachers to make use of the experience. Thus, a lot of things set me apart from the average person who is not having such memories coming up. Later, I lost interest in past lives; they have limited entertainment value. Just like the early years of our current life have little significance now,[2] so do our past lives. Continuing to go after memories of the past is going backwards…I wanted to go forwards. I wanted to understand God and my connection to this Life Force. I wanted to create my future not live in the past.

---

[1] Mostly this is true. However, after living in India for more than a year and all of the stresses of dealing with this radically different culture and truly ignorant people, getting involved with my new large family, and heaps of financial stresses, I have found myself facing these issues once again. Editing this book many times over has helped to remind me of the tools I have and kept my focus on practicing what I preach.

[2] Yes, the past shaped who we are today, but it is what we focus on **now** that will determine how we feel now and shape the events of tomorrow. The now moment is the only time you have a choice of which thoughts to focus on; the now moment is where your power lies.

Many Changes

My passion for spiritual growth and being of service to others led me to doing volunteer work at Bellevue Overlake Hospital. I started expressing interest a few months earlier, back in October of '92, but to work at the hospital as a volunteer required going through an orientation program. The timing was such that with all of the holidays, the next orientation wasn't until late January so it was the beginning of February of '93 before I could begin. I wanted to do massage work, and they had a program they called "Special Touch," but it required further training and I had to wait a few more months before the next training session. So I started out by taking the book cart around to patient's rooms in the evenings. I was eager to share what I was learning about life and healing and the book cart gave me the chance to talk to patients who I expected would actually want to learn to be healthy. It did not matter to me that I had only memorized concepts and not yet fully integrated the lessons into my being through experience. However it was all perfect...diving in, and clumsily applying what I had learned eventually gave me the experience and wisdom that I enjoy today.

Some of the people I met were regulars, in the same bed, in the same room week after week. Others were semi-regulars, in and out of the hospital but always in the same ward when they were there. Sherry was one of the semi-regulars. Sherry would tell me about all of her various problems and how she had been in and out of the hospital for over twenty two years. I would counsel Sherry and tell her how she could improve her health by changing her thinking and having energy treatments. Then Sherry would come up with more stories to support her position of being a victim of the ailments of her body.

Still I thought I could fix Sherry by bringing Kathryn in to see her. Because Kathryn had such a long medical history and then miraculously improved as soon as she removed the negative influences from her life, I thought Kathryn would be an inspiration to Sherry. Boy was I naive. All Sherry wanted to do was tell Kathryn, anyone, the story of how miserable the life of Sherry was. Any fresh pair of ears would do, so poor Kathryn got an earful of Sherry's medical history...and I got yet another dose of it too. A doctor rescued us when he came in to see Sherry as part of doing his rounds. Kathryn seized the opportunity and whispered to me, "Michael, get us out of here!" So I said to Sherry and the Doctor, "Excuse us, we'll let you have some privacy. We will be right back." And then we promptly left the hospital and went home. Even though I was embarrassed about saying that I would be right back and then leaving, I was pleased that Kathryn did what she needed to do to take care of herself. She often found herself in the presence of psychic vampires. Kathryn was an easy target, and they often sucked her dry. So this was progress for her.

The next day I called Sherry to apologize. I intended to explain our disappearance but she was not interested; she acted as if nothing had happened. Sherry does not want to know; all she wants to do is tell others about how life is for her. She feeds on the energy of her listener as she does so. She does not even consider healing to be an option. In these early days I found it difficult to not want to fix people who seemed in such need of fixing.[1] I was becoming aware of how pushy I was and learning to back off.

It was only a few days into my new job in Bothell and I was feeling insecure. My boss Sheldon was not very communicative so I was not sure if I was meeting his expectations or not. At one of our regular apprenticeship group meetings[2], I asked Isaiah about it and the following is a transcript of the conversation:

Mike: Isaiah, I started a new job last Wednesday and I've been going through some real paranoid kind of feelings about the job and the man that I'm working for. And I'd like to get more clarification on where it's coming.

Isaiah: You already have the answer you need.

Mike: So my feelings have been fairly accurate?

Ezekiel: No, but if you explore your feelings and ask yourself where they are coming from and why you will find that you have access to this information. You do not trust your boss. He reminds you of your father and he is someone that you cannot charm or manipulate. You are looking for approval and it is not forthcoming. Your usual techniques to impress people and get them to like you will not work with him. He is looking for results and you will have to be patient until you can deliver such results. There are times where he is friendly, but mostly he is distant, yes? (Yes) And this behavior has triggered your need for confirmation, especially just after you were laid off from your last job. Can you feel this, does it resonate? (Yes)

So not only is he a father figure, but he has also triggered your need to compete. Your pattern is to

---

[1] A further note of interest is that if someone like this actually did decide to change and embrace what we are teaching in this book they would quickly experience more profound and dramatic changes than someone in a less drastic circumstances.

[2] January 20th, 1993

attempt to be better than others, to be the best, and you cannot. He is in charge and you cannot buck this. So you feel nervous and thwarted. One minute he is there for you and the next he is not, just like your father.

Instead of trying to get him to approve of you can you try to feel what is going on for him? Such a compassionate turn of intention has power. This is the power of love. If you try to understand him you would find that he has a lot more going on in his personal life that you cannot see. He does not have the time, energy, nor the desire to soothe your fragile ego. He might be more responsive if he was aware of his behavior, but he is not. This is much like your father, can you see this? (Yes) And your inner being is always setting you up, especially you since you are asking for growth. The approval you seek is something that you need to give to yourself.

If you go through this fire you can learn to trust him. And like your father you want him to take you in and tell you that you are wonderful, doing a good job, and that they don't know what they ever did without you. Is this accurate? (Yes) And like your father that approval is not coming. You will continue to suffer the emotionally uneasiness as long as you seek your approval from the outside. Your paranoia has no real source; there is nothing about this job that warrants it. The anxiety is within you and it is coming to the surface because you are ready to be healed. And not unlike surgery, it can be a bit uncomfortable at times. Don't be surprised that opportunities for growth come when you have been asking for them.

Mike: I'm not real surprised. I just...the form always keeps surprising me. (Good) It just totally amazes me sometimes.

Ezekiel: The form is of your making.

Mike: (laughter) I'm responsible?

Isaiah: Yes, definitely.

Mike: Of course I am.

Isaiah Most certainly.

Mike: Oh God!

Isaiah:	You didn't know how creative you were did you?
Mike:	Oh wow, no, I guess not.
Isaiah:	Congratulations. You have begun a major piece of work. But remember, this has very little to do with him, this is your work not his. Notice your projections and take responsibility for them.
Mike:	I was feeling that it probably was my projections because it was getting to the point where there were crazy stuff that I was thinking (Um hum) and I've been through that enough times to know that's my own stuff. (Right, coming up for healing.) Well, thank you very much.

"It is in the dark that the seeds of growth are planted."
- Isaiah

Lack of awareness, not knowing what is going on in the minds of those around us, not knowing what will happen next, leads to a growing fear in the mind of the unaware person. This was just another example of how I was looking to the outside world to validate my existence and for my safety. I kept assuming that other people had the ability to deem me worthy or not. If a boss did not like me, I could lose my job. Not yet understanding that God has always and will always meet every one of my needs, I placed my fate in the hands of fickle humans. No wonder there was so much fear in me. It is frightening to think that humans are running our world...it is uplifting to think that God is running our world. Through a series of job related miracles, I learned this lesson well, that God indeed is running our world.

I had to accept that some things I just won't know when my worrisome mind demands to know. My intentions to become more spiritually aware, to improve my relationships and to do my best job at work are like seeds I am planting in the dark of the earth beneath the soil. From those seeds sprout fruitful life experiences. No person can take away that fruit, for it is rooted in my soul; it has become a part of me and it will flourish and continuously spring forth for all of eternity.

Over the next few weeks, my inner struggle with work continued and I also continued to ask Isaiah about it. Part of the reason I kept asking Isaiah was that I had nothing else on my mind to ask, and I did not want to pass up the chance to have a one-on-one chat with Spirit. It made me feel important and worthy, at least for the moment. Here is part of that transcript.[1]

---

[1] February 10th, 1993

Mike: Last week you mentioned that I was falling back into old patterns at work and so I've taken that this week and looked at it and tried to...tried to change my consciousness...and I'm not quite sure if I'm getting it all. I'm not sure if I really fully understand the meaning of what you said, if I've made any improvement this last week.

Isaiah: When you lost your job your mask as a gainfully employed person was shattered. You began to flounder. This caused you to search for a different way to be. You were frightened. You began thinking, "What are the possibilities? How is it that I can define myself? How can I get the validation I need?" In your creativity you found a few good ways and a few that were not so helpful. Ultimately you had glimpses that you were worthy, irregardless of your employment situation. And you even began letting go of the need to have your employment your way. Can you see this? (Yes)

However, you began to fall back into the old patterns once you got this new job. You immediately began accumulating some of the trappings of the old mask and falling back on you job for your validation. Do you understand? (Yes) You are again trying to make this your home.[1] Once again you are beginning to base your validity on the reinforcement you receive from work. Can you see this? (Okay?) This cannot define you. (Okay?) You will be going backwards if you continue to use work to define yourself. You are already forgetting what you learned during your unemployment. Do not let the fear stop you, it cannot hurt you. You are real, you are valid, and you have the right to be here even if you do not have a job.

Do you understand? (Okay, yes) We know that you understood this better last week. (Huh?) You are building mental structures again, you have to feel this. Do you see?

Mike: I guess I am having a hard time understanding this.

---

[1] Isaiah meant the home of my identity and self worth, not my body. At the time I did not understand this.

Isaiah:	Go back to feeling all of these things we have been talking about.[1] Feel what it is like for you now. Feel what it was like when you lost your job. Feel what it was like once you found your stability in your unemployment. (Um, okay, I see that.) Don't forget to use your heart too, not just your mind. You keep falling back on your thinking. Feel it, not just think about it.
Mike:	How...I guess I'm not quite sure with my job being a thinking job that it is, how I can achieve an appropriate balance where I'm still valuable to my employer and still moving forward in my own personal life.[2]
Isaiah:	Your work personality is the role you play to bring in a living. You are not this persona. You are having difficulties because it is fulfilling to believe you are the work persona. You thrive in that role because you are talented and can impress people with your skills. There is a certain criteria that you can and do meet at work which reinforces your sense of validity. Also your paycheck does very well to pay the bills which gives you power in your relationships. However you are not any of those things thus the real you doesn't have it so easy.[3] Do you see?
Mike:	Okay, that's why I'm having such difficulty grasping that. Okay, I see.
Isaiah:	You have helpers, others who will help you remember. (laughter)
Mike:	Yes, I do have a helper in that department.
Isaiah:	You are very lucky.
Mike:	Oh, I know.

---

[1] A that moment I was getting lost in thought trying to make sense of what Isaiah was telling me such that I was not able to hear everything he was telling me.

[2] Each time I reread this paragraph while editing this book I think, "Duh"...I was so off base at that time, I hadn't a clue what Isaiah was saying! Look, as dense as I was at the time and yet this stuff eventually sunk in. I am sure it will all become second nature for you too, once you apply and practice what you are learning.

[3] Nor is there anyone who is going to come forward and give the "real you" a stamp of approval. There is no one in this world with such power, save the individual self.

Isaiah: You will not need a heart attack to remind you.[1]

I never fully understood what Isaiah was trying to tell me at the time all of this was happening, yet today it is all too obvious to me. While conversing with Isaiah, I even got distracted and derailed by the fact that my job was a thinking job. These days I see it all the time when I am teaching others; they just don't get what I am trying to tell them. And I hate it when they say, "Yes" when I ask if they understand. It seems really weird to me because if they were paying attention to their own thoughts they should have already noticed what I am telling them about life and about themselves. Now that I am aware of what I am thinking, I often find myself expecting that everyone else is aware too, but they are not.

The issue was that I had low self-esteem, that I needed validation for my right to existence from somebody somewhere. Isaiah wanted me to experience how it felt, to need and seek and get validation from my job. During the time that I was laid off, I felt how it was to not be able to receive validation due to having an elite job, and to feel what it was like to have basically been fired from my job. There was a comparison to be felt and experienced...what was it like with the mask on, what was it like to have the mask shattered; what was it like to rebuild a new mask?

Changing the topic dramatically...I began having trouble with excessive farting again. At Kathryn's request, I tried to hold them back; I liked it better when she couldn't smell. My efforts were futile; with the farts coming every five minutes or so the build up of pressure in my abdomen was too strong. This went on for a couple of months, and the smell was awful. Early on into this experience, I asked Isaiah about it and the following conversation[2] ensued.

Mike: Yeah, Isaiah it's Mike again. I've had a bit of trouble with gas lately, having an abundance of gas, and I've been playing with my diet, changing things around, and sometimes it just doesn't seem that what I'm eating could be doing it. Is there any...is there something you can see that's causing this?

Isaiah: On one level you like change very much. It excites you and keeps life fresh and interesting. On the other hand you are resisting it. You are not able to digest all of the changes that are coming your way. On the physical level you can try using charcoal. This is a good

---

[1] My father had a couple of heart attacks and there was a part of me that worried that I too would end up having one. My father had similar behaviors based on self-esteem issues too.

[2] February 24th, 1993

practical thing that you can do until you have sorted through the thoughts and feelings that come from the changes you have created. You can find charcoal in capsule form at the health food stores. You keep asking for change and they keep coming. So much change that you cannot swallow it all. (Yeah) Your resistance to change is reflected in your inability to digest your experiences.

Certainly the amount of changes I was going through was immense. I did try the charcoal and it significantly reduced the frequency of escaping gas. I had this problem for at least six weeks more so I had plenty of opportunity to test the charcoal. Over the next few years, this problem came and went, always at times when I was making major internal changes. I kept a ready supply of charcoal capsules on hand; at work, at home, in the car. I am happy to report that as of May 2005 I have not had a long lasting bout of flatulence for at least seven years now. And my life is changing more than ever; I just find it easier to accept things as they come.

By this point, I had been journaling my thoughts and feelings and the details of significant events for many months. I had also been doing automatic writing. This writing did help me, for a few moments at least, become more aware than usual and get better answers to my pressing questions. I went through and read some of those past entries and could see how much I had already changed. I found my thoughts and actions had slowly come to match my expectations more often. For example, I was now accepting the suggestions Kathryn had to offer without criticizing them or thinking about it too much. As a result, I was finding great joy in a whole new world, one that Kathryn had lived in for quite some time. In the more distant past, I had not understood this world, I even criticized it, but I was now beginning to give it validity and to enjoy it.

I was also focusing my mind and heart on being with Kathryn when I was physically with her. I was reaching out to her more. I was finding it easy to really listen for longer periods of time. Kathryn was having concerns with one of her breasts, so she made an appointment to see her doctor in Portland, a three-hour drive away on a work day. She called me at work and asked me to go to Portland with her the next day. My first thought was, *She can do this without me. I don't feel like taking a day off from work to drive to Portland and back.* But I decided to ignore those thoughts and really listen to her. Then I heard the real message that came from deep inside her, the unspoken message, I could feel that she was frightened and really would not be asking me if she did not believe that she needed me with her. I knew that I had a great opportunity to nurture her like I had never before so I said yes. I even had to cancel a massage session with my favorite therapist who is always booked up in advance; it would be at least two weeks before I could get another appointment. My massages were very important to me, but now I was discovering other priorities.

It took me about ten seconds to make this decision. In the not too distant past, I would have taken a lot of time to decide on this one, and I would have needed a lot of convincing. Even then, I would have gone with a grudge, and I would have been looking for a negative outcome to use as a reason the next time to get out of such an obligation. Up to this point, my position was, *If you keep going to your doctors in Portland, you can go without me. Get a new doctor who is closer.*

It is amazing how such a simple thing like dropping a glass and breaking it can cause a person so much distress. It is very revealing about the kind of pain and trouble we are carrying around inside of ourselves. I dropped a glass and broke it. As a result, I got really upset and snapped at Kathryn. I did not throw a fit, or get really loud, or do anything really obnoxious, it was just that I was not nice when I tried to communicate with her. I am certain Kathryn noticed it; I did. I decided to look inside, this time without Kathryn's prodding, to find out why breaking a glass would trigger such a reaction in me. I thought about what that would have meant to young Mike. Mom and Dad would have gotten angry. Dad would have treated me like I was an idiot who could not do anything right. For a period of time I would have felt like I was not loved. Kathryn helped me to perpetuate this unlovable image I held of myself when she would criticize my clumsiness.[1]

I realized the amount of fear a simple event like this can hold. My defenses came up when this underlying disapproval of myself rose to the surface. These unclarified experiences from our past are like filters of pain and suffering that we pass the experience of certain present events through. At the time of this incident it felt overwhelming that such a simple thing could shake me from my peace of mind. I wondered if I would ever get past these seemingly endless landmines hidden deep within my psyche. Today breaking a glass is just breaking a glass. A small inconvenience, but nothing more. By years of practice, observation, contemplation, and challenging my thoughts, feelings and reactions, slowly over time the changes I was seeking have occurred and become the natural way I respond to life today. The practice came with each event like this. Mixed in amongst my everyday waking life were opportunities to become aware and to choose and develop new habits of thought. We do ourselves a great disservice to ignore issues because they are difficult,

---

[1] The problem was not the criticism from Kathryn or my father, the problem was that I believed the criticism was true. That's okay; now I know differently.

they only remain difficult for a longer period of time, and ultimately we still have to face them.

During a meditation, I told my guides that I wished that they would force their voice through all the noise that was going on in my head. This is the response I got. "We teach by example. We want you to remember who you are. If we forced our way through, we would be taking on the traits of a physical being and teach you nothing of being a spiritual being. You must decide to listen and that way you will hear our gentle, loving voice." Indeed, for that brief moment, I was hearing the voice of Spirit that I so longed to hear. At the time, I had no idea of how significant these bits of wisdom that came to me through my own mind were, yet they were precisely the thing I was looking for. Over time, the voice within me did not get stronger, I just got better at recognizing and appreciating it.

Kathryn and I were having trouble with the neighbors who lived below our apartment. Their cigarette smoke was coming up through the laundry room and stinking up our apartment. After a futile attempt to get the situation fixed, we decided it was time to rent a house. The only problem was that the houses in our price range were dumps. After raising our price range twice, we found a place that we were excited about. We applied, had our hearts set on it, and then the owner decided to sell it instead.

We were very disappointed, especially Kathryn. She worried about it for days and talked about ways to get them to change their mind. I explained to her that it would all work out. We had already been talking about moving before we got smoked out. I told her that God was looking after us and that the smoke was a sure sign that we were supposed to move.

Again we raised our price level two more times. Then we found it! It was a beautiful home, set on a hill with a lovely view of Lake Sammamish and the snow capped Cascade Mountains. Part of the walk around the neighborhood also had lake and mountain views. The neighborhood, the house, the location were all perfect, beyond my wildest dreams actually; this was a much better house than the one that got away from us. God certainly was looking out for us. However, the price seemed to be a big stretch. After explaining to our perspective landlord, Phylis, that my bad credit was in the past and that I had a good job and good income, we got accepted as tenants.

I was amazed at how accurate Kathryn was at knowing what was going on inside of me. A few days later, while we were getting ready to sign our lease agreement, she told me that she did not like my energy. My first reaction was to look at what I was doing, at my outward actions, like an outsider might do. From that perspective, one could see that I was working, washing the cars, running errands, and such—nothing wrong with that. Normally I would have gotten defensive, actually I started to, but I was changing. This time I took a short break, closed my eyes and noticed what I had been thinking about. In my mind I was rehearsing a major defense case. I was worried that Phylis might change her mind about renting to us due to my poor credit record. My energy gets very aggressive when I get frightened, and I really wanted to live in that house; I could even see us buying it. Energetically I was postured to defend myself. Kathryn felt this and told me about it, which helped me to shift my energy. I was amazed and so lucky to have her to bring to my attention what my thoughts were creating. Not only did it make a difference in this situation, but it helped me to learn how to use my mind properly.

We signed the lease without a hitch. On Saturday, March 6th, 1993, with the help of members of our apprenticeship group, Kathryn and I moved into our new house. Our new landlord, Phylis, was remodeling the kitchen and the work was still incomplete. This caused Kathryn a great deal of stress. She often felt she had to keep an eye on the contractors in order for them to do a good job. In the scheme of things, five weeks of inconvenience was really nothing, but at the time, Kathryn did not think so. Kathryn was getting lessons in being adaptable.

The following day we ran into our friends Steven and Drew at church. Drew was looking deathly ill. We went out to lunch with them and found out they were in the midst of a very traumatic event. We asked Isaiah for his help, here is the conversation.[1]

Mike:	Isaiah this is Mike. I have a friend that is going through some physical problems right now. His name is Drew, and I'd like to know if you can, what you can see with his physical condition and what can be done?
Isaiah:	We can see that his thymus is not working properly and that his immune system is severely weakened. What is your question?
Mike:	Well, the doctors are diagnosing cancer.
Isaiah:	Is it Hodgkin's?
Mike:	I'm not certain of the exact nature of it. And his friend[2] Steven, and I, and Kathryn were concerned, and we would like to help him in his healing process along with whatever the doctors decide they need to do. We'd

---

[1] March 17th, 1993

[2] Friend, partner and lover…indeed Steven thought of Drew as his husband.

like to know if there's anything that we can do to help and if....

Isaiah: It feels like he is only willing to go through so much, that if his treatments or the disease gets too tough he will just leave. Comfort is the best thing that you can offer him and the freedom to make his choice. He has a partner, right? (Yes) He has a lot of fear about this, yes? (I would think so.)

If you really want to grow with this event you will have to get out of your mental boxes of what healing is about. Your friend Drew has a choice. You cannot take it away from him just because you are learning to be a quote healer unquote. As a healer, your job is to support him in his choice, no matter what it is. It feels that he is too tired to fight. Will you be okay with this? (Uh, yes) His partner wants him to fight this. And you will need to be with him, supporting the partner in his anger and suffering while you are at the same time supporting Drew in his choices. Do you understand? (Yes) Do not try to influence the choices that are to be made. Simply be present with love and support.

Once the chemo-therapy and radiation degrade his body further, the discomfort may cause him to just slip out. This is only a strong possibility and not a prediction. He has freedom to choose anything around this issue including a full recovery. But currently he is thinking about what he has coming up and how much of it he will tolerate and he is considering leaving. Yet he still finds the diagnosis difficult to accept. He is also considering getting a second opinion. They are both panicked. How long have they been together? (Oh, two to three years.) Is the partner the younger of the two? (Yes)

They have talked about this already and the partner understands that Drew is not so willing to fight.[1] So he is understandably panicked. He loves Drew very much and does not want to loose him. He saw them spending the rest of their lives together. Can you be present with these intense emotions? (Yes) You both will find this

---

[1] Later Steven shared with me that Drew had always said if the HIV he had for years turned into AIDS and he got sick he wanted to go quickly. He was not up to hanging on and suffering.

difficult because you want to fix the body. [1] You are not in training to be auto mechanics are you? (No) This will be a good lesson for you. Be present, listen and do not react from your own emotions. Indeed learn to calm your emotions and keep the love of Spirit flowing through you for them. There will be anger, there will be pain, simply let it be and send love. They both will need to talk out their feelings. You may find yourself hearing about the anger of the partner and then hearing about the desire of the other to simply leave when it gets too tough. On a soul level, this has a grand purpose. This experience will accelerate their evolution. There is much more to this situation that meets the eye. Death is a part of life and the timing of it is always in perfection. Don't get too caught up in the appearance. Both will survive, it is only an experience.

The partner feels that he is nothing without Drew. He is having trouble seeing how he is to go on if Drew leaves. He thinks, "What is the point?" It will be a great learning experience for this younger one. And he must quickly come to understand that he can bring Drew great joy and love right now while he still has Drew here to do so. This is an intense situation that you are putting yourself into which will alter your lives too. If you can learn not to fix, your capacity as healers will increase. Learn to simply be God. (Oh, I want so much to get in there and fix it.) We understand that it will be a challenge. It will be your initiation. Give up the need to succeed at healing; it is okay to feel like a failure. This is ego and ego has no place in healing. Healing is about letting Love do the work not about taking away the pain or repairing the body. In reality it is your personalities that needs the healing, not the body. On a soul level if it takes your own death to accomplish this then so be it. If it takes the death of a loved one then so be it. You are all so much more than these bodies living in this now moment. Yet this now moment, including the pain and suffering, affects your soul evolution significantly. The development of the personality that is what is really important. It is the fear that needs to be healed not the body. (Thank you)

---

[1] Of course I wanted to fix him...Isaiah had told us we would be healers, I thought, "Why couldn't we heal him?"

Many Changes

Kathryn: Isaiah this is Kathryn and my question is just an extension of that. This whole issue with Drew brings up a lot of anger and fear for me because of the cancer I've had.[1] Is this an opportunity for me to work through this. I'm not...it's very difficult.

Isaiah: Most definitely. You may find there are times that you need to back off because of this. It is for you to learn what your limits are and even to forgive yourself for your perceived weakness. You cannot be all things to all people. Yet you have intentionally developed this trait in yourself over many lifetimes. This is called evolution, you try out a belief, see how it works, and then evolve it to fit your learnings. We suggest that it is time to change this outdated belief. Thus you may need to withdraw at times, honor this need if it comes up. Your own pain may need your time and energies for a time, then you can return to your healing work for others. Each time you recognize your own needs, and take care of them first, you will return to assist others, stronger and with greater ability. You need to clear out your own fear of cancer. Can you see how this fear will not help your friends? (Yes) This won't be your only opportunity to heal this fear. (Oh my.) Don't worry dear one, you can do this.

By this point in time Kathryn had created a great deal of distance between herself and her family. Not only by living physically three hours away, but also energetically by not continually going back to them for support that never came. At this point she only had a minimal involvement with her family, where as before she had regular phone calls and trips to Portland to visit them. The following conversation[2] between Kathryn and Isaiah reveals the leery state of mind Kathryn had regarding her relatives.

Kathryn: Isaiah this is Kathryn. And it appears that my mother and two sisters want to come up and see me in my new life. Could you tell me, is this going to...? Do you see this will transpire?

Isaiah: Are they coming sometime in May? It feels like that.

Kathryn: I don't know. And why are they coming really?

---

[1] Kathryn had three prior occurrences of melanoma, skin cancer.

[2] March 24th, 1993

Isaiah: You have changed and they have noticed. They are curious and want to find out what is going on. You can relax, they are not coming to attack you. Anyways, you have the home court advantage. They are coming to your turf. (laughter) Even though you see it somewhat differently, it will put them on their best behavior. Does this ease your concerns? (Um hum) These three are powerful women, they have bossed and bullied you and taken advantage of your good graces. Your identity as one who has to duck or hide when you hear them approach can slough off like a snake sheds its skin. That identity is old and tired and dried up and ready to simply fall off. You new skin is ready to be seen. Like fire toughens steel, the challenges that your old self has gone through has toughened you. You are strong enough now to handle anything. You can be happy without guilt. And you can be happy in your own home while your mother and sisters are there. Now that is power, especially when you consider where you have come from. You no longer have to apologize for who you are and they have noticed this already. They no longer mean what they meant to you before, for you have already grieved their loss. You are queen of the manor. (laughter) This is your home. And you don't have to let them know where the spare toilet paper is kept, unless you want to. (laughter...Yeah, thank you)

This story is coming to an end my love, the story of the meek and trembling weakling. As it is with any good story, there is a happy ending...when you experience that you are powerful enough to let your mother come, visit for a short while and then send her back home again, you will see that the past is finished. It is healed. (Oh, that's great.) This is the way to view their visit; this is the way to create your life as you want it to be. But more than that, this is the way that it really is. (Okay) You can always ask them to go home. (laughter...thank you)

A few weeks after moving into our new home, we did our budget and found ourselves wondering how we were going to pay the bills. This new rent payment pushed our spending about two hundred dollars per month beyond our income, and adjusting our already tight budget did not seem like an option. Again I had to explain to Kathryn, "Don't worry it will all work out. It always does." I had no idea how, but I knew it would. Kathryn accepted that answer much more readily this time than she did the first few times I used that line on her. I got very little argument from her, and noticed the difference, and for that I was grateful.

Two days later, only three months after getting this new job in Bothell, a woman came around to my office selling a dozen beautiful long stemmed red roses for $25. I thought it was a good price so I bought one for Kathryn. Once the rose lady left my office, the accountant came running in and said, "Quick, you can get your money back if you hurry. I was going to wait until the end of the day to let you know, but you are getting laid off today."

My first thought was, *Oh my God! Not again!* Then out loud I said, "No, I'll keep them. They are for my wife." After a short pause to think I asked, "I was told when I hired on that the company policy was to give thirty days notice. Is that what I am getting?"

"Yes" she replied. My previous boss Sheldon left the company about four weeks earlier, so now my new boss was this woman who had been his administrative assistant and accountant. I finished the project they hired me to complete only a few days prior. Since Sheldon had been the main driving force behind this project and he was no longer here, my employer found a buyer to take over the product and they simply let me go. I am certain they had this in mind when they hired me as it explained a few things that I thought was peculiar about the way they hired me and my insecure feelings with the energy at work.

I inquired further, "Well...I just finished the project I was working on the other day. I can't do anything of real value for the company in the next thirty days. Do you need me to stick around? Can I collect my final pay and leave? If you needed something else in the next thirty days I would come back and do it, but barring that...."

She responded, "I believe so. I'll have to check. In the meantime you can go home now."

Kathryn was surprised when I showed up at home mid-day bearing flowers. She again said to me, "What are we going to do? We can barely pay the rent on this place, now you don't even have a job."

I replied, "Don't worry, it will all work out." I did not know how but I really believed it would.

It was helpful to be off of work at that time because it gave me the time and energy to be supportive of both Steven and Drew. Steven's partner Drew died mid April 1993.

At the next apprenticeship group,[1] I had an enlightening conversation with Isaiah about my feelings and how out of touch with

---

[1] April 15th, 1993

them I was. I believe this confusion of feelings that Isaiah describes as going on for me is also going on for many people on a regular basis. On the surface most people would have seen strong confidence displayed in me, or even aggressive movement toward my goals; these were the energies I was the most aware of in myself. But underneath, I had a torrent of emotions and energies moving and shifting, I could feel the shakiness they added to my life but still did not fully grasp the reasons they were there. Again Isaiah clearly exposed what was nearly impossible for me to see...

Mike: Isaiah this is Mike. Yesterday in SOM III class...well I'll start with tonight and go backwards I guess. George and Lin and Dan mentioned that I looked angry in class. And then last night after class was over, I kind of jumped on Kathryn and Carla about their problem with the class. And I just...I processed some of it and I didn't realize I was angry in the class, though other people observed it in me. And I'm just real confused about what's going on right now.

Isaiah: You are used to processing your loose energy through your intellect. However, as you are stretching and reaching for new ways of being you are now processing much of this loose energy through your body. But you are not used to this technique and it is coming out in random ways. It is for you to feel how this energy is as it moves through the body and to become conscious and choose how you will deal with it. In the past you used your intellect to control the energies. By processing it through your body you are attempting to move beyond that phase. By the way, agitated was the word they used to describe your behavior. Do you realize that? It was not anger.

Mike: I knew anger wasn't quite it, but I was...

Isaiah: It is very interesting that you interpreted it as anger, don't you think? (Uh, yeah?) From your perspective you see this as anger, and perhaps when you take in to account the judgment then anger is an appropriate label. Do you think there is a problem with being angry and not realizing it?

Mike: (laughter) I suppose it is. I feel...

Isaiah: Anger will come, and when it does it is okay to feel it. You should feel it and you should recognize it. When irritation or agitation comes it is appropriate to feel it too. Perhaps the irritation leads to anger for you.

Perhaps you can even recognize the energy before it transitions and soften it. (I can get there...eventually) You need to take responsibility for it, and we can see that you are attempting this. Are you afraid that if you cannot identify it that it will get out of control and be dangerous?

Mike: I fear that and I don't like to hurt Kathryn, or my friends.

Isaiah: Kathryn will survive this, your friends too. They already have. (laughter) Especially for you Mike, you need to feel your emotional energy and to be okay that you have it. Your emotions are natural. If you can let go of the fear you can begin to differentiate the various vibrations of your emotional energy. Right now you lump it all together under the label of anger. But we are telling you that there is much more here; fear, grief, excitement, irritation and sorrow are all here. Do you see?

Mike: You're...let me see if I understand what you are telling me. I have this energy that I don't know what to call it so I'm calling it anger.

Isaiah: Yes, that is correct. Your emotional energy is quite intense. However, for the most part you only notice it when it comes out and especially when you have to explain yourself to others. At other times you are too much in your head and not paying attention to the emotions that course through you. If you were to pay attention, which requires stifling your reaction for long enough to do so, you would find that there are many different emotions involved. Because of your confusion and the sudden appearance of an outburst you find yourself too frequently giving it the label of anger. Try this the next time you find yourself feeling any sort of negative emotion...sit down, breath deeply, notice how you are feeling, review your recent thoughts and the events, correlate them with the feelings. Challenge your thoughts and ask, "Is this really true? Is this what is really happening? Is there more, something I don't understand?" But most of all notice the feelings. Don't ignore them. Do you like them? Can you change them? Can you change your thinking and where you place your attention? You will find that there is more than one emotion going on during any single event. There are many. Your emotions are good. (Oh, is that so?) They give you feedback on your thoughts and actions. You don't need to be afraid of abandonment for feeling. Your loved ones have had plenty of opportunity to ditch you because of your anger, but they have not and will not. Do you understand? (Yes) You will not be punished for feeling. But do not be surprised when you get a response after expressing your feelings. (laughter)

Mike: I guess I feel like I need to control those bursts of emotion, those outward bursts of emotion, and be responsible.

Isaiah: If you repress these feelings they will build up and then show up as if they are ambushing you.

Mike: Yeah, that is the way it feels at times. And I have noticed the build up a few times too.

Isaiah: Although you should not repress your feelings, this does not mean that you must express them to others either. You need to feel your feelings and you need to understand them. Then you must take responsibility for them. At first you will need to be quite deliberate about this. As often as you can ask yourself, "What am I feeling?" Try to notice when you are trying to suppress an emotional outburst, that will be a good time to check your state of mind and emotion. Merely suppressing them will guarantee an outburst at a later time. Give yourself time to make this change and love yourself through it.

Mike: Yeah. That was a part of the confusion because I felt like I was really enjoying the SOM class and getting a lot out of it. And...but then in the car when Kathryn was expressing her dissatisfaction with it, and Carla too, it was like I was...I don't know, I just got really upset and just...and...

Isaiah: Well now that some time has past can you feel what was going on? What were you feeling?

Mike: I suppose I felt maybe threatened that...I don't know, that maybe Kathryn might pull out of the class and that would mean I should pull out, or that I was inappropriate for liking the class...

Isaiah: Abandonment, that is the bottom line for you. Isn't it?

Many Changes

Mike: Yeah. Especially after I expressed the anger, and Kathryn was upset with me. I was very afraid of that.

Isaiah: Loosing your job once again also felt like abandonment to you. Is that correct? (Yes) But it is not so. You have been actively releasing the illusions that you hold about yourself. You have set this up. Once again you get to see that you are not your job. That your worth does not depend on, is not defined by, your job.

Mike: That's kind of a little more clear this time too.

Isaiah: You can create this differently next time. You don't have to loose your job to remember that you are not your job. (Oh, good!) This is not to say that you were the sole creator in this event, but that your creative energies were a definite match to the movements of energy in this company. Nor is there reason to blame yourself for the economic situation that appears to be going wrong. (Yes) Again this is a situation that requires feeling. Let go of all judgments and feel the feelings. That way anger won't need to spew out from of your mouth. Do you realize that you judge your emotions when you feel them? It is like you expect yourself to be good enough so that you don't have these feelings. The feelings are a natural gage, like the gages in your car. They give you information and help you to make choices. Yet they frighten you. (Okay) Remind yourself regularly that your emotions won't harm you and they are your friend. This should help.

Mike: Did the massage I had yesterday help release some of that so that more of it was on the surface, or....

Isaiah: Yes, but the current events, the daily, moment to moment energy and feelings that you feel, and being consciously aware of them, that will unlock so much more. It is a tremendous opportunity for you if you use it that way. Yes, the massage did unlock some energy that was held in your body. It makes the old energy available to be seen and the energy that is releasing will definitely draw you into certain events. Massage is helpful for you and particularly in your leg muscles and mid to lower back.

Mike: Yeah. There's a lot locked in there right now.

Isaiah: Keep reminding yourself that you will be okay. This is truth. But make sure you become consciously aware of the feelings, use these events to help you grow, to free yourself of these illusions. They need healing. It is time. You are strong enough and loved enough to walk into this darkness bearing the light of your consciousness.

In one of my morning meditations, shortly after losing my job, I got the impulse to write a check to myself. I thought this physical ritual would help me create a significantly larger paycheck. I wrote myself a check for $200 more than I was currently getting each fortnight.[1] I put "God" on the check in the upper left corner, the place where the business name would go, and I also signed it in the lower right "God." The next day, I did the very same thing, from scratch I drew up another paycheck for myself. After that I looked at the two checks every day and imagined what it would be like to have that extra money flowing through our life. It was exciting to dream about, yet quite a stretch for my mind to believe I could actually find such a good paying job.

My last employer did give me my thirty days severance pay without ever calling me back into the office. I also collected unemployment benefits for the next four weeks. And then I got a contractors job at Microsoft, which paid much better. My next paycheck turned out to be more than $500 larger than at the last job; this was nearly a forty percent increase. Even though I thought getting a $200 increase was a stretch, the Universe showed me how easily It could give to me way beyond my belief!

It was during a mediation in one of our weekly apprenticeship group meetings that I got the inspiration to start going by the name of Michael rather than Mike. I had always preferred Mike since it was shorter and easier to write and sign. Also Michael always seemed too formal and pretentious for me. But during this meditation, I got that it was time to let go of shortcuts and take on the responsibility that went with the new name. Thus, everyone at Microsoft knew me as Michael; they never knew Mike.

One day at work Kathryn called me, her voice was frantic, "Michael, while I was cleaning, I left the door open, and I saw an animal walk into the house. It is black; I think it might be a cat, but I am not sure. It ran into the guest bedroom. What should I do?"

Kathryn was afraid of cats. One time, with some effort, I got her to pet a friendly one, but she would never pick one up and hold it. I told her, "Get the broom, go into the bedroom and close the door behind you. Then open the sliding door. Next get behind the animal, leaving the path to the door clear and start shooing it out."

---

[1] A fortnight is a two week period of time.

Kathryn replied, "I am too afraid to do that."

"Okay, then I'll take care of it when I get home," I replied with a bit of cheekiness. It was around noon so that would have been a few more hours.

"I can't stay in the house that long with a stray animal on the loose!" Kathryn did not find much humor in my remark.

I encouraged her to try, "Kathryn, you can do this. You are bigger than the animal. It probably is a cat; I have seen a black cat in the back yard a few times. It will be more afraid of you than you are of it and will flee for the open door."

"Okay...hang on while I try." Kathryn put down the phone and was gone for a short time when she came back she said, "Oh, my heart is beating so fast...pant...pant...(she was breathing hard and had to catch her breath) When I went back with the broom it ran past me and out the front door. I am so glad that is over."

In the next few weeks the cat came around frequently. Kathryn would "let me" pet it outside. She also began feeding it. This was really quite funny because on one hand she just wanted it to go away. But on the other hand it was spending nearly all of its time sleeping on our back porch so Kathryn worried that it was not getting food. The mother in her was stronger than the frightened little girl so the cat got fed.

One day, I got Kathryn to hold the cat. We worked our way up to this of course. She had been holding it for about two minutes when a panic overcame her and she said, "Take it now, take it, take it...Michael, TAKE IT NOW. GET THIS CAT OUT OF MY ARMS NOW!"

I did not need to do anything, the cat sensing Kathryn's distress jumped from her arms and started sauntering around the inside of our house. Kathryn tried to make me put it outside but I told her, "It is only a matter of time before she becomes a full fledged member of the family. Maybe we should start thinking of a name for her." I laughed.

Over the next few days my words came true, Kathryn named her Miss Kitty. It was not long before Miss Kitty was sleeping in the bed with us, right above Kathryn's head, competing for her pillow which Kathryn often relinquished.

It was in May, just after I started working for Microsoft that Kathryn began the process of selling her home in Gresham. I was busy with work; it was an extra stressful time trying to understand my new job and to make a good impression. We were dealing with the intense energy shifts that were occurring in us both as a result of our participation with this spiritual group. All of the experiences we had been having—the group, job changes, home changes, relationship changes, deep-seated-wound-healing changes—all of these things had both of us living virtually in a whole new world than we had been only a few months prior. The outer world was the same, but still it was a completely different experience.

Here are the conversations we had in an apprenticeship group meeting.[1]

Kathryn: Isaiah this is Kathryn. Um, I've had a lot of anger because I don't feel loved or supported,[2] and last night it turned to grieving. Can you explain this to me?

Isaiah: Go on, be more specific.

Kathryn: Um, well there is just a lot of different scenarios that keep presenting themselves and I just don't feel supported. Um, things at the house in Gresham, things with Mike and I. Just a lot of different things happening over and over; it seems that I feel...holding it all up by myself.

Isaiah: And how does that feel?

Kathryn: Not good at all.

Isaiah: Yet in actuality you are holding it all up yourself, are you not?

Kathryn: No one else is there to...yes. I feel I don't have a choice, but I...

Isaiah: Does it feel like a part of you is dying? (Yes) And what part is that?

Kathryn: The nice, make-it-all right-for-everybody-else part.

Isaiah: And the part of you that believes you need someone else to rescue you because you don't believe you can do this yourself. This stronger part of you that is rising carries some anger with it, and you find this

---

[1] May 20th, 1993

[2] It would infuriate me to hear Kathryn say she did not feel supported. I was already working a job, and although she was being a housewife and working hard, she did not have a job per-se, which I considered more stressful. On top of that, I was always helping her with the many projects she would come up with that I would have rather skipped. This was on top of the many personal changes that I was going though.

Now a comment like this holds no energy for me. And from this now perspective I can see how that time was very difficult for Kathryn, too; now I have compassion for her. This realization took me years to come to. Now under similar circumstances, those involving the emotional outbursts of others who are close to me, I move much more easily to realization and compassion.

Many Changes

uncomfortable, don't you? (Um hum) Dear one, you have requested to release this weakling and to take back your own power. Do you remember? (Yes) How can you go forward with this work if you are supported and protected? This is a setup that you have given to yourself, with love. Can you see this? (Um hum) Until you become angry enough to cease believing that you need rescuing you will not heal physically. So that is what is going on.

This is a temporary state and the feeling of support will come back. And truly you are still supported and always will be by Spirit. But it is your own spirit, your own higher self, that has set things up this way for now so that you will get off your butt. (laughter, wow) So the anger is healthy and it is necessary.

Kathryn: So what you are saying then is I'm kind of being pushed to stand up there and do what I have to do.

Isaiah: Yes, you are being pushed to discover that you can do what you have to do. Alone if you have to. Can you feel how this exercise, and viewing it as an exercise would be helpful, can you feel how it will give you strength?

Kathryn: Oh yes. I feel healthier and stronger than I ever have.

Isaiah: So embrace the anger when it comes up and be angry. Let it be okay. Welcome it, when it comes, and be conscious as we have been asking Michael to do. You will find that you don't need a mother. You do not need a sister. You don't need a husband. Your self is all that you need, no one else but you. If you do not need them why do you let them stay in your life? This question might frighten you now, but don't let this cause you to move into resistance. For later you will experience the power this gives to you. It is time to re-evaluate your relationships and to enquire within of the true value they have for you.

Your relationship with your partner bears further scrutiny. You are not mutually dependent upon each other as you once believed you were. But you are afraid to look at this. You think that you will be abandoned if you become too strong. It even seems to be what is now happening, hmmm? (Yes) This is projection dear one. This one especially will love you even more if you become strong. Compare the person you were two years ago to who you are now. (Unrecognizable) Yes and it did not come without a struggle. Is that right? (Yes) Again you are not finding it comfortable.

What happens when a butterfly is ready to emerge from its cocoon and someone tries to help it? It dies. You are very much in a stage like that. You must fight your way out of the cocoon in order to have the strength to survive in this world. It may be a silly metaphor, but it is like you have just worked your way out of the cocoon and are exhausted by the struggle. It left you feeling a bit limp and lifeless. But this too will pass.

You were correct; grief is a part of this too. You are letting go of family and friends that you thought you needed. It is a bit like a death for you. Grief is present dear one. You have begun to see the reality that you are indeed already on your own. When you are ready you will find that your inner guidance is coming through much stronger and much clearer now than it ever has. There is a part of you that has died; the safe part. And there is grief for this too. A ritual would be helpful. Perhaps you can bury her in the back yard. And the cat can help.

Kathryn: Oh, thank you (said sarcastically because she was still just warming up to the cat.)

Isaiah: In all seriousness a ritual would be helpful. It will engrain the meaning of all of this in your mind and in the cells of your body. Find something that symbolizes the cocoon, this safety prison, this thing that bound and restricted you, and bury it in the ground. Then say a prayer and bless it. (Okay) It will transform and become something else.

Kathryn: Isaiah, so what do I need to focus on now then?

Isaiah: Sell your house; focus on accomplishing things. This has been very difficult for you for many years, now it is not. Butterfly, it is time to test out your new wings. You do have power in the outer world now. (Oh, okay) And balance is necessary. In private you need to address and feel your anger. Then, without emotion, deal with the outer world.

Many Changes

You also have a tendency to worry too much, yes? (Yes[1]) When you were powerless, you had good reason to worry. But you are a powerful butterfly now. You have transformed. Worry is the same thing as visualization, but it is visualization used incorrectly. Let worry be your signal to practice focusing your mind on what you do want, rather than on what you do not want. The most magical life you can imagine will be your reward if you make this one small change in your thinking. Visualize the life you wish to have. There is great power in this dear one.

Mike: Isaiah this is Mike.

Isaiah: Michael[2]

Michael: Michael, yes, Michael. Um, the last week has been rather difficult. Um…I don't even know what kind of words to put on it. Um, Saturday I lost my ring; Sunday I find myself questioning my relationship with Kathryn; Monday I find myself questioning why do I want to get out of technology and go into spiritual growth, healing kind of work. Um, and just a lot of question going on, a lot of doubting, and just not feeling quite right. And I'm not quite sure where I'm at. Am I trying to create chaos for something interesting to do or….

Isaiah: Noooh… that doesn't sound like something **you** would do. (sarcasm)

Michael: (laughter) Part of me thinks that might be something that's going on.

Isaiah: You are like a child who runs around doing all sorts of naughty things hoping to get attention. The ring was lost by this child. And it is this child that is questioning his relationship with someone who is changing so dramatically. Can you see this? (Um hum) There is a part of you that is resisting growing up and taking responsibility. This part is asking why it must

---

[1] She sure did! I had a pretty strong ability to worry too, but just about different things. It is a trick my mind used to play on me, because I was not worried about something Kathryn worried about, I could feel superior for a moment.

[2] I had just made the name change from Mike to Michael at the prior week's meeting and had not yet gotten used to using my new name.

be so hard. This is okay if you can see it and make a conscious choice of how to move forward.

You still have the adult within you that is capable of doing those things that are safe. Those things that bring positive reinforcement...like work. A little boy comes out when it is not safe. When you have to do things like truly connecting with someone or being consistent. There is part of you that wants to run and play when there is difficult work to be done. Okay, so perhaps we are being a bit harsh. It is meant to be a metaphor and not to be taken as a rebuke. Kathryn is changing, you are changing, and thus so must your relationship change. At times Kathryn has been like a mother to you. Does this resonate? (Yes) And your ego has enjoyed being her protector at times. Yes? (Hmmm) And her ego too has enjoyed nurturing you like a mother does. But you are both asking for change, and change is occurring. You are both coming into your own as independent adults. Adults that are able to be with and express ALL of their emotions. Your mutual neediness has all but vanished. Thus the confusion. Does this make sense? (Uh huh) On Saturday you simply tried flipping back to the past neediness. It was a twelve year old boy that lost the ring and got separated from the group. Was it not? [1] (Okay) And you are finding that the past ways no longer work. You each are finding your own points of balance. You may find yourself trying out the past energies again, the programming is still in there, but you will find they no longer work. When you feel this coming, you can stop it and reach for your new tools. The new tools will work and require just a bit more practice before they feel totally comfortable. And don't be surprised if even these new tools become worn and outdated. Later in the future, again you will find further changes that you will want to make, further adjustments. But for now

---

[1] Lin and her Husband Dan, her Daughter, Kathryn and I, all went out to a street fair on a Saturday. I got separated from the group because I got tired of keeping track of them while they were never keeping track of me. They would hang out at a booth they were interested in while I was bored with it, yet when I found a booth I liked, they moved on without taking notice if I was with them or not. Finally it just did not matter, I knew I would find them again eventually, and I did. I enjoyed and needed the time alone. I never was a herd animal. Although there is much accuracy in the part about the child within me coming out in destructive ways, Lin's personal opinions, her judgments toward me, did come out in the channelings.

these new tools work and will carry you forward. Do you understand? (Yes) If you can tolerate this change, you will find your relationship becomes stronger not weaker.[1] Because you each are now, or will shortly be, in a position to be able to walk away from this relationship, you will find that you need to renegotiate everything. Before this you could not leave because you needed what the other provided. Many relationships are like this and it is okay. But much more is possible and you both are beginning to see this. And you both have chosen to explore and create something better and stronger.

In the past health and wholeness was not the goal, but it is now. This could not be accomplished within the old boundaries of the old relationship. New boundaries are required and are being created. Your relationship must change just as you both have changed. This is not so much an ending as it is a new beginning. What you have already experienced are growing pains; a signal that you are growing into a new life. For the two of you, the end would have come if you remained needy. You both are craving much more than that.

So this is why you find yourself questioning why you want to make these changes. "Why do I want to be a healer? Why can't I just stay in the computer world where it is safe? I understand this and there is stability." Right? (Yeah) Deep inside of you there is this inner urging, pushing you forward. Truly you are dissatisfied with the status quo. But when the going gets tough you begin to question your choices. This is normal but do not let it derail you. You can feel that there is a higher level at which you can love. The question you should be asking is, "Do I need this other person or do I love her?" It may scare you to ask, but ask you must if you wish to complete this movement you both have already begun. You will not break up; your relationship will become stronger, if you can simply love one another through this process. Not because you cannot part company, but because you find that your love and strength is mutually supportive. Each of you will no longer drain the other, but you will be of great help to each other in many

---

[1] Time proved this to be a very true statement.

ways. For in the past you have each drained the other. Totally. Especially you Michael, you have totally drained Kathryn at times. Do you recognize this? (Yes, I do) It was the neediness. It is the neediness that is dying. Have we answered your question sufficiently?

Michael: Yes it does. Um, one other...It seems like you touched on something that I've been wondering about. I've been real objectionable at times to Kathryn going forward with doing so much. And I've given myself a couple of reasons. But I'm starting to wonder if it's because I don't want to feel responsible and have to do as much as she is doing.

Isaiah: You often find an answer that seems to fit neat and tidy, but it covers up the deeper reason that you are not quite ready to face. You have fear, fear that she will leave you. (Okay) You need to acknowledge this fear and understand that you have it if you are to overcome it. Do you understand? (Yes) You are afraid that she will leave you if she becomes too strong. Can you see that? Can you accept that this fear is inside of you?

Michael: Well I can, it does resonate with truth. But one of my fears has been that she's...I see her at night time when she is in a lot of pain from doing so much during the day, and I'm just kind of concerned with that too. Is that something I should not be concerned about?

Isaiah: This is her concern, not yours. (Okay) But if you look deeper you will find that wrapped up in all of this is the fear that there will not be enough of mommy left for you. That she will not be there for you. (Okay) If you can let go of your fear of saying, "No, I have no energy for this project," you will find that you have other options. You will find that you are free to encourage her and even that you can help in small ways. You can listen to her when she needs to vent. It does not mean that you need to come to her rescue. This will make room for her energy to flow. She does not need to slow down because you are afraid. She has the right to find and stretch her limits. She needs to expand in this way. It is part of the process.

So it is for you to differentiate between your concern for her and your fears of getting what you perceive as your needs met.[1] For truly your lesson here is that you can meet your own needs. If you can do this you will find that you are stronger and more loving than you think. Do you see? (Yes I do) Too often this love and strength is suppressed because the little boy in you is worried about getting his. And he gets angry when he thinks this way. But you are capable of so much more. One day you will see just how much more love you have to offer. Search yourself and you will find this strength inside. Negotiation may be necessary at times, but let go of the fear, the anger, the worry. Neediness can no longer be the basis for this relationship for either of you. It will no longer hold together this way. (Thank you)

It might sound like both of our lives had become an emotional hell. It was not that bad. We had plenty of times where we held each other, loved each other, had wonderful outings together, and spent hours staying up late talking with great excitement and enthusiasm about the changes and insights that were coming to us. We did not know how long this fantastic Master teacher was going to be with us. We were making sure we were utilizing Isaiah to the fullest while we could. By facing the issues, walking through the fire, and asking for clarity about what we discovered on the journey, we made the best use we could of this safety net that seemed to be always waiting beneath us. The Indian culture and Yogi traditions are strong on the disciple-guru relationship, because they knew that having a Master to light your path can help you understand where you are and keep you heading in the chosen direction. Having Isaiah helped Kathryn and me make quick progress clarifying the mess we had created in our minds. It is much easier and safer to work in the light than it is in the dark.

---

[1] Isaiah was spot on with this insight.

Be Careful What You Ask For

This next conversation with Isaiah is a prelude to what was coming next.[1]

Michael: Isaiah this is Michael. Um, I've been planning, or thinking I should say, about a hypnotherapy class, um, for quite awhile now. And there's two time periods in which I've got in my mind that I'm considering. And one is this summer in August and the other is this fall starting in October.

Isaiah: We see that fall will be a much better time for you as you will find that a great number of emotional disturbances are occurring within you this summer. [2] We see that you will be facing the IRS issue very soon. [3] But that is not the only issue, there is another. By the end of September your energy should be clear again and you will have much more energy for study.[4]

It was the end of June, nearly two months had passed in my new job at Microsoft. During a meditation with our apprenticeship group I was inspired to ask for help releasing my arrogance. This was a silent and sincere asking that came from the depths of my heart. It was a prayer to God to help me release this arrogance that was clearly plaguing my life and was causing me to blindly offend so many people. I should have added, "And please be gentle!" Well my prayer was answered swiftly and not so gently.

We held a combination house warming and birthday party for Kathryn, most of our apprenticeship group as well as many other friends were there. A few days later Lin, the one who was channeling Isaiah, called me about a problem. During the party, while talking to a friend, I let slip a private detail about Lin's family. At the time, I immediately felt that I had made a mistake, but I did not realize just how private this issue was for Lin, I thought it was common knowledge. Even though I noticed my mistake, the words were out and I continued on with my conversation. When Lin called she was emotional and very upset with me. She was hurting and felt that I had betrayed her trust. She told me

---

[1] June 17th, 1993

[2] Isaiah was predicting the biggest emotional upheaval of my life up until this point!

[3] Yes the IRS issue did come up, but that barely made a blip on the radar compared to what was coming.

[4] As the story will show these statements did come true.

that I was caught up in showing off and trying to look important and said things in front of her son that he should not have heard. This was a crushing blow to me. I don't want to hurt people but so often I found myself being offensive in some way. My own judgments attacked my already low self-esteem. In my world of friends and teachers, it was important to me that Lin trusted and liked me. Now it looked like I lost her trust forever.

At the next apprenticeship group meeting, Isaiah announced that the group would be coming to an end in September. This was disappointing news for all of us. We had gotten so much wisdom, guidance and support from Isaiah, many of us had physical and emotional healings, it was natural for us to feel like something of value was being taken away. Of course I could not help but feel that I was a major catalyst in this situation; that I was the one to blame. I have included most of the transcript of this meeting below because it is such a powerful lesson about healing.

> In the dimension of what you call time this is July 1st, 1993. Give us a moment...[1] Self doubt can be a challenging obstruction between the dimension of Spirit and that of the physical plane. But do not let this discourage you from continuing on your path. Do not give in to the idea that this is an impossible path or that you are powerless. For you are the light, the source, you are the All That Is. You are timeless, beginningless and endless; there is nothing that is impossible for you. Even when you have forgotten this, it is still so.
>
> It is time for all of you to come back to conscious awareness of the reasons that you are here, in this particular grouping, in this specific configuration. And to become aware of the effect you have on one another. The time has come for the baby birds to leave the nest so to speak as we have other work for this one whom we are speaking through. Also you each have your own individual paths to tread as healers. Two of you are ready now to begin your own work. The others still have their own self doubt to face. But face it you must for indeed you too are ready to be of assistance to others who need your light.
>
> The reason for the existence of this group has been to make you aware of your own inner ability to assist others in their healing process. If you go back through the transcripts you will find that we have been removing that which has blocked your conscious awareness of your true self, of your natural God given ability to heal. An ability

---

[1] Lin would often get started then have to stop and go just a bit deeper so that she could be clear enough to channel. Often her own resistance, judgments, and opinions would cause her to stumble a bit and even interfere with the channeling. She freely admitted this herself. Even still, the lessons we got from Isaiah and her wise counsel was extremely valuable to us.

shared by all of humanity, yet each of you were that close to demonstrating these abilities and this is why you are here. You had fewer blocks than the majority of humanity is what we are saying. This does not make you better or elite in some way; it just means that you were prepared to take the step you have all taken in this last year's time. This group has been of great service to her in that she has had difficulty allowing us to move through her in this way. Each of you has functioned as transformers, lending your bodies to this process and allowing our energy to flow through her in a much more complete way. For this we offer our most sincere gratitude. For this message needed a time and place to be expressed.

You have all been affected, quite literally on a cellular level, by this energy. [1] Many times we have told you of these cellular changes, this has not been a game. Yet right now, while you remain so close in this grouping, you do not recognize the full depth and scope of these changes. But once you are cut loose you will begin to notice just how deeply you have been affected. You will see that each of you ARE ready. The gift that will come with this separation is that you will see how capable you are. Those of you who have a tendency to resist change will find some pain in this, but you need this push for we wish you to begin assisting others. We salute those of you who have been working hard through the difficulties and the pain.

It is important to note that our entire focus has been to remove the blocks you hold in your consciousness so that you can become successful healers. **Healing is simple; it is God who is doing the work. Your job is to be a clear channel for the healing energy to flow to the one who needs the healing. It is not complicated.** [2] What makes it seem complicated are the beliefs and ideas you hold, the programming that exists in your subconscious. Some call these blocks karma. Some say, "This is my personality, this is how I am." Yet we have been teaching you that all of this can change. And indeed you have seen how your personalities have changed. As you find the courage to move out of your shell and begin your healing work you will find a new challenge facing you...your ego. One of the biggest blocks of this healing power is allowing your ego to take credit for it. [3] Those who don't understand this are ready to heap compliments and credit upon you for being able to transmit healing

---

[1] Every person in the group reported odd sensations in their bodies and dramatic changes in their thinking and emotional states.

[2] I want to emphasize the importance of these last few statements to anyone who is considering the path of a healer. It really is that simple and anyone can do it...if they choose.

[3] There is a very good example of this on page 70.

energy. You however should not go there. At such times you must remind yourselves that this is God's energy doing the work. Although there is no part of you that is not God, your personality, your ego, that which you call you, are only a single focal point in an infinite creation, a channel, for this energy that is emanated from God as you. And you will block the energy by taking credit for it. If you do not allow yourself to become more important in your own mind because you have become a servant you will find that you too are served by this energy. Ego and fear are what blocks this energy. Judgment, the idea of separation, seeing yourself as better **or worse** than others these are all based on fear and will block the flow of Spirit's healing energy.

Fear is essentially the thing that keeps your good from coming into your awareness, and thus excludes it from your experience. Fear is the thing that prevents you from serving clearly as a healer. Fear that you are not good enough, not pretty enough, that you are not loveable. Fear that you do not matter, that others won't see how grand you really are. This fear is what we have been addressing all these many months that we have been together by answering your individual questions.

Discretion and integrity are two essential qualities of a healer. Your thoughts must be tempered by your heart before you speak or take action in the world. If not it is likely to be coming from your ego alone. The heart and mind must be integrated, otherwise you have separation. "Is this harmless? Is this loving? Does this serve the highest good?" These are the questions you should ask yourself before you speak or act. The answer will be clear. If it is not, then do not act, do not speak. We promise you that nothing will be lost if you do not act from your unclarity.

Compassion is another essential quality of a healer. Can you walk into another being's energy and feel what they are feeling? We have done this exercise in this in this group. You all found, much to your amazement, that you can walk into another person's energy and you can feel what they are feeling. You must do this without judging your feelings or theirs. In this way you can understand **their perspective** and you will have compassion. Again discretion is important. Discretion in what, and with whom, and in what way you share this private information that you pick up. You must be sensitive to those things that are painful, those things that may cause judgment in others. Much like a doctor, attorney or priest you must maintain privacy. And you must also use discretion with those things that are not ready to be embraced by the one you are healing. Have compassion and not judgment. BE present and BE the presence of God.

Once you begin your work in earnest you will find yourself in the middle of family dynamics. Even in the most horrific of situations you will need to be able to release your judgment and bring forth compassion. If you are allowing God to flow through you, you will find this occurs automatically. But you must be prepared for this and not react from judgment. As a healer this is your job. You are not expected to be in this state at all times, that would leave you open to others who would take advantage of your open and receptive state. However, when someone is ready, when they are sincere, and they are asking rather than taking, make it your intention to serve as a healer. It is by your intention that you open up to allow the pure energy from the Source of All Life to flow through you to this other for healing. BE with them without fear, without ego, without judgment, without anything that blocks this energy from flowing.

Secrets are difficult to keep but keep them you must. For it will not be long before they discover your lack of integrity if you let secrets slip out. If you are to do this work in a consistent way this is a must! And being consistent is what we are asking of you. And indeed we feel that you have made this commitment within yourself to be so.

Although we are kicking you out of the nest, you can rest assured that you can and will fly. At all times you have access to this guidance; there is nothing to stop you except your own blocks, which we enumerated earlier. You also have the transcripts which you can refer to for inspiration, motivation, and to remember just how far you really have come. And you each have your own guides as well. Call on us and we will be there.

So with all of that in mind we will open up to receiving your questions.

Kathryn: Isaiah this is Kathryn. And, I am very grateful to have had the opportunity this last year to deal with issues that block me from becoming a healer. And as that time obviously is becoming closer, can you please help me by telling me what is left standing in my way?

Isaiah: There is nothing, you are fully prepared dear one. Truly nothing stands in your way. (Okay) Perhaps it is time for you to take a look in the mirror, for you will see a whole new person. One who is strong, capable and without fear. For not only have you fully embraced your healing capacity, but you have also embraced the warrior too. You have always been a healer, yet it was the protection you were lacking, and the discernment of when to be open and when to protect yourself. You now have that warrior capacity to protect your vulnerable side if someone tries to take advantage, tries to harm you. Can you see this? (Oh yes) Once you become comfortable with this new side of yourself there will be nothing to stop you from sitting down at your computer and writing. Receiving Spirit through your hands like this will be quite ironic, will it not? [1] (Um hum) When you are ready you can allow it to come through your voice.

You are out of danger now with the warrior protecting your vulnerable side. [2] Yet the warrior is a signal. When she comes out it is it is time for you to go inside to find out who is threatening the inner child and what the threat is. And then it is for you to find out how you can come back into balance. For the appearance of the warrior is a very good sign that you are feeling unsafe and that something is out of balance. (Um hum) It is not to reject the warrior as being wrong but it is to accept and integrate her into your personality. And to know that she comes with a message for you. Let her do her work, and she will alleviate your fears about being able to serve. Although you may not be quite ready to accept this we tell you that you are ready now. (Thank you)

This was my beloved partner that Isaiah was talking about. Many people looked up to Kathryn, trusted her, and sought out her wise counsel; Kathryn's opinion mattered to other people. No longer was she a doormat that other people wiped their feet on; she was standing up for herself; and she had become a whole new person. I felt such pride that she would want me for her partner, this Master who had cleared most of her karma and was such a powerful healer. Although Kathryn still had challenges come up, this truly was a major turning point for her.

As strong as my desire to be healed and be a healer was, I was still struggling. My blocks were still firmly in place. During that same apprenticeship group meeting I had the following conversation with Isaiah.

Michael: Isaiah this is Michael. Um, my question is about…part of it I know I need to be patient with myself, but I also,

---

[1] This comment was made due to the strange condition with her skin that was mentioned on page 68. It was ironic because this condition was due to Kathryn stopping the flow of spiritual energy at the wrists, and now she was ready to let it flow.

[2] I can vouch for that as we had many battles yet still to fight. I also witnessed her warrior with other people. Kathryn was not someone to mess with. Yet she was as loving as the best mother.

part of me believes there is something I'm missing here that I need to process, I need to be going through, or working on, or I'm not sure what. But it's around the issue of um, always looking, seeking attention. Seeking to be the smartest, the brightest, the quickest, the one who's best. Um, it's around that issue. And um, I know it has a lot to do with not feeling adequate, not feeling worthy. Um, feeling like I'm going to be abandoned. But it just seems to take over me right now at times and I'm frustrated with that.

Isaiah: Yes this is so...but what is your real question?

Michael: Is this just a matter of being patient and I'm doing the right things I need to be doing, or is there something that I'm not looking at right now that I could be?

Isaiah: We have already spoken of the things that blocks Spirit from moving through you Michael. Your ego is right at the top of your list and you need to understand when it engages. Pay attention when you find yourself thinking or saying "I. I want. I need. I. I. I." Then you need to come back to bringing your thoughts and words through you heart and ask youself, "Why am I separating myself from others?" At the moment you begin to speak in terms of I, you have instantly separated yourself from the others you wish to engage with.

You also need to take notice when you feel an urgency to tell your story, when you feel that you need to be the one who is speaking. [1] Do you understand? Do you realize that you have just made yourself more important? Why is it that you cannot listen? Do you not know that the other person may be suffering and in need of your loving support? We know that you have it within you to listen and to offer support. But when you find yourself needing to be special, needing to be acknowledged, needing to be seen as someone with great insight and wisdom this is your signal that you have just cut your connection with others. Yes, you are accurate. This is the biggest cause of your distress. This is the reason for your most serious errors in judgment that cause you and others pain. And to heal this you must pay attention and notice what is really

---

[1] Ouch! That one hit me right between the eyes. Isaiah knew me inside and out.

going on inside on a deeper level. And you cannot pay attention while you are jockeying for position in a conversation. Do you see? (Yes)

Pay attention to when you feel like there is something that you must have. This is another signal for you. It will change everything for you if you can simply attain that level of awareness. It will give you the chance to ask yourself, "Is this something that I really need right now?" Don't let yourself go unconscious in these moments, because that is what you have been doing. Does this make sense? (Yes it does) It is okay to have wants, needs and desires and to set out to get them. But not if you hurt others in the process, not if it causes you to feel that your needs are more important than others. This is programming that you have developed in yourself in past lifetimes. And now is the time to change those programs, especially since it interferes with your discretion and ability to be compassionate. You cannot be the healer you wish to be with these programs in place.

To be compassionate you need to be aware of the emotions of other people. You need to let go of your own ego long enough to feel what they are feeling. But your fear that your needs will not be met causes your ego to lock in. At those times you have nothing to offer others. Indeed others come to see you as an irritation, a pest. This is exactly the opposite of what your ego is desperately grasping for. So not only are you making life more difficult for others but you are also thwarting your own goals. The ego's need to be special is not met in this way, nor is your spiritual goal of being a healer being met. This old programming is not serving you in any way, can you see this? (Yes) And because you are asking to move forward this issue is hitting a peak at this time. It is coming to the surface. And others are saying to you, "We won't take this from you anymore." It has happened recently, and it will happen again.[1] It is you who have set this in motion. Because even you can feel that this is intolerable for one who claims to be a healer. (Yes it is) And you can no longer stand the pain you are causing yourself and pain you are causing others. Once you become fixated on getting what you

---

[1] An accurate prediction of what was next to come.

feel you need you go unconscious, everything else becomes invisible. Do you understand? (Yes)

So you need to be keenly aware of the signs and stop the process before it goes too far. You need to notice when you start to feel numb and feel anxiety in your abdomen. It will feel like a pulling towards something you want. That is the time to stop and ask yourself, "What is happening? What is it that is pulling on me? Can I change my direction; can I satisfy this need in some other way? Is what I am about to do loving, is it for the highest good?" (Okay, thank you[1]) This is the time for you to take care of the little boy inside of you. This when he begins to shout, "Look at me. Notice me. Can't you see that I am special? I must be special." A little boy can be cute, but not when he is wrapped up inside of an adult man. Others cannot trust you when he is active. And this one is not cute, not happy. This is not a sweet expressive child. This is a child who says, "I am more important than anything else. If you don't pay attention to me I will kick you." Do you understand? (Yes) Although we are exaggerating he is very much like a six year old child.

Michael: It feels like that a lot of times.

Isaiah: It is like this boy would burn the house down if it was exciting enough, if it got him the attention he wanted.[2] This little boy will take any kind of attention, even if it is negative. Can you see?

Michael: Yes. Um, well…I understand what you are saying. It doesn't make sense to me. But I understand it.

Isaiah: Good. So it is you that must pay attention to this little boy. If you do then you can chose consciously what you want to do with those feelings. And what are the feelings that are causing him to act out in this way? Do you know? (No) You need to become aware of them. You cannot begin to heal others until this is healed within you.[3] Right now you cannot be trusted. Do you

---

[1] I was so hoping Isaiah would stop now, I was feeling small enough.

[2] I would have never actually burnt down a house to get attention. Even though I felt Isaiah/Lin had gone a bit too far, at times when I was angry I held images that were as destructive as this in my mind.

[3] What a crushing blow that was to my fragile ego. But Isaiah was very accurate; I was not ready to heal others, nowhere near ready.

see? (Yes) We can feel that your little boy is feeling scolded, judged, and this is not the point. It is information for the adult to take in and decide what he will do with it. There are many people with swollen egos who call themselves healers. You have recently met one such as this.[1] Their neediness gets in the way and they end up manipulating others because they think they are right. Are you with us? (Yes) This is not good enough for you. (No) This is not how we are teaching you to be. So it is right now in your face and it will keep getting bigger until you make the necessary internal changes. So be grateful and pay attention. Ask the people who love you to help by pointing it out. (Okay)

Are there any other questions? She is having trouble staying out of the way...[2]

A few days later Kathryn got in her automatic writing that her "hands are ready to test the waters, so to speak." We discovered that her hands had more tolerance for exposure to warm water, but still were not healed completely.

Over the next week, Kathryn began feeling a lot of pain in her body, like the fibromyalgia was returning. At the next apprenticeship group meeting Isaiah told her it was due to her resisting the next step of becoming an active and visible healer. Part of her resistance was due to her fear that she would lose her relationship with me. That she feared I could not handle such a powerful woman, and that she could not continue to tolerate the dramas I created through my insecurities. Isaiah told Kathryn that she did not have to worry about these things, but to simply move forward. He told her that when her pain got great enough, she would do so.

Kathryn did not wait. We had taken our Reiki levels I & II class and initiations together. Due to everything that was happening in her growth process Kathryn felt drawn to continue on and take the Master level Reiki initiation and class. Because I was not feeling the energy movements yet, and because of my emotional and mental confusion, I did not think it was at all appropriate for me to be taking a Master's level class just yet. I knew a single initiation and class would not give me what I needed to be calling myself a Master of anything.

---

[1] Referring to our workshop with Jerry mentioned on page 70.

[2] Lin was having trouble staying out of the way. I expect that was due to the fact that Lin had been stung by this issue in me so the topic was involving her ego. This is where the evening of lecture and questions ended.

Kathryn decided to use a different Reiki teacher for her Masters level class and initiation which occurred on July 10th, 1993.

Kathryn also continued her automatic writing, in private at home. She was stretching herself to go deeper with it and she was successful. She began taking requests from people in the group as well. Sometimes she would spontaneously get information for other people we knew, even though they had not asked Kathryn a question. Her writing always proved helpful to the persons involved. For many months she did this writing nearly daily, then she backed off to doing it only when she felt like doing it, which was only a few times a month.

At the very next apprenticeship group meeting Martha was sharing with the group her pain about a situation. I butted in like a know-it-all with advice and how "I" dealt with those situations. Martha then proceeded to tell me off in front of the whole group. Martha was someone else I looked up to, so offending her and being told off in front of others was quite humiliating. I nearly went insane as Martha continued to tell her story while I sat there in my humiliation. There was no rock available to crawl under. After the meeting was over and some of the others had left Martha laid in to me again. She told me that my interruption that day reminded her of how I had done the same thing to others in the Science of Mind I & II classes we took together and how she used to get sick of hearing me talk.

Next it was Kathryn's turn to have a go at me. Over the next few days I discounted her ideas about some things we were doing together and had not been that attentive when listening to her as well. Kathryn told me off a few times and was even threatening that our relationship might not last.

The final straw, the one that broke me, came from work. David, my boss from my contracting agency, came into my office to have a talk with me. "Michael, I have some concerns that your contract will not be renewed at the end of the month. I am hearing that you are a loose cannon. Everyone says that you act superior to the others on the team, no one likes working with you." Dave went on to relay the embarrassing details of a few reports he had received about me.

Although I wanted to disagree that it was a fault in my code that caused Willie and Jim to spend the weekend working, I knew such words would not go over well. I said, "I am so sorry about this. I am certain I can solve this problem if you give me a chance."

Dave was only slightly moved by my plea, "If you can get the other five members of the team to agree to keep you on, then you can stay. Otherwise your contract will expire at the end of the month."

I knew it was no coincidence that all of these people, Lin, Martha, Kathryn and the people I worked with, were coming down hard on me all in this short period of a few weeks. It was happening so quickly, and the impact of each blow was so severe that it seemed to all happened in a matter of days not a few weeks. I knew beyond any form of doubt that my prayer to release my arrogance was being answered by these events. I made my mind up that I would keep my big mouth shut and just listen, for many months if need be. I decided that when someone else said, "Lets do it this way." I would blindly follow rather than trying to show them how my way was superior. This was not easy, but I was able to do it.

My first challenge was directly in front of me; Jim was standing at my door. Jim was blaming my code changes for a nasty bug that they still had not figured out. I was pretty certain it was something else unrelated to my changes. In my own testing I had already proved this to my own satisfaction, yet I was not even allowed to present my proof to the others because he and Willie spent the whole weekend throwing out most of the work I had done in the last two weeks. I was steaming mad about the seeming injustice of this all. I thought to myself, *This is why I am arrogant, because other people don't know what they are doing, refuse to view the proof about facts, and go off emotionally thinking they have it right. And because I hold my ground they label me as the trouble maker and call me arrogant. Besides having my code ripped from the project, I now also have to go and kiss their asses.* Although much of this may have been true, to treat other people as less than oneself is arrogance and will never be received well by others.

I had to deal with my ego issue and just apologize to Jim for this problem and everything else. I spent at least seventy percent of the next few days arguing with him in my head. My job and career were on the line. I didn't need to lose the third job in less than a year. Yet my mind still wanted to have a show down. ARRRGGGG, I had totally gone insane! I knew I needed to let go of it and cooperate, and that is what I did on the outside, but inside I was steaming and wanted so badly to prove that I was right and that they were wrong…and they were too. ;-)

Even still, I swallowed my pride and went with the flow. I started out by apologizing to everyone and asking them for a second chance. My apology was sincere; I did feel sorry for offending them. It was not possible for me to choke back all of the tears as I went through this process. They all agreed to give me another chance, and my contract was renewed.

For the first few months, I was very careful about my communications. People would say things to me that I disagreed with and had a hard time hearing. I decided that for the time being I would try out other people's ideas and perspectives and just put my own aside. This was an extremely difficult and painful time for me, as well as a major turning point in my growth. I began seeing myself in a different light. I discovered that I did not like myself very much. I did a lot of crying. As time moved on and I gave respect to other people, I found a new respect for myself at a much deeper level. I also discovered something very interesting…even though the shortest distance between two points is a straight line, there are other paths that may be preferable due to factors such as greater beauty, greater ease in making the journey, or meeting up with experiences that are necessary in order to appreciate the destination. I learned that other people had good ideas too; they were different from mine but they worked.

I'd like to say that I no longer have any trace of arrogance in my personality; but that would not be true. Once an energy is created, the pattern and possibility is always there. However with my intention shifted and the passage of time, today I quickly recognize the onset of this pattern. I subdue the arrogance with the simple reminder to myself that "All is well. I am one with All Of This." The love that radiates from me far outshines any traces of arrogance that remains.[1]

It was in this time that I noticed that I had a complete healing of those nightly back pains[2] that were due to my arrogance. Since the prior November they had continued to occur about once a fortnight, but the pains went away completely within a few months of making this change in my behavior. I could feel my inner experience change greatly in this same time period too, there was much more peace was in my life. That is significant because the reason I was injured was due to my arrogance, and now that I had healed the arrogance, my back pains were completely gone. However, my back is still the part of my body that lets me know when I am under too much stress, but my pains are not in the same place and do not come on in the same way or with the same intensity.

Years later, at a time that I was receiving weekly chiropractic treatments an interesting thing happened. My chiropractor David had a different approach to finding where his client's spine was out of alignment. He would move his hand up and down my spine, without touching my back at all, until he felt something. He would find the spot by feeling the energy. Then he tapped the point on my spine where he felt the energy and would say, "There it is," and make the appropriate adjustment using various methods. On one of my visits he pinpointed the precise spot on my back where I used to get those nightly pains. I wasn't having pain there at the time but he said something about the energy in that spot was affecting the spot where I was having pain and that, "It had

---

[1] Usually! I am presenting these examples to show that we all can change, and that it is worth making the change. I am not trying to assert that I have achieved perfection. I still have room for growth.

[2] The back pains I described on page 69.

something to do with my brother in a past life." I took that as a third confirmation of the reality of past lives and the validity of my understanding of this healing experience.

A New Chapter Begins

August 5th, 1993 was the last meeting of our apprenticeship group. We had one other purely social gathering, a meal at Dan and Lin's home. After that, as individuals we each kept in touch with a few of the other members, but we were no longer in close contact with all of them or as a group. Lin's energy toward me never warmed up again. Carla, one of the other women who had spent a lot of time with Kathryn, was telling Kathryn that she should leave me. Kathryn just got tired of hearing it and stopped seeing her.

So for Kathryn and me, this was the beginning of a new chapter of our lives. It was a time of vacancy; there was an emptiness just waiting to be filled. Whatever it is that we focus our minds upon is what will fill the void. Fortunately for us, we spent very little time lamenting what we were losing and focused on creating what was to come next.

Kathryn was beginning to have concerns about the leadership of the church. She had been doing volunteer work in their office[1] for many months by the time August rolled around, so she had a chance to see what the minister was like in her everyday working life. Kathryn was not impressed with the way she managed her emotions and treated other people. This was another good lesson for us in learning to feel the difference between people who walked the talk and those who only talked the talk. The timing for this lesson was also good; it reflected to me what my arrogance could easily lead me to. Thank God I was already changing that part of myself.

Even still, we decided to go to the week-long church retreat held in Seabeck Washington. It was an annual event, held every year near the end of August. It was a nice break from the busyness of our everyday lives. It also gave us a chance to enjoy a week with a very motivating new thought minister from a church in Southern California. We had heard him speak once before and loved the music of his choir. This was a man that we felt walked his talk.

There were many sweet romantic moments in that week for Kathryn and me. Even though there seemed to be non stop challenges between us, there were more times where the true strength and love that our relationship had shone through the thickest muck we could create. Thus, a lot of the single people at the church looked up to us and saw our relationship as something to aspire to. One short-lived relationship in particular began at this retreat, and their emotional buttons were

---

[1] This was in addition to the greeting and ushering volunteer work we had been doing there for over a year by this point.

already being pushed. This gave Kathryn and me each a chance to do some counseling for the two individuals, which we both enjoyed thoroughly.

While taking a walk alongside the bay one evening, Kathryn and I came across a pigeon that had landed in the water. It was now struggling to get out. Within a few minutes it had exhausted itself and was floating nearly motionless on the surface of the icy cold Puget Sound waters. Being the animal lover that she was, Kathryn insisted that I go in and rescue it. After a bit of arguing[1] with her about it, I began removing my clothes. I stripped down bare naked because I wanted dry clothes to put on when I got out of that cold water. Fortunately no one else was around.

Except for faint breathing the bird remained lifeless in Kathryn's hands as she dried it using my t-shirt...I mean really, this woman had no compassion! Now I had to put on a dirty wet t-shirt or...I made do without it. Being a skinny sort of guy, I get cold easily. In fact I even get cold quicker than most of the women friends I have known throughout my life. I insisted that we walk back to the retreat center at a brisk pace, which did warm me up sufficiently as I had hoped it would.

Meanwhile back at the main lodge, they had just begun making a fire.[2] How lucky for me, it was as if God was telling them we were coming. We sat next to the fire, and Kathryn began to give the pigeon Reiki, I transitioned between warming my bones by the fire and assisting Kathryn with the Reiki work. Of course this brought a considerable amount of attention to Kathryn and the bird.

It took about twenty minutes before the Pigeon began to move. It had been lying down in Kathryn's lap but now it was insisting on standing up. Kathryn protectively held her hands over it to keep it from flying off into the big open room. The bird was content to raise all of its feathers a little bit and shake the whole body once. From then on it rested, standing up on Kathryn's lap, as she continued to give it healing energy.

Someone brought us a box and some newspaper. I punched some holes in the sides and top, then shredded the paper and put it into the bottom. Fast asleep the pigeon fell, what with its harrowing swim and soothing energy treatment, wouldn't you?

Kisses and sweetness were my rewards for being so patient with Kathryn as she nurtured this bird. We meant it to have been a romantic

---

[1] Even though I knew it was futile, I had to try. I did not want to go out into that icy cold water.

[2] Puget Sound islands can get quite cold at night even in August.

night for just the two of us, to get away from the hyper activity of a predominantly single group of people. Side tracked by only a few hours, we made up for lost time. Holding Kathryn in my arms, I could feel what real love was truly like.

The next morning, many people gathered on a grassy lawn, as the pigeon prepared for his morning flight. Perched on my finger, it was reluctant to let go even after three attempts I made to make it fly. Finally I had to take the pigeon with both hands; I grabbed it by its body and tossed it into the air. It took flight and circled the cheering crowd. Within a few minutes we all went into the dinning hall for breakfast...including the pigeon which followed us in. The staff chased it out. Not being offended deeply enough, the pigeon returned at lunch time, to again fly around the dining hall. It seem to get the message the second time it was chased away because it never returned. We definitely got the message that the pigeon was grateful to us for saving its life.

Many months had passed since we felt like we were getting anything really meaningful from our church. With our teachings from Master Isaiah we really had outgrown it. In fact by the new year, we had enough of that experience and called it quits with the church. However, we were enjoying that Southern California minister's talks immensely as well as the choir rehearsal's that made us all high on spiritual music. A group of us that hung out together decided to go to his church in Southern California for the Sunday service following Thanksgiving. This would give us the chance to hear him lecture and his choir sing live again and see what their church was like. I could easily justify the costs of this journey because it gave me the chance to visit my family in San Diego. Everyone else had the dual purpose of visiting some of the entertainment attractions such as Universal Studios and Disneyland in mind. For me these were minor benefits, since it was a "been there, done that" sort of thing. The trip turned out to be a lot of fun for everyone.

August of 1993 was a very busy month for us. We also started the process of buying the house we were living in from Phylis. This meant I had to deal with my outstanding IRS debt. Phylis's resistance to letting go of this house also complicated things a bit, especially for Kathryn.

When we first moved into the house, Phylis was a frequent visitor. She came by often with the pretense of working in the garden, but she really had a few ulterior motives. First she wanted to make sure her new tenants were taking care of the place. Second she needed someone to talk to and suck energy from. It still took Kathryn a little while to catch on and do something about it, but after a few months of Phylis's weekly visits Kathryn got her to stop by taking on the gardening responsibilities herself. But now that we were trying to buy the house, Phylis began coming by again.

Before going to Seabeck, we changed the locks on the door because we expected that Phylis would try to enter, she knew we would be gone for a week. When we came back it felt to us that Phylis had come by the house and tried to get in, there was no physical evidence, but we both just felt it. On Monday while at work I got a call from Kathryn. "Michael, I need you to come home right away."

Kathryn's tone of voice worried me. "Why, what's up? Are you okay?"

"I just shoved Phylis out the door and locked her out. I am not sure what she is going to do next. I need you to come home right away."

Kathryn defended her home like a true Cancerian. I inquired with a laugh, "She doesn't have grounds to charge you with assault and battery, does she? The workers[1] are still there, right? ...Did they see all of this? Why do you need me to come home?"

When I got home and talked to the workers they thought the whole thing was funny. They did get a bit worried about Phylis's behavior when she got aggressive. Kathryn told me that Phylis had first complained that we changed the locks. When Kathryn inquired how she knew, she gave a lame excuse of suspecting that we would change the locks so she was only trying to verify her suspicion. At which point Kathryn accused her of trying to come in while we were gone. Phylis then proceeded to do an inspection of the house, without permission, and tried to claim a few things that could be easily removed from the house; she said they were excluded from the sale. This is when Kathryn kicked her out and locked the door behind her. By the time Phylis came back later I had looked over the sales contract we had signed with her and found support for our case. When we presented this to Phylis she gave up her fighting.

The three years I needed to wait to bankrupt the IRS had passed. Back in May I made one attempt to negotiate with them on the phone; that conversation went nowhere. I had just filed bankruptcy papers the day before when the loan officer for our house loan told me not to. We had planned on getting the loan in Kathryn's name alone, but the loan officer told us he could get us a better loan if my name was on it too. He told me that I must pull out of the bankruptcy proceedings and negotiate some sort of settlement and that they could tie it into the loan on the home. Because a considerable down payment came from the sale of Kathryn's Gresham home she insisted this be done through a second loan only in my name and not in hers. The lender was amiable.

---

[1] Some minor repair work was being done to the house so that it would pass inspection for sale.

This time I went to the Bellevue IRS office and talked to an agent face-to-face. The bank told me they could lend me sixteen thousand so this is what I offered. The IRS agent told me that was not enough, that it would need to be at least twenty thousand. I went back to the lending officer and he approved the higher loan amount. Again I went back to the IRS in person. This time a different agent handled the short negotiations which amounted to the same conversation, "Not enough, your offer needs to be four thousand dollars higher to be considered." Not being one to give up easily I got one more loan approval, then paid yet again another visit to the IRS, and for the third time I got, "Not enough, your offer needs to be four thousand dollars higher to be considered." This was the third agent I spoke to; I could only assume that it must be written in the IRS employee handbook, "Always ask for four thousand dollars more whenever a client makes a settlement offer." That was the last time I needed to play that game. I filed bankruptcy and paid the IRS nothing.

The bankruptcy however, left us scrambling to get a low document loan under Kathryn's name only. Tax laws can be so annoying...for fourteen years Kathryn lived in the home she was now trying to sell, but due to the fact that for eighteen months she rented the home out it now fell into some sort of business tax category. There was one loophole we were trying to jump through which left us pushing to have the sale of the house closed by the beginning of November or Kathryn would take a huge capital gains tax hit.

It wasn't easy, but we pulled it off. It seemed nothing was impossible. If we persisted, if we kept our minds clearly focused on where we were going, we always found what we needed to help us get there. It's funny; this is just what the Masters teach. A loan we thought, and were told by many, that we could not get...really was possible. This huge IRS debt vanished virtually of its own accord. One day at a time, I just did what I needed to do that day, and I was kept safe the entire time. I did not worry about this debt every day; in fact I rarely did worry about it. The job move to Lake Oswego, then the timely job offer in Bellevue, kept my income in my pocket for that entire time. Having lived through this experience, the synchronicity of all of it totally amazes me. Many of my friends expected some sort of horrible ending to this problem, yet that never came.

Never worry; it is a waste of time. It is a painful experience. It makes you physically ill. Isn't it true? How many times has this been proven scientifically? So then why do you do this to yourself? Because you don't have control over your mind, that is why! That is why the Masters stress meditation, contemplation and becoming aware of each and every thought you think. Worry has the power to create a future that contains the very thing you worry about. That is worth repeating...Worry has the power to create a future that contains the very thing you worry about.

Indeed your present and current reality already has just such creations within it. If you could only cease all worry, and you can, you would be astonished at how it transforms both your inner and outer experience of life. To cease it, practice focusing your mind on what you do want, as often as you can. When worry enters your mind, again shift your focus to what you do want, the worry will disappear. When you worry you become aware of the potential hazards on the road ahead and focus intensely on them. It is fine to become aware, but if you focus on the hazards, you will tend to drive your car right into them. Instead, you need to move from awareness to focusing on the clear patches of road you can see, those beautiful visions of what you do want, and you drive safely past the worries to your intended destination. If you practice focusing your mind when it is still and peaceful, as it is when you are walking in nature or meditating, then when times of worry come, it is easy to focus your mind on that which you have already practiced focusing upon.

Amoram Our Second Master

With September came planning; what to do next? I always enjoyed being a teacher, and spiritual growth was my favorite topic. I had a little bit to offer, but not yet enough to create an income from it. In this last year, the idea of being a healer had also become very enticing to me; indeed the two paths are intimately linked. I was learning that being a healer first involved being healed, and to be a teacher, one must have experiential knowledge of that which he is teaching. The more of myself I healed, the more I experienced and learned...and the more I realized that I had to heal within myself. At times it felt overwhelming, yet it was exciting to see how far I had already come. Kathryn and I often commented that every three months we were both noticeably different people. For example, the arrogance that was all too present in June, by September it was replaced with a willingness to listen to others without judgment and the ability to do things their way without suffering while doing so.

In my excitement over these beneficial changes and all that I was learning, I tried to share it with others. I found that most people did not want to know. Often I took it personally.[1] In many ways, it probably was a personal rejection, understandably so. Because of low self-esteem, I had a strong desire for my accomplishments to be recognized. These desires factor into our energy; others could sense this in me as I spoke. My enthusiasm to teach came out something like, *Hey, listen to what I have learned. Then you can appreciate me for showing you how to use this power that you have been misusing all of your life.* When the self-esteem is healed, one is then able to come from a place of compassion when they teach. The desire to help comes out something like, *I understand that you are suffering, yet I know you are capable of eliminating it. Would you like to know how powerful you are?*

Even though we were already doing some healing work for others, we weren't being paid for it. We wanted to be doing it as a business, to earn our income from it; it felt like a waste of time for such gifted healers to be programming computers and cleaning house. Yet it did not feel as if others believed that there was value in what we had to offer; there were times that I did not either. Our skills were limited so I was looking for classes to take that would augment our skills and give us greater credibility. Mental understanding is not the same as experiential

---

[1] I have since come to understand that all Masters experience this apathy to personal and spiritual growth. Jesus referred to it many times; the parable of the wedding banquet where no one would attend, then later those that did come came shabbily dressed, is just one such example.

knowledge, yet that is all the world at large seems to want to pay for. Going the typical route of taking university courses to get some sort of degree in psychology did not appeal at all. I felt these academics had little to teach in the wake of Master Isaiah. I wasn't willing to pay the price of time, money, and stress to jump through their hoops just so I could charge money to insurance companies for servicing their clients. The system sucked, and I wanted a reasonably acceptable alternative.

After considering many of the modalities of healing available, we decided to take a course in hypnotherapy. We put more energy into interviewing our teachers this time than we did for the Reiki class or for Jerry's energy class. This time we met Mack, the instructor, in person. Kathryn and I both felt good about him...at first. Later, during the class, Kathryn had some trouble with him and his energy. However we did learn a lot in his class. This included what we were continuing to learn about picking our teachers. It is a process. We won't always do it to our human ideal of perfection, but if we pay attention, we learn to understand and recognize the movements of energy. The next time we feel similar energies, we have information about what to expect. So we always have advanced warning about what is coming, good or bad; it is just that we are not skilled at reading and recognizing it. Bad experiences contribute greatly to our skill of reading energy. If we are paying attention that is...are you?

Everyone who comes into our lives is a perfect match to our energy, especially teachers and others who play significant roles. Thus, it is not truthful to try and find someone who is responsible or to blame for how the exchanges of energy between two or more people turn out. Everyone involved have contributed their energy to the situation. Rather than blame others for their behavior, which may have been contemptible, understand what it is in your own energy that makes you a match to them and their actions, and then change your own energy. It is important to ask ourselves, "Why couldn't we tell in advance?" Everything we need to know about a person is present in their energy, yet most people are not aware of this. Don't blame others if you can't pick these things up, learn to read energy better. It is important for our own evolution to understand why such things happen in our experience and reality.

Mack's Hypnotherapy class met four hours Friday evening, ten hours on Saturday, and eight hours on Sunday...which pretty much blew away an entire weekend. Fortunately we always had the following weekend free from classes. For eight weeks we were involved with classes, home study and practice. It was extensive and incorporated much profound wisdom from Buddhist teachings, modern psychology and the field of Neurolinguistic Programming. Mack was good at presenting relevant bits from the Buddhist teachings without it becoming a religious discourse. He had gained much awareness from his life experiences, only a small portion of which he had time to share with the class. However, I could tell he was a wellspring of experiential wisdom. I did not aspire to be like him in personality and style, but it was definitely worth taking his hypnotherapy class.

We practiced the techniques on each other during the class, rotating so that we worked with different people. So we each had our own experience with being hypnotized. I had the impression from all the stage acts I had seen, and some of the incredible accounts I had read from those who had had verifiable psychic experiences, that I would have a stronger inner experience than I had. I expected that the hypnotist would actually gain control of the subject, and I could not understand how this could happen to me. And it did not.

What I discovered was that the subject voluntarily gives control to the therapist. If the subject has much familiarity and comfort with the actions the therapist is commanding or even a strong subconscious desire toward those actions, even if their words say otherwise, they are most likely to comply with the therapists commands. The wide variety of trance states that are experienced are a result of the wide variety of mental states the subject is willing to experience. Deep meditation gives us access to more information about our inner world and access to inner resources, so does the state of hypnosis. Indeed states of meditation and states of hypnosis are one and the same, except with hypnosis there is a therapist who is guiding the mediation and keeping the mind of the subject focused on the desired goal and encouraging them to go after something they do not consciously know how to access themselves.

No one ever loses control of themselves under hypnosis. If a suggestion is made that does not fit their values, then it is ignored. This can be a difficult thing to grasp for many people since they say one thing with their mouth, yet think differently in the privacy of their mind. People tend to think their values are the ones they speak out loud, even if they hold conflicting values in their mind. Thus, it appears that they lose control as they act out their true values, which may be in conflict with the ones they publicly live and speak.

Early in December, we received a box of Christmas gifts. The outside of the box was addressed to Michael and Maria Skowronski. Kathryn was furious. I tried to calm her down and explain that it was a natural mistake but she said, "No, your parents have never accepted me. They want Maria back in your life and they want me out of it. Send the presents back." I was shocked at Kathryn's reaction, it seemed too extreme to me.

I did not send the presents back. I did however call my parents and I told them what had happened. It turned out that my father was the one who had addressed the box, and absentmindedly wrote Maria's name.

I accepted their apology and explanation; I told Kathryn that she was making too big a deal of this situation.

Last September, before we began our hypnotherapy class, we had no apprenticeship groups with Isaiah to go to, nor were we continuing with classes at the church, so we needed some other social spiritual activity to fill our time. We decided to start a Master Mind group, based on the work of Jack Boland, a deceased Unity Minister. Martha from the church and from the apprenticeship group was one of the members of our Master Mind group. Just after Christmas she suggested that as a group we arrange a private group session with Brenda who channels Amoram. In January of 1994 we had that session.

When we arrived at the door, we were greeted by Bren, who invited us to come inside. Her house was neat and tidy, except for the occasional toy that was scattered about the floor. "Do you have kids?" Kathryn asked.

Bren replied, "No, but plenty of children come with their parents. The toys are to give them something to do and to help keep them quiet while we do our work downstairs. Come, let's go down and get started. I have another appointment immediately following your group."

Bren began by explaining a bit about Amoram and who he was. Amoram was an ancient European mystic in his last life. He roamed about various Europe towns and villages, healing, and teaching, and then disappearing before people could become too attached to him. He was well known to those who were true seekers, but others had no idea of his immense wisdom and mystical powers. In each place he visited he was known by different names, which made it easy for him to avoid the attention of the frightened and superstitious masses. Amoram was his favorite name at that time and it personified the energy of inner strength and love that he brought to us through Brenda. He had become enlightened many life times prior and completed his cycles of reincarnation in his lifetime as Amoram. He now helps many people from his perspective in other dimensions.

I was more skeptical this time than when I attended the Isaiah groups. I did not expect this experience to be nearly as wonderful or enlightening. But I was wrong.

I was having difficulties with feeling sleepy much of the time. So I asked Amoram about it. He told me there was a cord between my solar plexus and my parents; it was like an energetic umbilical cord. That it was my mother who was especially taking energy from me through it. My mother was not getting her needs fulfilled by my father so she looked to me to fill them. Amoram suggested that I cut the cord in my meditations and release my parents to get their own energy.

I followed Amoram's advice. For the next week, in my morning meditation, I would visualize cutting the cord at my mother's and my own solar plexus and then I tied the cord in a knot and buried it. An interesting thing occurred as a result of doing this exercise. Ever since I left home, my mother and I had talked on the phone every other weekend. One weekend I would call her, then, two weeks later, she would call me. This had been the pattern for many years. So then I started doing this visualization and it was my mother's turn to call me but she didn't call. Many weeks passed, and I wondered if I should call her because there were usually hurt feelings if I did not call her when I should. But I wanted to see how long it would be before she called me so I waited. Two months passed before I got a phone call from my mother. When I asked her why it had been so long she simply said she had been very busy and made no big deal about it at all. There was a certain co-dependency that was forever missing from our relationship from that point onwards.

It was too big of a coincidence that this pattern with my mother changed to not consider this visualization and my intentions to be the catalyst that caused the change. By this point in my life, the "coincidences" were mounting quite high. It was clear to me that these Masters were right...our thoughts do create our reality, even our outer physical reality. This experience left me wondering, *If taking control of my thinking for only a few minutes at a time has this much power, what sort of random world am I creating with my mind which is normally way out of control? How do I bring the rest of my mind under control so that I am consciously creating much more of my reality than I now am?* Although I hoped I would get to that place in this lifetime, at the time the task seemed overwhelming and impossible.[1]

Amoram's exercise did not solve my problem with being too tired. Although Amoram pointed out one of the places I was losing energy there were many others. It took many years of study and introspection to understand the relationship between my thoughts and actions and the degree to which I was either tired or awake with life force energy. The solution to this problem was the same as it was with all other problems. The answer lies in our connection with our Source, or God, in how open or closed we are in this connection. The more we are allowing, accepting, appreciating and finding joy in life the more open we are and the more vital, alert, awake and alive we feel. The more we are resisting, the more

---

[1] By the time I wrote this book in 2005 I had come to be in conscious control of my mind most of the time, and even when it gets out of control, I am aware of what I am thinking, and I attempt, most often with success, to redirect it. The "coincidences" and miracles have also increased in a phenomenal way. Although it is not in the scope of this book to fully describe what brought me to this place, the change in thinking, disciplines and practices related in this book were essential to me.

we push against life and what it is bringing to us the more we deplete ourselves while at the same time we are also closing ourselves off from the flow of life force energy.[1]

We liked the session with Amoram enough to join a regular apprenticeship group. Unlike Lin, whose group meetings were free, Bren was charging one hundred dollars per person for the meetings, which made me just a little bit skeptical. To Bren's credit, she had been channeling for many years, she had five individual groups which each met every month and was very busy with private sessions. Bren also made alternate financial arrangements for those in need, which often meant she got no payment at all. So I had mixed feelings about Bren and Amoram. My mind kept wanting to make it an all or nothing sort of thing, but the inner urging of my Soul to awaken, and the hope of achieving awareness with the help of Amoram prompted me to give this teacher a try. Both Kathryn and I put a sincere effort into applying what we were given and practicing the exercises.

With the new year of 1994 came our first attempts to begin a healing practice. We registered with the state of Washington as counselors and hypnotherapists. This was not a validation of our credentials. It was a necessity for a business license to work from home and it permitted us to advertise as "registered" counselors and hypnotherapists. We had to have a large sign made and placed out in our front yard. It told our neighbors what we were intending to do and gave them time to raise objections at a specific community council meeting. And that is what they did. One neighbor in particular objected strongly and found a couple of others that he incited into action. Together, they rallied the support of other neighbors who signed a petition against our business license and brought it personally to the council meeting. Their objections were solely based on fear; their strongest argument against us was the amount of traffic increase it would cause in the neighborhood. Yet the license specifically stated the boundaries and limited us to only a few clients per day. We fully intended to move into office space once our schedule grew busy enough to warrant such a place for our business. Our neighbors did not stop us from getting our license, but they did create enough problems to postpone the decision for another month while the council gathered more data.

Kathryn and I decided to hold an open house for all of the neighbors so they could come and meet us and see that we were nice

---

[1] By integrating the teachings contained in this book and those of similar teachers you too can come to an understanding of how to enhance and increase the flow of your own vital life force energies. If it sounds like it is too big of a task to undertake, consider this...What else will you do with eternity? Continue to do the same things you are currently doing and just coping with low levels of vitality, or will you slowly, one day at a time transform your entire existence and become the powerful being of light that you really are?

people. We were hoping to gain enough support to proceed with our plans. Our very first visitor was a woman who had not signed the petition. She had no real worries about our plans; she was just curious and wanted to meet us. She told us, "Gerry who lives down on the corner came around and told us that you could be bringing potential criminal elements into our neighborhood, then hypnotizing them to do God-knows-what and letting them go." I replied, "If they are worried about that, then they should go after the entertainment industry, you know…motion pictures and TV. They are already doing a bang up job of that." My sarcastic humor went over her head.[1]

Only two of the people who signed the petition came around to visit. They signed the petition because their neighbors did such a good job of convincing them that this business would be a bad thing. Later they both regretted signing without first getting more information. We got those two and a few others to sign a statement saying they supported us receiving our business license. However, we did not have enough visitors to have any real impact, more people showed up at the council meeting to object than turned up at our house to meet us. This is a big statement about the general population. We have the ignorant and frightened making decisions for us all. People without information or awareness should not have these rights. It amazes me that with humanity being as old as it is, that still today, in this "modern era," most if not all governments give so much power to such weak and immature people. America is supposed to be the land of the free and home of the brave; instead it has become the land of the frightened and the home of the enslaved.[2]

We took our dilemma to Amoram who asked us, "Beloveds, is this a business or a healing practice?"

"A healing practice," replied Kathryn in answer to Amoram's question; I was still trying to figure out what he meant and why he was asking that question.

Amoram continued to inquire, "So then why are you trying to get approval from the world for the healing work you do?" There it was again, that same issue of seeking approval rears its ugly head in me and still I am oblivious to it. Amoram continued, "You could go out into the world

---

[1] Whether conscious or not, deliberate or not, the movie industry is hypnotizing people in so many ways. One of the most predominant messages is that violence is the way of the world and the way to solve all of our problems. Are you aware of the many and various beliefs and attitudes that are being programmed into you by these entertainments? This is mass hypnosis. I suggest you choose the messages you subject yourself to wisely.

[2] This statement is only a reaction to America's strong national pride, while it remains intentionally unaware of the culture it is developing. All nations on this planet, not just America, face this very same problem.

and get many degrees, licenses and papers and all such things to give legitimacy to your work or you can simply begin the work...simply. We suggest that you need no business license, that you are healers and that you can begin your work without needing the approval of your government or those in your neighborhood."

Kathryn and I liked this idea. Later, after the session with Amoram was over, we inquired a little more of Bren as to what she has done to operate her practice and was surprised to find out...well lets just say she had not been seeking outside approval for her healing practice. So we took the sign down and withdrew our request for a business license. We also continued with our plans to have clients and students come to our home for healing and learning.

A Unique Wedding

Both Kathryn and I saw Steven pretty regularly, sometimes weekly. We were there to support him through his grief, but mostly we got to observe as he showed us how strong his spirit was. Since the death of Drew, Steven matured dramatically. He faced many challenges with Drew's family who started out appreciating how he took care of Drew during and after his death. Later, Drew's family began attacking Steven for being Drew's gay lover and used it as an excuse to take many valuable items from Steven's home, items that Drew and Steven bought together, yet it was Steven who had the job and paid for these things. Steven came to peace with this far easier than I expected. Steven's grief for Drew was strong, reflecting how strong his love and connection was. As a result, Steven was still having experiences with Drew after his physical death. Sometimes he would visually perceive Drew; sometimes it was a physical touch sort of perception of him, there was certainly a telepathic communication of information occurring as well.

I could feel the difference with Steven, that he had more depth and maturity. I often asked him about his inner experience. He confided that in the past he never fully believed there was something more after death. He feared that death was the end. This surprised me since he was a regular church goer and studied spiritual books too. But now that he was still communicating with Drew he knew there was something more. Steven shared with us that Drew had been telling him what it is like on the other side and teaching him about energy. It was amazing to listen to Steven share because much of it was nearly identical to what Amoram was teaching us; especially the part about an increase of energy that was coming to the planet at the time, and how it was affecting people.

Both Kathryn and Steven had come to a remarkable clarity of being at the same time, even though they each got there by facing different issues. They had become assertive, not aggressive nor passive, but assertive. If somebody mistreated them in some way, they each had the clarity to speak their mind without worry what others thought. When they spoke up it was not in a vindictive, negative, or scolding way, but in a way that asserted their right to be and to receive fair treatment and to have peace in their life. They had inner strength and power and nothing to prove to anyone. I admired this about them and wished to attain such an inner calmness and power myself.

Kathryn and I already considered ourselves to be a married couple, but we never held a ceremony nor were we legally married. The first time I felt like I wanted to marry Kathryn was when we were at the top of Multnomah Falls and she was talking about her future as if I was in it. By the time we saw fireworks later that day, in my mind I was committed. We had been wearing rings for more than a year and calling each other husband and wife. So for me, it had been a done deal for a long time now. But for Kathryn, the form was missing. She asked Amoram about it, "Amoram...Michael and I have felt married for a long time now. But we have not held a ceremony nor...will we change our relationship if we get legally married?"

Amoram replied, "Beloveds, do you want the world mind attached to your relationship? Because that is what you are asking. Do you need legal sanctioning of your relationship? Or is this about each of you and your commitment to each other in Spirit and Love?"

Kathryn replied, "Our commitment to each other," at the very same time I replied, "Our commitment in Love and Spirit." We looked at each other and smiled.

Amoram continued, "Very well then, it is for you to sit down and discuss, 'In what way do we wish to celebrate our commitment to each other? Who do we want to have present? Is this to be a sacred ritual...what is our ceremony to look like? What will we say to each other, what commitments will you make?'"

Kathryn needed more information, "But don't we need to have a minister and to file the legal paperwork?"

"Beloved this is a choice, whether you want the world mind attached to your relationship, or whether your commitment is enough for you. For there is much energy that goes with legal papers and governments and the expectations of society...is this what you wish to attach to your relationship? It is a question, a simple decision for you to make. We do not see that making this choice will put a curse on your relationship, but it is for you to decide, 'Do we need the approval of the world mind? How are we to go forward into the world as a couple? What is important in our marriage and what part of the world expectations and dramas can we leave behind?'"

Kathryn inquired further, "What about our families, do we invite them to the ceremony?"

Amoram responded, "Indeed this is one of the choices you need to make. How much world mind energy is attached to this choice? How does it feel to you to imagine them coming to your ceremony? What is the purpose of your ceremony, to satisfy others or to invite Spirit into your heart and relationship? Will those you invite contribute to the energy you wish to create or will they dampen it? Can you see how with a 'traditional legal marriage' you are also carrying with it the traditional ideas of inviting any random energy in? It is time to think outside of the boxes beloveds. Be with this and give this some time, then you can create the perfect ceremony that is a reflection of who you are."

Over the next few weeks Kathryn and I talked about our ceremony many times. Finally we came to a decision; Kathryn and I were to be the only two people at the ceremony. We could not invite just a few people without worrying that others would be offended, so we invited no one. We did not even have a minister, nor did we tell anyone we were getting married. We wrote out our own vows, we selected music to play and created the flow of the ceremony together.

When we were ready we held our ceremony on a Sunday morning. It was a powerful and moving experience for us both. As soon as we finished, I had just left the altar to turn off the music, when the phone rang...it was Steven calling. Of all the people in our lives that we considered inviting, Steven was at the top of the list. It was appropriate that we were able to announce our marriage to Steven first. After this time we went about our lives like any other married couple does. We told people, including our family that we got married; we signed legal documents as husband and wife. We did not need anyone's approval, no one needed to know what form the ceremony took or that there was no minister. We loved each other and we were married, end of story.

The Invisible Woman

By March of 1994, I had just completed my second project at Microsoft. They had no real immediate work for me, but were anticipating some soon, so they did not want to let me go. Thus, they gave me the project of learning MAPI and then rewriting a mail gateway being used by the Microsoft's helpdesk. Version one of MAPI had been released to the world at this time, but version two, the one currently in use today, was still in the process of being written. I needed some of those new features so I had to learn about this new product. I was excited because I felt it added value to me as a contractor...it was more than just a feeling. I had a very strong suspicion that this new experience was going to be quite valuable to me.

In June of 1994, a year after starting my Microsoft Job, my boss Dave came into my office to tell me that Microsoft had closed my contract, immediately, effective that day. I was to pack up my stuff and leave. I was told it was due to a company wide reorganization, many people were changing groups, they let go of many contractors. I was also told that due to the difficulties that had occurred early in my job last year, and my unwillingness to work weekends and long hours,[1] Dave's agency could not get me another Microsoft job. Dave did say they would try to find me something somewhere else.

I was a bit concerned about this twist. I liked working for Microsoft. I did not mind changing groups, but I did mind going to another company to work. This group had even offered me a permanent job at Microsoft[2] as an employee, but I turned it down because the pay was so much less than I was currently making. Since I was always doing things that others told me were impossible I thought it must be possible to get another Microsoft job. I decided that this agency was not the best company I could be working for. So I contacted a few of the other contract agencies and had them looking for Microsoft jobs for me. I rejected the few job leads that Dave's agency sent my way; I always found some good excuse why I was not a match to the job.

I enjoyed a few weeks of time off during a particularly beautiful summer and was consciously grateful for the timing. Then in early

---

[1] It is interesting to note here two events. I was just told that my unwillingness to work long hours prevented me from being hirable at Microsoft. When I was laid off from Raima I was told that one of the reasons that I was the first one was because I was the least willing to work long hours. Yet I persisted in going to interviews and setting a limit to the number of hours I was willing to work in a week. Don't believe the limitations that others set for you.

[2] I got this permanent employment offer from Microsoft a few months after we resolved the arrogance problem they had experienced with me earlier in my contract with them.

August I had an interview with a Microsoft group. This group was looking for someone with MAPI II experience, which was very difficult to find since it had not been released to the general public yet. I was excited and it felt right to me since I previously had the feeling that the MAPI experience I got in the last job would come in handy.

When Malcolm interviewed me for the job, I told him about the problems that occurred during my previous Microsoft contract. I told him that I understood my part in it and had already resolved those issues...he would not have to face them with me. I also told him I was only available to work forty hours per week. After Malcolm checked a few of my references he hired me for the job. I got a fifty percent increase in my hourly rate[1] and this contract agency was much easier to work for than my prior one. I would be writing sample code for cutting edge email technology. Other developers would be looking at my code to find out how to do things with MAPI. My source code would be sent out to thousand of developers and large corporations. I was ecstatic!

After a few weeks of working in my new job, I spoke to Amoram about an interesting thing that was happening in me, "Amoram, at my new job, there are these boxes of software lying around; actually they are stacked up along one particular hallway, one I am always walking down. I keep wanting to steal a couple of the software packages. The really weird thing, besides the fact that I don't steal things, is that it is the Spanish version of Word. Why would I be obsessed wanting to steal a copy of software in Spanish?"

Amoram replied, "Beloved, we ask you to ask yourself, 'Is this my energy or does it belong to someone else?'"

I asked, "What energy? Wanting to steal?"

"Yes beloved...Is it in your energy, this wanting to steal these software packages?" Amoram's voice was strong, his question was not rhetorical and he really wanted me to answer this question.

"No...I mean yes, I don't know...in the past I have stolen, and I guess if I am totally honest I still do in very small ways, but not like this...." After a short pause I continued, "If this is not my energy, whose is it?"

"Indeed, beloved, that is the question, whose energy is it? Has it ever occurred to you to ask, 'Whose energy is this?' This is not just for

---

[1] This was only one year after getting a forty percent raise in pay. Over the proceeding years I had done a lot of workshops and exercises designed to create abundance, but it was slow in coming. It was in the years that followed when I was working on healing my own self worth and correcting my understanding of how life works that the abundance began showing up. It was only after I had opened up enough in these later years that I could receive the fruits of the work done in the prior years.

Michael, this is for each and every one of you beloveds to ask yourselves, whose energy is this? Whose? Is this mine? Is this yours? Does it belong to someone else? Do you know you can feel this, that you can discern this? You can indeed come to know whose energy this is."

"We would say no beloved; it is no longer in your energy to steal. That this does indeed belong to some of those who occupy the office space near the boxes."

This whole concept was new to me, or so it felt. I did not realize that some of the thoughts in my head belonged to other people. That my mind was merely picking up on them. Since this experience I have come to know that even though I may have a seemingly separate physical brain, the mind we all share is one. Your brain and my brain both have its existence in a common mind. So it is not such a big leap for the thoughts held in the mind of us all to exist in your brain as well as mine.[1] Very few people realize this is possible, let alone realize that it is going on for them all of the time. If only you paid more attention to your thoughts, you would come see that this is true.

The desire to steal the boxes persisted for the next few months until there was an office reshuffle. The people who had occupied those offices moved elsewhere, for a few days the offices remained vacant. Then new people moved in. The first time that I noticed the thoughts to steal the software had disappeared from my mind was two days after the move, while the offices were still vacant. Once they were filled again, the desire never returned. I did wonder who it was that wanted to steal the software.

Eventually friends were asking Kathryn when she would begin teaching Reiki classes. They were impressed with the treatments she gave and how strong she had become as a person. She put them off as long as she could but eventually she succumbed. This meant becoming visible, that final step that she had been resisting. We began planning and promoting our classes.

At the end of June 1994 my parents came up from San Diego to visit for a few days before going on to Vancouver where they were catching a cruise ship to Alaska. Kathryn was upset about how my parents did not respect her so she was planning to spend the entire time in Portland with her family. I convinced her to stay. I told her that she could always leave later if she did not like the way it felt. I tried to convince her that she was making too much out of a few simple mistakes.

---

[1] Concepts such as this are difficult to grasp on this plane of existence. For once you fully do understand, it this world disappears; you vibrate out of it and into other more luminous worlds. This whole world is designed specifically to shroud these illusions with a sense of reality. But the truth is always available and perceptible to those who sincerely seek it.

But she would not hear of it. She threatened to have it out with my parents when they came. We had more than one argument about this issue.

While showing my parents around Seattle, they called Kathryn "Maria" a number of times. On the second day of their visit, Kathryn remained true to her word. She sat my parents down and had it out with them. She told them that either they would have to get over Maria and accept her into the family or she would be absent from Skowronski family events. My parents denied their lack of acceptance of Kathryn and defended their actions as simple mistakes. My mother especially found plenty of excuses. There was a lot of crying; many hurtful things were said. In the end Kathryn declared she was going to Portland. She was packed and out the door in less than an hour.

I had two more days to spend with my folks. I did not want to face this mess all alone...but I had to, and it was not so bad. My father broke down and cried. He apologized to me for offending Kathryn, and he asked for help in becoming a better person. My mother remained determined that she had accepted Kathryn as my wife, but I could feel that she was looking to me to reassure her that I still loved her.

The next day, while exploring the Seattle Science center with my parents, I noticed a woman who reminded me of Kathryn and how she was with children. As I began to tell my parents about it, the name "Maria" came out of my mouth when I wanted to say "Kathryn." Neither of my parents seemed to notice, but I did. I reflected back and realized that this had happened before, but only when I was with them or talking with them on the phone. At no other time did I speak the wrong name for my wife. Amoram's question came to my mind, "Whose energy is it?" I thought, *Is this my parent's energy tripping me up when I talk about Kathryn?* That evening I contemplated the feelings that occurred earlier that day at the science center and I could feel a total lack of Kathryn in the slot of my wife, while Maria remained there.

My parents left for their cruise; Kathryn returned home. I said to her, "I think I finally understand what you mean when you say my parents have not accepted you into the family. I had something happen...." and I told Kathryn the story.

The next time we saw Amoram, Kathryn asked him about my parents and what was happening. Amoram said, "Beloved, is it not interesting that people who cannot see you would come and move into your home while you are preparing to become visible? You are finding that you can no longer tolerate such a thing. And you have found your voice, have you not? Were you not worried that you could not speak when the time came? Now you know that you can speak...and you can roar...the lion roars!" With that everyone laughed.

"Michael's parents have not let go of Maria. They have a past connection with her, and in the past, they were left behind too. So they are revisiting this energy, which has nothing to do with you. They do not see you...they have not made space for you in the family. Someone else is still in that space in their mind and hearts. This comes as no surprise to you, for you have known this all along. You have known that they have no room for you." Amoram had a way of helping us see life as nothing more than a play of energy, which took the emotional charge out of it. That is not to say there is no emotional energy present, the drama is merely replaced with awareness which causes great peace and joy.

I asked Amoram, "Is the experience I had with calling Kathryn "Maria" while being with my parents about my energy or theirs?"

"Theirs...." Amoram said slowly with a strong and authoritative tone, yet there was a hint of questioning why this was not obvious to me.

I wanted a clearer answer, more words, from Amoram, "Well, I just wanted to make sure I am understanding correctly. Like that time with wanting to steal things at Microsoft, am I picking up on my parent's energy around Maria so her name comes out even when I am thinking about Kathryn?"

"Yes, beloved. Maria occupies the slot of wife in your life...in your parents' mind...Kathryn does not exist. It is not exactly that way, but the impact on Kathryn is the same. Why are you surprised that you are picking this information up? We have already told you that you are doing this all of the time without realization. This is a good lesson for you, one you will never forget."

Indeed there were many unforgettable experiences in my life lately; this was certainly one of them. By the time the following Christmas came my parents had made room for Kathryn in their hearts, minds and in our family. I could tell when this happened; in fact, I was the one who told Kathryn; she confirmed that she felt it too. I knew when it happened because I stopped thinking and saying Maria's name when referring to my wife while talking on the phone with my mother and father.

Kathryn was finally ready to become visible, she was ready to teach Reiki classes, and she asked me to assist her and give initiations. This required that I too take my Master level class and initiation. It was at this point that I could see how appropriate it was that I waited...now it was Kathryn who got to initiate me into this level, she was my Guru Master in this respect, rather than someone else who only spent a few hours teaching me. Because it was at Kathryn's feet that I had the most profound and practical experiences that helped my understanding of these energies grow.

We taught our first Reiki class on July 9th and 10th, 1994. We had only three new students, and two friends, we hoped for more, but still teaching five people was a start. It felt right to be Kathryn's assistant rather than the teacher.

Shortly after she began teaching, she began testing the water again. She started out slowly, putting her hands in warm water for just a little bit of exposure at a time. Then she waited a few days to see if any skin problems occurred. With each successful try she became brave enough to go further. Within a few weeks she was showering and washing dishes without the gloves. Kathryn was healed! Kathryn was now able to put her hands in water! We knew that the transition had occurred because of her becoming visible; advertising her healing services and teaching classes was a very big step for Kathryn. Only six months before she began doing this, she still had indications that the skin problem was still there...now it was gone; it never returned!

It occurred to me that we might get more students for our classes if one of us published an article in the same newspaper that we are advertising in. So in July of 1994 I wrote my first article for the *New Times* which was published in August. This article described what I had been doing and experiencing over the last few years as I had been integrating both Isaiah's and Amoram's teachings.

Releasing Our Sharp Corners

A wise master[1] teacher recently told me "Your sharp corners would not be sticking out so much if they were not leaving the body." One of the things that are happening for me, and for many others, is that our issues are coming to the surface to be released. We are in a time where a great deal of energy is coming into this planet to assist us in releasing that which no longer serves us. This energy is here to shake us up and to accelerate us forward for the purpose of a great healing—individually, collectively, and for our planet.[2]

It has been my experience, especially over the last two years, that when I ask my guides for assistance in spiritual growth, all that is unlike what I requested shows up for my observation and release.[3] This used to concern me. Here I am meditating, doing my spiritual practice, sending out love, and along comes "someone" or "some event" that knocks me off my cloud. This is not what I had in mind. I was expecting to realize spiritual bliss which I have read about when studying the lives and teachings of Yogananda and other Masters.[4]

How short-sighted I can be in those times when I find events occurring that bring me to a place where I feel irritation, judgment, and friction. I have come to realize that it is in these times that I can give thanks, and know that my prayers have been answered. These events, which seem to be outside of ourselves, are an external manifestation of that which is truly inside. We are being assisted, as we have asked, to move forward. This requires us to release old patterns that no longer serve us. We need to make room in our vessel for the new person we wish to become.

One of the questions I typically ask in trying times is, "What can I do to fix this?" The answer I get over and over again is to do nothing. It

---

[1] Amoram

[2] Amoram had been telling us this in our apprenticeship group meetings. Also Steven had been telling us that he was getting this very same message from his deceased partner Drew. I myself could only observe the world and my own life and confirm that it did feel like a new energy was present just as Amoram had been saying.

[3] Although these unwanted experiences seem to come from the world outside of ourselves, they are showing us what really does exist within our minds. Once it has been observed it can be released by changing the programming. It really becomes deactivated, the energy will always exist within us, but we deactivate it and activate something else more desirable.

[4] Here is where patience comes in...I have finally experienced some of that bliss I was seeking. It only took me about nine more years to release, from my own mind, the things that were keeping me from my bliss.

is a time to BE[1]. This answer usually causes panic in my mind[2] and it responds with thoughts like "I have to do something! I must change them so that they won't treat me like this anymore." or "I'll punish them by taking away something I do for them so that they will realize my worth."

The point of interest here is that it is my mind that is racing around coming up with ways to fix the problem and prevent the pain. It becomes a very contracting experience. The time has come to face the fear, to face the pain, and to walk through it. Great insight can occur by quieting the mind and just being with and observing what is occurring internally. The first thing I usually notice is that I am not this limiting and contracting experience that I am having, that I am not my mind, that I am much more than all of this.

When I expand my energy and am connected to the essence of my being, all judgment is released, both of self and others. It becomes easier to take responsibility for the way I have acted, for my thoughts and feelings. I remember that Spirit is present and always offers perfect guidance, not the frantic quick-fix solutions that come from the mind. The guidance that comes from Spirit may even be to take the same action that the mind suggested. But the difference is in the energy that is behind the action. Now the intention is service to the Whole, not just to serve ourselves. We can slow down and trust that Spirit is guiding us through this release, and we can improve upon the quality of the journey now.

Even if the external events do not seem to be changing,[3] it is important to be who we are, spiritual beings of light. The fact that we have a physical body and are experiencing fear and discomfort is a normal part of being on this plane of existence. Even the Masters experienced these things. Yet they walked through the experience and remained spiritually present in their bodies. It is in these traumatic times that we sometimes allow our spiritual presence to leave our physical, mental, and emotional body, and we deal with events from a place of separation. By fleeing in this way, we lock the

---

[1] BEing is about going on with your life and trusting the Universe to guide you to each necessary step. It is a time to focus your mind on something else entirely, something that brings you to a positive feeling emotion.

[2] I no longer panic, not for more than a few seconds, I just calm my mind...it has become quite easy with practice.

[3] It is only because we hold our perspective on a few moments or hours of time rather on the bigger picture of a season or a life time or eternity. Even though things seem not to change, change is always present; change your perspective, and you will see them.

energies that have surfaced for release in our bodies.[1] When we remain spiritually present, we allow the release to occur as an unfoldment—like a flower that is blooming.[2]

Don't be surprised if you experience physical symptoms of discomfort. As we continue to grow as spiritual beings and release that which no longer serves us, we make room for new energy to enter. It is during this time that our vibrations actually shift, and our bodies go through physical changes.[3] This can cause discomfort and even concern of disease. Notice that I have used the word discomfort and not pain. Pain is a marker of where we are separate from Spirit and it does not usually cease until one listens. Discomfort will last a little while and then go away. It may even be a few days, but I have found it seems to come and go, and then it is gone.

Reiki and other forms of energy treatments are of assistance in accelerating release. Ask your guides to work with your energy, or to guide you to someone who can assist you. Even though we each must do our own inner work, we can be greatly assisted by another who has released those things that we are releasing. They have the vibration and energy that you are seeking to replace that which is being released. Being with their energy can accelerate this healing and ease the discomfort that often occurs in the release unfoldment.[4]

If you find yourself called to assist another in this way, find that place within you that is of compassion and of pure intent to heal. Release any notion of what form that healing needs to take, leaving this to Spirit. Touch them in a way that is appropriate for the relationship you have with them. Listen if they need to share.[5] Avoid

---

[1] What actually happens is that we create a habitual energy pattern of not dealing with the trauma and accepting any outcome. The fleeing and the emotional response, too, becomes a habit.

[2] By remaining present, we have the ability to make choices and develop new habits, ones that serve us rather than ones that leave us a victim to the coming and goings of life.

[3] Isaiah told us this would happen in the very first meeting we had with him. Yet I had no idea of how such a thing could happen, nor did I really believe that it would. However, over the years that led up to writing this article, I had many of such experiences with these movements of energy. Most people become concerned that they are getting a disease, but if you hold the proper perspective in your mind, you can ensure this is a shift of energy rather than a state of becoming diseased.

[4] Although this was written as a form of advertisement, these statements are true. I had weekly treatments from Brenda for many years, on top of what I got from Kathryn. It was expensive, but the result was priceless.

[5] Listening to others is only valid to a point. If the person you are listening to is going on about things that make you or them feel bad when they talk about them, this is not helpful to either of you. Instead you should try to bring them to a place of seeing the good that is present in their lives. Get them to talk about this instead. Get them to dream of how they would like life to be.

falling into the savior role, the ego consciousness that tells you what a great person you are that you can help them in such a way.[1]

Release is a natural process that occurs in all of us. You are not alone. Sometimes it brings with it physical, mental, and emotional discomfort. The discomfort is temporary and can confirm that you are progressing on your spiritual path. Release opens the door for a new and grander you to emerge.

    I got one nice phone call from someone who liked the article and also we got one student for our next Reiki class because he read it. We got a few other students in that class as well but they told us they had not read the article. I was very disappointed; I had hoped more people would at least call to let us know they got something out of it. In many ways I saw how humanity suffered and was confused, and I wanted to help. I felt like I could at least point people in the right direction and provide some comfort for their journey. I wanted to be there to witness people when they had their moments of awakening. I was just beginning to understand and accept the frustration and loneliness of this path I was on.

    Over the next sixteen months, we held nearly one Reiki class per month. Often we had as few as three students and a few times as many as ten. It was nice to have the extra income, but it was only enough to offset the expenses we incurred in our own training and advertising; we were not making a profit. Still we were happy to be doing our healing work and people were getting benefit from it. At the end of every class, Kathryn and I felt a deep sense of satisfaction, like we were in service to God.

    In September, our friend Steven met a man named Peter and a romance began. We first met Peter at an end of summer dinner party that our friend Martha held at her new house. It was a time of great joy for all of us as Kathryn and I were following our dream of being teachers and healers, Steven had found new love, and Martha had purchased a home of her own, something she had been trying to create for quite some time. As time went on, the five of us formed the core members of a spiritual dinner group; others came and went, but this core group held together for a few years. We met monthly, in restaurants at first, then later in our homes. It evolved to the point where the host would come up with a ritual, and if necessary, ask the others to do some homework and come prepared for it. Before we had dinner, we would have prayer and perform the ritual. There is much power when many people gather

---

[1] Although I had much practical experience with these things by the time I wrote this article, I was still very much lost in the illusions of physical life. It often took me much time, and much drama, before I came to follow this advice myself.

together with the purpose of expanding their spiritual awareness, and our group felt this power. Much joy, laughter, and even a few tears were shared in these groups. Many months later, Steven and Peter got married, and it was Kathryn who was the minister of their wedding ceremony. The attendees were mostly gay men; they liked Kathryn and complemented her for helping to create such a nice ceremony.[1]

Another New Year came around...in a channeling session held on January 2nd, 1995, Amoram put it very well when he said to us, "...you both spent much of the last year mucking out the stalls. This is what you needed to do. New learnings came, you no longer wanted the old ways, and you released many of them. Although this was quite painful at times, your intention to move forward remained strong and carried you through. You must continue to integrate what you have leaned into your life such that your personality is shaped by it, such that it becomes your automatic response." I was not happy to hear it put quite that way, but as the words left Bren's lips I knew it was true. I wanted to think that all of our study and learning was firmly in place, but time proved that Amoram was correct. I still had much more work to do.

Once a person learns new skills, it is only an intellectual exercise until those skills become integrated into their life and experiential awareness grows within them. Yet the old crap is still lying around our minds and needing to be cleaned out; it comes to our awareness slowly, over a long period of time. As life presents you with events which activate those old energies, notice them, and then remember and put into practice your new understandings. The new energies will gain strength and the old ones will eventually become deactivated. Prior to 1994, Kathryn and I integrated many of the teachings we had been given and had grown skillful in applying them in our lives and helping others to do the same. Still, 1994 was a year where much came up in us to be released, so many past ways of dealing with life and relationships came out of us as old, worn-out habits. Even though we had new skills, the habitual way of dealing with life was still present. Each time an old pattern came up for us, we got to look at it and say, "This no longer serves us, how can we change this?" We had many new tools, new ways of responding to life, now we were using them to consciously change; we were forming new habits to replace the old.

As this new year began we were having troubles with one of our neighbors; she was bothering Kathryn more than she was bothering me. First, this neighbor woman threw dog shit at our house as a way to get our attention...it stuck to the walls. Then a few times she burned her rubbish in her back yard, it is illegal and just not done in these suburbs these days. One time last fall when she did that, it was a dry and windy

---

[1] Nine years later, when this book was written in 2005, Steven and Peter are still married.

day, which was a big fire hazard given all of the dry shrubbery around. Another time, she came over drunk asking us to hypnotize her husband, who had recently left her. She wanted us to make him return to her. She was one of the craziest people I had ever met. Now she was beginning to cut down trees and bushes that were on our property.

So Kathryn wanted to build a fence around our property...actually she wanted me to build a fence. My general attitude about such things was that I worked forty hours a week in a job and when I came home all I wanted to do was relax, study and play. Even though we were both very much attached to our position, we were able to have a calm discussion about this situation. At first paying someone else to do the job did not even seem like an option, especially in Kathryn's mind. We were already in debt to a point that was becoming uncomfortable. Our goal had been to pay off our debts quickly, not go deeper. This was more of an issue for Kathryn than it was for me, as I had faith the money would come. After our discussions started becoming redundant, I calmly said to Kathryn, "I am not going to build a fence; I don't have the time, the desire, or the skills. This is your project not mine. So if you want a fence, you build it. If that means you hire someone to do the job, then do it."

Kathryn replied, "But we are partners and we should do these sorts of things together. This is our home not just mine. How can I build a fence if you don't want one?"

"It is not that I don't want one; I really don't care either way. I just don't want to do the work; it is not my priority. This is a situation where we don't see eye to eye, so we must agree to disagree, just like Amoram has taught us. And I don't think it is fair for me to prevent you from doing something you really want just because I don't want to do it. So just do it and leave me out of it."

Kathryn accepted that answer and decided to give it some more thought. She spoke to Bren and our apprenticeship group about it. Then while we were talking to Amoram, Kathryn had the following dialog...

Kathryn: Amoram, what would you share with me for this year, or what would be helpful to me to bring forth energy in a more expanded way as a healer? And also, what would be most helpful for me to protect myself from negative energy?

Amoram: The first thing you can do is look at your definitions because there is no such thing as negative energy. If you focus your mind in the world of duality you will bring negative energy into your life since in this world energy is split into positive and negative. However, if you focus your mind on the truth and remember who you are then you can again experience all of the energies as a whole instead of experiencing the positive and negative.

Kathryn: Oh, okay, (laughter) that was very helpful. (laughter)

Amoram: You are such a masterful creator beloved and your current situation is a grand demonstration of this. We find much humor in this for you. It is incredible. They are cutting down your trees and you are talking about building fences of separation. You want to build separation. Do you see the duality of this?

Kathryn: Well not totally because if I did I wouldn't be thinking of that.

Amoram: Yes beloved, this is how it is. In your mind you wish to create separation between you and she. Have you considered sitting down and sending this one the energy of love, compassion and tenderness? This would reunite the energy in your experience. We are not advising you to go to her home and in some physical form assist her. Not at all. Nor would this one appreciate such assistance. But rather than creating barriers in your mind, send forth wholeness, which is the truth of all that you and she are. Send it knowing that if this is what you send, even if she rejects it, wholeness is what will return unto you. The love, the compassion, the blessing they are all contained in the wholeness. Beloved Kathryn, if you continue to look at things as positive and negative, you will remain attached to the forms of duality and will indeed experience negativity. But what if you decided to see such events as opportunities? What is the opportunity for you? Could this be the chance for you to send love and compassion and experience how it returns to you? Could this be the chance for you to see the truth that the outside world cannot encroach upon your inner sanctuary unless you allow it to? This is an opportunity for you to discover this sanctuary beloved. What a gift! And you will find that the world is attracted to your light. The world is always attracted to the Light and often it seeks it in the in the most dramatic of ways. Did you catch our choice of words? Seeking it dramatically. Many people seek to reach the light through drama. It is the only way they know of to create, through seeking attention. Most people know nothing of attention and intention. So they attempt to bring forth the energy they need through drama.

Kathryn: But how can I respond in nothing but total love if they are cutting down my trees and my bushes? That's very difficult.

Amoram: Yes beloved we agree that for you, at this time, it is very difficult to respond in nothing but total love. That is because you need practice. And that is why this experience is a blessing to you; it is the opportunity to practice. We are not saying that you need to let them cut down your trees. We do however want you to become aware of how you respond to others and their actions. Not react, but respond.[1] Dearest Kathryn, this does not mean that you cannot build a fence. But not in separation beloved, not in separation. Build the fence because it is time to build a fence, because you wish to create this now at this time. Do not build this fence to protect yourself, use your energy and intention to accomplish this. Build this fence for the simple reason that it brings you joy. This is a big difference in intention from building it to separate you from the negativity outside of your perimeter. This requires practice beloved. You must stop your mind when you find it running frightening scenarios about the woman next door. You must stop your mind when you find it lecturing that woman about her crappy neighbor policy. You must bring clarity to your mind about these issues and come to realize the only reason this experience is in your life this very now minute is because you have a habit of letting your mind run rampant instead of choosing consciously and intentionally what it is that you wish to think about and there by create in your immediate energy and in your future.

So you see beloved, we have come full circle and both of your original questions were really one and the same. How do you expand as a healer and how do you protect yourself from negative energy? This change in your habits of thinking will propel you forward as a healer. Because as you practice the new way of thinking it will become the habit. Even your automatic reactions will

---

[1] Dear reader, please pay attention to the subtle difference Amoram is talking about here. The inner intention is everything, the outer world actions mean very little compared to this.

come from a choice that you consciously made sometime earlier through your practice. This practice will shape your energy, your experience, and your life; indeed it will shape your very personality. Each time you align your subconscious thought process with Spirit then the intensity, power, and effectiveness of your energy is naturally turned up a notch or two. And disciplined practice is the path to this goal.

Also for you beloved you should schedule people to come to you for energy treatments. Ask people to come, not to make money but for your practice. Ask them to come for the joy of doing the work, for the love of serving God as God is in those others that you will be working upon. There is no other special preparation necessary. You just show up and do the work, that will be the practice. Greater experience will come, new habits will form, and your energy will increase. We also see you giving your classes and you should continue to give life to this vision too. Alow it to be and when you feel the words coming forth beloved, speak them. Your guides are there and the words are with them as they are also with your own higher self. (Thank you)

Kathryn did go ahead and build the fence. When it was done I liked it and told her so. She tried to convince me that I should trust her more in such matters. I told her, "I do trust you. That is why I told you to do it even though I did not see the need for it. But that still does not mean I have the same vision as you. I could not see how good it would be until it was done. Now I see it, and I like it."

Even though we had been giving Reiki classes, the students were few. No one was coming for hypnotherapy. I wanted to be doing more, to be having an impact on others like Isaiah and Amoram had on Kathryn and me. It was during that same apprenticeship group meeting that I had the following conversation with Amoram.

Michael: I'd like to know, I'm curious, what's up for me in this year? I know that there will be a transition period between what I'm doing presently and what I'll be doing, but I'm curious about that and I'm just curious in general, what's up?

Amoram: Beloved this is a year where you can begin to speak for yourself in truth and without the judgment which has hung around you like a dark cloud for such a long time. Your conversations with Kathryn around the decision for the fence has been a grand demonstration of this. (laughter) When you speak, as you so eloquently put it, "without the blooming of your arrogance," you can and will have a different impact on the world. This is the year for taking this new energy, this new way of being, and expressing yourself fully in the world. Not to declare and proclaim how wonderful you are. But to be available and to be seen as you are being. To shine like the sun and the moon. To express the joy that is in you. This is the year to begin being this new self you have created and for it to be enough that you and only you recognize it. The more you let go of being seen by others all the more that others will see you.[1] Consciously choose to be more available. Do not wait, nor expect, anyone to take you up on your availability. Just practice being available, with no other motive than joy. Not because you are growing, not because you want to do healing work and not because you want to do a different job. Practice being available for the sake of being available. Move beyond the structures, the organization, the plans and the lists. Just be. This year is about learning that no matter whether others recognize your accomplishments or not that you are progressing and changes are becoming a part of who you are. (I see it.) And that is all that matters beloved, if you can see it rejoice and be glad, for it is your own beautiful creation and the only thing of importance in this regard.

Although Amoram's answer was full of truth, it was not satisfactory for me. I wanted out of computer software and to be doing this teaching and healing work. Since I needed an income to pay my bills, I expected the healing work to provide that. In March of 1995, I began creating a class, an apprenticeship training of my own. After creating the basic layout, I began advertising using the *New Times* monthly newspaper and the bulletin boards at Microsoft. Only one person responded, and he never even committed to the class. This was frustrating to me and I thought, *What is it going to take to get more people interested in taking classes and receiving treatments from us?* I saw other people who seemed to be successful, was this just a popularity contest? I

---

[1] It took many more years for me to fully understand this lesson. Life just wore me out. I got tired of trying to prove myself and my worth. I just started being who I was, a being of light. Most people did not and still do not see the light that comes from me; it matters not, I see it, and it is brilliant. But as I let myself be this light more and more, without trying to make others see it, more people have come to see it. God put people who really needed this light in my life, and we both received wonderful blessings as a result.

never have been the most popular guy around. At the time I could not see that Amoram had already answered these very questions. I wanted the inner work I was doing, the preparation for the outer work, and the advertising to pay off now, not at some unknown time in the future. This attitude, this desire, left me deaf, dumb, and blind to what Amoram was trying to teach me.

Every six months or so, the apprenticeship groups would reorganize. Some people left and other new people joined. Some people had changes in their schedules. So this regular reorganization kept up with these changes. In May of 1995, Kathryn moved into a women only apprenticeship group...without me of course. I was very disappointed because this was one way that Kathryn and I could spend time together doing something we both enjoyed. Also because I liked the women that were in Kathryn's group, in my mind they were the most powerful people of those who came to these groups. I did not like the energy or the people who formed the group I was in. I learned to live with my disappointment and make the best of it.

Kathryn was a very strong woman and very good at handling physical pain and suffering without mentioning it. In July, Amoram gave Kathryn some advice about the nausea she was experiencing. She told me nothing about it.[1] Amoram told her[2] it had to do with her family, especially her sister Bridget. That she needed to do release work.

> Beloved Kathryn, the nausea that you asked Brenda about has to do with your family. Brenda has been assisting you during your energy treatments and will continue to do so. She has been assisting to release from within you this nauseating energy from your family and especially your twin sister. You can no longer hold this energy in your body; it is time for it to leave. And you must cease to identify yourself as her mirror. This must be a conscious choice and you must recognize the habit when it arises and remind yourself once again that you are not her mirror twin.[3] This statement, this way of viewing your relationship to her, keeps this energy trapped within you.

> Beloved the word that we would use to describe your twin is malevolent. She is predatory in her thought, energy, and actions. You no longer need to be her prey; you no longer need to mirror her pain

---

[1] Maybe Kathryn did tell me and I was not listening, or maybe I gave it such little importance in my mind that I forgot. Either way, the first I can recall learning about this was many years later as I was going through old transcripts in preparation for writing this book.

[2] At her women's apprenticeship group held on July 5th, 1995.

[3] Whenever Kathryn told someone about her sister, she said they were "mirror twins," so it was quite common for her to use this phrase.

back to her. Do you understand that you have been reflecting her incapability, her pain, and her suffering? And you have been reflecting not just from her but from many in the family.

Kathryn heard from her twin sister Bridget that her ex-dog Gus was not being looked after well, that he was living under harsh conditions. Kathryn had given the dog to a nice man who took it for walks daily…until he fell seriously ill and Gus was then passed on to another person who did not look after him properly. We had no awareness of this situation or control over who Gus was given to. Nevertheless, Kathryn's guilt over abandoning Gus got the better of her, and she made an attempt to rescue him. Bridget lived near Gus' new home so she was able to tell Kathryn where he was. Kathryn made a trip, five to six hours of driving one way, to rescue him. She was intending to just take him, but she got caught in the process by the current owners. She asked them if she could buy Gus back. They refused to let Gus go and claimed he was being taken care of. But Kathryn saw his living conditions, tied up outside by a rope, and body shape, fat with matted hair; she felt the energy, so she knew these owners were clueless about caring for a dog.[1]

A few days after Kathryn returned home, no longer able to take the mental torture knowing how her abandoned dog was living, she convinced me to go back to try and rescue him again. This time we would be sneakier. Since Kathryn had been there, she had it all figured out, and we were totally prepared to take him and run. This suited my sense of adventure and desire to protect and defend my wife's honor. However, this attempt was doomed to failure too. Gus was not there when we arrived. We waited for his owners to come home under the pretense of trying yet again to buy him back, this time for a very large sum of money. They told us an accident had happened and Gus was killed. Kathryn took the news badly but she accepted it. We went to the beach and held a ceremony for Gus. It was a very moving and powerful experience, just one of the many that made our relationship strong and beautiful.

Kathryn had a dear friend named Lester; I had met him a couple of times when he came to Seattle, and I liked him too. Lester was a very interesting business man with a great sense of humor. One weekend, we decided to drive out to Spokane, Washington to visit Lester and also to spend a few days in Coeur d'Alene, Idaho. Spokane was a five hour drive from our home, much of it through open desert that we did not find very

---

[1] Dogs are social animals and should not be left to live alone outside. Tied up on a short rope or living in a small cage is not acceptable! They need to be inside with the family and have access to the outdoors. If this is not possible, then they should have at least one companion dog, room to move, run and play, also a dry comfortable place to sleep. Fencing them in is much more preferable to a rope around their necks. Dogs will give you a great deal of love if you treat them with only a little bit of kindness, it is worth the extra effort to really love them and make them true members of your family.

scenic. I had tunnel vision; I was focused on getting the tedious part of the drive over quickly. This did not make me the best travel companion, nor did it make the trip comfortable for Kathryn. We made a few stops along the way and we had a few dramas because I was taking offense at the comments Kathryn was making about my driving. At one point Kathryn requested that I pull over and talk with her about it. This was a good move on Kathryn's part, even though I did not think so at the moment she asked me.

Kathryn calmed herself down; our egos had been battling long enough. She looked me in the eyes, and with love in her heart she asked me to be her partner and friend and listen to her. With her asking me so nicely, how could I refuse? I calmed my emotions down and made myself open to understanding. I listened attentively as she carefully explained to me that it was physically uncomfortable for her when I would take off from a stand still and speed up to freeway speed, 70-80 mph, in only a matter of seconds. It was just too much for her; she wanted me to build up speed gradually. She needed to get used to the speed slowly.

I really heard her this time. My desire to win the battle vanished and I had compassion for her. I wanted to make her comfortable. From that point on, for the years ever since, I did my best to remember and make a calmer, slower take off whenever we hit the road. Now that kind of driving has become habit for me...unless I consciously and deliberately choose to have some fun, and that is usually when I am in the car alone.

Kathryn conveyed her message to me in a way that made it easy to listen. Too bad all of our conversations did not go so smoothly. It takes clarity of mind and confidence in oneself to be able to do what Kathryn did. When you have that kind of consistent clarity, you can also consistently diffuse almost any conflict you find yourself in the midst of.

Lester was wealthy and as such, his home, which was modest in size, was well adorned with antiques and various works of art. Some of them, such as a hand carved wooden horse, were quite large. I enjoyed getting the tour and hearing the stories behind the treasures he possessed. However, Lester was not just a superficial man. He was intelligent, articulate, had a big heart, and treated others with respect.

We enjoyed a few days with Lester before heading out to Coeur d'Alene. We got into a conversation about birds, and since I had a few in the past, Lester introduced us to a friend of his who raised parrots; specifically hand-fed, baby Moluccan cockatoos. Much to the dismay of Kathryn, I fell in love with one of the birds. We spent a great deal of time over many days talking about this issue.[1] Kathryn used the, "it cost too

---

[1] It was with this experience that I really came to understand that the source of our difficulties came when we tried to control the other person. If one of us had a strong desire

much, we can't afford it" argument. I never liked that one, especially since I was the one earning the money, and more frequently, she was the one spending it.

This issue with the bird also came up at the same time I wanted to enroll in massage school. Kathryn did not like this idea either. She knew it involved a lot of nudity and putting my hands on naked women. After all, it was pretty obvious that I should not spend $3,500 on a parrot, $4,000 for tuition and a year of my time working less and touching naked bodies more. Yet, that is exactly what I wanted to do. My primary motivation was to augment my healing skills, to utilize a natural talent I already had, and to use it as a tool to get people to talk to me and learn from what I had to teach…but it had not escaped my notice that it would involve touching naked bodies!

At first, I thought I might have to give up my desire for the parrot. But I did not hold onto that thinking for long. I became firm in my conviction that I could have it all, including happiness and Kathryn.

We took the issue to Amoram. It never ceased to amaze me how impartial he could be. My shame buttons were so big at the time. Kathryn, and what I felt to be the rest of the world, all seemed to have judgments around the things I wanted. There were many ways in which I just did not fit into this society and its structure. Amoram, on the other hand, did not judge me or anyone else, for that matter. He simply shed light on our lack of understanding and helped us both to be better partners for each other.

---

for something, and the other had a strong desire in the opposite direction, it invariably resulted in manipulations from both parties. Manipulation is the fruit of fear. Fear is a state of insanity.

Ali the Psychic Dog

I got my Cockatoo and named her Sedona. We hit it off great and quickly became best friends. Sedona's cage was large and took up a lot of space. We placed it between the dining and living rooms giving her a prominent place in the home. With her cage in this spot we could see Sedona from many places in the house, and she could watch us too. This is very important for parrots since they are curious and social creatures. In the early evening, at dusk, she would go crazy bobbing her head and body up and down, screeching and chattering very loudly. She would fluff her feathers up to make herself look big and scary while she was attacking imaginary foes that were flying at her in all directions. It was quite an amusing sight to watch. Kathryn enjoyed watching Sedona's antics, but mostly she was tolerating the bird. Because Kathryn liked everything neat and tidy she was forever cleaning up the stray seeds, feathers, and down that would end up on the floor near Sedona's cage.

Kathryn decided that if I could have a parrot, she could have a dog. As a result, we went to the nearby humane society to look for one. However, we did not just take the first cute dog we saw. We were looking for the right feeling, which we did not get with any of the dogs we found at the pound near our house. So then we tried another animal shelter, which was much further away. It was there that we found our dog. Although she already had a name, Kathryn gave her a new one, "Ali" (pronounced alley).

Earlier that same day, a woman brought Ali in and dropped her off. She told the shelter that her husband was beating and abusing the dog so she wanted Ali to go to a new home. I couldn't help but feel sorry for the poor woman as I suspect that she was the one that got the beating that evening. Kathryn and I both felt this was a case of perfect timing, God's timing. Had we not picked up Ali, the woman may have told the husband where Ali was and he may have gone and picked Ali right back up again. So it was good that Ali got to escape from the pound on the same day she was brought in.

We were on our way to the car, out in the parking lot and we almost lost Ali right at the start. Ali had been behaving so well that Kathryn let her off of her leash just outside the front door of the dog pound. Ali took that opportunity to go wandering. She did not run off, but walked fast enough that it took some effort to get her back. Once Kathryn and I rounded Ali up Kathryn sat in the back seat with Ali and lavished her with love as I drove us all home.

Ali was about one and half years old; she was a small, sweet Black Labrador mixed with some other breed. For awhile, Ali would flinch when we reached to pet her. After a few weeks she finally got over that and learned to trust us. Ali understood the most common commands and obeyed very well. The previous owner must have put in a lot of work and effort to train her this well, we figured he probably beat her into submission...still, I was grateful that I did not have to do the training. When we took Ali for a walk, she usually ignored other people, but occasionally she would find interest in a stranger and politely pay them some attention.

It was nearly six months before we ever heard Ali bark. We figured that the previous owner had her vocal cords surgically removed. One day we were out walking Ali in our neighborhood when some children approached us and wanted to pet her. Ali began to bark and growl and she did not stop until the kids ran off to play. We were very surprised! Ali had never ever barked, let alone become defensive like this. Kathryn said to me, "I knew she was psychic. Those kids are cruel to animals, and Ali knew it. That's why she was barking at them so much."

I couldn't believe it; these kids lived right across the street from us. I liked them and Kathryn had no physical evidence to support her statement about those kids. By now I should have trusted Kathryn's intuition, but I did not. You can imagine how frustrating that would have been for her, but she did pretty well putting up with my skepticism. A few weeks later, I witnessed the kids mishandling a cat, and I knew that Kathryn was right.

One night a young man knocked on the door. Ali and I answered...no barking, not yet. The visitor explained to me how he lived a few doors down, I replied, "Yes I know, I have seen you working on your car." His parents were not home, and he needed a few dollars for gas so he could get their car back to the house. I gave him some money and we continued to chat for a bit. Kathryn had been standing near by, out of eyesight but she could hear our conversation. She came to the door to meet the man and when she did, Ali began to bark at him and would not stop. After he left, Kathryn told me, "He would have made sexual advances on me if you and Ali weren't here. I am certain of it."

Kathryn was wearing her night gown; it was a simple cotton gown, pretty but not revealing in anyway. Maybe he was lusting after her, but how could she tell? When I questioned how she knew this she said in a frustrated tone of voice, "Couldn't you feel how his energy changed? When he saw me, his energy turned aggressive and sexual. That's why Ali started barking. His intention was harmless until he saw me." I never discovered evidence to prove or disprove her allegations. But today I have no doubt that Kathryn and Ali were correct. I can clearly remember how Kathryn used to make such statements to me as if they were obvious, as if it were standing right in front of us in full living color and I was denying that I could see it. Now I often feel that same frustration with others because they don't see or feel what I can. I usually laugh because it seems preposterous that I ever had difficulties picking up such energies.

One day, Steven and I went for a hike at Twin Falls National Park, a thirty minute drive from our house; we took Ali with us. Our destination was a bridge overlooking a lovely set of waterfalls. From the very start of our walk I let Ali off the leash to roam free. This was never a problem with Ali because she was so well behaved. Along the way, we passed many people that Ali did not bark at; this was the case nearly all of the time. We were almost at the bridge that overlooks the falls when Ali started to bark like crazy. I yelled at her, "Ali! Be quiet! Come!" And then I hurried after her and put her leash back on. I was not worried she would hurt someone; I was worried someone would take offense or be frightened. That is when I discovered that it was a forest ranger just up ahead on the trail that Ali was barking at.

I got irritated with Ali because she would not shut up. As we started to pass the ranger by he stopped us and said to me, "You know it is illegal to walk your dog without a leash. I could write you a ticket right now." I apologized and the ranger let us pass without a citation. "He was mean," Steven said in a feminine way that gay men often use to talk about other men. "I did not like the feel of him at all." Steven was not saying this because Ali tipped him off; he was only relaying his own intuitive feelings to me. I was the only one who was not aware of the negative energies emanating from this man. My first reaction to Ali was to scold her for being bad, but after Steven's statement it finally occurred to me that Ali had once again picked out the bad guy. How could I be so oblivious? I mentally flogged myself a little, *I should know enough to trust Ali by now...she only barks when there was some sort of danger near by. Here I am getting irritated with her and she is doing the right thing. How could I be so stupid...so unaware?* [1]

Once we got to the bridge, I left Ali on the leash, my feeling sense, which I was now paying attention to, told me that this was not the last we would see of the ranger. So we sat on the bridge for a while with poor Ali stuck on her leash. It was not long before the forest ranger came back, hoping to catch Ali on the loose. When he saw that we were obeying the law he turned back around and continued back to the car park. A little later I set Ali free once again.

---

[1] Over the years, many dogs have lived in my home that are clearly aware of harmful people approaching, barking only at those times and not when other harmless people approach. These dogs all had experienced prior abuse. Another dog I had that was never abused had this ability too, but she waited until the danger came much nearer to her before she would respond by barking.

The other thing that used to amaze me about Ali was that she could tell when I was going to take her for a walk before I said anything out loud. I could be upstairs in my bedroom and decide I was going to go for a walk, at that very same moment I would hear Ali coming. She would run up the stairs, full of enthusiasm and excitement, stand near my feet, dancing back and forth with her tail and bottom wagging like crazy, and look up at me with her big brown eyes that said, "I'm ready, let's go!" I could talk about walking all day long; just speaking the word "walk" out loud would not trigger a response from her. But if I actually had the intention of going on a walk, then she would respond. She was clearly responding to the energy of my thoughts and not to my words. This happened many more times than I can count.

Dogs give so much unconditional love that they are role models that people should aspire to; Ali was no exception. There were many times that Ali gave me love and comfort when it seemed that it was nowhere else to be found. I had other dogs before, but I had been incapable of realizing and experiencing just how deep and loving they are. Those past experiences got me ready for this one, but it was Kathryn that helped to wake me up enough to see what was obvious in the animal kingdom. I am so glad she did; my relationship with all animals, especially dogs, will ever be blessed with the richness of such love.

Massage School

  Not only did I get my bird, but I also enrolled in massage school. This required that I find a job that would let me work part time and be much more flexible with my schedule. I asked my current boss, Malcolm, if I could switch to working part time, only twenty to thirty hours per week, but he would not agree to that. He did, however, introduce me to Michael C. who was looking for someone with my skills, especially the MAPI skills! He had a great project that was much more challenging and fun than the sample code I had been writing. I got the job and ended up making an extra $7/hour[1] and working only the hours I had time to work.

  During the summer, I took a pre-anatomy class. Memorizing names and labels has never been one of my strong points. I have no interest in them, except to communicate, so I don't pay much attention to them. I would rather understand the concept, function, and reason behind the label. So I decided that taking this class would help me get through the full time class easier by giving me more time to absorb the names of the body parts. It also gave me an outlet for an excited energy that was craving for some way to express itself. Once I decided to go to massage school, I could not wait to get started. This was my first chance to do so.

  I enjoyed the pre-anatomy class, but it made me even more enthusiastic about getting into the actual hands-on massage training. I was also finishing up my contract at Microsoft and anticipating the break my new job would give me from thinking about computer software so much. Time seemed to crawl along very slowly, but finally the anticipated day arrived...my first hands-on massage class. This was the prerequisite, two day, *Massage Therapy for the Novice* class.

  Since we were going to be massaging the legs first, the class organized itself into groups of three; one body on the table and two therapists (one for each leg). After doing one full leg massage a new body hit the table and the prior body became a therapist. This way everyone had at least one shot at giving a massage; one person gave two massages and did not receive one.

---

[1] How disappointing, only a fifteen percent increase in pay instead of forty or fifty! (Sarcastic humor) Everything I had been wanting, greater freedom and flexibility, more money and more interesting work had been delivered to me on a silver platter. God and this Life we live are incredible, amazing and beyond belief when you really look at it closely. Nothing is denied us, NOTHING, when we are fully aligned with God. Because it truly is God's Life we are living. When we accept this and go with it, instead of resisting, complaining, and trying too hard to change it, when we accept that this IS God's Life and go with it nothing is denied us. Even though in many ways I was still very closed off, the little bit of opening I had allowed for brought this much wonderful synchronicity into my life.

I keenly observed as people quickly disrobed and got naked behind a sheet. I was hoping to get a peek of someone who fumbled with their sheet. This inevitably happened many times through out my massage school experience and became quite passé. As time went on, I found myself more interested in observing and feeling people's reaction to this interaction with nudity in a classroom setting.

One of the first things we were taught was how to "drape"[1] the person we were working on. First the teacher demonstrated on one of the bodies that we just happened to have lying around. Then the rest of us followed suit and draped our body the same way. The lesson continued until we had massaged the back side of the leg we were working on; the leg included the gluteus muscles which make up the butt, my favorite body part.

Although I never got over the enjoyment of seeing and touching naked flesh,[2] the novelty of it quickly wore off. I was left with the understanding that my overly perverted obsession with nudity was a mere product of the way this natural desire has been suppressed and erroneously made out to be filthy by religion and culture. For me, massage provided a safe outlet for an energy that needed to be expressed and explored, yet it was only one small part of what I came into this world to learn and experience.

In the state of Washington, massage is regulated. In order to legally practice, it is required to take approximately five hundred hours of training. To maintain your license, you must take ongoing training each year. We must be able to communicate clearly with doctors and chiropractors, as well as understand how to heal and not do harm to the body. Thus, anatomy and physiology are a big part of the course.

I thoroughly enjoyed massage school; learning something new, being involved with other healers, it was fantastic! I was thirty-seven years old and up until that point mostly hung out with computer nerds[3] and people in their forties or older. Now I was spending a lot of time in an environment with most of the other students being in their twenties. This was a different crowd for me. It gave me a new perspective from which to see life, which helped me to understand myself and other people better. The best part was that right now I was doing less software writing and

---

[1] Draping means to cover the body so as to expose only the body part that was being worked on at that moment and thus preserve the privacy of the client. Draping also helps to keeps the client warm.

[2] Neither did I get so excited that I embarrassed myself in front of anyone in the classroom.

[3] At work only. In my private life, computer nerds were only part of the picture if they too were into spiritual study and practice.

looking forward to the day when I could begin my new career as a healer in earnest. I was only a year away from that goal, or so I thought....

Temptation Rears Her Lovely Head

Kathryn and I continued to hold our Reiki healing circles. Hilda one of Kathryn's clients, later became a Reiki student and then started coming to the healing circles. One time both Kathryn and I gave Hilda a Reiki treatment together. Later that evening, while Kathryn and I were sitting up in bed talking, Kathryn asked me, "Did you pick anything up about Hilda?"

I replied with hesitation, "Well...I did, but I was going to wait until some proof showed up before saying anything."

"Proof...what? Like a big fat tummy?" Kathryn said with a giggle. "So, what do you think it is...a boy or a girl?" Kathryn took for granted that I was picking up the same thing she had picked up, did she know I knew or just suspect? The more I think about it the more I suspect that she knew that I knew.

"A boy...it feels strong, confident and ready to go like a boy." I replied. Kathryn had the same feeling.

The next day, Kathryn called Hilda at home, "Hilda, I don't want to get your hopes up or worry you, but I was curious, are you and your husband planning on having children?"

Hilda replied with enthusiasm, "Kathryn, why do you ask, do you know something?"

"Well, I could be wrong, but...both Michael and I felt that you might be pregnant. Do you know anything yet?" Kathryn asked echoing Hilda's enthusiasm.

"I am only one week late. I suspected that I was pregnant but I did not want to tell you anything last night for fear that I might not be. I haven't told my husband yet or even had a pregnancy test. Now that you have picked up on it, I'll buy a test kit today."

About nine months later, Hilda had a son and Kathryn was invited to do a Christening ceremony. This was new for Kathryn, and she had to create a ritual herself. It turned out to be a lovely day for Hilda and her family, and the ceremony was well received.

One evening, our healing circle had a small turnout of only one person, which was not unusual. Kathryn and I had already begun giving this woman a treatment when there was a knock at the door. Kathryn told me to get it and help whoever it was, that she wanted to continue working on this woman.

There was a very attractive, twenty-something woman at the door. She asked if this was the Reiki healing circle and I told her yes and invited her in. Michelle was her name. I was immediately struck by a sense of physical chemistry, Michelle was hot and I would be happy to spend time putting my hands on her lovely body. Yet I had to control myself and do healing work instead. I took her into the healing room where we had two massage tables setup. I started the treatment in the usual way, by getting centered and saying a prayer. I tried pushing sexual ideas out of the way, but in time this became too difficult. I could feel her sexual energy and I was sure she was enjoying having my hands on her. Before having Michelle roll over to work on her back I used a rocking technique on her that I had just learned in Massage school the weekend before. She liked it, so I used it on her back side too before I finished the Reiki treatment. Before Michelle left we had the chance to talk a little bit because Kathryn was still intensely involved with her client. I had not felt such strong mutual chemistry in a long time, and I was totally soaking it up.

Silly me, I should have known that such a thing would not escape Kathryn's finely tuned radar system. She was on my case like I had cheated on her and desecrated the temple all at the same time. I defended myself with the excuse that all I was doing was giving her an energy treatment. We had a long talk about this one. Kathryn would not let me slip into unconsciousness about this issue. Eventually I had to own up to the fact that I was turned on and totally flirting with Michelle.

When Michelle left she told Kathryn and me that she would be coming back next week. Kathryn wanted me to call her and let her know that she was in no way welcome in our home. I called Michelle from work the next day, where I knew I could have some privacy. It was quite embarrassing for me to call her and give her this message. Michelle was shocked at Kathryn's reaction and openly admitted that she was flirting with me, and that she liked it. She saw no harm in it. I liked this attitude, and in many ways shared similar views as she did. However, I was pretty keen to keep my wife and made it clear that this would have to be the end of our communications.

About thirty minutes after hanging up with Michelle, I got a call from Kathryn. Michelle had called Kathryn right after we hung up, and she gave Kathryn a piece of her mind. Apparently Kathryn maintained her composure and made it once again clear that Michelle was not welcome at our front door. Kathryn was not sure what to do or say but she made me promise that this woman would not be calling her or coming around again. I told her I would take care of it.

The worst thing about all of this was that I really wanted to have an affair with Michelle. On one hand, I experienced a lot of guilt for this desire, and on the other hand, I was ecstatically involved with a wild sexual fantasy in my mind. My mind was in a spin...I could not focus on my work. I used my time to write Michelle a letter thinking this would solve something. I never sent it, but the writing helped me to sort though my thoughts and desires to the point it wore me out. Instead I called Michelle and asked her nicely to just let this thing go and not make anymore trouble. She told me she already had. It took a few days for Kathryn to calm down from this episode.

A Shocking Turn of Events

It was Friday December 8th, 1995. Since massage school began, for nearly three months, I had been looking forward to a weekend workshop in a Hawaiian massage technique called Lomi Lomi. One of the massage therapists I went to, a woman who also attended this same school, used a lot of Lomi Lomi techniques in the massages she gave me. I enjoyed how the Hawaiian techniques flowed; also they are more nurturing and sensual in nature than pure Swedish technique. I had even heard a rumor that breast massage was taught and practiced in this workshop, so you know that I was seriously looking forward to this class.

However, it was beginning to look like I might not be able to attend, and I was torn between my feelings of disappointment for missing this class and my concern for Kathryn's health. Kathryn had been complaining of having stomach trouble for the past month or so, and it had been getting increasingly worse over the prior few weeks and days. Earlier in the week, she got to a point where she could hardly eat, and she often felt like she was going to vomit. On this particular morning, I took Kathryn to Dr. Jane, a naturopathic doctor who prescribed some herbal remedies to help Kathryn's digestion and get her feeling better. Dr. Jane was concerned that this was a bigger problem than these herbs could handle and gave us her home phone number in case we needed any other help from her over the weekend.

In the evening Kathryn did not have any dinner; she only had a small portion for lunch and she skipped breakfast in the morning. She also skipped dinner the prior evening as well. Shortly after I finished eating my dinner and cleaning up the mess, I settled down on the sofa to enjoy watching some TV with Kathryn. All of a sudden Kathryn mumbles to me in a barely audible voice, "eeit mee a...bowl...qwi I'm ona thhoow up." I could see that she was looking very bad and I ran to the kitchen for a stainless steel mixing bowl. I got it to her just in time for her to hurl what little food her stomach held in to the bowl.

I thought to myself, *This is horrible! What is going on?* I was feeling irritation more than compassion at the moment. I was tired after a long week of study, work, and helping Kathryn out due to her ailing health. It had already been a stressful day, and then just when I sat down to rest and relax, I had to deal with this smelly mess! God damn it I was pissed off! It only took a moment before I noticed where my head was at. Then I felt bad because I was worrying about myself and missing my Lomi Lomi workshop the next day while Kathryn obviously has something seriously going wrong in her body. I straightened out my head enough to ask, "Are you all right?" with an appropriately concerned tone in my voice.

Kathryn replied with a quiet and weary voice, "No, this is just getting worse. Now I am vomiting? Michael, what is going on with me?" I could see tears in her eyes, but she would not let them flow. "Please, call Dr. Jane for me," she asked.

When I got Jane on the phone I explained to her what had just happened. She asked me if Kathryn could talk to her so I handed Kathryn the phone. With all of the strength and clarity she could muster Kathryn talked to Dr. Jane in a reasonably normal tone of voice. Dr. Jane suggested that Kathryn go to the emergency room of the hospital and Kathryn explained how afraid she was of hospitals and doctors. After having had so many bad hospital experiences, and four years of reasonably good health, she thought she was done with all of that. A visit to a hospital was not what she wanted at all. Dr. Jane then went on to let Kathryn know that Kathryn's condition was beyond her ability to help, she had nothing else to offer. She insisted that Kathryn go to the hospital.

After hanging up the phone Kathryn told me about the conversation with Dr. Jane. She said, "I hope I don't have to go to the hospital. I'll wait awhile before deciding to do that."

I was getting frustrated and wanted to start yelling at her. I thought to myself, *If she continues to get worse at this pace, we will be going to the hospital in the middle of the night, in the middle of my sleep, or right before I need to leave for my massage workshop.* Then out loud I said, "But sweetheart, it looks inevitable, can't we just go now? Won't that be easier?" I tried to maintain the tone of concern in my voice but stress showed in my energy and facial expressions.

"No," Kathryn whimpered weakly, she would have snapped at me but she did not have the strength for that. "I hate hospitals. You know what I have been through with doctors and hospitals. They don't know anything about healing."

I knew there was no point in arguing with her, she was way too strong willed for that. So I settled down to watch some television with her. We were both tired so it was not long before we were ready for sleep. Kathryn was too nauseous to sleep lying down in bed so she decided to sleep in her recliner. We had a wireless doorbell so I removed the button press from outside the front door and left it by her side. She could use it to call me if she needed anything in the middle of the night. I went upstairs to sleep in our bed alone.

Well it happened just like I worried it would. I was in a very deep sleep when I first heard the doorbell ringing…it was like the ringing was part of my dream and I could not figure out what was going on. It took me a moment, but when I finally realized what the noise was I rushed downstairs as quickly as possible. When I reached Kathryn she said,

"Take me to the hospital. I can't take this anymore." It was nearly 2:00 AM; I briefly thought about how tired I would be during my massage class in the morning and then I put it out of my mind and got us ready to go.

I rushed Kathryn to Bellevue's Overlake Hospital and parked right outside of the entrance to emergency. As I helped Kathryn out of the car, I realized the rush and panic I was in. I calmed my energy down and slowly helped her to walk over to the triage nurse. I noticed a half dozen people in the waiting room. Two different men, sitting at different ends of the waiting room, looked as if they each had been in a fight, I wondered if it had been with each other. They also looked drunk, or stoned, perhaps both. There was a woman with her daughter; I could not tell what was wrong with them. If I had to guess the daughter was sick of listening to her mother nag on and on, which she was still doing at this hour of the night. There was a father sitting with his young son, lying with his head in dad's lap. The boy had his jammies on and dad's coat over him for a blanket. Dad looked calm and reassuring.

I was about to leave Kathryn with the triage nurse to go and park the car in a legal spot when Kathryn said in a quiet whisper, "Don't leave me here alone." Not wanting to miss my chance for easy parking I replied as I quickly walked away, "I saw a couple of ER spots a few feet from the door. It will only be a minute."

When I returned Kathryn's admittance forms were nearly filled out. An emergency bed had just cleared up and the nurse said, "I have enough information from you now Kathryn. We can take you to a bed and your husband can finish with the paperwork."

"NO! I want Michael to come with me." Kathryn said in a week yet determined voice.

"We don't normally allow family members to be present in the emergency room. He'll be near by in the waiting room."

In exasperation I thought, *They just don't understand.* I replied to the nurse, "No, I will need to join her, and I know that I can so let's not discuss this anymore." Then I turned to Kathryn and said. "Kathryn, I will only be a minute to finish with these forms. I will come back and join you as soon as I am finished. Don't worry. It won't take long. They will help make you comfortable." Kathryn was reluctant to leave my side but they were already pushing her wheelchair away.

The forms only took another few minutes to finish up and I was again standing by Kathryn's side, holding her hand and attempting to comfort her through all of this. Soon a doctor came in, looked at her chart and started asking all the same questions. The doctor told the nurse to give Kathryn two different medications and then started to leave the room. Kathryn and I both stopped him to ask what it was they were giving her. The doctor explained that one was to stop the nausea and the other was a painkiller. He then walked away.

Intravenous drugs work quickly and Kathryn was already looking much better than she had in days. Relief moved through me as I too could feel Kathryn's discomfort release. I could hear the goings on all around us. Our curtain enclosed space was smack-dab in the middle of the emergency room. The woman next to us had just completed her visit with the doctor and was talking on her mobile phone to her husband explaining how she wrapped her car around a telephone pole. I could hear the doctor telling one of the drunken men that he had to remain awake to make sure he did not have a concussion. The little boy got a bed to lie down in, dad was not with him. Apparently dad was better than me at followed orders when the nurses told him to wait in the waiting room.

About ten minutes passed then a new doctor came to visit Kathryn. He quickly read Kathryn's chart and asked all of the same questions. "I was briefed by Dr. Sullivan and I would like to start with an endoscopy. We will give Kathryn a drug that knocks her out, well nearly, but not completely...she will not remember anything when the procedure is done."

"Wait a minute," I said in objection, "She won't remember anything? Does that mean this will hurt her but she just won't remember the pain or does that mean she won't feel anything?"

"I had this done to me when I went through Medical school and I did not remember anything. We need to look inside of her stomach to assess her condition, and she does need to have a certain level of consciousness while we do."

"What exactly is this procedure?" I asked.

"We will put a tiny camera down her throat and into her stomach to see what we can find in there. We will also take a tissue sample to biopsy. This is a fairly quick procedure but we will need to give the drug a little time to take affect. You can take a rest in the waiting room and we will let you know when we are done."

I objected, "No, I would like to observe this procedure if I can. Kathryn wants me with her as much as possible. She is very afraid of doctors. As you can see from her history she has had a lot of experience with hospitals and doctors. What the history does not show is how often it has gone wrong. Please...can I stay with her as much as possible?"

"Okay," said the doctor. "You may be able to help us if we need to restrain her."

"Restrain her!" I said in shock. "Why, won't the drugs you give her work?"

"As I said before, she won't remember anything. But she will be somewhat aware of the procedure as it is occurring, and apparently, it is not always comfortable."

I was at once excited to be able to watch this procedure and also concerned about what Kathryn was getting into. This would be a great experience for me considering all of the anatomy and physiology I was learning in massage school. Yet, I could not help but wonder how much experimenting on my sweetheart they would do before they found the cause of her problems.

About forty minutes had passed before they were ready to begin the endoscopy procedure. They sat Kathryn down in a chair that was much like a dentist's chair. A nurse stood at one side holding Kathryn's arms down. Kathryn seemed to be asleep and I was holding her hand. The doctor demonstrated how good the little camera was by showing me a video of the buttons on my shirt and then he started inserting the instrument into Kathryn's throat. Within moments of him doing that Kathryn awoke from her peaceful state of rest and began to struggle. The nurse was not holding Kathryn well enough and Kathryn swatted near her mouth like one would swat at a pesky fly. The nurse got Kathryn's arm and held it down again. At first I was amused at her mild look of discomfort. Kathryn seemed unaware of what was happening; she just wanted to sleep. But as the doctor moved the device down her throat her annoyed and uncomfortable look turned to one of horror, like she was being tortured. She also became much more violent in her attempts to stop the procedure.

For a moment, which seemed like forever, I contemplated whether to assist in restraining her or to make the doctor stop. I decided to help them and hold Kathryn's arms down. I watched the video monitor in amazement as the camera moved further down and into her stomach. It was all pink and soft and moist looking inside. I could see little bits of food hanging on the walls of her esophagus. Even though the doctor demonstrated the clarity of the image before he began, I was surprised and impressed at how clear it was inside of her body. I have seen enough illustrated text books and photos of dead cadavers who had been opened up to expose the inside of the body. But never had I seen video footage of the inside of someone's living body. It was truly amazing.

Kathryn began to relax again, making only mild gestures to stop the annoying procedure, as the camera made it to the stomach. I could see a bit of pasta still intact enough to clearly recognize it. Then the doctor activated a claw that grabbed, pulled, stretched and tore a bit of the stomach tissue out. This seemed unnecessarily violent, I am certain there must be a way of cutting it rather than tearing it like that. Kathryn began to fight again as I continued to hold her arms down. I wanted to object. I wanted to cry. But by that point I knew it was futile. I felt bad about what I was helping them do to my sweetheart. From the camera images the doctor said it all looked normal. So why did he have to pull out a bit of her flesh in such a violent way then?

There were no more dramas as the doctor removed the endoscope from the inside of Kathryn; she slept peacefully. I was told they would be taking her to a room to look after her and that further testing would be done later. I decided to go home to get Kathryn a nightgown and other things necessary to make her comfortable in the hospital. This only took me about fifty minutes, perhaps an hour, but no more. When I got back to the hospital I found out that they had done an ultra sound on her abdomen and found a tumor the size of an orange sitting on her intestine. It was this tumor that was pinching her intestinal tract closed so that food could not pass all the way through her. I was in shock. I felt like I should have never left her alone in the hospital. It was almost like I believed they would not have found cancer if I had stayed there by her side. This can't be happening…not to us. What did this mean? "Is this cancer?" I asked.

"It could be," said the nurse, "but we need to collect a fluid sample and take a biopsy to be certain. We are about to perform that procedure now."

"How will you do that?" I asked.

"We will use the ultra sound equipment to locate the tumor and insert a collecting needle into the fluid and tumor. Please take a seat in the waiting room and we will let you know when we are done."

"I'd like to be there and watch. Kathryn wants that too…I know she will feel comforted by my presence. Please let me be there." I was very concerned that they were going to keep me out of all of this.

"Okay, you can be there for the procedure. Follow me." She took me to the ultrasound room. Kathryn was there and mostly sleeping. She would occasionally wake up and was happy to see me. "Where did you go, what is happening?" Kathryn asked. "They think you might have cancer, they found a large tumor…the size of an orange." I said as I choked on my words. I could not believe this. Would she die? Kathryn looked worried and sad, but within moments she closed her eyes and went back to sleep.

They prepared Kathryn for another ultrasound by placing lubricating jelly on the paddle like instrument and on Kathryn's bare stomach. Kathryn woke up again when she felt the cold pressing on her belly. "What is happening?" She said, "Where am I?" As I started to explain she closed her eyes again. Kathryn remained sleeping as they moved the device over her stomach. There were times I could see the tumor, but I had to look carefully. I hoped they were wrong. But they had done this before; they knew what they were doing and they knew what they were looking at.

Kathryn woke again when they inserted the needle into her abdomen. I held her hand and comforted her. "What is happening?" Kathryn asked again; this was not the last time she asked either. She was not remembering anything from our previous conversation. How could I keep delivering the bad news over and over again for what must seem like the first time to her? I tried to soothe her with my words but I was not very convincing; I was in too much of a frightened and confused state myself. I was thinking, *How could this be happening? We have been on such a path of growth and healing. We have been helping others to heal. We have been teaching healing with energy. What did all of this mean? How would I go on without her? How much time did we have left?* The thoughts of attending my Lomi Lomi class was a desire long past. I just wanted to wake up from this nightmare and find my lovely bride healthy and whole.

The uncomfortable procedures were not over yet. Now they wanted to do a CT scan of her abdomen. To do this Kathryn had to drink nearly three glasses of a liquid chemical which provides contrast for the x-rays. They told her it tasted like tang. Luckily Kathryn was mostly awake at this point but she did drift off a couple of times while she was supposed to be drinking. She had to be reminded why she had to drink this nasty tasting substance each time she woke up. And each time Kathryn tried to get out of drinking it by explaining that nothing would stay down and that it would just make her sick. I felt like I was going to go insane in this Loony-Tune drama that had much too quickly become my world. Luckily the anti-nausea medications were working well and the liquids did stay down. Kathryn drank most but not all of it, maintaining her own sense of control. I watched as they spent nearly forty minutes positioning Kathryn's body and films and taking one x-ray after another. Kathryn did not look comfortable and now she had to pee too. Her strength as she went through this was amazing. I on the other hand, was barely able to cope.

Kathryn's room in the oncology ward was ready and waiting for her after the CT scan was complete. An elderly volunteer pushing Kathryn's wheelchair took us to her room. He was a nice man and he tried to make idle chitchat, but neither Kathryn nor I were in the mood so the conversation was strained. A senior nurse and another one who was in training followed us into Kathryn's private room. The senior nurse took the usual vital statistics; temperature, pulse and blood pressure. Kathryn was mostly awake by now, still a little groggy from her medications and her ordeal of the last week. But now she was able to carry on a reasonable conversation.

"What is wrong with me?" Kathryn asked the nurse. "This is the oncology ward, my dear." The nurse replied with a compassionate tone of voice as she continued her job of hooking up bags of fluids and medications to the tube and needle in Kathryn's arm. "It looks like you may have cancer. They have taken a biopsy of the tumor and some fluid samples." The nurse paused to give some instructions to the junior nurse and then turned her attention back to Kathryn. "Your doctor will come around shortly to talk with you and explain what they have found and what course of treatment he believes you should take. I really don't have enough information to say more than that at this time."

The nurse went on to explain how to operate the bed, how to call a nurse, how Kathryn was to pee in the special measuring cup sitting inside of her toilet. She told me about the visitors lounge around the corner and where a small kitchen was. I informed her that I had volunteered at the hospital a year ago and was familiar with the facilities. I asked if they could arrange a cot for me to sleep on as I was planning on staying with Kathryn as much as possible. The nurse was happy to accommodate me. As we continued our conversation, the doctor showed up at the door.

"Hello Kathryn, I'm Doctor Howard Jones. I can see that you have had a rough morning." With his introduction, the nurses excused themselves and left.

"This is my husband, Michael. I'd like him to stay with me overnight, I hope that is all right." Kathryn replied.

"Of course he can stay...actually we'd like to see more of that here."

"Dr. Jones, is the tumor cancerous? Will I have to have chemotherapy?"

"Please call me Howard. We are not certain about the tumor yet. Based on its location and what you have told us of the gradual build up of discomfort the chances are very likely that it is malignant." Howard sat on the bed next to Kathryn and held her hand as he talked. I could tell that he was a caring man, and Kathryn was receptive to his gentle way. "We have to wait for the test results of the biopsy to know what type it is and to determine which course of treatment to recommend. We should have those results by the late afternoon. I will come back around to discuss them with you both. The best thing you can do is to relax and let the nurses make you comfortable. I have prescribed some medications for the nausea and to reduce your pain. You just need to let the nurses know how it is going for you and they can increase or reduce your dosage to help keep you comfortable. Don't let yourself get too discouraged at this stage. Twenty years ago, a Cancer diagnosis was the same thing as a death sentence. Medicine has come along way since then. We have a high rate of healing in this day and age, and even in the worst cases, we have so many specialty medicines to help you to cope with the discomfort and side affects of the treatment medicines. This does not have to be the horror story of the past era."

Kathryn responded, "That's reassuring...Where is your accent from Howard? You don't sound like you come from the States?"

"I'm a Kiwi...from New Zealand. My first time in America was when I began medical school, which was in Hawaii. Except for occasional visits home, I have lived in the States ever since." Howard placed his free hand over the hand of Kathryn that he was holding, patted and stroked it gently and said; "I have to go on to see other patients now. I'll be back to see you around dinnertime. It was a pleasure to meet you, Kathryn."

"Thank you Dr. ...uh, Howard. I am glad you are my doctor." Kathryn said as Howard left the room.

I moved closer, right next to Kathryn's bed and sat where Howard had been sitting, put my hand on Kathryn's leg and said, "It looks like you have a good one this time. Maybe this experience is just to help you heal your history with the medical community, and you will survive. Dr. Jones seems like a very nice man, a true healer."

"Yes," Kathryn replied. "Let's hope that is all this is about. Oh, Michael, I am afraid. I'm so sorry you have to go through this. Thank you for being here and being so gentle. I really need you now, please stay with me."

"I will, I already asked the nurse to bring a cot into the room for me to spend the night. I am not going anywhere while they have my beautiful wife held hostage here. I'll make sure they set you free."

"No, that's not what I mean. Please don't let me go though this alone. I love you and I can handle anything if I have you by my side." Tears were in Kathryn's eyes as she barely choked out these words.

"Silly woman! Of course...I won't leave you because you have cancer. I want to be a part of your healing. What would kind of person would I be if I left you now...what kind of healer? Knowing what I know now today, if I could go back in time and change things so I never met you...I would not do that, I would choose to meet you and fall in love with you all over again, knowing that one day I would end up here having to face this with you. I would choose it so don't worry. Just focus on healing."

"What if I don't heal; what if it looks like I will die from this? Will you stay with me?"

Choking on my tears, I hugged Kathryn close and said, "If these are your last days, I don't want to miss a single one of them. You are so precious to me. Anyway, you can't die, I love you too much."

Howard returned in the evening as promised, just after Kathryn's liquid dinner arrived. It didn't matter; she didn't want it anyway. As Kathryn tried to engage Dr. Jones in a bit of frivolous chitchat it became obvious that he was in more of a hurry this time. Kathryn picked up on this and moved onto business, "Howard, you must have family to get home to. Do tell me what the tests turned up?"

"The tests from your biopsy were not conclusive...confusing actually. It appears as if you have Ovarian Cancer...and yes, we are aware that you had a complete hysterectomy nearly two decades ago. The test results were weak so we will need to do further testing on new tissue samples before we can be conclusive about this diagnosis."

"More tests? I don't think I can handle more poking and prodding Dr. Jones." Kathryn said in a weary tone.

"Please call me Howard."

"Oh, yes, I almost forgot. You're not like the other doctors I have had. They loved their title and wanted it used with reverence."

"Kathryn, I recommend that you have surgery to remove that tumor. It is blocking your bowels, which is why you are having trouble with nausea and eating. It will kill you if you leave it that way. We will do further testing on the tissue samples we gather from surgery."

"Surgery! Oh no, not another surgery." Kathryn said exhausted and full of doubt.

"I have scheduled you with Dr. Levington on Monday evening. He is very good; we are lucky that he had room in his schedule."

"Monday evening? What day is it now?"

"It's Saturday." Both Howard Jones and I replied in harmony. It was hard to believe that Kathryn could not remember. A few days ago she was sharp as a tack. Not very comfortable but she was clear headed. Today she was sickly and confused. She still was clear about what she wanted and did not want; current events, however, took a few explanations to sink in.

"I've got to go now. The nurses have instructions to prepare you for surgery. I am off tomorrow so my colleague Dr. Carlton will be doing my rounds for me. I'll see you Monday morning."

"Goodbye Howard. Thank you for being so patient with me."

"Goodbye Kathryn, Michael. It's my pleasure."

Dr. Jones left and it was not long before a nurse came in for the usual vital sign readings. She gave Kathryn her dinner and told her to eat it all since it was the last meal she would have for a long time. Kathryn drank only the juice and left the rest.

That night I was quite restless, my mind was reeling with all that was happening. I recalled an experience that happened about six weeks earlier, right before Kathryn began reporting her stomach problems to me. Her Sister Bridget had called to tell Kathryn that she was going to the doctor the next day for a biopsy. She was having stomach problems; they suspected that it might be cancer. Bridget was very frightened. Kathryn talked with her and calmed her down. A few days later Bridget reported that her biopsy turned out clear and her problems had disappeared. About nine days later Kathryn began reporting her stomach problems to me and now, only a few weeks later, Kathryn has cancer. I wondered, *Is Kathryn helping Bridget heal empathically? What is she doing?!? Bridget does not deserve this kind of help!*

At this time, I was not aware that Kathryn had been experiencing these problems since last July. Even back then, Amoram said it had to do with her family.[1] I have read many accounts of empathic healings done by Masters such as the Greek Mystic Daskalos.[2] The events that occurred in Kathryn's life seemed to match these accounts in their nature. Based on such accounts, and conversations with Amoram and Isaiah on this topic, I am still convinced that this theory is sound and likely to be true. In the end it does not really matter if this was a cause or not, the impact on our life was the same no matter what the cause was, and God was still in full control of the Universe and All of Life. Today I understand that I did not have the ability at that time, nor at this time, to judge whether Bridget "deserved" the help Kathryn gave her or not. A Master only follows the inner guidance that is given to Her from Spirit, from the outer circumstances alone the actions cannot be fully understood.

---

[1] See transcript on page 172.

[2] Dr. Stylianos Atteshlis is Daskalos in the books, "The Magus of Strovolos," 'Fire in the Heart," and "Homage to the Sun." http://gr8Wisdom.com/Books/Daskalos (proper capitalization is important when locating this website)

Surgery

Around 1:00 Sunday afternoon, a nurse brought in a gallon jug of liquid and said, "You will have to drink all of this. It will cleanse your bowels."

"I can't drink that much. Nothing is staying down." Kathryn tried to explain to yet another nurse.

"You will have to find a way, dear...I know it will be difficult, but you need to do this. The drugs you are on should help you to keep it down. And once you get about a third of the way through, your bowels will make room for more. You can't have anything in your bowels when they perform the surgery on them. It could lead to a deadly contamination inside of you. You have more than 24 hours...let's get started now, shall we?"

"Are you offering to drink the first glass?" Kathryn replied with a sarcastic and exhausted tone. Then Kathryn complied once again and started to make her way through that gallon of cleansing laxative. At first she made a few nasty faces; then she gasped in terror when she saw how much more she had to drink; finally she just did what had to be done. She was strong and did very well drinking it all down. Indeed, she did finish off the entire jug. By the time she got to the third glass she was on the toilet more than she was off of it. The worst of the experience did not last all that long; it only took a few hours. It probably helped that she did not eat much in the last week.

Neither of us slept very well that night. With the usual nurses rounds every few hours, and Kathryn needing my help to get her to the toilet, we were up and awake more than we slept. Normally I don't do so well with such a lack of sleep; I get irritated and offend people with my attitude. This time however, I found an inner strength and softness that surprised even me. I knew it was me who had to keep the energy peaceful and nurturing, I knew that getting frustrated, angry, or agitated in any way would be detrimental to her frail health.

The busyness of Monday morning came as quite a shock. We had only been at the hospital during their quiet period, the weekend. But Monday morning is one of their most busy times. Most surgeries and procedures are done during the week. People don't want to ruin their weekend with a hospital stay, so they wait until Monday to check in, by that time there is often a heightened sense of urgency. It felt like an invasion of our safe haven; we had to get used to this new and busier energy of the weekday.

This evening Kathryn was due to go into surgery. We had not yet told her parents that she was in the hospital. Kathryn did not want to have them come to visit, nor did she want to explain to them why. This was the first hospital stay she had where she had a supportive husband around and a doctor she trusted and nurses that were sweet and compassionate. She did not want to spoil it with a visit from "the family of pain".

We got a phone call from a couple of our friends. Brenda was planning on coming by around 1:30 PM to do some energy work on Kathryn. Martha called Kathryn to let her know that she could not make it until after Kathryn was scheduled to go into surgery and that she had to leave before Kathryn came out. Even though Kathryn would be in surgery and Martha could not see her, Martha came anyways to be there in support of me and to pray. Martha also had another surprise for us. She had attended a weekend workshop at church. The main speaker was a successful hypnotherapist that Martha thought would be able to help Kathryn heal her condition or at least make the surgery less of a problem. Kathryn accepted the gift, a very expensive one at $150 per hour.

Bren arrived on time with her friend, Leslie, who had driven her to the hospital. She sat with Kathryn chatting and laughing for a while then Bren got down to doing her energy work on Kathryn. The nurses came in at one point to take Kathryn's vitals and change her saline solution bag. They seemed at ease with Bren while she did her magic.

Bren was still chatting with Kathryn when Fred the Hypnotherapist arrived. Bren excused herself saying she had already stayed longer than she intended, and then left. We made sure the nurses did not need to interrupt us for anything for the next hour and then shut the door. Fred sat with Kathryn and talked a bit to her about his experience with helping people like Kathryn find their inner resources. Kathryn listened politely for a while then told Fred that we too had studied Hypnotherapy and understood how all of this worked.

Fred discussed with Kathryn how she wanted to proceed with her session and they decided to focus on making her body receptive to the surgery and to keep bleeding to a minimum. She also wanted him to implant the suggestion that her body would recover quickly from the surgery and clear itself of all cancer.

When someone charges that much for their work you expect something amazing, special, or different. You expect them to have a higher degree of success and you expect it to be obvious somehow when you meet them. Neither Kathryn nor I had such feelings about Fred. I believe that Kathryn went through with this because she was trying to be polite and fully receive Martha's generous gift. Kathryn and I did not really need Fred coming in to keep us busy at this point in time. For someone else, this may have been more powerful, as for Kathryn and me...we were already doing the visualizations before Fred came to help us do them. Over time this would become a theme, some well meaning person knows of some supposed cure or way to heal cancer and they expect us to dive in and try it. It was an interesting lesson for two people who want to help others to heal their lives.

Kathryn was a bit nervous about her upcoming surgery. She had plenty of past experiences to give her good reason to worry.[1] There was the time a surgeon left a small towel inside of her abdominal cavity. After many days of pain that would not go away they opened her up again to find the towel that had been left inside. There was also the time a surgeon cut open her kidney because he did not recognize what it was. She had plenty of other stories of the incompetence of doctors and surgeons. Thinking about these past difficulties did not feel good, nor could I see them improving our current situation. I tried my best to distract and redirect Kathryn's mind toward healing. This was difficult because she felt betrayed by her body.

Kathryn got permission from the doctor for me to be present with her as she was anesthetized and up until she went into the operating room. I held her hand for as long as I could, sometimes I had to release it so the doctors and nurses could do their work. As she was being taken to the operating theater, I said a prayer for her and visualized her being returned to her room after a successful surgery. Martha had arrived just as I came out into the waiting room. She stayed with me for about half an hour and then had to leave. I went back to Kathryn's room and slept for twenty minutes. When I woke up I found out that Kathryn's operation was finished. I was surprised as I was expecting it to last at least a few hours. I quickly made my way to find the surgeon to learn what he had found.

The surgeon Dr. Levington saw me at the same time as I saw him; immediately he began walking toward me. "Mr. Skowronski, the surgery went well and your wife is in the recovery room where we can watch her vital signs until the anesthesia wears off."

My mouth said, "How is she? Did you get it all, did you get all of the cancer?" But in my mind I was thinking, *I must have some good news, please pronounce her well!*

"Your wife is a long ways from being in remission from this cancer. Oh, and it still looks like ovarian cancer to me. We will have

---

[1] We use the past as an excuse to worry, and indeed if you contemplate bad experiences and superimpose them on current ones you will worry. A Master gains control of their mind and emotions and understands that all is well and in Divine order at all times.

results from the biopsy later this evening. I will let you know. There is about an eighty percent chance of remission with this disease using the treatments we have today."

I was shocked, "You mean..." I took a deep breath and nearly cried, "you didn't get it all? Does she still have cancer inside of her? What are you saying...what did you see?"

Dr. Levington guided me by the arm to a chair and we talked further, "First I want you to know that we did all that we could with surgery. We removed two feet of bowel which contained the large tumor and a smaller one too. We also removed her omentum; it had little rice size bits of cancer scattered all over it."

"What is an omentum? Doesn't she need that?!?" I could hear how anxious I sounded and I tried to calm myself down. "Please doctor; tell me everything and I will just try and listen. Don't leave anything out."

The doctor went on to describe Kathryn's medical condition in great detail. She still had a lot of rice sized bits of cancer scattered all over her abdominal cavity. They planned on treating this with chemotherapy. I hoped and expected that Kathryn was going to reject that plan. I felt that we could treat this better using natural therapies and I believed that Kathryn would agree.

I went back to Kathryn's room while she was still in the recovery room. It was time to make the dreaded phone call to her mother. I promised Kathryn I would do it at this point in the program, just after we had more news from the surgeons. I was keen to get it done before Kathryn returned; I did not want to disturb her. "Hello, Irene, this is Michael. How are you?"

"Oh...I'm doing okay." Irene said with a shaky voice; her tone picked up some energy when she asked, "How is Kathryn? I am a bit worried about her I have left two messages and she has not called me back. Is everything all right?"

"No..." I said with a sad tone in my voice, "everything is not all right. I am afraid I have some bad news. Kathryn is in the hospital. I had to bring her in very early on Saturday morning."

"Saturday!" Irene interrupted with an expression of shock.

"Now wait and listen, please...." my tone of sadness turned to impatience and now I was keen to get this conversation over with, "Kathryn has cancer and has just come out of surgery. They found a tumor the size of an orange. It has been pressing in on her intestines and blocking them. This is why she was having so much trouble eating and keeping food down. So they just removed that tumor as well as another one of significant size. They also had to remove her omentum and gallbladder. The surgeon said there was still rice sized tumors sprinkled all over the interior of her abdominal cavity but that chemotherapy should be able to get rid of that. He also said she should have about an 80% chance of full recovery, and a 95% chance she will live at least a few years more. But I am not so sure that we will go with chemo...."

I was interrupted again when Irene said, "Surgery?" Her concerned voice quickly changed to disturbed and demanding when she said, "Kat has been in the hospital since Saturday and neither of you have called to let us know? Why, what is going on?"

"Kathryn did not want you to worry until we knew more."

"Well I have been worried. I knew something was wrong, and when she did not call back, I was very worried. I would have come down to help her if I had known. Her own mother, you don't even call to let her own mother know!?!" Irene's tone was now angry and strong.

"Kathryn is not having any visitors." I wanted to add *especially you* but I restrained myself. "She just wanted to get the surgery over before she saw anyone."

"Visitor! I am not a visitor! I am her mother. Why wouldn't she want her own mother there to comfort her and take care of her? What is wrong with you?"

I tried to be tactful, "Kathryn is capable of deciding what she wants and needs. She is going through a very difficult time right now and she is in a lot of pain and discomfort. She does not want a lot of company. She would feel that she needs to talk and entertain. She just wanted to be alone with me."

"Whoever heard of such a thing! I am her mother; her mother should be with her at a time like this. Every other time she was in the hospital, I was the one who came and looked after her. I made sure she felt loved and that she knew her family was behind her. How dare you keep her mother away from her at a time like this! I am going to get Sam to drive me down there first thing tomorrow morning. What hospital is she in?"

"No, Irene. Kathryn does not want that. You will have to wait until she says it is okay to visit. It should only be a week or two after she gets out of the hospital. Look, Kathryn has just returned from the recovery room. I have to go now. We will call you tomorrow. Bye." Without giving Irene a chance to reply I hung up the phone. I wanted to give her the message that I was not going to put up with any of her games. Their energy was not conducive to healing and I was firm that they would not get anywhere near Kathryn until she was ready. My only fear was that Kathryn would break down and let them come. But I figured she would only do that if she felt like her death was imminent. Fortunately it was not.

Kathryn was awake for a short time after her surgery, but after awhile the pain got the better of her. She had a button that injected pain medicine into her veins and soon the medications sedated her too much. She slept all night long.

The next day both Dr. Jones and Dr. Levington came to visit Kathryn. They discussed with us a couple of treatment options but kept heading us in the direction of a specific chemotherapy course. Kathryn surprised me by agreeing to have a course of six treatments and then decide what to do next from there depending on the results. She was too afraid and too tired to mess around looking for alternative treatments. I was not happy with Kathryn's decision but I did not want to make things worse either; I gave her my full support. We planned on beginning the treatments after the start of the new year, so we still had time to change our minds. Later we talked with Amoram about this option. We also talked about many other possible healing options, but Amoram told us it was important for Kathryn to become clear of which option she had the most belief in. Because Kathryn understood and had the most faith that chemotherapy would at least buy her some time, we became firm in our commitment to go through this process. I found it easier to support Kathryn after talking to Amoram.

Irene called Kathryn at the hospital the day after her surgery. Kathryn was polite and talked to her mother, but I could tell it was difficult for her. Soon the conversation turned into a battle of wills. I could only hear Kathryn's end of the conversation but I got angrier and angrier at Irene as it continued, "Mother, please wait until I am feeling better before you come and visit. I just want some peace and quiet for a few days while I am at the hospital." Kathryn paused to listen to Irene, then replied, "I really don't want any visitors right now, please just listen to me." Again Kathryn paused for Irene and then continued to plead with her, "I don't feel well and this conversation is not helping. I am insisting that you do not come here. Stay home and I will call you when I am up to it." There was a short pause for Irene to speak, then Kathryn raised her voice a little and said, "No mother. You're not listening to me." At this point I motioned to Kathryn to hand me the phone. She quickly said, "Good bye mother, Michael wants to talk to you," and handed me the phone.

I had been stewing for a little while and was quite ready to let Irene have it with both barrels, "What part of 'NO' don't you understand? Hmmm? YOU WILL NOT COME AND VISIT US. YOU WILL STAY HOME. AND IF YOU DO COME HERE, SECURITY WILL BE

INSTRUCTED TO TURN YOU AWAY." Then I slammed the phone down.[1]

Kathryn had a look of shock on her face. "That's not what I had in mind when I handed you the phone! Now how am I going to face her?"

I shrugged my shoulders and said, "She needed to hear that. I think she got the message." Kathryn was too ill for another confrontation so I got away with it.

I stayed with Kathryn most of the time she was in the hospital. I took a few breaks every day; I usually left the hospital for an hour or two once a day. One night I had to go home just to get some uninterrupted sleep; I left the hospital late and returned early in the morning. Every other night I slept in Kathryn's room at the hospital. I watched over every procedure that was done on her and double checked the medicines she was given and monitored the frequency as well. I wanted to make sure human error or neglect did not make things worse for her. I also motivated Kathryn to get up and walk around and took her outside into a small garden at the hospital so she could have fresh air and sunlight. I brought my computer into the hospital; I got a little bit of work done while it was there but not much. It is debatable if it was worth the effort.

Kathryn surprised me with how quickly she recovered from her surgery. By Friday morning we were getting her ready to return home, just in time for the weekend. I was a little bit sad and frightened. It was comforting being at the hospital where I knew they had everything necessary to take care of her. I wasn't sure if I was up to the task of looking after Kathryn at home. I did fine; however, especially since I did not have to go into the office to work. I only had about twenty hours of work to complete on my current contract job and I had nearly three weeks left to complete it in, so it was easy to find the time for that.

We had planned on going to San Diego for Christmas but those plans had to change. When we called my family to let them know about Kathryn's surgery, they offered to come out to visit us. But Kathryn did not want to deal with my family living with us for five days or more. My mother begged to come and after a few debates between Kathryn and me, we decided they could come if they stayed in a motel.

At first my parents were not happy about this arrangement, but in the end it worked out best for us all. The last time my parents had

---

[1] Although at the time I felt justified in my position I now realize that I wish to do better in my relationships with ALL other people, even those I perceive as having caused me or a loved one harm. I have been working on this issue with a great deal of success but am sad to report I still have my blow ups and outbursts of anger. I am however happy to report that such incidences are short lived. Persistence is the key and I continue to reprogram my mind in this regard.

visited us, Kathryn told them off about not accepting her into the family. Although by this point they had already made the necessary changes in their mind to accept Kathryn, they were still feeling wounded about that last confrontation. Having their own room to go back to gave them a break from feeling like they had to watch everything they said and did, and we all got a necessary break from each other's energy.

My mother was very helpful during the time she was at our house, which was most of the day each of the eight days they stayed. Mom did much of the cooking; I did the rest. Mom also did most of the cleaning, Kathryn helped...she could not resist doing some of it herself. I wanted Kathryn to just sit down and relax, but there was no stopping her. At the time it frustrated me, now I understand that she needed to do this. Kathryn wanted to do something from her usual routine so that she could begin to feel normal again. It was more therapeutic than I realized at the time. When my parents and brother left, I was a bit sad. I would have liked it if my mother stayed longer; I enjoyed her company and her help.

Whenever we were in Seattle for Christmas, we opened our home to friends for dinner and celebration. This year we had fifteen people including my parents and brother Pat. We asked everyone to bring an inexpensive gift that was worth about ten dollars, twenty at tops, for our traditional gift grabbing game. These gifts were wrapped as usual but no names were assigned to them. Instead we all drew numbers to see who would go first and then we started picking gifts. From the second person onward there was a choice to either take a gift from someone who had already opened a gift, or to take a chance and choose a wrapped gift. The first person had to pick a wrapped gift since there were no opened ones to choose from. If a person took a gift from someone else, the one who just lost their gift got to choose again. Once a gift had been taken three times it had to remain with the third person who took it. At the end of the game we were free to exchange gifts if we choose to, but not before.

In the past couple of years, mostly people were just being nice and not taking gifts from others; nearly everyone opened a fresh gift which was not as much fun. But this year, there were a few gag gifts and a few really good ones too. A couple of cheeky people stirred up the energy and got us all taking gifts that others had opened. It became quite competitive, but in a fun way, everyone was laughing and having a great time. I contemplated how this was like life. Sometimes we make things so serious; we are careful and make the most thoughtful choices...it can become boring and our intellect can cause us to miss out on inner guidance. At other times, we follow our inner calling; our desire gets the better of logic and reason; we make choices that may even seem harmful; it stirs up the energy and is often more interesting...we feel alive. This is the world of duality and contrast. The balance of all that happens is what gives life its character and color. I was beginning to understand what Amoram had been telling us about judgment; it was not so much about what we choose, but that we choose consciously.

Chemotherapy

With the new year of 1996, came a whole new set of experiences for us. First I got a new Microsoft Job, one that allowed me to work part time from home. Part time from home! If you go looking for jobs like that, they are difficult to find. This one easily fell into my lap. Time after time the Universe shows me just how much it loves me as it delivers to me exactly what I need.

Kathryn began her chemo treatments the second week of January. We checked her into Overlake Hospital's Oncology ward on Tuesday morning at ten AM. First they took her vital signs and a few blood samples for testing. Then they hooked up an IV with a saline bag. Using the IV port, they injected Kathryn with anti-nausea medicine, which we called "ants in the pants" because of the feeling it gave Kathryn around her anus. They also used this port to deliver pain medicine and the chemotherapy which dripped into her veins for about twenty hours. She had another day of rest and monitoring. Kathryn then left mid-day on Thursday.

Thus we stayed two nights with each visit. Kathryn had six of these treatments scheduled three weeks apart. For each visit I stayed with Kathryn the entire time she was in the hospital, leaving for only a few hours each day to maintain my own sanity and run errands.

The treatments were extremely taxing on Kathryn. Each successive treatment took a greater toll on her body. We had to delay both the fifth and sixth treatments by one week each because the chemo drugs kill the white blood cells and not enough new ones had regenerated. The white blood cells are important to fight off infections and viruses. We experienced just how important they are when a few days after her sixth treatment we had to return to the hospital for four nights because Kathryn became very ill with a high fever. Personally, I find that the discomfort of a fever is bad enough; I cannot imagine having to face life threatening illness on top of the after effects of chemo therapy. I felt helpless as my best friend suffered; I did not know what to **do**. The drugs they gave Kathryn controlled her fever and pain. A blood transfusion helped to bring her white blood cell count up again. Yet it was the way I was **being**, the love and support that I offered, that gave Kathryn the strength and courage to continue on in an effort to survive and become healthy again. I could not have been this way without the training I had already received from Amoram, Isaiah and from Kathryn herself.

Kathryn made many friends with the nurses who were on the whole very gracious and generous with their time and compassion.

Although Kathryn did not want to be in the hospital, she had many positive experiences that offset most of the negative ones of her past medical treatments.

After Kathryn's first chemo treatment, I called the massage school and officially dropped out for the term. Previously my intention had been to try to make it to enough classes to qualify for my certificate. But by early January, I had already missed nearly my quota of classes and I had only been able to get in half of the practice time required. When I witnessed the after affects of Kathryn's first treatment, I knew I could not leave her home alone for the long periods of time necessary to attend classes. I did not want to drop out, but I could see no other choice. This was incredibly painful for me to see my dream of getting out of computer software delayed even further. Over the next few months, I continued to exchange massages with some of the other students. I planned on continuing my massage training as soon as I could.

Kathryn's first week after chemo gave us just a taste of the horrors to come. Kathryn was starving yet it was very difficult for her to get anything down; she would have an immediate gag response to many foods. Right after her first Chemo treatment, on the way home from the hospital, Kathryn surprised me when she asked me to stop at the grocery store to purchase baby food. Many years before I met Kathryn, she fell down and broke her jaw bone in a couple of places. For a few months, she had her mouth wired shut. Thus, Kathryn had prior adult experience with eating baby food.

The baby food was not enough, Kathryn wanted some normal food as well—something with more flavor in it. Unfortunately many flavors would trigger a nauseous reaction. There were times I would cook three different things for Kathryn before we found something she could eat. Most of the time, if she got it down, it stayed down, but not always. Sometimes I would try feeding her something that she enjoyed eating a few days prior, but this time she could not tolerate it. Then she would ask for it again a few days later. I was not sure if I wanted to waste my time cooking it, but I would. Even if she asked for it, once it was under her nose and she took a taste she might push it away. It was frustrating to put that much love and hope into preparing some food only to have it rejected. It was a lot of work too!

One of the strangest foods that Kathryn was able to consistently eat was a Mexican bean and egg tostada. This was made from either a fried corn tortilla, or a raw one warmed on the grill or in the microwave oven. I spread it with warm refried beans, and topped that with a fried egg, parmesan cheese, salsa and guacamole. We discovered this one afternoon when I was serving baby food to Kathryn and preparing my own tostada. Kathryn liked the aroma so much that she asked for a bite, then another, and before I knew it she ate my whole tostada and was asking for one more! Not only did she not eat things with such strong flavors, but she was not eating such large quantities of other things either. When I look back on this today, I suspect the joy I put into making them helped in some way. I loved the flavors so much that I enjoyed every moment of making them. For me it was like creating a masterpiece.

Unfortunately not everything went down as well for her as those tostadas did, not even the baby food. "Get the bowl," became a common phrase in our house. Often Kathryn said it in a muffled and distorted way since her mouth was closed trying to hold back the contents of her stomach. But I quickly learned to recognize the many subtle and frantic ways in which she would make this request.

It took nearly a week before we got Kathryn's anti-nausea medications right. For the first few days, she ate very little but was starving much of the time. At first when she ate, she vomited. We always had one bowl ready and waiting, but one day we learned the hard way that two stainless steel bowls were necessary. From that point on whenever I took a bowl away from Kathryn so that I could empty it, I gave her the clean one that was waiting. Then I immediately emptied and cleaned the dirty one so it was ready and waiting.

Through all of this I had to learn to control my anger and frustration. This experience was both physically and emotionally exhausting. And the more physically exhausted I got, the more anger would rise up in me. I knew Kathryn did not need this nor did she deserve it. Even though my training and practice was to observe such thoughts and let them go, I felt compelled to blame these feelings on someone. Usually Kathryn was the one I blamed, it was a knee-jerk reaction. If I came too close to her when I was experiencing these strong negative emotions she would get nauseous. Then Kathryn would ask me to clean up my energy. At times, this only made my anger and frustration grow bigger because I felt like I was being blamed for making Kathryn feel worse when I had not done a thing. But I got used to searching for new thoughts in my mind until Kathryn would tell me, "There, that's it; that feels much better." The new thoughts that would trigger this response from Kathryn were always something of a loving and compassionate nature directed toward Kathryn. It is amazing how difficult it can be to generate such true and pure thoughts in the midst of such outer and inner turmoil, but it was not until my thoughts became pure and true that Kathryn would respond positively.

Just days before Kathryn's second chemo treatment, while we were in a Thai restaurant, we noticed a small pile of Kathryn's hair lying in a clump on top of her menu. We had already talked about the coming of this event; when her hair began falling out, I was going to shave her head. That day finally arrived. Kathryn did not want to suffer the agony of watching as each clump fell out, she was keen to get it over with. As soon as we got home, we set up the kitchen for the shaving.

I thought I was going to enjoy shaving Kathryn's head, but the awareness of why I was doing this was all too present in my mind. Pleasure was not what I experienced; this was incredibly difficult and painful for me. Kathryn tried to make a joke about it, but I could not hold back the tears. All I could think was, "How many more degrading things will I witness? What else will happen to my sweetheart? How many more things like this will I have to do to her?"

The onslaught of negative experiences became overwhelming at times. I could not help it; I worried that Kathryn was going to die. What would I do without her? How much suffering would she go through before that happened? How much more would I suffer watching her go through it?

On the upside, we had our spiritual support; all of our recent training was a big help. Both Kathryn and I continued our meditation and visualization practices, we prayed regularly, and found inspiration in books and lectures. We had many people who were offering love and assistance; many synchronistic events occurred. In more ways, this was a positive learning experience for us and for many other people too. We learned that we were able to make it through life's most difficult challenges and still have love and joy frequent our experience.

Kathryn's oncologist, Howard, suggested a hair dresser named Wayne to Kathryn. Wayne did the hairdressing for the wigs used in local Seattle theaters. He also dealt regularly with chemotherapy patients and their special needs and had a lot of compassionate energy to offer. Wayne fit Kathryn for a custom made wig designed to look just like her hair before she began chemo. Although Wayne sold it to us at his cost, it was still expensive. I got a lesson in letting go of trivial things like wasting money when Kathryn decided she could not wear the wig. How could I be angry with my wife at a time like this? Fortunately Wayne also had a good lead for hats, Kathryn found a few that she liked and wore those most of the time.

Kathryn finally allowed her family to drive up from Portland for a visit about ten days after her second chemotherapy treatment was complete. They came to visit in Kathryn's territory and in her timing. More than two months had passed since her initial hospitalization. They had requested to come and visit many times and been denied, yet Kathryn's mother Irene and the other the family members were softer and gentler than usual. Although Kathryn privately received a few lectures about the way I talked to her mother on the phone, Irene never said a thing to me directly about that event. Irene knew she had no hypnotic effect on me, only on Kathryn so she did not waste any energy trying to shame me for my behavior.

While Kathryn was undergoing her second chemotherapy treatment, I went out for lunch at a nearby sushi restaurant. I decided to have a glass of white wine with my meal. I had not spent any time considering having a drink prior to this time, I saw someone else having a glass and it looked good. I just ordered the glass of wine without giving it any thought. While I was waiting three or four minutes for the waiter to bring it, I considered that I would be giving up nearly ten years of sobriety. I tried to muster up some remorse for giving up my sobriety only months before reaching the ten year mark, but I could not. A glass of wine sounded good, in no way did it sound like a bad idea to me.

I had a second glass before returning to the hospital. I enjoyed the feeling but didn't want any more. I did not tell Kathryn about it; she did not need to worry. At the time, it seemed like a one-off event. I had not planned on continuing to drink or hiding it from Kathryn. But that is precisely what I started doing on that very day. Every few days or so, I would take the opportunity to have a quick drink, or I would buy one or two single serve bottles of wine to consume at my leisure. Eventually, I started bringing full sized bottles of wine home, one at a time, and even some vodka...I kept it inside the access port to the shower pipes, behind a false wall board inside of our bedroom closet. In the years we lived there we never opened that up; except once when we first moved in to see what was behind it. I drank three or four times a week, usually I kept it to the evening only. Normally it was two, sometimes three standard drinks. Sometimes I might have a midday drink, but I never liked how it made me feel. A few hours after drinking, I felt blah for the rest of the day, and I was not about to drink all day and night, I just didn't enjoy that.

I carefully monitored my mood and how Kathryn responded to me while I was drinking. I knew that someday I would have to answer for these actions, and I wanted to be able to say that she enjoyed my company as much or even more when I had been drinking. For the most part, this was the case. I was also hoping that I was over any sort of addictive tendencies and was being watchful for that.

For the first five or six weeks, I kept it under pretty good control. But then a few times came when I was bored with my life of work and nursing, a life that seemed not to have any fun in it; I was so upset at how much suffering I was witnessing in Kathryn, that I did not care about keeping it under control. I just wanted to be smashed out of my mind on something. Twice I drank a full bottle of wine in one evening. One of these times I got the spins; usually an entire bottle by myself is enough to make me sick. I was not happy with this behavior, and I didn't enjoy the spins. A couple of other times I took some of Kathryn's pain medications, but I did not like how it felt. I was starting to consider getting some pot to smoke, but where would I find it?

Easter was approaching. Kathryn and I had an invitation to have dinner with some friends; it would be a large gathering. I knew there would be wine and drinking at the party and I did not want to be left out. It took me many days to get up the courage to ask Kathryn if she would allow me to have a few drinks of wine socially on Easter. I practiced many lines trying to find just the right way to convince her. One of my ideas was to tell her that I had already been drinking, I was keeping it under control, and that she did enjoy me when I had a few glasses of wine. I finally got enough courage to bring up the subject, yet I did not confess to the drinking I had already been doing. Kathryn rejected the idea and left no room for discussion. There was a lot of shameful energy involved in this conversation.

On Easter Sunday, I went for a walk a few hours before we were to leave for our social event. I stopped at a convenience store and bought a four pack of single serve wine. I drank two before returning home, and hid two more in the car. While at our friends house I was able to sneak out to drink the other two bottles over the course of the day. However, I got caught by Kathryn finishing off a glass of wine left on the table by one of the other guests. She found a private place to scold me; I felt like a bad little boy again. We had a longer talk about this event when we were driving home. Still I did not tell her I had been drinking prior to this. Kathryn made me promise not to try drinking again. I felt badly and secretly dumped out the rest of the vodka I had hidden away.

For a few days, I tried to keep my promise, but finally I gave in and snuck some more wine home. One evening, a few days later, Kathryn and I had a big fight. I was angry and so I went for a drive to cool off. I thought about going to a bar but the atmosphere did not appeal to me. Then I decided I would go downtown and try to score some pot. I went to Pioneer Square and walked around for a short time before I got the courage up to approach someone. I was able to purchase a single joint from one man, that was all he had yet I wanted more. I got ripped off when I tried to buy a bigger bag from someone else. After ten years of not smoking, it only took three hits to get very high. In that moment I was reminded why I liked marijuana so much.

Scoring more dope was a problem, and I did want more. I decided to try the University district during the day. It took about forty minutes of walking around and asking strangers if they knew where to get it before I finally found a young man who could help me out. This was humiliating, and I couldn't believe I was doing this at my age. I bought a forty dollar bag, which I thought would last for quite a few months, but it only lasted a few weeks. I planned on smoking only once or twice a week, however it quickly became a daily habit.

A few days before I ran out of my stash, I realized I had to do something to get more. The process of finding it was embarrassing so I did not want to keep buying such small quantities. However, Kathryn would notice it if I spent a few hundred dollars. I decided to create a fake pay stub using our computer and printer. I made it out for two hundred dollars less than it should have been. Since my working hours fluctuated greatly at that time, I knew Kathryn would not notice. I was able to pinch another one hundred dollars from my pocket cash and buy a much larger bag this time. From that point on I began taking ten and twenty dollars from my wallet every few days and putting it aside.

I hated this deception, but I knew that Kathryn would not allow me to smoke pot and remain with her. I did not know what else to do. In every other way I felt like the same person. I was a good husband; I was taking very good care of my sick wife; I was earning an income and satisfying my employer; I continued with my spiritual practices and meditation...and I was enjoying smoking dope. I had forgotten how much of a spiritual opening it gave to my mind and how creative I became. Except for the paranoia, I was thoroughly enjoying the experience. As I observed my paranoia and the thoughts I held, I realized it was directly linked to the judgments that society had against smoking marijuana; judgments I had allowed to live in my own mind too.

I found that I could release the paranoia completely by consciously choosing to come to my own personal approval of my actions. At first, I objected to this technique; it seemed to fall under the category of justification, but I could not deny that it did work. Then I began to understand that my truth, my justification, was just as valid as those who complain about the evils of smoking dope. Soon I began to face each judgment that came to my mind about my dope smoking with an aware and critical mind. I found that under scrutiny each judgment was baseless because I remained responsible, prayerful, and aware in my thoughts and actions. I continued to make choices that were the most loving ones I could make at the time. I was reminded of the lessons given by Amoram and Isaiah about not needing to have everybody's approval. As long as I could see that it was not impacting their lives, I did not think they needed to know. I thought to myself, *Once I have demonstrated that they can live with me this way, then I can tell them.*

During this time, Sedona, our Moluccan Cockatoo, had become more of a nuisance than a beloved pet. She was very needy and wanted a lot of time and attention. We understood how appropriate her needs were, but I just could not keep up with her. Kathryn had no desire to even try. If I let her out of her cage or kept her near me, she would always get into things, or chew the furniture. She had not become potty trained as I had hoped she would. I was not patient enough to train her to fit in better or I was just not good at training birds; either way, it was beginning to show in Sedona's behavior, and I did not want to ruin her. With all that was going on in our life, Kathryn asked me to get rid of her. I was not ready to face the embarrassment of making that suggestion myself, but I had been thinking that way too, so I was happy she suggested it. We found a pet store that specialized in Moluccan cockatoos, and I left Sedona with him. Within two days she had a home with a male Moluccan. We wished her a happy married life.

Women's Apprenticeship Group Acquires a Man

As it often happened, Bren and Amoram's apprenticeship groups underwent another change of membership. Two of the women in the women's apprenticeship group that Kathryn attended moved on to other things. As the remaining members, Joanne, Hilda, Kathryn, and Bren talked about who to have join them, I was the only person they considered; they did not even consider Bren's husband. I felt honored at this selection as I held all of these women in high regard. Of all the groups that Bren held, it was in this group that she most actively participated as a member and not just as the host and channeler. The following is most of the transcript of this first meeting.[1]

> You are Masters. Do you not know this? There is nothing in you that is missing. YOU are a Master, you are One with the All That Is. Yes, in this now moment, even though you are not aware of it, you are a Master.
>
> God is All That Is. Indeed many use this phrase, "All That Is" as a name for God. There is no place that God is not. So where does that leave you? Can God be some sort of figure outside of you? Objectified, solidified, all contained within some form while there exists anything else outside of It's Divine Self? If that were possible it would mean that God is not ALL powerful. Would it not? You see there would be some power outside of God. The more that exists outside of God, the less of that "ALL power" that God would have. Yet ALL religions state that God is ALL powerful.
>
> If God is All That Is, then every thought must be God's thought. Is it not so? Every touch must be God's touch; every breath must be God's breath. Thus your actions must be God's actions, your experience must be God's experience...indeed, your very life is God's Life. So why is it that you do not know this? Why is it that you do not remember who you are? Because this is the divine game you are playing with yourself.
>
> As we begin in this new configuration[2] it is time to start at the beginning. We know some of you are mentally rolling your eyes, "Amoram, we know all of this, you have covered this before." But we

---

[1] March 3rd, 1996

[2] Referring to the new grouping of individuals that made up this particular apprenticeship group.

say to you beloveds, you do **not** know this. You do **not** remember these things. For you they are only concepts, ideas and beliefs in your mind. As such you move blindly through life bumping into reality and not understanding what you have come up against. You don't understand how you have created the reality you live in.

So life comes in cycles. You will come across the same ground, the same teachings, and the same experiences over and over again, this has its purpose. These are reflections of where you are, of how you most often use your mind and of what you are calling to yourself through your desire and the way you focus your mind. If you pay attention you will learn and consciously experience. Once you have gained the experience you desire then understanding will occur. However, your programming, that which lives in your subconscious, your automatic reactions, this will be the same...unless you consciously make new choices. At first you must consciously choose to think and act differently. You must practice the new thoughts if you wish for them to become the new programming. Then and only then will your personality change. Then and only then will your reality change. Once that occurs then wisdom is also yours. Then you will know and understand and then you are consciously and deliberately changing your reality.

Is that not the definition of a Master? All of you have already done this many times. All of you have consciously chosen to change in some small way and have made that change and experienced the new way of reacting and of being. Yet, because you are still largely unaware of your programming, programming that gets in the way of your awareness, you easily forget the power you hold. Thus we repeat, and we cover the same ground, the same teachings over and over again. You expect some great new revelation to come from us, some single magical point where the lights come on and you see perfectly clearly. Beloveds that will happen for you, but it will occur slowly, incrementally, as you deactivate the ideas and desires that blind you and replace them with ideas and desires that allow the truth of who you are to shine through. The revelation is the Master that lives within you; the revelation is in the seeing of that which is blinding you.

You are Masters, right now, in this now moment, you are Masters. Because you do not remember who you are, you do not remember that you are indeed a master. Yet it is only a portion of the real you that is unaware, the Master in you is quite aware of your predicament. The Master in you is always reaching to you to remind you. Even though it would be more appropriate to say, "The Master you live within." While you focus your attention through your physical senses you remain unaware of this larger part of your own self. You see the world and all things in it as being outside of yourself. Desire and fear result from your outward focus and they distract you and prevent you from looking within.

To overcome this you must go within. Contemplation, introspection and meditation are required to know who you really are. They are not optional; they are required to know who you really are. You must study your mind. You must know what lies within it. You must understand your subconscious mind, your programming, your automatic ways of thinking. You must become consciously aware of that which you assume is a fact and ask yourself, "Is this really so?"

Michael: But Amoram, whenever I meditate I don't seem to get anywhere. I get bored and my mind wanders. I don't...

Amoram: Beloved, yes this is so. Your mind does not just wander, it is very busy, wanting this, worrying about that, judging others, *"He said this, she said that, she shouldn't have done this, he should have done that, when I see him next time I will say this."* Is this not so?

Michael: Yes, but I am expecting all of this bliss and wonderful astral travel that others talk about.

Amoram: Ah yes, expectation. Expectation is very creative beloved. And it often brings on hallucinations. But what we are talking about is meditation and contemplation. You must first understand what lives in your mind. What is it that occupies your subconscious beloved? Do you know? It is a simple matter to know. Whatever worry, whatever conversation is going on in your mind, whatever thing or event you are fantasizing about while you are supposed to be meditating, that is what lives in your subconscious. That is what you believe is important in life. And because you do not have conscious control of your mind, because you do not exercise your conscious mind, the subconscious mind is that which is creating. Your subconscious is a masterful creator...is it not?

Yes beloveds, true astral travel is possible. By going within you can travel to distant places. You can even physically manifest a body and be physically present. You can witness and interact with events that are occurring and later receive confirmation from someone who was there physically. This is different from hallucination. Many great beings are adept at this even now.

Michael: Living masters, in the flesh, on the planet now?

Amoram: Yes beloved, they are indeed living on this planet now.

But those skills will develop naturally as you gain conscious control of your mind and once you have deliberately programmed your subconscious mind to be in harmony with All That Is. This power does not come to the novice mediator. The beginner is not in control. It takes time, practice, patience, and perseverance. We are talking years of time in most cases. But what else is there to do with time? It is eternal is it not? You have eternity to master your mind and become conscious. But why wait? Right now you are ignorant of the power that lives within you. You often misuse this power, creating things you would not consciously choose to create. Your worry is creative. Does not your outer world reflect the worry that you allow to occupy your thoughts? This shows you the power of your mind. By consciously focusing your mind, by creating mental scenarios that you consciously want to occur, you can direct the same power of your mind that you are currently directing with worry. Do you wish to remain blind for a few more years, a few more lifetimes? We are talking about healing the blindness and starting now. You must start somewhere, you must start someday, why not here and now? Why prolong the blindness?

We come back full circle beloveds. The reason that you prolong the blindness is that you do not know who you are or why things happen the way that they do or how you can change things you wish to change. This is why we come back around to the truth that you are already Masters. You are God, and you must come to discover this for yourself, within yourself, within your experience of life. And more over you must change your outlook on life to reflect this truth and let your thoughts and actions be motivated by this truth. If you contemplate these ideas this will motivate you to go further and practice meditation, practice gaining control of your mind. Practice.

Your mind got into this disheveled shape by practice. Every day you rehearse and practice thinking in a certain way. Your life is in cycles. You get up, you brush your teeth or not. You have your coffee, or perhaps a cigarette or you shower and meditate. Which ever way it is, it is a habit. You talk and listen to others, read the news or watch it on TV, you watch other entertainment which influences your way of thinking and culture. All of this is practice, repetition which reinforces your subconscious programming. All of this practice happens subconsciously and automatically and with ease. Thus if you want to change you must first consciously choose to change and then you must practice the new way of being either in your mind or physically. In this way it will become automatic. Eventually the act of becoming conscious will also become automatic and you will find yourself consciously aware much more often.

Women's Apprenticeship Group Acquires a Man

Then Amoram asked if there were any questions. As was often the case people began asking personal questions about their life. It was as if they were waiting for Amoram's talk to be over so they could get to the good part, the part about themselves and their specific life issues. I had been frustrated with meditation for years and asked for further clarity on how to meditate.

Michael: Amoram, this is Michael. I still am not sure how to change my meditation practice. What am I doing wrong, what do I need to do? I mean, um...what should I expect?

Amoram: First of all beloved, you should drop your expectations. You should be in a state of curiosity. You should quiet your mind, focus on simple words and phrases, like "detach...let go." At some point other more complex thoughts will return and disturb the silence. Notice those thoughts. Ask yourself, *"Why is this thought so important?"* Then you should remind yourself of your goal and again attempt to quiet your mind. At first this will be difficult. A chattering unruly mind is the habit you have developed. I am not just talking about Michael here; this is the case with everyone. You have made certain things important in your world. By this practice of stilling the mind you will discover what those things are. Those things disturb your peace, even if they are exciting. If you make quieting the mind and letting go of excessive thought more important within your being then you will find the peace you are seeking.

Michael you have a tendency to think too much. This is not new information for you, you have been told this many times. You need to learn to quiet your mind and feel what is in your heart and emotions. As you pay attention to how you feel you can determine which thoughts feel good and which ones do not. You will not notice how you feel if you keep your mind so busy. And especially with you there is much excess energy moving through you. A walking meditation out in nature would be more helpful for you at times. Get out and move your body to release that excess energy. This will allow your mind to become still and then you will be able to hear the voice of the Master inside of you.

This was the first group that we went to after I had begun smoking pot. I was a bit worried that Amoram might ask me to deal with my addictive nature, or even tell me my meditations practice was lacking due to my pot smoking. I felt great relief that he left this issue alone.

Amoram did something unusual, he asked us to return the next day for another session. He told us that he wanted to quickly create a deeper bond in this particular configuration of people who were meeting. Then on March 4th 1996 he gave the following lecture.

> Today we will focus on creativity, and specifically, "How is it that I can create what I want and need for myself?" Yes, we know that a spiritual person should not be selfish and should be busy creating for another. Isn't that what all the religious people say? But we will tell you this, unless you are willing to be selfish long enough to create for yourself you will have nothing to offer another. You will only engage in a battle of taking energy which will deplete both yourself and the other. You must give from your excess not from your essence. You must be willing to create for yourself in order to have the energy and vitality to be of service to others. If you have not created peace in your own life, how can you offer peace to another? If you have not created abundance in your own life, how can you offer abundance to another?
>
> You must be consciously present to create. Being scattered and unfocused will not produce the desired result, you cannot create while being absent. You must be focused in the now moment of today.
>
> Each of you are very masterful creators in one area of your life or another. For Michael creating jobs is very easy, but for others it is a constant struggle. Why is this? And for Michael there are other areas of his life where he hasn't a clue how to create this or that. So we ask each of you to contemplate, "Why is it that in this one area I can create masterfully and in this other area it is a struggle?" Ask this question around your hot issues and be with the feelings that come. Ask us to come and comfort you and enlighten your mind in this process, we will come, we will be there.
>
> Pay attention to your feelings. They have much to tell you. Good feelings tell you that you are moving towards your highest good and bad feelings tell you that you are moving away from it. With that in mind how do you suppose fear and guilt affect your creations? We agree that fear and guilt are great motivators, but they leave you blind and attempting to create in the dark. Creating from a place of joy and love is far more pleasant and much more powerfully creative. There is light in this energy and the way is made clear. Assistance from seemingly outside forces arrive in various and amazing ways.
>
> What are your motivators? What motivates you to create? It is time for you to begin asking yourself this question. Not just once, but on a regular basis until your awareness of the answer is constant. Do you create because you will be destitute if you do not create a job? Do you

create to avoid punishment or coming off as the bad guy? Or do you create because you know that you are God and for the joy of expressing your Divine Self in a specific way? We suggest the latter beloveds; create to make your hearts sing![1]

There are unpleasant activities in your lives, ones you would rather do without, yet many times these can lead you to joy. Most of the unpleasantness is due to your ego and the way you think about the activity, rather than the activity itself. Yet still there are those activities that are simply unpleasant. For example, you can find great relief and joy after having an unpleasant conversation that you have been putting off. And if you can let go of your ego, let go of your judgments, to let it simply be a conversation about what is and how you feel and what you want, then it might not be unpleasant at all.

Keep your heart open. Keep your heart open even in the most difficult of situations. If you do then your Spirit is able to assist you in a way you are sure to recognize, in a way that will bring tears of joy to your eyes. You do not have to deal with the challenges of life alone beloveds. This apparent separation is a creation of the ego, the result of forgetting that you and everything outside of you is God. Instead forget the idea of "I" and that of, "I must do this alone." Come to recognize the "We" that you are and that surrounds you at ALL TIMES. Yes ALL TIMES, you are surrounded and infused by Spirit at all times.

To be a brilliant creator you must pay attention to the energies that surround you. You must come to know where the depleting energies come from and where it is that you are infused with energy. What physical activities, which thoughts, which people, which places? How does it feel to be in the city as opposed to being out in nature? In the city you have all of the fears, worries, and the striving to rise above by standing on backs and necks of others. In nature you find the feeling that "All is well." Do you spend too much time in the company of others or do you give yourself time alone for contemplation and meditation? How does each activity feel? How much time is appropriate to engage in each of these activities? In order to create you need to infuse yourself with energy, life giving energy. What music are you listening to? What are you reading? What are you watching on TV or at the movies?[2] How do these things make you

---

[1] I tried for many years to write this book out of financial necessity. It was very difficult and slow going. Today I am writing it because I know what a great benefit and joy it will bring to so many people. This awareness does make my heart sing. Consequently I am now filled with life force energy each time I sit down to work on this book.

[2] Consider the events of 9/11 and how much it was like America's favorite kind of movie, violent and destructive and vengeful. The things we read or view cause our minds to focus; it is with the focus of our mind and thoughts that we create. Thus, it should be obvious that

feel? Are you energized or depleted? You must be conscious and present for this, you cannot discern these things if you are absent.

You must also become aware of the timing. At one point in your life an energy, an activity, a person, place or thing, may be depleting while at a later time it might be uplifting and energizing. And you too may find that the reverse is true. In order to create consciously and deliberately you must discern and not hold on too tightly to the learnings from the past. You must be available to feel in the now and present moment what is helpful to you and what is harmful.

...

We observe that you dear Kathryn are creating a new relationship with your body. This is what you are focusing on at this time. It would serve you best to allow all other creative projects to expand from this place of creating a new body. This is your current practice, a Goddess-like practice of creating bodies. You are in the process of creating a new body for yourself, is it not true? (Yes Amoram, I want to create a new healthy body.) We understand this beloved. You are letting go of what you no longer desire, but you must also purposefully focus on and create that which you desire to be. It will be much more fun if you can shift to seeing it in this way. This may take you longer than the few days it took to create the world, but indeed (laughter) this is still a creative endeavor. In time and with play, you will come up to speed. (laughter)

...

And for you Michael, one of the greatest blockages for you is your judgment. So we ask you to be creative with your judgment. (laughter) Beloved, you will have such fun with this exercise, if you allow it. You see, you can either judge yourself for your judgments or you can laugh and play with them in order to diffuse the energy they contain. You can catch yourself in judgment and say, "Wait let me first put on my robes and get out my gavel. Ah, now that's better. Bang! Bang! Bang! I declare that court is now in session!" (laughter) Allow yourself to play with your judgment. If you find that there comes a day where court is in session all day, then so be it. This is creativity at its finest! In this way you can see how easily your judgments are merely a stance and that as easily as you create this different position to stand in, you can also create a non judgmental

---

we must take great care in our choice of entertainment as it provokes us to focus our thinking in certain ways. In other words...Is destruction what you wish to create?

position as well.[1] (Okay) This will be much fun for you Michael (laugher).

It is interesting that Amoram was asking me to deal with my judgmental nature, he did not ask me to deal with my addictive nature. The very desires of marijuana and alcohol usage were moving through me during this period of time, I was drinking and smoking pot, yet Amoram was commenting on my judgmental nature. It was this judgment that I noticed was at the root of my paranoia while I was high on pot. No one else knew I was smoking…so whose judgment was it I was really facing? Previously Amoram asked us to face our dark sides. Something is dark because it is kept hidden and separate from the light. We face our darkness by looking at it, by bringing the light to it, and then choosing how to respond to it from a place of awareness. Not by exposing ourselves to others but by exposing ourselves to ourselves, clearly and honestly. This desire to smoke pot and drink alcohol was in me. As I allowed myself to become more natural, this desire came to the surface. I knew that it was more important to face my judgments about what I was doing. I also knew that right now I needed to be exploring my dark side just as I was doing. I had fear mixed in with all of this as well as jubilation at the new freedom I had found—the freedom to break out of the box.

---

[1] In those days judgment was ever present and I thought I would never be rid of it. It used to consume my mind for hours on end. Now judgment comes, I recognize it, and it goes all fairly quickly. Today I fully understand how destructive judgment is, and I leave it alone. I have learned to choose, discern, and how to allow.

Memories

In the following transcript, which came in the next month, Amoram talks about memory. Given that Kathryn and I were facing such a big health issue I was expecting something in these channelings that would give us specific advice for healing her cancer quickly. I expected Amoram to point out what we were doing wrong, why was it we were not getting an instant result with Kathryn's health and recovery. Yet Amoram continued to teach us about energy and life and creativity and…memory?!? I just could not understand how all of these things were related to solving our current health crisis and other physically manifest experiences. In time I finally got it…now it seems obvious to me. I watch most other people flounder around in ignorance. As we did then, I see people now, who want to know which surgery, which pill, which technique will cure what ails them. The ignorant don't want to hear of this spiritual mumbo-jumbo about energy and awareness. Yet no permanent change can occur without it.

[1] On this fine spring day we will discuss the subject of memory, what it's about and how to use it. If you think about it you will realize that most people consider memory to be an energy from the past. Something that is finished or complete. Unmalleable, unchangeable. But as we have discussed before, although there is a cycle of time, in reality there is no such thing as past. So it is that which we call our memory is also a part of our now moment. Our past is part of today, part of what is happening right now. The past, like memory, is another dimension. You should begin to engage your memory as if you were entering another dimension, as a place you might visit. It is a place you have been before, and it is familiar. But there are also things within memory that you have not seen before, things which can be tools to help you in this now moment.

This is not to say that you are going to go and live in the past or in that memory. We are not advocating that you even use memory as a place of comparison between the past and the present. But it is to be willing to experience your memories with an open heart and mind.

Do not allow yourself to be deceived by calling your memories your past. This will only create distance between you and your memories. In truth your memories are living things. That which you learned and experienced in your memories can be called upon in your daily life, in your now moment, to be utilized in your creative endeavors. To understand the value of this, you need only contemplate the condition

---

[1] April 3rd, 1996

of one who has a disease that affects their memory. There is a flow of energy between your memories and this now moment, without which you would be crippled and impotent.

While looking at memory in this light it is easy to see the tragedy in being unwilling to face your memories. Being unwilling to look, being unwilling to utilize the tools and the learnings, is worse than having a disease. If you are not willing to look how will you ever discover the gifts that you missed in what you call your past? You should be willing to be with all of your memories. This will give access to what many would call your soul history. For the dimension of memory contains more than just this lifetime alone, it also contains those gems from all of your lifetimes. Your memory is a like a grand library. You may enter it and take down vast volumes of information and experience. And yet many have chosen to put a limitation on remembrance by holding on to beliefs they are unwilling to bring to the light of truth. Is this not a disease?

Everyone is familiar with the concept of pain and trauma being stored in the cellular memory of the body, correct? But why is it that you have jumped to the conclusion that only pain and suffering is stored there? Could it be that there is also joy and masterful experiences stored there as well? Shouldn't you consider taking a look to see? If you do you just might find that there is a great deal of your soul history stored in your physical structure as well. Make it your desire to read this history as if it were an open book.

Beloveds, many people are afraid that they might discover that they were once a mass murderer or something else equally distasteful. So they choose to use this as an excuse to turn away from their memories. Yet wouldn't such a memory help you to generate compassion and understanding rather than judgment towards another in this now moment. Wouldn't such a memory help you to discover how your programming came to be the way it currently is, and help you to have compassion and understanding for yourself? Wouldn't such memories help you to avoid paths you have already explored and found empty of life, substance and satisfaction?

The dimension of memory is changeable. This statement will surprise many and intrigue others. But it is true. As you become aware of your soul history, as you change who you are now, and how you think and focus your attention, the changes that occur within you ripple out to the concentric circles of who you are in the various dimensions of memory. You are not static beings beloveds. Just as the food and chemicals you now consume flow through your body and affect all of your organs and limbs, so do the thoughts and changes in your programming flow through the entirety of your dimensional experience affecting who you are in each and every dimension. With such understanding you can even repattern your very DNA.[1] In this way you may rid yourself of any generic tendency towards any disease.

Abuse is abundant and rampant in this world, but how much more sad is self-abuse? Yet many people use their memories as an excuse for self-abuse. "Oh what a terrible thing I have done. I can never live this down. I will never be worthy of such and such. This is how I am. I am stuck with this way of responding to others." Yet those very same memories can be used instead as a means of understanding. You can use it to recognize the vibration of a path you no longer wish to travel and set your sites firmly on a path you are now consciously choosing. The memory was nothing more than a stepping stone, a small event in your infinite life. You should be willing to ask yourself, "What truly was hurt, rejected or pained? How was it that it really happened? What was it that caused me to close myself off to my memories? Am I not still here? Were the wounds real? Or do I have more power to change things than I ever thought possible?"

You must remember yourself. Re-member, to take what you have separated into many pieces and reconnect the various members. Do this with love and the conscious understanding that you are once again remembering that you are a Master, that you are God, and that you contain all of the talent, wisdom, and abilities of God.

There is nothing so terrible that you cannot remember it. There is nothing so bad that it will annihilate you if you recall it. God has already witnessed and experienced where you have been and what you have done. There are no hidden corners even though you hide your head in the sand. It is time now for you to re-member yourself and come to know the beauty and grace that resides within you.

I found it interesting that Amoram talked so much about facing the shadow and darkness, embracing it and re-membering it. Now, as I am writing this book, I understand the awareness that comes with remembering. At the time of this channeling, I was frightened of what I was remembering. Yet I was beginning to see the pot I was smoking more as a tool than as a problem in my life. The "problems" in my past were due to my mental problems and not to the pot or other drugs I used. The drugs I used only brought my mental state to the surface and exaggerated it to be more easily seen. Those problems from the past would bleed into my now moment, they would become part of my now experience, anytime I fell back into the old patterns of judging myself for

---

[1] Kryon gives a lot of information about repatterning our DNA including a bit of the physics involved. You can find out more by visiting http://gr8Wisdom.com/Books/Kryon (proper capitalization is important when locating this website)

smoking. If I viewed my desire to use pot through the eyes of that man who quit smoking pot ten years prior, through the mentality of the 12-step programs I attended, then I experienced the pain that came from that vantage point and feared my life would again tailspin out of control into more suffering. Yet when I focused on who I was and the new intentions with which I lived and created my life, marijuana became a powerful tool that soothed me and opened me up to greater levels of awareness.[1]

By this point, a few years had passed since the last past life memory came up for me. It was no longer necessary for more past life memories to come to the surface. There were other memories that were more important, and they were coming...of this lifetime, of family and friends and eras of my own life and how my energy was in that era and how it changed from one era to another. There was a part of me, the part that was looking for excitement, that wanted to get at more fantastic memories of past life experiences. But practicality was becoming more important; I wanted mental and emotional healing and I was seeking to know God more clearly. Thus, the memories that came to me were a perfect match to my needs. At the time of this channeling, some of the events that were occurring were frightening, and confusing; at the time I would have liked it to have been different. Now, as I am remembering those times to write this book, I understand that they were the foundation that my present awareness is based upon, I would not change a thing. Just the process of remembering while rereading this past channeling changed me in this book writing moment and it will affect my future.

At the end of April, the Microsoft group I was working for reorganized and let me go. I didn't mind; dealing with Kathryn's health had been extremely stressful so I welcomed the break from work. Amoram commented on this in our next apprenticeship group.[2]

> Michael is a master at creating work. His recent circumstances has given him the chance to demonstration this in a grand way. Insteady of saying, "What a terrible thing this is. I have lost my job. What will I do? Those horrible people how could they lay me off." Michael has instead embraced this as an opportunity for play. There is a lightness in his energy and he is creating his next situation without panic. He is aware that other work will come, in the right timing, and that all is

---

[1] I am not promoting the use of marijuana or any other drug...however, if you have chosen this as your path, or someone you love has done so, I am suggesting that you look at the illnesses of the mind rather than what is being put into the body as the cause of any difficulties that may arise. By blaming problems on the drugs, you are only side tracking yourself from the real issues.

[2] May 7th, 1996

in divine order. What another would perceive as a humiliating obstacle, Michael has perceived differently. And so it should be with all of the circumstances and events of your lives.

My break from work was not long lived; a few weeks later near the end of May, I got a job with Asymetrix Corporation; it was another part time working from home contract. Finding this one was easy too. There have been many times that I tried for part time and working from home contracts, just because I liked the idea of it, but they were too difficult to find…actually I never found any. Yet this time when we really needed for me to be working from home, finding these kinds of jobs was easy. God always gives us what we need, often it is what we consciously want, but sometimes it is not, but even then it is what we need.

Healing Separation between Healers

We were not satisfied with the outcome of our advertising in the *New Times*; too few people responded. We had enough clients to pay our advertising costs, but we were expecting much more from it than that. We noticed a lot of people advertising how their system was the latest or greatest form of energy work, almost indicating that other systems did not work. This motivated Kathryn to write the following article for the *New Times*...

Healing Separation between Healers by Kathryn

It is clear that focus in the Reiki community has been bringing forth the energy of separation between Reiki practitioners and teachers. It is disconcerting to see and hear different claims of how each type of Reiki is more powerful, faster, takes less time to learn, and is better than another's form. I wish to state that the form is not nearly as important as the intention behind it. And the intention of wanting or needing to be better than others has nothing to do with healing. That energy comes from the ego, where someone has to win and someone has to lose. It is not based in the heart of knowing that there is room for all to join the circle.

Reiki's philosophy is very simple. (Not easy, but simple.) "It is to speak the truth without judgment or blame. It is the willingness to recognize prejudice in one's self and replace it with truth and love. It is respect for the right of others to form their own values and beliefs. Placing greater value on learning from experience and inner guidance than on the teachings of an authority. It is promoting a friendly cooperation with other Reiki practitioners and masters and alliances and schools. It is to bring forth the energy of unconditional love."

By creating separation in stating that one's way is better than another's is to muddy the waters for all who enter this stream of consciousness. It is not so important how each healer brings their own unique gift of treatment or teaching. It IS important however that we each bring forth the energy of respect and honor for all who have stepped forth as healers. And for each one of us to be in appreciation for the many gifts that each bring to the table. To be willing to come to the table and to co-create the space of Namaste, which means I honor the place in you in which the entire universe dwells. I honor the place in you which is love, of truth, of light, and of peace. When you are in that place in you, and I am in that place in me—we are one!

This is where true healing begins—inside each one of us. It is futile to attempt to heal any other until we are first willing to look inside ourselves. Where is our motivation? I mean where is our true motivation? It is all well and good to speak the words, "I am here as a healer to assist others." But judging or condemning anyone else along the way has nothing to do with healing. How can a Reiki practitioner claim to heal others while causing injury to the Reiki community by practicing elitism?

Mother earth is inviting all those to come forth who choose to be a part of the healing force that is so needed and welcome now. And when one claims to be a part of this healing force, and yet spends energy stating that theirs is the best and/or the only way, is to separate themselves from the circle. For in the end, it doesn't matter how many more clients one saw than another. Or that one brought in more money than another. The only thing that will matter is, *What was the quality of our love?*

The division that has been created in the Reiki community is confusing to those who have a desire to bring this energy into their lives. For Reiki masters to attempt to put down other Reiki masters by claiming that their way is better is child's play. And more importantly, we are losing valuable gifted souls who desire to enter this circle, but won't participate in this energy. And so, until we heal our own separation, how can we truly teach anyone else to heal theirs?

This does not have to be a time of contraction into the consciousness of lack and the need to be better. It can, instead, be a time to choose expanding this wonderful circle, and of allowing each the freedom to fly its own exquisite flight. For this allows each student to choose what is perfect for them in that moment. And for the student to be the teacher, as the teacher is also the student. And if it is time for students to choose in their apprentice another instructor; it is to remember that one is not better than any other. It is that all colors of the rainbow are necessary. Even though you may not like a certain color, it is not to say that all others should not like that color. Or that it is any less valuable in the full spectrum of light. For our purpose is only to bring the light of love and joy to each situation. Not to be the judge and jury about which colors we bring light to. For it is not up to us to determine that anyone needs to be anywhere other than where they are. For each is a sacred space, and each human is capable of bringing forth love and light to whatever experience they have chosen.

I recently experienced first-hand that out of darkness can come great light. After extensive surgery for ovarian cancer and a grueling six months of chemotherapy, I discovered a deeper meaning of God's ever presence in whatever color of the rainbow we are experiencing. No matter how dark it may seem. Although this has been the most difficult year of my life, it has also been the most blessed. My healing included traditional and nontraditional medical treatments. It was also about my willingness to receive love from the most unexpected places. So many people who do not consider themselves "healers" brought me immeasurable assistance through heart-felt concern and love. Their gifts were just as important to my full recovery as the "healers" medical assistance I received. Thank you, God, for allowing me to realize that we are all healers, that there is not just one way.

So I ask all healers, are you willing to embrace the love of unity that brings us together in that sacred space where healing truly begins? Are you willing to listen to your heart as you allow the circle to expand from exclusiveness to inclusiveness? I invite you, encourage you, and welcome you to walk together in the light that we share.

Radiating and Reflecting

Kathryn's health had improved dramatically. She had plenty of energy and was back to eating well again. Her blood tests showed a decrease in cancer fighting enzymes, which indicated there was less cancer present in her body. We were happy and optimistic that this trend would continue. Kathryn was ill for so much of her life that whenever she had any energy, she would spend it as fast as she could. I could see that she would be stable and healthy, and then later wear herself out so badly that I was again afraid for her health. Amoram addressed this in our next apprenticeship group. But the most interesting part about this meeting was the topic of "Radiating and Reflecting." Here is the transcript.[1]

> For today beloveds we will focus on two qualities of energy; radiating and reflecting. Radiating is a creative and powerful expression of energy which comes from deep inside. Reflecting is a reactive expression of energy that results from the energy coming from another person or event. Radiating is much more powerful than reflecting and is a result of being clear and aware of one's own self-sufficiency. Reflecting is a much weaker expression leaving a person at the whims and fancy of others and outside circumstances. With practice; introspection, contemplation, and meditation, one can develop and improve their ability to radiate and come to consciously choose when to reflect and when to radiate.
>
> Let us explain...when you are reflecting you are mirroring the behavior of another, or you are witnessing your behavior mirrored back to you by another individual. This is ego behavior that we are referring to. Behavior that has a belief in separation as it's source. Reflected energy is an expression of your habits of thoughts, your programming, and it needs to be seen so that you can understand the stances you hold and the position you have put yourself in. When you are radiating you are expressing your inner God like nature, you are expressing your creativity. Not for the purpose of impressing another or for acquiring something you are lacking, but for the soul purpose of expressing who you are. Radiating is done from a place of love and joy.
>
> So the time has come for you all to begin to ask yourself, "When are the times, under what circumstances am I radiating energy and under what circumstances am I reflecting energy? When am I comfortable enough with who I am that I am naturally and spontaneously generating energy in a creative and loving way? How

---

[1] June 5th, 1996

can I heal myself such that I no longer reflect my ego?" Beloveds, the purpose of this personal inquiry is to understand in what situations you retain your power. You can learn from this and expand your awareness of your wholeness such that you are reflecting less and radiating more. You can catch yourself in your smallness, while you are reflecting and immediately stop reflecting and begin radiating. It can be a conscious choice. As a healer or teacher you may even consciously choose to reflect in order to show another something that needs to be seen, but by doing this consciously and lovingly you are actually radiating energy. The distinction of these two energies in this case revolves around whether it is conscious or not and whether the energy comes from fear or from love. And it is for you to reflect on your actions carefully to understand which position that you are truly coming from. (laughter) Use your feelings beloveds to assist you. You will feel good, peaceful and loving if you are radiating and you will feel bad, agitated, superior or inferior if you are reflecting.

You have all had experiences where you are radiating the creativity that is within you and others have reacted by reflecting certain qualities, qualities that may appear slightly or even significantly distorted. It is at these times that you need to become aware that this has nothing to do with you, but that it has to do with the other person and how they have developed their personality. A common example of this is when someone is spouting off how you are, or rather how they perceive you to be, and it bears no resemblance to you whatsoever. None at all. You can look at that person and understand that they are describing themselves rather than you. It may be that they are describing a great fear they hold of being a victim of such a person as they are describing, or it may be that they indeed hold and directly express the energy they are projecting on to you. In either case they are describing their own inner state of being. For example, they may be calling you a liar and enumerating the ways in which you lie, when indeed it is they who are untruthful. Or it may be that they have been hurt many times by the lies of others and are hyper vigilant and paranoid about being lied to. Either way it is their energy that they are expressing. If you are clear in your own energy, and understand who you really are, then you can see past their outburst and understand the truth of their communication. It is for you to bring forth peace, love, gentleness and compassion. You are there to be of assistance as a healer and a teacher.

Now is the time to consider simplifying your lives beloveds. As life brings you change, as you feel yourself begin to contract, consider simplifying things in your life. There is no need for complications or struggle. It is not necessary to run around and fix this, or change that, or to bend over backwards trying to be all things to all people. At these times there is only the need for simplicity. Come back to the simple truth of who you are. Take a deep breath and come back to the understanding that all is well. That the outside is the same as the inside and that all events are offering you the opportunity to have what you have been asking for. For far too often you waste your energy trying to change the flow instead of going with it. To simplify is to go with the flow of Life instead of resisting it and shoring up all sorts of obstacles in protection of the fragile ego being that you have created. Breath is essential to mastering this. Sometime soon, take notice of your breath when you are calm and then again later when you are agitated. Notice that when you are calm, your breath is steady, deep and even. When you are agitated, your breath is short, haphazard and shallow. Slow your breath down, make it deep, even and steady and your mind will also calm down and become peaceful. This is simplicity beloveds. Compare this to running around and attempting to manipulate outer circumstances. Compare the difference in feelings and ask yourself, "Which feeling do I prefer?"

You see the complications in your life come from the fact that you are attempting to separate you from you. Although it is impossible to do this, you have created the illusion that it is so. Maintaining the illusion that this separation is real, is the real cause of your complications. It is simplicity itself to realize that you and all that you experience as outside of yourself is in reality truly One.

Imagine for just a moment what it would be like if you really and truly remembered and knew that you and everything outside of you were God. What would that be like? If someone treated you unkindly, knowing that they were God you would try to understand why. You would try to make what ever was wrong right. Wouldn't you? If the synchronicity of life prevented you from doing or having what you wanted, you would know it was God guiding and directing you on the path that is best for you, best for your place in the dance of life. If you really and truly remembered and understood that it was God you were entertaining with your thoughts, words and actions, would you be on your best behavior? Wouldn't everything you thought, said and did come from a place of love and a profound desire to serve? Holding this perspective is simplicity itself. For truth needs nothing to hold it up. It needs no support. Lies and illusions on the other hand can only exist with continuous support. It is this continuous expenditure of energy supporting that which is not real, and can never become real, that depletes you and makes you confused and ill. Thus it is simplicity itself to come to rest in the truth of who you are. Practice, breathe, be still and know that you are God.

Is this difficult to comprehend? Have you ever had someone you considered so special that you did anything for them? You even forgave them for any pain or suffering they caused? Somehow you found it easy in their case. That is the energy we are talking about. Seeing life and everything about it with such reverence that you are willing to stretch your mind and change your way of seeing life to make it all well. And this includes yourself too. If you really understood life this way you would treat your own self with the same love, reverence and tolerance. And once you gain enough wisdom from this practice you will then evolve to knowing when it was your job, and when it was not, to help correct life in a loving way, from the intention of love and light and harmony.

So it is your motivations that need to be looked at beloveds. For if you knew the motivations of the majority of those living in the world you would be very sad indeed. Most people are not motivated by love. They are not motivated by Spirit. It is for you to ask yourself, "Is this action I am about to take loving? Is this action harmless?" And the first point of action is your thoughts. Practice changing all of your thoughts such that they are loving and harmless and your actions will follow.

Along the lines of simplifying your life you will need to ask yourselves, "What is it that I want in my life? Where is it that I feel unfulfilled and am seeking fulfillment? And why is it that I feel that I need this thing, this person, or this event to be fulfilled?" Use discernment while asking these questions beloveds. Discern between the voice of Spirit and the voice of your ego and use restraint when it is your ego speaking. With practice you will find that most of the ego's desires will dissolve easily in the still, quite place within and that the voice of Spirit will become stronger and more powerful within you. This does not need to be difficult or boring, take your time and go slowly, but this should be your daily work and practice.

By living in this way you will naturally develop a deep and abiding respect for yourself and for all others around you. When you are motivated by love, when all of your thoughts, actions, words and deeds are motivated by love, then respect must follow. Once you have developed discretion, restraint, and respect then responsibility must follow. You will find yourself naturally, easily and automatically responding to life in a loving way. That is our definition of responsibility beloveds. **To be responsible is the ability to respond in love.** Being responsible is not a burden it is a quality that we are asking you to develop. To say, "I do not want to be responsible." Is to say, "I do not want to be conscious. I do not want to love or be loved." We are not telling you that to be responsible means you must answer to someone else for your actions, we are telling you that responsibility will occur naturally within you once you decide to simplify your life and make Love your primary motivation. Love of self, love of others and love for God which contains both self and all others.

So this is the practice. We know that you have something in your life that you want to change. And it is not changing. You keep practicing, and studying and praying for it to be different but it does not seem to change. This is because in some way this thing you want to change still serves you. With one hand you are pushing it away and with the other you are pulling it toward you. While even with your voice you are proclaiming your distaste, judgment, or rejection of said thing, you are energetically hanging on to it with all the power of your being. When you notice this struggle within you it is time to ask, "What part of this thing I do not want still serves me? In what way do I believe I cannot live without it?"

Often people use this as an excuse to forgo their spiritual practice, "This spiritual mumbo jumbo is a waste of time. I am not getting what I want." Is what they say. They change a single thought and expect results. What about the millions of other thoughts they hold? Do they not also require scrutiny? Do they not also need to change? There are millions of thoughts that you give time and energy to every day. If you create a habit of correct thinking, then you can run on automatic pilot until you feel negative emotion, at which point you have found a new pattern of thought that needs changing. This is where the work, exercise, and practice of changing thoughts begin.

So in the theme of simplifying your life, of making Love your primary motive, we are asking you dearest Kathryn to allow yourself to take rest. Do not judge yourself for your body needs this and your peace of mind needs this. You have a tendency to get caught up with your todo list. "I have so many things that need to be done, and even yesterday's list is not complete, so I must work even harder today." There is time for work and there is time for rest beloved. Make this a gift that you give to yourself, to the God within you. Allow yourself the time to digest your life's experiences. Allow your body the rest to rebuild its resources. For you are no longer in the recovery phase so much as you are in the rebuilding of your strength phase. And it is for you to discern between when to speak your truth to your family and when to remain silent. We can feel that they are pulling you back into their dramas. Now that you are doing well they want to see you as the same weak victim they love to torment. They have no desire to recognize how you have transformed or the power you have acquired. It is for you to discern how much energy you have to offer towards this endeavor and how much you wish to reserve for your own sustenance. Go into your knowing and listen.

Your relationship with Michael too is going through many changes beloved. Michael is again moving out into the world to engage in other opportunities and activities.[1] This is necessary and purposeful for him. It is not for you to fill the space with so many activities as has been your pattern. Be actively doing as long as it brings you joy and make an equal time for rest. It is not for you to wait until Michael returns home to take your rest. That is far too stressful for even a healthy person to live this way. For you need the rest to rebuild your full strength. You also need the practice of giving yourself this necessity. You even need the practice in recognizing that rest is a necessity. (laughter) It is for you to let go of at least one activity per day.[2] You must get past the idea that these things "must be done." For there are many living in this world that never engage in the activities that you believe must be done. And joy is often present in their lives. So it is for you beloved to simplify your life with Love.

...

Simplicity for you Michael, is to cease trying to be all things to all people. As you reengage yourself with the world and find yourself being with more people, more energy, it is to watch that you do not deplete yourself. Do not let yourself become so involved in trying to be the best, or the greatest, or the one who has all of the answers. It is your pattern to use your accomplishments to put yourself in an elite position. It is not that you should not try, or should not learn, but it is not for you to be so out there. You are not to be up on the stage. It is for you to achieve for the purpose of developing your skills and for you to be aware for your inner experience. You have nothing to prove, except that you do not need external validation. You know who you are and it is for you to simplify your life by ceasing to seek outside approval. This seeking actually depletes you and leads you to seek outer approval even more; a vicious circle. Simplify your life by retaining your vital life force energy. It is yours, you have gathered it...you have earned it. Do not diminish it by attempting to exchange your valuable energy for the worthless approval of others.[3]

Amoram's comments to me were accurate...although I had mostly stopped the arrogant behavior and thinking, this need to be the best was still very strong in me. I was coming to realize I did not need to prove anything; there were times I was at peace with this realization, but more often than not, this old habit of competing would unconsciously kick in.

---

[1] In a few weeks time, I would return to Massage School.

[2] The way I saw it, Kathryn needed to let go of about ten activities per day.

[3] Many years later, once I came to love and accept myself, this need to compete left automatically. My automatic reaction now is to back off and let others stand out and compete. Because I know who I am, the opinions that other people hold of me are irrelevant. Because my intention is to be loving and harmless in all of my actions, I can walk through life with confidence and not care what others think.

For the first few months after receiving this advice from Divine Mother and Amoram, I became a little more diligent at watching for this. Each time I caught myself competing, which came up fairly regularly at school, I backed off and reminded myself that I have nothing to prove. I waited to give other students a chance to answer questions or be the one to do a task. I did not debate when I thought someone else was wrong, I even let go of the thought that they were wrong. A few times I noticed that this was difficult to do; I noticed that I really did believe that I needed to impress someone. When this happened, I went further by trying to understand what I hoped to get from this person. Ultimately my inner questioning led to the same conclusion, I wanted to know that I was okay, appropriate, and worthy to take up the space that I occupied. Yet no one I met, no one, had the ability to grant me a certificate of worthiness...no one but me.

Many times I have read about reflecting, or mirroring as some called it, but I never really understood it. I got so much from this lecture that I listened to the tape in the car on the way home and finished listening to it when we got home. I had a breakthrough in my understanding. Later in the day I observed the crazy woman next door abusing her dog. I went into rageful judgment of her behavior. In my mind I even brought up other offenses she had committed that did not involve her dog. After about five minutes of this I noticed what I was doing. Actually it was the uncomfortable churning sensation in my stomach that I noticed first. I did not feel good at all. Then when I asked myself what the pain was about I realized that I was hanging out in the court room again with my robes on and gavel in hand.

So then I asked myself, *In what way am I reflecting her energy?* Because I knew that I was not "radiating from a place of love and joy," as Amoram had said, I knew that I was mirroring, that I was reflecting something back to this woman next door. By simply asking myself this question, I received the answer: *You are reflecting back to her the harm she is doing. However, because you are emotionally involved with this energy, perhaps it is wise to also ask, 'In what way is she a mirror for me?' The answer of course is that she is reflecting back to you your own judgment of yourself, for how you have treated animals, especially how you have mistreated dogs.*

I knew I was receiving wise counsel. I did have judgment of myself in this regard. There were many times in frustration, usually from being hungry, tired, or after arguing with Kathryn, that I would kick Ali if she did not move out of my way fast enough. I always regretted it, I judged myself severely for this. I tried to create enough resolve to never repeat it, but I had to admit that I was not certain I would never do that again. I felt unreliable in this way and I judged myself for this. I had no idea what I could do about it. Then I realized...I had to love myself anyway. Even if no one else loved me because of this quality, I had to love myself. Then I found it easy and natural to love the woman next door. Immediately I felt compassion for the anger, frustration, and confusion she must be in to abuse her dog in this way. It became clear to me that I needed to send love her way, not anger and judgment.

Facing Rejection

I found the work I was doing at Asymetrix interesting. It was not my usual sort of work with PCs; this time I was writing software for a portable handheld device. The device was missing some of the basic database tools that we would find on a PC so my job was to create a database and an interface to it so that the other team members could easily get at the data. Because the task was so repetitive, I wrote a rather clever tool to automate the job. The project leader did not like my implementation, ended my contract, and took the work away from me.

This was the first time I was fired from a software job. On one hand I felt confident in the approach I took to solve this engineering problem, so I felt I should defend myself and my solution. I wanted to go to the development team and show them why I had done it this way and why it was so good, but because Amoram had recently warned me about competing, I decided to back off and accept the abrupt end of my contract. Then I started seeing this as a blessing, it was the Universe's way of giving me a break from work during the summer. I decided to just go to massage school and take a few months off from working. Neither Kathryn nor the unemployment office liked this idea, so I had to go through the motions of applying and interviewing for jobs.

This was an enlightening process for me, one where I got to discover just how powerful intention is. I did everything I normally would do to get a job, but I was getting nowhere. I did not want a job, but I applied for appropriate sounding jobs like I was supposed to do only to satisfy the unemployment office and Kathryn. However, to satisfy Kathryn I had to apply for more than the minimum of three jobs required by the unemployment office, I had to apply for ALL appropriate advertised jobs. Some weeks I sent out as many as ten resumes. I had a few telephone interviews, but they were either not the right match for me, or I was not right for them. I had one live interview, they even offered me the job, but the work they had for me was not exciting enough to make me want to wake up in the morning to go into the office, so I turned it down.

With the end of August came a few days of cold rainy weather. I began to think more seriously about finding a job, but still I did not feel like taking one. Then we had a few more weeks of warm sunny weather, still I had no motivation. Then, in the second week of September, it became obvious that summer was over. Our budget was also beginning to suffer, thus I became motivated to find a job. Within a few days of firming up my intention to go back to work, I had a job again.

Another interesting thing happened during this process. The reason I got fired from the Asymetrix job was for the way I wrote a specific piece of code. I was proud of that code so I used it at the interview as an example of the work I was capable of. A few days into working my new job at Microsoft, my boss told me that he was impressed with that specific piece of code and the ingenuity it took to create it. It made me stand out amongst the other top contenders for the job. Amoram, indeed all of the Masters, was teaching us that our reality was in our minds. Someone with less experience than I might have taken that firing, or any of the other difficulties I had with jobs, and come to the conclusion that he was not worthy of being a software engineer, or that he needed to settle for any job he could find because his skills were not good enough. I, on the other hand, was reveling in the way I was learning to walk though fire; I was becoming so strong that nothing could shake my confidence.

Jumping back in time just a bit, back to June...I enjoyed my second quarter of massage school, especially once I did not have to work anymore. I had plenty of time for study and practice as well as time at the lake and walking my dog. I continued to smoke marijuana during this time period and was just a bit concerned that it would affect my studies and grades at school. However this proved not to be the case, I scored 95% or better in all of my tests, even though I smoked only an hour before taking them.

At the beginning of August, during one of the weekend workshops, I got to work with Marion, a woman who I found quite attractive. I felt that she was interested in me too. She liked my deep tissue technique, yet she was having difficulty with doing deep work herself. I offered to help her, she accepted, and we met up at her place to do an exchange. We enjoyed each other's company so much that we ended up working nearly three hours each on the other, thus we spent nearly seven hours together that day. I had the free time for this because Kathryn had gone to Portland for the day to visit her family.

Marion had breast reduction surgery as a teenager because her breasts grew too big and they were giving her back pains. These many years later she still had discomfort in the breast tissue. Normally she had a woman therapist who worked on her and massaged her breasts too. So it was not too difficult for me to talk Marion into letting me massage her breasts...actually it seemed to me that it was the other way around, like she led me into offering to massage her breasts. It seemed that by telling me the saga of her breasts, she was trying to get me to offer to massage them. Anyway, it happened...I massaged her breasts and she consented to it. Even though I was sexually interested in Marion, during the massage I did my best to keep it polite and professional. I kept my mind focused on healing and soothing her body rather than on any sexual fantasy.

That evening however was a different story. I began to fantasize about having an affair with Marion. It had been a long time since Kathryn and I had any kind of normal sexual life. Now that Kathryn was in better health, I had expected this to change, but it did not. Kathryn still had no sexual motivation. After a few days, my fantasies got the better of me, I wrote Marion a letter. In it I explained to Marion how difficult it had been for me with Kathryn being so ill. I told Marion that even if Kathryn was not able or interested in sex that I still had my own needs. In the letter I asked Marion if she would be my mistress, if we could have a secret affair.

Apparently this freaked Marion out. She showed the letter to the female founder and president of the school who asked me come to her office for a special meeting with her and two other teachers. Marion was not present. The president asked me to leave the school in a few weeks once I had finished the second quarter, the other teachers supported her. I objected to their decision. I agreed that I may have done something wrong as far as my wife was concerned, but that I felt that I had done nothing wrong as a massage practitioner. I was willing to leave Marion alone if she declined my invitation, I had no intentions of stalking her. Marion attended classes at night and I was a day student, so I might only run into her at weekend workshops, and only if she took the same ones as me. But they said that other people had complained about me too. When I asked who and what their complaints were, they refused to give me details. Whether or not this was true, that someone else had complained about me, I knew that I had not given anybody a reason for complaint.

This was a problem; how would I explain being kicked out of massage school to Kathryn? I hated the place I found myself in, a place I knew I created, yet I still hated it. I did a little research first, looking for a massage school that was close by. Then I decided to tell Kathryn that I had heard about this school from another student who was going there. It had the advantage of being closer to work and home, thus I could save commuting time. Also the schedule of this school was easier on working people. I told Kathryn I was too tired to face going back to work while attending massage school so I was trying to reduce my stress.

At first Kathryn asked only a few questions and did not raise any objections, but over the next few weeks she questioned my choice many times. Then one day she asked me, point blank, what was going on. She knew something was up. She knew I really liked the massage school I was going to. She wanted to know the real reason I was changing schools. She was insisting and not going to take another lie for an answer.

I had to tell her. I hated lying to her and now she was too suspicious. She knew I was lying. It took me a few minutes to muster up the strength. I was not sure if I was going to tell her about the pot and alcohol. I had to think about it for a moment. So first I told her the real reason I got kicked out of massage school. Kathryn remained calm but I could tell that she was shocked and hurt. While Kathryn was digesting this news, I was thinking about whether to reveal the rest or not. Then Kathryn demanded, "Is there anything else I need to know? You better give it all to me now. If I keep discovering more later down the track, I will be very angry. I want to know everything now!"

Then I told her the rest of the story. We sat and talked, rather calmly, for about an hour. I gave my best shot at justifying my behaviors. I tried to sooth Kathryn and re-assure her that I loved her and was not intending to leave her, it was just that I had needs to fulfill and she could not do it. Kathryn did not have much to say. She asked many questions. She would not accept the blame I tried to place on her for my choices, nor did she spend much time trying to make me out to be a horrible monster or anything. I knew that she was keeping a lot inside. She cried, but I knew there were deeper tears and rage inside that she was not letting out.

After we got tired of discussing the whys and hows of these events, Kathryn asked me to dump out my stash of marijuana and alcohol. I agreed, and we went upstairs, removed it from its hiding place, and flushed it all down the toilet. I felt like I did when I was a teenager and got caught doing some "very bad things." I felt unworthy to make any choice for myself at this point. Like I had to beg for forgiveness, and I felt deeply ashamed. I felt like I had to explain my actions in a way that others would somehow accept. This required twisting my own mind and thinking in ways that were not always honest. Fear makes us dishonest,[1] not only to others but to ourselves. We all take on dishonest behavior as a way to appease others. A "good" person thinks, *I am doing the right thing.* But not so deep inside, doing "the right thing" is dishonest to their self. It is not true to what they desire or really choose. If set free from the expectations of others, or under the cloak of secrecy, they dream in their mind or act out in the world these desires.

I wanted to be the way others[2] wanted me to be, but I wanted my life my way even more. I thought to myself, *I want the pot and I want other more interesting and diverse sexual experiences with other women...and I want to keep Kathryn in my life as my wife. I did not want the pain and suffering that we had just gone through with her illness. I went through it because I love Kathryn and would do anything I could for*

---

[1] See references to this in "A Course in Miracles." Fear makes us dishonest until we become Self-Aware, after which time we quickly move past fear into realization of the truth of our being. Then we can be honest or dishonest as the situation requires knowing we are in harmony with Divine will.

[2] Others as in Kathryn and our friends, society, anyone who would look at the outer circumstances and judge what happened.

her. I did my best, and my best was very good too...Kathryn often told our friends this...she often told me this. Many times Kathryn held me and cried, she told me how she could not make it though this experience without all of the wonderful support I had been giving her. She thanked me for my company and told me over and over how much she enjoyed it. It was just that I had to take care of myself too. Something had to give somewhere, a person can only hold so much in. It is just too bad that others don't like how I did this. And I don't deserve to be kicked out of massage school either!*

This kind of thinking was not going to make my current situation any better. These thoughts and desires had to be suppressed and I had to somehow act contrite and be sincere if I had any chance of keeping my wife. I lied to myself as well as everyone else in this respect. I was sincerely in emotional pain and suffering and guilt over "what I had done." I wanted to do the right thing. I wanted other people to like me. I wanted my wife to stay with me. I lied to myself, I judged myself, *What I did was wrong. I must be a better person and make it up to Kathryn and everyone else.* I used this position to plead for my life with Kathryn and friends to continue as normal.

Kathryn then proceeded to gather up my personal toiletry items, like shaver and toothbrush, and some of my clothes. She took them down to the guest bedroom and dumped them on the bed. She did not say a thing, she did not have to, I was the guilty one and she got to decide what happened next. I could not help but wonder, "Will she kick me out? Will she divorce me? What is going to happen next? I'm going to be really pissed off if I went through all of this illness with her for nothing...if she just kicks me out of her life for these trivial things!"

The next morning we had to get ready for a Reiki class that we were teaching. I wondered how effective we would be. Would our students get anything out of the class? We rose to the occasion. Throughout the class, I could feel a much nicer energy flowing between Kathryn and me than we were expressing the night before. The energy was so nice that it was a very big shock when the class was over, our students had left, and we were alone together again. All of that beautiful energy was gone, like it had been sucked out the door and taken with our students. Now we were left to suffer in this hell that we were co-creating together.

Kathryn decided she wanted me to move out. I was to find someplace new by Tuesday. "Tuesday!" I exclaimed, "How can I possibly find a place and move out in two days? I am also trying to find a job? We can't afford for me to take an apartment by myself...and who wants an unemployed man who is separating from his wife moving in with them? You have to give me more time, like a week...at least."

I began looking for an apartment and continued looking for a job. Again, I was only going through the motions, my intention to actually find either was nil. It seemed like my life was not my own. I wanted to be in massage school. I wanted to be having a happy loving life. I worked hard to earn this house I was being kicked out of. For many months I worked hard to save my wife's life, most of that time I worked a paying job and did the cooking and some of the other housework too. I paid the medical bills. It felt like it was my turn to get what I wanted and needed. I have done all of these things for Kathryn and still she is not happy, still she feels that she can mess with my life and my happiness. I was lost in my own pain and suffering. I found it very difficult to find peace in the first few weeks after I revealed my activities to Kathryn.

I went to an AA meeting. I am not sure what I expected to find there. I guess I just needed to go again. It certainly did not work for me anymore. I mean it could work for me if I went backward in my progress, and allowed myself to be hypnotized by their view on life and mind altering substances. But I knew theirs was only a mental stance, one I could no longer accept. My life was not unmanageable. It was the people in my life who were unmanageable. So I stopped trying to manage them and their feelings and gave them what they wanted. I stopped chasing tail and stopped getting stoned. I could quit because I did not need this stuff. I needed my wife and friends more. I needed peace more, so I was giving this stuff up and I gave up trying to change them. I also gave up going to twelve-step meetings.

As the week progressed, Kathryn and I got a little closer, but then she would shut the door. At one point she almost allowed me to stay at home in the guest room. But finally she insisted that I get out. I went to stay with Steven.

Steven was very supportive of me. He understood my situation and did not shame me in the least for my choices. He did not like the drama I ended up creating and he also understood Kathryn's perspective, but he did not judge me for these things. It was a bit odd for me to be living with him and Peter. I never really felt welcome at their home and I mostly blamed Peter for this. Years later Steven and I had a talk and I discovered that he too was not all that keen to have me around. Even though we were good friends, living in the same home with him was too much. It explained the energy I felt while living there.

I stayed only a few days with Steven and Peter and then went to San Diego for a week. It was my father's sixtieth birthday so I went to celebrate with my family and get away from Seattle for a week. I was honest with my mother and father and told them what had been happening; they were not impressed with my behavior. Yet they took me in and supported me as best they could. When I returned back to Seattle I returned to Steven and Peter's home.

Coming to Acceptance

After about five days, Kathryn decided I could come home and live in the guest room. She wanted me in her life but was not yet ready to share a bed with me. I was happy just to be invited back.

These events ended my massage school training. I was too busy trying to piece my life back together to consider continuing. It was not even discussed; I knew that if I continued with massage school, Kathryn would no longer be a part of my life.

Of course we had many talks with Amoram about all of this. In our first conversation Amoram addressed the real problem we were facing. Amoram asked Kathryn if she could fulfill all of my needs, especially my sexual ones. Even Kathryn was clear that she could not do so. Amoram told Kathryn that she should expect that I would try to get my needs fulfilled somehow. Amoram then went on to ask me if I thought having sex with others would satisfy my needs. Through our discussion Amoram helped me to realize that I would find an endless pit of desire, that what I was really looking for was a deep spiritual connection. He told us that when we were truly connecting in love that our sexuality could take us to new spiritual heights.

Amoram told us both that we were not free with each other in bed, that in some ways we each held back. He acknowledged the love we had for each other, but that we each needed to get in touch with what we were holding back. My first reaction was surprise because I felt like I gave it my all when it comes to sexuality. Amoram pointed out that there had been times where I had given much more of my energy in past casual sexual affairs than I had with Kathryn. When I thought about it that way, and I remembered a couple of those other experiences, I knew what he meant. At other times, I knew I could be free and so I was, and with Kathryn I knew in some ways I must limit the way I express myself and so I could not be free.

There were many ways in which I judged Kathryn's openness in bed. I loved her so I accepted this limitation, but deep inside, the comparisons between her and other lovers were there, so was judgment. Thus, by holding these kinds of limiting thoughts, my ability to physically express love was also limited. There was a part of me that missed my full sexual freedom; it would have been nice to experience it with Kathryn, yet somehow in my mind this did not seem possible. This was my darkside; it was calling for the light. It was forcing its way through the barriers of expectations and obligations, trying to find expression. My pain was due to suppressing it, not from expressing it. Now as I faced this issue with the help of Amoram, it did not seem so big and nasty. It seemed smaller and more manageable. It seemed liked we could find a way to shift this.

Amoram went on to explain that with the basic biological differences between man and women, these sorts of dramas will often play out. In general, women or feminine energy needs love and security to be sexually open and aroused; they tend to try and own and monopolize their men. Men or masculine energy is easily sexually aroused and that most men are not monogamous in their energy, that they often have fantasies going on in their mind. These differing urges and behaviors are largely a result of the physical biology of men and women; they are natural, but even still, conscious choices could be made.

Amoram told us there was little difference between holding sexual fantasies about other people and actually having sex with other people. It is the same energy. Actually, doing it just means it has been thought about more and given more creative energy. Thus, Amoram said, most men are not monogamous. This was congruent with everything else that Amoram, and others, had been teaching us. As time went on and I came to feel, experience, and understand energy better I realized the truth of Amoram's statements. When my mind is focused on something, it could be anything other than the person I am spending time with, then the energy between us is diminished, and this can be felt by the other person. If, while I am having sex with my partner, I am fantasizing about someone else, then the same wonderful depth of connection will not be there. The fantasies may create more sexual stimulation, but that is not the same energy as a loving connection. The same comments hold true for non-sexual interactions, if while I am spending time with Kathryn my mind is on another woman, or on some other project, Kathryn would not have the same experience of my presence with her.

So finally we were facing what had always been a source of separation in our relationship. Because it had become visible, because others had noticed, we were finding more discomfort with this, and we had a desire to do something about it. But what?

I was in total agreement with Amoram that Kathryn needed to focus on renewing and strengthening her physical health; it was not for her to attempt to fulfill all of my sexual fantasies, nor was it possible for her to do that. Amoram then suggested that I find some books on the topic of male sexuality and begin to understand myself better. He suggested that I take care of my own needs; he called masturbation "self-love." In these last few years that Kathryn and I had been together, I had not been masturbating very much. Before I met Kathryn, I did it regularly. Years earlier, I had thought there was something wrong with the pornographic magazines that I would use to achieve the visual stimulation that got me going. I felt it was wrong to support the exploitation of women. When I stopped buying and looking at pornography, I also stopped masturbating.

I went to the bookstore and found a couple of books about male sexuality. I also bought a couple of pornographic magazines. Amoram had not suggested this, nor did he say anything against it, but he did comment on a book of nude art that Bren had enjoyed. I did not find any nude art books that interested me so I figured pornography was just as good. At this point I figured that these girls that were posing for these magazines had free choice and were choosing to do this, so I was willing to enjoy.

From these books, I learned a few things that I did not already know. I enjoyed them, but the benefit I received was not so much from any specific thing or technique that it taught as it was from the topic in general. By exposing myself to these sexual topics, I came to clear out my own shame and guilt around my sexual desires. I came to realize that my sexuality was natural and normal. Still, I had the desire for sexual diversity; I wanted sex with other women. Even though I had to suppress this urge in order to keep my relationship with my wife, it was easier to suppress when I engaged in regular masturbation. No other suggestions were coming forth that would help me to deal with this issue, and Kathryn was not willing to allow me the freedom of sex with other women. Slowly, over the next six months, Kathryn's health continued to improve, and our sex life returned to its normal state.

During my last week of massage school, at the end of August, I began experiencing a great deal of pain in my knees, especially my left one. By September I was using a cane to walk. At first I worried that arthritis was beginning to set in.[1] Amoram told me my pains were due to all of the stress I had been undergoing, that it was an energy thing. Earlier in August, Kathryn began working with a naturopathic doctor to rid her body of any remaining traces of cancer. Amoram suggested that I try Kathryn's naturopath for treatment.

On my first visit, we discussed everything that had been going on for me. Your typical doctor may only talk about physical things, but the naturopath also wanted to know about emotional stresses. He knew about Kathryn's cancer but I also had to tell him about getting kicked out of massage school and that I had been smoking pot.

The doctor tested me for food allergies which turned out to be an educational experience for me. Using an electronic device and electrodes attached to my fingers the nurse was able to determine which foods I had

---

[1] This kind of thinking is so common...whenever people have something unusual happen in their bodies, they search their mind for what they know and try to label it. Then their subconscious begins transforming a short term energy shift into a long term disease.

allergies to. One at a time I would hold a small glass vile that contained a particular food substance, their electronic device would do its thing and the results were noted. Then we ran the test over again with a different substance, many times, until they had tried about forty different things. They found that I was allergic to wheat, milk products, turkey, broccoli, and the night shade vegetables which included tomato, potato, bell peppers (capsicum) and a few other things. I was allergic to cane sugar, but not beet sugar, nor dextrose, nor fructose. I was surprised that beet sugar was not a problem for me because I thought it was chemically the same thing as cane sugar; energetically it must be different.

I was skeptical of this process and the validity of the results it yielded. I asked Dr. Simpson why all of a sudden my body was allergic to these foods. Why is it that I could eat these things all of my life and have no problem but now he was blaming the problems I had with my knees on the food I was eating? I was especially concerned because he wanted me to stop eating these foods which included many of my favorites. Wheat and sugar is in just about everything that is processed and packaged in the USA, so I wondered how I was going to stick to this diet.

Dr. Simpson told me that the body is equipped to deal with stress, up to a certain point. As each new stress is added on, they begin to overwhelm the body's ability to deal with it and soon the final straw comes, the straw that breaks the camel's back. Something in the body just breaks down all at once and manifests as some sort of disease. He said if I could eliminate one or two of the stresses, I should get immediate relief, the foods that I was allergic to were the easiest thing to eliminate in that moment. He told me to cease eating all of these foods for the next two weeks, then to slowly begin assimilating them back into my diet one at a time and observe the results.

It was difficult to follow the doctor's advice, especially abstaining from the sugar. I loved candy, ice-cream and most things that contained sugar. We were eating take-away or meals out a lot of the time. We could not prepare our own food for the cost we could buy it at the Microsoft cafeteria[1] plus it was very convenient. I ate breakfast and lunch at work and even dinner I had been bringing home from work with me. For a while I had to go back to making most of my food myself. When I ate out, I had to ask what was in it. I had to be careful of things like soy sauce, because it had wheat in it, and sugar which was added to nearly everything as well.

It only took five days on my new diet for my knee pains to subside. I was surprised that it actually made a difference, but it did. By the time a few weeks had gone by I nearly forgot I ever had a problem.

---

[1] At that time the prices were much better than they were in 2004-2006 and so was the food.

Then one Friday evening Kathryn and I went out for our regular Friday night date; dinner and a movie. I decided to have mashed potatoes with my meal. Boy it tasted good, especially after those weeks of abstaining from my favorite foods. While we were walking from the restaurant to the movie theater, which was in the same shopping complex, my knee began to hurt. It was in so much pain that I was limping again and we had to stop at the car so I could get my cane from the trunk. I was surprised that those potatoes could cause me that much pain, and so quickly too. But it was the only thing I ate that was against my diet. It took about thirty six hours, until Sunday evening, for the pain to go away and for me to be free of the cane again.

After about four more weeks, I slowly began trying small portions of the restricted foods. In the beginning I had the same difficulties, but later my body gave me less painful reactions to these foods. I remained on this restricted diet for about nine weeks when I discovered that I could eat normally again. All during that time, I was receiving energy treatments from Brenda and counseling sessions with Amoram. My physical recovery coincided with my emotional recovery. I was feeling much better about myself and my life, and Kathryn's health continued to improve.

In December, just a week before Christmas, I came into work only to find out that the project I was working on was canceled. I was disappointed because we were working on a software installation tool; anyone who installs software on Windows would have used this tool. It would have been the first large scale commercial software package that I had written. I could have told people, "I wrote that." But another team of developers, in a totally different Microsoft group, had also been working on a software installation tool. Unfortunately Microsoft decided to continue development of the other tool and scrapped the one I was working on…now I was unemployed again.

I was so disappointed that I did not even feel like collecting my things to take home. Every other time I got laid off, I collected my things right away and went home. There were about five boxes of stuff, and normally I would just get it over with so I would not have to return. But for some unknown reason, on this day, I did not feel like doing this. I went home and left the packing for the next day.

When I returned around eleven o'clock the next morning to collect my stuff, I ran into Saud, he was the manager of a different Microsoft project. Saud had a job that would last four or five weeks that he asked me to do. He needed to get it started right away but he was short on staff due to the holiday season. By that time I had already accepted the fact that I was out of a job. I had adjusted my mind to having a few weeks off over the Christmas holidays. Yet I could not turn this job down; if Kathryn found out she would throw a fit. So this new job offer came as a bit of a disappointment. However, it was easier to readjust my mind once again than it was to pack up my stuff, take it home, only to return with it all again the next day. I don't like packing and moving things, so I marveled at how the Universe continued to look after my every need; even in matters that seemed trivial like this.

In January of 1997, after they had a chance to review the work I was doing, Saud offered me a job as a permanent Microsoft employee in his group. This was the third time I received a job offer from Microsoft. A few years ago, when Malcolm asked if I wanted to convert from being a contractor to being an employee working for the Exchange group, I did not even ask how much money they would pay, but this time I thought I would like to find out before turning it down. I was shocked to learn that it was less than half of what I was currently making. I found it difficult to comprehend how Microsoft could afford to pay more than double to such a large staff of contractors. I knew there were other benefits, but one could buy these benefits themselves and still have extra money left over in their pocket at the end of the month. I expect that job security was the real answer, it seemed to reflect the fear that most people walked through life with.

Whenever I went to job interviews, I let my prospective boss know that I was only available to work forty hours per week, on the rare occasion at crunch time was I willing to do more, but only for a few weeks. I tried to let them know early in the interview; there was no sense in wasting time if they were expecting more. A few times, this revelation ended my interview; this happened while I was looking for my next job. It was nice that I was still working because the rejection had no effect on me at all. I had the confidence to set this limit because I knew there was always someone who was happy to have forty hours of work from a good engineer. And I knew I needed to set this limit for my own sanity, even forty hours of work per week is too much unless you really love what you are doing.

It was at this same time that I found my next Microsoft job. Again when interviewing for this job, I used that code sample that got me fired from my Asymetrix contract. And again it was instrumental in getting me this job. My boss Jeromy liked what he saw and told me, "I already have plans of writing a code generator for our databases. Your ideas could be useful for this project."

I was able to create a good impression in this group within the first few weeks of working for them. For years they had been trying to make a complex data entry task easy for the user. They had a set of questions and answers pertaining to their sales processes that needed to be entered into a database; the set of questions changed depending upon the answers that were previously given. They had tried a couple of solutions, but the solution always fell short of their expectations. I was able to create a solution that they fell in love with. I have since seen such types of user interfaces in other software, but before I wrote this, none of us had ever seen it done the way I did it. Actually my best software ideas are given to me from my soul, from God. In those days, I rarely gave myself credit for having much psychic ability, yet I have always known that I received this inspiration from beyond the physical me. Some of my ideas have been so fantastic and new, I just knew that they had to come from beyond this being I consciously understood to be myself.

The next project was that code generator that Jeromy had told me about when he first interviewed me. It was a tool that took the design of a database, which we call a schema, and generated C++ source code. This source code could be compiled using standard compilers into a program that would run as a service under Windows and give easy access to the database from any program or language that supported the COM interface. This project was made easier by the work I had done at Asymetrix. Not because I was able to reuse the code, I did not, but because I had to do similar thinking and planning in this project as I had to do when I created that code for Asymetrix. This project was challenging and also a lot of fun because it drew an intense creativity out of me. I had my own office, the work and people were fantastic, and I did get a bit of a pay increase; I enjoyed this job immensely.

Back Pains, Again!?!

In March of 1997 I began having extremely painful back pains and difficulties with acid reflux along with some stomach pain. The back pains were not in the same place, nor were they of the same nature, as the difficulties I previously described in this book. The back pains were continuous throughout the day; most of the time it was a minor irritation, but at night however, about half an hour after going to sleep, I would wake up in what seemed to be intolerable pain. The pain was located in the thoracic part of my back, around the T3 vertebrae. This was accompanied by a very unpleasant burning sensation in my esophagus.

At first I began taking Kathryn's pain medicine. I hoped the back pains would go away on its own in a few days. Kathryn did not approve of me doing this without a doctor's prescription, so after a few days I went to see a medical doctor. He had no real solution to offer, but he did prescribe the same pain medication I was already taking since that was working with no apparent side effects. He also told me to take some antacid and another drug to stop my stomach from producing acid at night while I slept. Taking this medication became a problem within about a week because the pain and acid reflux continued. I was taking way too many of the pain pills and they were just barely giving me relief; I could still feel a great deal of the pain.

This was worrisome to me. I started pulling out all of those wise thoughts[1] that were handed down to me by my elders over these last thirty-eight years, *The older we get, the more aches and pains we can expect. I am not getting any younger. Am I stuck with this for the rest of my life?* Yet even though I thought this way, I was not catching myself. I barely ever noticed when I did this, but I know I used to think this way a lot.

I went to Amoram to get his advice. The first thing that Amoram told me was that I needed to change my thinking about illness. That I need to pay attention to my energy, my thoughts, and ask myself, *What is in this creation for me to see? How can I see this differently?* Amoram told me to visit David, the chiropractor that Bren and Kathryn went to. Amoram also suggested that I give up the pain pills completely and find the inner strength to deal with the pain; some of the breathing exercises he had taught us would help. He told me to sleep in a semi-reclined position, that this would minimize the acid reflux.

I went to the chiropractor right away. David had an interesting technique for diagnosis; he used his hand to feel the energy of my back.

---

[1] I am being sarcastic.

He did not touch my back; he held his hand an inch or two away from my spine and moved up and down feeling the energy field. When he found a spot that was out of alignment he touched it with his finger and pressed gently saying, "there," indicating that he had found the spot that needed adjusting.

David also used muscle testing as a diagnostic tool. There was one technique that he used a lot that totally amazed me. I would be lying down on my back, arms at my side, with my legs together, my spine was straight. David would extend one of my legs out to the side and ask me to resist while he tried to push my leg back to the medial position, next to the other leg. He did this a number of times and each time he would ask me to look at a different part of the room, he picked a specific spot and told me to look at it while he pushed. I was not supposed to move my head. I was only to move my eyes to look at the spot he pointed at. If I could resist David's pushing, all was well, but if not, then he would make an adjustment and try again. It was very funny to me because when I was strong and could resist, there was nothing David could do to push my legs together. But when I could not resist there was nothing I could do to keep my leg extended. With my eyes looking in one place, I could resist, but by moving ONLY my eyes to a new focal point I could not resist. Moving my eyes made the difference between having strength or not in certain leg muscles. He would make the adjustment to my spine, and then try again. Now I had strength and could resist his pushing. So having my spine in proper alignment was also a factor in whether certain muscles had full strength or not. This was just one more piece of evidence that the body is amazing beyond the understanding of most people. This helped me open my mind more to greater possibilities in healing.

I stopped using the pain pills and began sleeping in a recliner at night. Sleeping in a semi-upright position in the recliner was a big help in keeping the stomach acid down. I was left with a mild discomfort in the stomach, but the burning sensations were gone. As for the pain, the first couple of nights were a bit difficult but I managed. Although my chiropractic adjustment gave me some relief, it was short lived; usually it only lasted a few hours. I could feel when the vertebrae would go out of alignment again but did not know how to fix it myself. So the pain was still there at night.

Every night, in my mind, I kept my focus on my breathing and bringing in healing energy through my crown chakra. I let go of worrying that this was a permanent problem that I would have to live with. I would fall asleep for a short time and be awakened again by the pain. Then I would go right back to the breathing exercises, fully accepting that this was my new routine, until I fell asleep again. By the third night the pains began to slowly decrease each night until about a week had passed and it stabilized to being just noticeable, but easily ignored.

The other worry that I had to get over was about going to work the next day. When I couldn't sleep I worried that it would be excruciatingly painful to stay awake at work. Yet the next day, it was not too difficult. Because I was enjoying the work I was doing, it was easy to stay awake. So from that point on, whenever I would have difficulties sleeping at night, I would stop myself from worrying by remembering how many times I had done well at work after a restless night of sleep and then go on to meditating peacefully. I did not allow my mind to dwell on times where I was falling asleep at my desk.

So although I still had some physical components that were out of alignment to deal with, my pain and suffering were becoming a great lesson in the power of my mind. I was being forced to exercise my mind and control my thinking; the level to which I was successful with this was reflected in a decrease in the level of pain I was experiencing. The better I got at controlling my mind, the less pain I experienced and the longer I slept before the pains returned.

When I returned back to David a few days after my first chiropractic visit, I told him that I still had the pains and that they were still severe. He suggested I go and see a visceral manipulation[1] specialist named Peter. I had to wait a few weeks to get in for my first appointment, but after that I was able to see him three times in the first week and once a week for the next three weeks.

Peter basically massaged and pushed my stomach down with his fingers. It wasn't the most comfortable massage I had ever had, but it was effective. He told me that part of my stomach was being pulled up through a sphincter muscle into the space where the esophagus was; he was basically pushing it back down. He also told me to eat less food at night and give myself plenty of time between eating dinner and going to bed. I followed his instructions.

I had six appointments with Peter, and within three weeks I was reasonably back to normal. From that point on, I continued to keep my evening meals small as often as possible. Occasionally I would eat too much at dinner and the acid reflux problem would re-occur. I learned to keep antacid and over-the-counter acid control medicine around for those occasions. I had to continue visiting the chiropractor at least once, sometimes twice a week for the next year and a half.

I stopped seeing the chiropractor when I discovered Yoga. I discovered that some of the Yoga postures did the same thing the chiropractor was doing; it stretched and straightened my spine and the vertebrae moved returning it to its proper position. Yoga postures also massage the muscles and internal organs. In a body that does not stretch,

---

[1] Visceral manipulation is manipulation of the internal organs.

adhesions can develop between muscle tissues, causing a restricted range of motion. This can also lead to the spine being pulled one way or the other thus pulling it out of alignment. A spine out of alignment can be the physical cause[1] of numerous illnesses. Sitting in front of a computer eight hours a day without exercising and without stretching leads to such conditions in the body. There have also been many times where I have not had a software engineering job for many months at a time. At those times, I was not in front of a computer for eight or more hours a day, and I was usually out doing something highly energetic and physical at least once a day. At those times, I did not have the same difficulties with my back.

In 2005 at the time of writing this book, I was forty-six years old. I was far healthier in my forties than I was in my thirties. I have learned so much about health and energy that I have learned to look at every ache and pain as a passing thing. I no longer allow my mind to think, "Oh, I am getting old so I will accept this." That is how I used to see these things in my thirties. Now I think, "This pain is just a shifting of energy. My body knows how to bring itself back into balance. My body is amazing; it has healed itself of many problems. All is well." Most of the time, just thinking those thoughts sent the pain away, some of the time it took a little while longer.[2] Pain is a result of resisting what is, of being frightened by what is occurring, and it is also a warning letting you know that you are not connected to your Source, that you are disconnected from God.

Between work, chiropractor visits, apprenticeship groups, energy treatments, and private sessions with Amoram, the spring of 1997 was very busy for both Kathryn and me. Still we found the time to go on our usual Friday night date and out for a walk or drive somewhere beautiful. The love we had for each other was strong. We had just weathered a major storm and made it through. It was because of this that the minor squalls became a cake walk; we had become accustomed to working out our issues with each other and were getting through them much more quickly and with much less pain and suffering. But still, there was a part of us that liked to fight, especially in Kathryn. She grew up having to do a fair amount of it. Our friend Martha had been doing a lot of things with Kathryn in the last few years. Martha too was a Scorpio, and her

---

[1] The mind is always the root cause of all illnesses. Even physical illnesses that are caused by vertebrae pinching nerves are ultimately caused by a person who is not being aware of their body, its needs and its warning signals. People are deliberately ignorant about how to care for and maintain their body. This is a mental problem.

[2] In 2003 I healed a severely sprained wrist in eighteen hours using this kind of thinking. That story is in my next book and in an audio program that can be found on my website http://gr8Wisdom.com/Audio, look for the title "All Illness is Mental Illness." (proper capitalization is important when locating this website)

relationship with Kathryn was beginning to experience the same sort of dramas that Kathryn and I experienced. I guess Kathryn had a bit more to release and needed the extra person to do that with; Martha, on some level, signed up to do this dance with her.

In an apprenticeship group, Kathryn asked Amoram a question about her relationship difficulty. Amoram's answer is so powerful and precise; it would be useful for anyone[1] in a relationship to contemplate. However, the entire lecture that Amoram gave was so good I had to include it too. So here is most of that transcript. [2]

> Beloveds, we are pleased you are all here for this gathering today. For today we will discuss a topic that is an intimate part of your daily lives and personalities. We will discuss relationships, judgments and projection. As you move through your lives you find yourself having to negotiate and deal with a wide variety of energies. Indeed at this time on the planet, with the population at such a high point, there are many energies for you to negotiate with. Even if you tried going about your own business and basically ignoring others, the vibrations of the minds of millions of people are around you daily. It is much like walking through the busy shopping mall or train station; you cannot help but bump into a wide variety of people, people you might not consciously choose to come into contact with. And so it is with the thoughts and projections of the world mind. It is all around you and it encroaches on your personal space. As such it is impossible for you to escape the judgments of the world mind. Your point of power in this situation is what you choose to do with these stray and random ideas and ideals that are constantly bombarding you.
>
> So it is time to become clear and aware of which thoughts, which projections of mind, serve you and which ones do not. Along with observing and evaluating your own private thoughts and ideas come the thoughts that occur as a result of colliding with the minds of others. Mental collisions are happening all around you, but they are not by accident as you might suppose. And how is it that you will survive these collisions with the least damage? Indeed how is it that you can make it to your intended destination in one piece, in peace, love and harmony?
>
> With so many people on the planet at this time you are finding that there is also a great deal of projections bombarding you at every turn. Everyone has their own plans, their own ideas of how life should be and what your part in it should be. Even strangers have projections about other strangers. "You should be this way and not that way that

---

[1] That means you. We ALL have relationships.

[2] April 8th, 1997

you are now being. You should turn right at this place and never left and you gave the wrong signal too. Only bad people dress and act like you do. I was expecting you do the job this way and you did it that way. I love you so you should love me back and in exactly the way I am expecting you to love me."

So often the projections of others come to our awareness when they come in the form of a judgment. This is the time that we think we need to do something about it. But what happens when someone projects a complementary energy towards you? Do you not accept it blindly, without question, and with a smile? Can you really separate a positive projection from a negative one? We all know that in this world of duality all things must balance out. And so it is too with positive and negative projections. If you allow someone to define you with their positive statements about you, then you will also allow another person, or even the same person, to define you with their negative projections. Do you really wish to be defined by the whims and fancies of others? Indeed you are all doing this and it is cause for much of your pain.

There is something beyond projections beloveds and that is Truth. No matter what the projections are, they are still projections. If you are willing to embrace the positive ones then you are sure to find yourself wearing the negative ones too. But Truth is Truth. If you come to understand the Truth of who You are then you can rise above the projections of others.

Now there are judgments and there are observations beloveds. You are judged on whether or not you are meeting the expectations of another's projections. But there is also observation. Simply observing someone with your eyes and seeing that they are a beautiful individual. You may observe that, experience the truth of that, and you may even speak it out loud. It is an observation of the heart. The difference between the observation and the judgment is the projection. Judgment is the comparison between what is expected and what is witnessed. You are judged as good or bad because of this or that. With an observation there are no extra thoughts attached to it. An observation is pure energy.

Today everyone was glad to see Joanne return to group. You were not glad because it was Joanne that showed up today and not Fred. You were not glad to see her because she brought some exotic treat for you to all enjoy. You were simply glad to see her. You were simply glad to be in the same room with this one and continue on your journey of Spirit together.

Comparison is related to judgment just as contrasting is related to observation. With comparison you will always find an ego-based thought attached. Contrasting is an observation of the differentiation between one thing and another. It is not the idea that one thing is better than the other, but that the contrast helps to distinguish where one thing ends and another begins. You may look at all of the colors in the rainbow and observe the contrast of one color to the other. But you are not judging one as being appropriate and the other as not. You are only observing the different qualities of each.

As an example let's consider the colors you choose to wear. Why is it that you choose one color and not another? Is it because you see one color as being evil, or one color as being better or worse than another? For there are many in your world who are having a difficult time in seeing it any other way. Oh she might choose to wear red, but never pink. Because to that woman pink is a horrible color or because it is stereotypical of a certain type of woman to wear pink. And this is quite different from choosing not to wear pink because it does not feel right with their vibration. The difference being that one is an observation of how the energies merge together, a feeling, and the other as being an analytical thought, a judgment of how one is good and the other bad. This is an important and profound distinction beloveds. Can you feel the difference between observing and feeling that something is compatible with you or not, and to judge one as being of value and the other…well, we can all just do without that one can't we. Let's just make that one illegal. (laughter) Let's prohibit it and destroy all of it that we can find.

Now it is not for you to abandon your mind. But it is for you to begin to play with this and learn to feel when something works for you and when something just does not feel like it goes with the flow. It is for you to ask, "Why is it that this choice feels good and the other does not?" If you find judgment in your answer, how is it that you can change your perspective on this choice? Do you need to prevent others from making a choice that does not feel right for you, or can you let them decide for themselves if they can choose something different than you? You do not go to a buffet dinner and demand that they remove the foods you do not like from the table. No, you simply go and choose what you like and put it on your plate leaving the rest for another to choose. This is what we are talking about beloveds.

It is time to give up judging how certain people, things or events fit into your life. We are here to tell you that all things happen in divine perfection. If you step back and observe your life from a distance, such that you can see the big picture, the whole of who you are and the purpose of each event, you will find that it all fits in divine perfection. But here you are sitting in this single now moment, and you are in judgment with one thing or another. Duality is about separation. By separating one thing from all of the rest of creation and focusing upon its individual energy you are finding judgment. How to get past this problem beloveds?

You can begin with letting go of your addiction to the whys. (Amoram began pointing to each person in the room) "Tell me, why? Why did you do that? Why did life deliver this? Why? Why did this thing I did not want to happen, happen?" You are each addicted to the whys as if life were that simple. You try to spiritualize your query by attempting to find out the spiritual reason for all things that happen. You try to make yourself out to be a grand spiritual person as you explain to others the spiritual reasons why things happen. It is true that there is a purpose and perfection in everything, your spiritual reason why. But you may not be able to discover the spiritual reason for certain events until much time has passed. Try as you will to figure it all out based on past experiences, and based on possibilities of what could happen, you will still only find yourself grappling in the dark. It is just another mental exercise. Let go of the needing to know why and practice observing the perfection that is obviously in front of you. Practice observing the perfection of Life beloveds.

In so many of your relationships you are finding frustrations. You want things to be one way and yet some things, some "important things", are the opposite of what you want. And we would ask you beloveds, are you working with the correct materials? Have you given up your ability to observe, discern and say, "A hammer is great for pounding nails but it is not meant to cut wood. Sharon is the fastest typist we have, but she gets lost running errands in city traffic and takes too long." We suggest that punishing or manipulating some person, or some situation to change, so that you can move forward towards some goal is the least effective approach that you can take. And to judge the situation will only waste time and make everyone feel bad. It is wonderful to look at the spiritual masters who have walked the planet and think if they can do miracles so can I. But it is a different thing to believe you are going to wave your magic wand and make it all change right here and now. We see you when others do not. Soon you are beating this thing you want to change with your magic wand and trying to force it into submission. Until you observe from your own first hand experience that you can transform one thing into another we suggest that you do not rely on manifesting that ability in some urgent and important situation. You might be in for a let down. (laughter)

Get real beloveds. Observe where you are, do not judge it. Observe the tools, the materials, the people you are working with, do not judge them. Make choices based on these observations. Observe the results, do not judge them. Learn, grow and make your next choices from there. And cease asking people and situations to be something they are not and cannot be. Your true point of power is in your ability to change you, not another. Yet when you gain this power of self-transformation all things around you will also change.

Which brings us to another important lesson in relationship where others are expecting you to shape-shift. You will never be able to satisfy all the wants, whims and expectations of others. If you change how you are to satisfy one person, another person will find fault. If you change for them too you will find an abundance of others who will take offense at you for one reason or another. Even if you become a fully perfected self-realized master there will be someone somewhere who will want to crucify you. The world has always been this way. So it is to let go of this need, this addiction of pleasing others. It will make you crazy. You will become exhausted by all of the running around in circles and fall over. If you go inside, and communicate with your heart and soul, you will know how it is for you to be. You will receive the strength and conviction to live your life from a place of love.

Judgments, projections, compliments, observations…beloveds are you understanding all of this? What are your questions?

Joanne: Concerning my relationship, if you can call it that. Bill tells me that he loves me and that he enjoys spending time with me, but then he goes off and spends three days away. He doesn't call, and often I can't find or call him either. When I try talking to him about this he gets defensive and tells me I am making too much of this. He's a nice guy and everything but sometimes…I just don't know what to do.

Amoram: Beloved, we understand your frustration with the current situation. But it is as we said earlier, you are trying make him change into something he is not. And you are doing that with life too. There are many things that you desire to bring into your life, and they will come in time. Actually in perfect timing. You wanted a lover and Bill came. You…

Joanne: Yes, but I wanted a relationship. A lasting one. I am not sure I can make this work.

Amoram: You wanted a lover and Bill came. You also want a lasting relationship and have been asking for that. We are aware of this. However, that has not come yet. And it does neither Bill nor you any good to try to make Bill out to be that person who will be your life partner. Yet we are telling you that Bill is essential to you at this time in causing you to change so that you can be with

	that man who is coming to be your life partner. Without your experiences with Bill, you will not be a suitable partner for the one you seek. All things are in perfection beloved. Keep in mind that if you are feeling negative emotion such as frustration that you are not understanding something. If you go inside and bring yourself to clarity the time you do get to spend with Bill will be really special. The time will come for you to have your life partner, but it is you who is not ready for it. And Bill is living in his divine perfection too.
Joanne:	Thank you Amoram. I'll try to keep that in mind.
Amoram:	Go easy with all of this and go easy on Bill and yourself too.

Well Kathryn, how are you with all of this conversation? Does any of it resonate with you?

Kathryn:	I'm digesting a lot of it. Um, my question would be in this relationship that I'm struggling with my girlfriend. Um, was I seeing an appearency of what really wasn't there, and now I'm seeing it differently?
Amoram:	Beloved right now you are open to love. However once your buttons get pressed, your habits of thought engage, and your ego engages all of your well practiced stances about life and how things should be. [1] This blocks your vision beloved. You are not a bad person. She is not a bad person. There is love here. We know that you have a deep and abiding love for this one, and she also for you. It is simplicity to let go of those positions and just love, isn't it?
Kathryn:	Yes...I mean no...I know how to love, but sometimes it is just difficult.
Amoram:	We know beloved, we understand. But let go of the stances you must if you wish for the love to be experienced. You can practice this beloved. Indeed she is giving you the opportunity to practice and evolve in a way that is helpful to you in all of your relationships not just this one. For you are both locking into your ego

---

[1] This same thing happened with Kathryn and myself. It is interesting to note that her girlfriend Martha was also a Scorpio like I am. In my life I have found that I got caught up in locking ego positions the most with Cancerians, is this typical of the Scorpio/Cancer relationship? These days I let go of ego positions pretty easily, it causes too much pain to hang on to them.

position and projecting ideas and realities on the other that are just not there. True understanding is absent. If you can come to understand that you don't understand then at least you can let go of your position of being right and it having to be a certain way. If you really understood her there would be compassion. If she really understood you, there would be compassion, there would be love. So seek first to understand her. Go beyond the surface of her words. Feel how her heart aches and her words are her walls of protection. What is she really telling you? And is she really telling you about you or is her communication about her and her pain? You can see this in your own words and energy beloved. If you can remember some of the words you have said to her, do they really reflect how you feel about her or are they about protecting yourself?

Kathryn: Um uh, I can see that I am trying to protect myself. But it also feels like my words are accurate that they really are about her.

Amoram: Really about her or really about her pain and the way she is expressing her pain in words?

Kathryn: Okay, I see...my words are about the way she is expressing her pain in words. I want her to stop criticizing and attacking me.

Amoram: For your relationship it would be good if you can bring forth a third person to anchor the light, a spiritual referee so to speak. [1] You must become willing to let go of who said what, be willing to let go of your position in all of this. It would help too if you practiced this in your quite time. By going inside you can find the inner strength to renounce your position. This is true renunciation. So many religions stress renunciation, fasting or giving something up for lent, and everyone goes around giving up candy and meat and all such nonsense. Why not give up your stances? The true source of your pain, that which is really blocking the love, are your stances. If you will only give them up you will come to understand the illusions they contain. Look for the love. It is there. If you focus your mind on

---

[1] Seeking the counsel of third party when you are stuck in an ego stance is essential. Let go of your pride and just do it; it will ease your suffering. Let go of your purse strings and just do it; it will cost you less in the long run.

the love while you are engaging with her, letting go of your position will be much easier.

And so Michael...

Michael: Well, judgment is a very well worn groove in me. When you were first talking about well, you know, glad Joanne's here. However you put that. And...but it couldn't be someone else. And I was thinking, I am glad Joanne's here. I'm glad Hilda's here. I'm glad we're all here. I'm glad that this group is in the configuration it's in. And, um, and I really do feel it from a place of it just flows. And it just works. And I'm very happy to be with that. And conversely I'm also in a position of knowing it didn't feel to me the way I, it didn't feel comfortable, it didn't feel joy-filled the other groups that I was in, in the mix of energy. Um, and so I'm hoping that that's the feeling you're talking about there. And that's just not a judgment.

Amoram: No beloved, it is not a judgment. This group is quite compatible and you are aware of this and enjoy the feeling. You are also aware that the other groups you were in had a different feeling, one that was not compatible with you and your energy. This too is not a judgment. Judgment enters the picture when you begin comparing the two groups and labeling one of them bad and the other good. The other groups were not bad, they were not wrong, you were just learning something different in them that is all.

Michael: So I guess for me it's, I guess I keep fearing that the judgment's always going to be there.

Amoram: Ah yes, judgment will always be a part of living in the world of duality. But what is it that you do with your judgment? That is the key beloved.

Michael: It brings so much pain into my life.

Amoram: Because you are making your judgments real.[1]

Michael: Okay?

---

[1] A Master has judgments too; they just don't make them real. The unaware person takes a judgment and contemplates it in their mind and worries and mentally finds ways it can affect their lives. This kind of thinking causes much mental anxiety, pain and suffering. Indeed it is the root of all suffering.

Amoram:	The judgments become a problem because you make them real. Because you contemplate them, and make them important, and mull over what you will do for revenge or to teach them or to protect yourself in the future. In the midst of all of this thought truth gets lost.

In the world of duality you cannot do without judgment. Even your very language is built on it. Comparison is essential when you describe one thing it is often compared to another. This is bigger than that. She is prettier than me. Oh he is not so funny, but so and so is a real hoot. This is the nature of the duality.

So you will have to begin asking yourselves, "How is it that I can live in the world of duality and not get lost in the judgments?" It will take diligence and awareness but we know you can do it beloveds. The secret is in keeping your hearts open. The secret is in remembering...re-member-ing, to bring together once again the members that duality has separated. You must remember that all of it, the good and the bad, the black and the white, the tall and the short, are all a part of the All That Is. And yes it is true that right now in the duality you need this and not that. And perhaps you even got that and you needed this other thing. And it could even be that someone is intentionally messing with you for what ever reason. But yet the truth of the matter still remains that all is well. You still exist and always will exist. That you can control how you feel in this right now moment by what you choose to focus on. And that you can choose your response and that you can even change you automatic reactions. And you can be with the uncomfortable side of life and still remain comfortable. Your experience is your reality, no matter what is going on outside of you, your inner experience is under your control and it is your responsibility. So you get to choose whether to make judgment real or whether to make love real.

> "Practice observing the perfection of Life beloveds."
>
> - Amoram

Hawaii

By the time May came around, Kathryn and I were doing pretty well. We both felt reasonably healthy. We had been enjoying whatever sunny days we could find to get outdoors and just be together. Sometimes we would take our dog Ali for a walk together; other times we might drive around looking at nice houses and their landscaping. Or maybe we would drive a few hours up north to Marysville to see the flowers in bloom, then we would go to La Conner to have lunch and see the art shops...inevitably we would buy something beautiful. If I caught Kathryn admiring something small, I would quickly and discretely buy it for her while she was looking around the shop. Then I would leave it sitting somewhere at home that I knew she'd be looking, like her bathroom sink. She was often amazed at her discovery, even the placement at home seemed impossible at times. It must be a skill I carried over from my past life as a pickpocket. Even our darkest skills can be put to good use with awareness.

Even though it might seem like we were always busy with some sort of personal growth class or apprenticeship group, this was not the case. We did make a lot of time for fun and loving each other. In fact, we had done so many things in our area that we were exhausting the beautiful places to go for entertainment so we decided to go a little further this time...to Hawaii.

Kathryn was a Cancerian woman, and as such, she was totally hooked on her home. Those crabs love having their home close by so that they can crawl back in at the first sight of danger; this may be slightly distorted, but Kathryn did love her home. So when I suggested that we go to Hawaii, Kathryn said, "I could enjoy spending five days in Hawaii."

"Five days!" I exclaimed, "Yeah right...that gives us just enough time to unpack our bags, have a good sleep, and then pack our bags to get back on the plane to go home. I am not going to Hawaii for only five days! How about three weeks?"

Kathryn replied, "Three weeks! We can't afford that. Michael, you know I am afraid of the sun. I don't need to get melanoma on top of everything. Three weeks is way too long."

"No it's not! Three weeks is not long enough, but I know it would be impossible to talk you into going for longer than that." I went into a long dissertation of how we needed this break and had deserved it because of all of the hard work we had done. I gave it my best shot; it did little good. Kathryn agreed to spend nine days in Hawaii, with travel time, the whole trip took us just a bit more than ten days.

From the plane, I could clearly see the islands of our fiftieth state as we approached for landing. I was surprised to feel fear move through me when I first saw them. I was not sure why, so I contemplated this feeling. After all of those hours of flying over the vast ocean, with no other land in sight, we approached those tiny little islands and were going to land. The isolation from the rest of the world was a little more than I was comfortable with. But I knew it was more than just that. I knew that no matter how much I liked this place, it was not the place for us to move to. Both Kathryn and I had begun talking about moving somewhere else, but where? Neither of us had a specific place in mind, but from that feeling, I knew that Hawaii would not be it. It was almost as if the reaction I had in my body was telling me, "NO, this is not the place for you to live."

After picking up our rental car, we drove to our bed and breakfast accommodation which was near the city of Waikiki. It was a very large and beautiful home from the twenties. The house had been restored to pristine condition and was stylishly decorated with a combination of antiques and modern antique looking fixtures. Kathryn enjoyed the wallpaper; she inspected it closely to see if they did a good job hanging it; it met with her approval. There was a large porch on the second floor which looked out over the garden. The neighborhood was quiet. It was enjoyable to lounge and have breakfast outdoors in the fresh warm air, with the sounds of the tropical birds singing in the background. This place was a real treat coming from Seattle.

We were further from the beach than we wanted to walk so we drove into downtown Waikiki to enjoy the beach. Once we got there, we discovered it would cost $20 per hour for parking; arggg what a hassle! One way or another, they pay for that expensive real-estate. We found a free parking place quite a distance from the main beach and the shops we wanted to visit, so we ended up walking into the city anyway. After visiting the beach and having lunch in a quaint market square, we drove about half an hour east to another beach where I got to snorkel with the turtles. It was enjoyable, but it was a little on the cool side with sun often hiding behind clouds and the occasional bit of rain falling. I had an idea in my mind of what it would be like to spend time in the tropics, yet there were too many things that were spoiling my first day, and I was counting each of my nine days here with an awareness of how short this vacation was. Crowded beaches, expensive parking, cool weather...I wanted to be hot, hot enough to want to spend a lot of time in the water. Even the water was cooler than I expected it to be. Sometimes the air temperature was hotter than this in Seattle in May, how could Hawaii be so cool? I thought the tropics were always hot. It did not make sense to me. I was allowing outside circumstances to dictate how much I enjoyed the experience. There were so many things I could have been enjoying, yet I was noticing how many things were not going right. On the whole it was an ordinary experience, my judgment and resistance kept it from being an extraordinary one. Its funny how at the time I did not notice this was judgment, based on comparison, just like Amoram had recently been lecturing us about.

Even though the beach was not Kathryn's favorite place to be, she waited patiently for me while I enjoyed having a swim. Being out in the water with the turtles helped to wash away some of my disappointment. I relaxed a little bit more and also focused on enjoying the moment. Eventually I worried that I was leaving Kathryn alone too long so I returned to our blanket. I found her happily chatting with the mother of three children and enjoying the antics of the little ones. Kathryn was not expecting as much from this vacation as I was, and she was enjoying it much more, too. When I noticed this, it helped me to let go of my expectations and just go with the flow.

The next day, we went to the Polynesian Cultural Center. Kathryn had been here before with her ex-husband. She had spoken highly about this place so I was looking forward to this experience. It was very much a tourist attraction but still it gave us an interesting peek at what life was like for the Polynesian people before civilization had its way with them. We enjoyed a dance performance by the Maoris, the native people of New Zealand. We were also fortunate enough to be there on the award night of an international fire dancing competition. We got to see the best of the best play with fire.

As interesting and beautiful as our day was, it was Kathryn's company that I enjoyed the most. When we walked, we often held hands, and we did it with awareness of the love we had for each other. We both could feel an almost magnetic-electrical field of energy surround us when we tuned into our love for each other as we were at this time doing. I couldn't believe how lucky we were to be given this second chance to be together. I was grateful that Kathryn had recovered her health. She was my best friend, and I thoroughly enjoyed her company.

The next day we had to pack our bags to leave for our flight to the island of Kauai, this was the home of the TV show "Fantasy Island." Unfortunately packing, driving to the airport, waiting for our flight, driving to our next Bed and Breakfast accommodation ate up most of one of our days in the tropics. I was doubly disappointed with this realization because we had two more such days in our schedule when we would go to Molokai and then back to the main Island to return home. It was then that I realized that these nine days in Hawaii were really only six. The rest of the time was travel…arg! Amoram kept telling us to enjoy the journey and not put so much emphasis on the destination. I was beginning to realize how important this was.

This B&B was fantastic! It was a beautiful modern timber home that was luxuriously decorated. In the main living room area, windows stretched from the ground floor to the second floor ceiling and filled the home with daylight. Our room opened up wide to the never ending ocean with its waves crashing on the rocky shore. Palm trees and tropical flowers were everywhere to be seen. This was my idea of paradise; this was what we came to Hawaii for.

The next day we started out enjoying some time on the beach, but due to windy conditions, it was not warm enough for me to swim very long. We then headed west for sight seeing and to meet up with a helicopter that flew us over most of the island of Kauai. The views were fantastic but I was not sure I would make it to the ground before I had to let go of my breakfast. Surprisingly Kathryn had less trouble with motion sickness than I did, but once we were back on the ground, she began having trouble with nausea. We considered this a side effect from the helicopter ride and did not worry about it. We just went back to our lovely room, relaxed and enjoyed the ambience.

It took the entire next day to see the east and north coast of the island. While exploring a northeastern cliff with a light house, we saw many dolphins swimming only half a mile off of the coast. I had been hoping to find dolphins near the beach and wanted to swim with them. Seeing them from the cliff was the closest we would get on this trip. Many times along the way, we stopped for a break from the driving. We sat in the shade and I held Kathryn in my arms. Occasionally we would talk about how much has happened in the six years that we had been together and how it had changed and shaped our personalities many times over. Although there were painful times in our life together, due to our spiritual growth these had been the best years of both of our lives. We enjoyed a powerful feeling of love and accomplishment.

The next day we went to the island of Molokai. We were extremely disappointed when we arrived at our bed and breakfast. We wanted to turn around and go somewhere else before the owners saw us drive up, but our reservation was fully prepaid. We sat in the car looking at the dingy little shack in disbelief and discussing what we would do when the owners walked up to the car to welcome us. There was only one room for guests so there was no chance to enjoy the company of other travelers, something that most B&Bs in the Seattle area gave us the chance to experience. Their advertisements told us it was walking distance to the beach; however the ad did not say it was through private property that was posted with no trespassing signs. Also this part of the ocean was rocky, not what I would call a beach. In reality, we were located just about as far away from a beautiful tropical beach as one could get on this island. Their idea of breakfast was a bowl of fruit and a loaf of bread, meant to last us the three days of our stay. Our idea was a gourmet meal, or at least something home cooked with a chance to chit-chat with our hosts and other guests. This place did not meet our expectations; in fact, it sucked! I was very annoyed that we would be spending our last three days here.

We had plenty of daylight left on the day we arrived so we took a drive to a beach on the west end of the island. We enjoyed a meal at a nice resort and walked some of the trails that led to the beach. The next day we drove to the eastern end of the island. We enjoyed that drive and found a few hours of privacy on a lovely eastern point beach; private enough to get in a little bit of nude bathing...me, not Kathryn of course. She enjoyed my lack of modesty though; she even took photos.

On the following day, we took a tour of Kalaupapa, a leper colony that was located on a beautiful beach that was accessible only by boat, plane, or by walking a few miles down a winding trail along some very high and steep cliffs. This location was chosen so the lepers could not escape. I was amazed at Kathryn's ability to make this walking journey; I was thoroughly exhausted when we reached the bottom. We made it just in time to meet up with the other tourists who came down that same trail on horseback. Fortunately for us we reserved a couple of seats on the airplane to take us back to the top, neither one of us were up to walking that trail again.

We could not bear the thought of spending another day on this island at this particular B&B so we decided to leave one day early. Our hosts tried arguing with us, like we were obligated to stay. We weren't asking for our money back, we just wanted out of there; our vacation time was more valuable to us than the money. We booked an expensive room right on the beach at Waikiki; however the room was inexpensive by Waikiki standards. Because there were so many things in walking distance from our hotel, we did not rent a car. Instead we hired a limousine at the Honolulu airport to take us to our hotel; it was the same price as a taxi. This was my first ride in a limo, and it was very cool! I enjoyed watching as other people passing by looked our way to see who was inside. The deep black windows hid the fact that it was just us, ordinary people; no one rich or famous.

We enjoyed our last day in Hawaii the best of all. When we had a car we were so busy trying to see all of the sights and finding the best places to hang out that we did not do much relaxing and hanging out. The combination of natural beauty and man-made luxury here in Waikiki was just our style, at least for a short while. We had dinner at a lovely hotel with a large banyan tree in the middle of the dining area. Everything about this day was perfect. The next day we had plenty of time before our flight home. I got to enjoy surfing on a long board that I rented right outside of our hotel.

I cried as we were leaving our hotel to head to the airport; why couldn't we stay a few more days now that we found the best place to be? Kathryn would not hear of it; she was looking forward to being in her own home with her beloved cat and dog. After taking this trip, I realized that in the future I needed to plan more time for such vacations; Kathryn could return early on her own if she wished, I would stay longer. The first week or two is necessary to explore and slow down from all of the doingness we are used to in our everyday life. After that it is much easier to just hang out and go with the flow. It takes time to unwind, and then to actually relax takes even more time still.

What Do I Feel?

One day late in July, while Kathryn and I were making love, I felt like there was no room inside of Kathryn for me. The last two times we had sex, I noticed that she felt different inside, but I did not want to give it much thought. This time however, I was certain something was wrong. I could not help but think this was the result of tumors growing inside of her. How could I tell her what I had found? We had just made love and it was a very beautiful moment. I tried to wait as long as I could before I told Kathryn what I feared, but she could tell that something was wrong and she asked about it. When I explained to her what I had noticed, she reached up and felt inside; it felt irregular to her too. We held each other and cried for at least half an hour before calling her doctor for advice.

Dr. Howard Jones scheduled Kathryn to have blood tests, an ultra sound and a CT scan. Oh how I dreaded taking Kathryn back into that hospital; we had been free of it for over a year now. Kathryn was very frightened; she had no idea of where she would find the strength to go through all of this again. The test results were not good. It was clear that her cancer had returned. Dr. Jones tried more than once to convince Kathryn to resume chemotherapy treatments. She would not hear of it. We tried to convince Dr. Jones to schedule another surgery to remove the large tumors. That strategy worked reasonably well the last time; we thought it was worth a try. After that we would try alternative therapies to get rid of the remaining cancer. It took a lot of effort and more than one conversation to make this happen, but we finally convinced Howard and the surgeon to do another surgery against their better judgment.

On the morning of Kathryn's surgery, Brenda, Joanne, Hilda, Leslie, and Steven all came to the hospital to support us. We met down in the cafeteria. We had light hearted conversation with plenty of laughter. Five minutes before her appointed time we all stopped for a short prayer and meditation. When I took Kathryn to surgery Steven stayed and everyone else went on with their day. Again, like the last time, I stayed with Kathryn until the last possible moment. I then went down to the cafeteria to hang out with Steven and wait.

Steven and I had another cup of coffee and talked for about half an hour. Then we decided that we should go up to the waiting room. When we got there, I told the receptionist, "I am Michael Skowronski; my wife Kathryn is having surgery right now. Please let me know when they are done with her."

The receptionist responded, "Mr. Skowronski, we have been looking for you. Your wife's surgery is finished. The doctor will be out to talk to you shortly."

"Finished? What? How can that be? She only went in a few minutes ago...what's the time...." I looked at the clock that was behind her and continued, "about forty minutes now."

"I'm sorry I don't have any news for you, all I know is that your wife is in the recovery room, and the doctor wants to talk to you. Please have a seat and he will be out shortly."

Steven and I sat down. We decided that this could not be good. Steven held me as I cried. I could feel that he was choking back the tears too. It wasn't long before the doctor came out and confirmed our worst fears. "Mr. Skowronski, I am sorry, there is nothing we can do for Kathryn. We took a small tissue sample for a biopsy, standard procedure really, but the cancer is everywhere. There is just too much of it to operate."

Even though I already suspected the worst, I was shocked to get this news. "How much time does she have left?" I asked.

"With chemotherapy her lifespan could be measured in years, without chemo, only a few more months, if that." The surgeon was sympathetic but also detached, "I need to get going now. Please speak with Dr. Jones; he will help you evaluate your options. There is nothing more I can do...I am very sorry." With those words he turned around and walked away.

"Oh Michael, I am so sorry." Steven held his arms open, ready to receive me. I did not move; I was in too much shock. Steven came to me and grabbed me, and held me tight.

I cried silent tears and thought about what just happened. *I can't believe the doctor just told me it was hopeless, that Kathryn was going to die. This can't be. I have been hoping for and expecting a miracle. I've been expecting all of this healing work we have been doing to mean something, like we can actually heal ourselves and each other. How can she die? Nothing is going right. We have already been doing so many things to help Kathryn heal. Why isn't it working? This stuff is useless. Why have we wasted so much time and money on this training? Why didn't Amoram tell us this was happening? Why didn't Amoram tell us Kathryn was going to die from this?*

Steven interrupted my morose thoughts, "Michael, are you going to be okay? If you need anything you need to let me know. Peter and I are here to help you in any way we can. You only have to ask. I know how difficult it can be to have everyone trying too hard to help, so I won't bother you too much...but don't be afraid to ask. You also need support during a time like this. This is not just happening to Kathryn; it is happening to you, too."

Steven went home, and I went up to the oncology ward to await Kathryn's return. Instead of a single person's room, they put Kathryn in a double room. I was a little upset about this. I wanted Kathryn to have a private room; there should be no problem since our insurance covered that. I was told, "There are no more private rooms available. Don't worry; they won't be putting anyone else in this room with Kathryn."

I was please to hear this. I inquired further, "I will be staying here with Kathryn. Can I use the extra hospital bed, or do you need to bring a cot in for me?"

"We were told that you would be staying...you can use this one." Although I had never met these nurses, they knew who I was. Apparently some of the other nurses who had helped Kathryn during her chemotherapy stays had told them about us. Later, we found out that they had been told how nice Kathryn was and that I stayed with my wife. Although it was not uncommon for a husband to stay at the hospital with his wife, it was rare. Later, when I was walking around, I noticed that there were two single rooms that were vacant. I asked an orderly about it and he said that everything was fine with those rooms, that nothing was broken. I came to the conclusion that the nurses were just being nice to us but could not come out and say it because of legal reasons. They had given us this double room so that we had plenty of space and I could use the nice bed instead of sleeping on a cot.

They wheeled Kathryn into the room on a stretcher and carefully put her into bed. A couple of nurses came and began taking Kathryn's vital signs and hooking up the appropriate IVs. Kathryn woke up for a short time during these movements and asked me how it all went. "Honey, you were only in surgery for a very short time. When they opened you up they found too much cancer, they didn't remove anything. They couldn't...I don't know what we are going to do."

"Michael," Kathryn said with a slurred voice, "its okay; I am not going to die. I am a survivor."

"Do you plan on having chemotherapy again?" I asked.

"No." Kathryn was clearly tired and saving her breath.

"But the surgeon said, 'With chemotherapy your lifespan would be measured in years, without chemo, only a few more months.' Are you sure you don't want to take chemo long enough to get better, to give you more time to heal this?"

"Shhhh. We can talk about this later." Kathryn held my hand and looked into my eyes. I could feel her love for me. It was at moments like this that all of our fights seemed so silly and such a waste of time. How could we waste even a single moment of our life creating such suffering for ourselves? Our time with loved ones seemed so short.

Kathryn slept for many hours. I busied myself by bringing my computer in from the car and setting it up. My boss said it was okay for me to work from the hospital and let me take a computer in. I thought this was very nice considering that I was only a contractor and not a Microsoft employee.

Setting up the computer was as far as I got. Even though my mind was telling me to work while Kathryn was asleep so that I could be free to spend time with her when she was awake, I could not bring myself to sit down and work. I turned on the TV and began flipping through the channels. I passed by a dramatic looking news cast and switched back to see what it was. They were reporting that both Mother Theresa and Princess Diana were also near death's door that day. I was in shock. I thought to myself, "Kathryn is like a combination of these two great women; the world is about to lose all three of them soon. What a sad day this is for the world." The song, *There Ain't No Sunshine When You're Gone* began to run through my head. Now I was crying for the world as well as for myself.

Many thoughts passed through my mind in those first few hours at the hospital while Kathryn slept, *Who would I be without Kathryn in my life? What is the point of living if I don't have someone to share it with? How will I ever find another woman as perfect for me as Kathryn? What was I going to do with all of the money I would save when Kathryn is not here to spend it? How am I going to take care of this big house on my own? I will move away from Seattle. I want to live some place sunny and warm. How long will this take for her to die? How horrible is this going to be? I hope I can be present with her at her moment of death.* I could not even focus on a television program with all of the thoughts that were running amuck in my mind. At no time did my mind entertain the thought that Kathryn would survive this. It seemed inevitable that she was going to die soon.

"I am not going to die," Came a muffled voice from the next bed. It was as if Kathryn was reading my mind, or was she just picking up the conversation where we had left off a few hours ago? "Sweetheart, I can beat this, I need you to believe in me. We have much help from higher places."

I got up from my bed and went and sat next to Kathryn. I held her hand and said, "Of course you are going to survive this. I have fears about this, but I trust that you can do this if you want." I was lying to her, but I did not want Kathryn to know I had lost my faith in her survival. "Maybe we should just sell everything and move to some tropical island and relax and meditate...just like Bernie Segal[1] talks about. So many of his patients were healed by...."

Kathryn cut me off, "No, we are not going to run away from our problems. We can stay here and face them. I don't want to go anywhere; I like my home. But I am not going to go through chemotherapy again. Western medicine is not the only therapy available; we can find some other way to heal this."

Physically Kathryn's strength was weak. However, her determination to survive was strong. She made me start to think that she might actually survive this. At first my feelings confused me. I felt disappointment to hear her talk like this. I spent some time contemplating why, and I realized that I was not ready to go into another long stretch of dealing with such intense illness. I was feeling disappointment that she planned on fighting this. There was a part of me that wanted this all to be over...I just wanted Kathryn to die and to move on with my life. I was shocked to find myself thinking this way and began to judge myself. Then I decided it was natural to not want to go through the difficulties of fighting this disease. I realized that it was my limited mind that saw death as the only option, as my easy way out of these difficulties. I still wanted Kathryn to live. I reminded myself that we have had many miracles in the past, and a miracle was entirely possible here in this situation. Perhaps God was setting us up for a really profound miracle to occur to give us more credibility in our healing practice. It really was the disease that I wanted to die and not Kathryn. I had to get clear in my mind how I felt about this, how I wanted to see this, and what I believed. I prayed to God to help give me the strength to support Kathryn in love.

There were a number of times that Kathryn was worried about what I would do, and how I would handle all of this. A few times she said to me, "Michael, I am very sorry that you have to go through this. Please stick with me, don't leave me. I really need you right now."

"Oh sweetheart, you don't have to worry about this." I went to Kathryn's side and held her hand, "Of course I will not leave you. I am your best friend. If this is the end I want to have every minute with you that I can...if it is not, then I don't want to be the fool that left you when it got rough. Don't you worry about this; you have enough on your plate to deal with. I will be okay. I have support too."

Many days passed yet Kathryn did not seem to be recovering from this surgery. She remained weak. She wanted to eat so badly, but the

---

[1] Dr. Bernie Segal is a true healer and author of many books dealing with cancer and alternative therapies. Visit http://gr8Wisdom.com/Books/Bernie (proper capitalization is important when locating this website)

doctors told her that she had to wait until her stomach began making normal sounds again. I questioned this logic because they had not cut into her bowels, but the doctor insisted that it was necessary. They told me her system was in shock due to the little bit of surgery that they had done, and it would not be ready to handle food until the sounds returned.

Not only did Kathryn want to eat, but she wanted to go home. I could not believe she was thinking this way. How could she want to go home when she was doing so badly? This freaked me out a bit because I did not want to be the one having to take care of so many things. It was comforting to me to be in the hospital knowing they had all of the equipment to take care of her. Thankfully, Kathryn did not have the strength to fight the doctors who insisted that Kathryn remain in the hospital.

More than a week passed and Kathryn still had not recovered. She was now eating a little, but she was still weak. She wanted to go home and talked about it all of the time, but the doctors would not let her go. To me, it was starting to feel like Kathryn was going to die very soon. We called her family and asked them to come and visit Kathryn. We called my parents and my mother insisted on coming up to see Kathryn and to help out when we got her home. Once my mother arrived at the hospital, I left her to visit with Kathryn while I took the opportunity to get together with our friend Joanne for dinner and a movie. I needed a break from all of this dreary hospital business; I enjoyed my time away and found it easy not to think about Kathryn or the hospital for the few hours I was gone. When I returned to the hospital, Kathryn's family had just finished their visit and was getting ready to check into a hotel room. I was relieved that they were on their way out as I was returning. I did not want my wonderful evening ruined by their energy.

That evening I was exhausted. I had slept at the hospital for nine evenings already, each night my sleep was interrupted many times for various reasons. On this particular evening, it was taking me nearly an hour to fall back to sleep after the nurses came in and did their business, and then something would wake me up again. In the privacy of my mind an insane rage was brewing which only made my insomnia worse. I was on the brink of running down the hall shouting obscenities at the top of my voice. Thankfully, reason took hold, and I decided I needed to go somewhere else to sleep. But where? My mother was sleeping in my bed and Petra, our house sitter, was in the guest bed. I did not want to make do on the sofa, nor did I want to be woken early in the morning, nor did I want to wake them at two AM. So I decided to get a motel room near the hospital. I had to call a few places before I found one at a reasonable rate, but as soon as I did I was on my way.

My head hit the pillow around 2:30 AM and I fell asleep immediately. I slept until 10:15 AM; I felt refreshed and alive. I wanted to sleep more but I figured people would be looking for me. I phoned the hospital to let Kathryn know where I was.

"Michael, where are you?" Kathryn asked with a concerned tone in her voice.

"I am at a motel. I just needed to get some sleep. I really needed that, I feel much better now. And you too, you sound much better, what has happened?"

Kathryn responded, "Everyone was wondering what happened to you. We were starting to get a bit worried. You need to get over here right away; I am ready to check out."

What? Did she mean she was going to check out of the hospital or die? She was too sick to check out, yet she sounded fine. People often sound much better right before they die. "Kathryn, check out of the hospital…is that what you mean? How can you?"

"Yes, I am checking out of the hospital. All of our stuff is packed and on its way home, I need you to come and get me. I was just about to call a taxi."

"But, are you feeling okay? Does the doctor think this is a good idea?" This just seemed too impossible to believe. Yesterday she looked deathly ill. Last night she seemed totally drained from all of the visitors she had.

"Yes, I am feeling much better. The doctor said it was okay. Now please come down here and get me."

I quickly got dressed and checked out of the motel. When I arrived at Kathryn's room she was dressed in her favorite top and overall jeans and sitting up in the bed. There were no tubes sticking out of her. She looked happy and was smiling like a radiant goddess. My mind spun; how could she make such a transition in such a short period of time? [1]

I looked around the room, my computer and all of our things were gone. Quite a few things made it from our house to the hospital in the ten days that we were there. There were also many flowers and cards. I hated

---

[1] When I wrote this section of the book it was the first time I had put these events together this way in my mind. Once I collected all of the events as they have been written I discovered an interesting coincidence…that Kathryn felt alive and refreshed on the very same day that I did. What does this mean? Could it be that my energy, my doubts and worries about Kathryn's survival, were actually dragging her energy down? There is never only one reason for big events like Kathryn's slow recovery that magically shifted overnight. I would say that because of my close emotional and physical proximity to Kathryn my energy was one of the contributing factors; in my absence she bounced right back.

packing and moving things, [1] so this was quite a gift to have this done for me. I was beginning to love having all of this family around to help. I needed it nearly as much as Kathryn did.

The first thing through the front door of our house Kathryn sees a leaf lying on the floor in the entry way...she bends over to pick it up. I was in shock; she just had her stomach cut open and sewn back together. I snapped at her, "Kathryn! Don't! Ask me...I can do that for you." There was a look of pain on her face. My mind went off on a judgment trip about her needing everything to be so clean and tidy, even at the expense of re-injuring her surgical wounds.

Kathryn's family stuck around for about another hour, and then they drove home. They were just as happy as I was to see Kathryn looking and feeling so good. I had to admit, that their energy had changed. They were genuinely concerned for Kathryn and clearly expressing a lot of love. This was a side of them I had not seen before; maybe I had briefly seen this in some of them, but not to this extent. Kathryn's illness seemed to be bringing this family to a place of greater understanding and maturity. It was heart warming to witness this transformation.

My mother remained at the house for another four days and was very helpful. Even Kathryn was grateful for my mother's help. Petra, who had been house and pet sitting for us while we were in Hawaii, also stayed at our house while we were in the hospital. My mother and Petra hit it off famously and became good friends. We invited Petra to stay longer, rent free, and asked her to help me look after Kathryn. She agreed.

Petra was a beautiful woman in her late forties. She had been a massage therapist, but now she had severe arthritis which prevented her from doing any serious work with her hands. She gave me a short massage a couple of times, but it became clear that it hurt her too much to continue. I felt a physical attraction for Petra, and soon it became an emotional one too. I began to fantasize about being with her. I also gave her a few massages, which only added fuel to the fire of my inner passion. The second time I gave her a massage Kathryn picked up on the energy and cautioned me to pay more attention to what I was doing with my

---

[1] This is a very interesting coincidence. When I wrote this line I realized it was just one more time where I did not have to do my own packing and moving. There have been many times in my life, prior to this experience and since, that I was saved from the job of packing and moving. Always life seems to orchestrate events such that this task gets done for me. Rarely do I deliberately plan it this way myself, not consciously that is. This is just one more example of how life is always adjusting itself to our consciousness. In this case my desire is to have the packing and moving done for me. I don't resist the subtle ways that life pushes and pulls me which makes me available for this to happen.

energy. I never made any overtly sexual advance toward Petra, but I often wondered if she noticed. I figured she had to.

Petra stayed with us only a few months. Then she moved to an Osho community out in the sticks, on the outskirts of Redmond. They had an indoor heated swimming pool that I was permitted to use. This was no usual swimming pool. They used a diatomaceous earth filter and did not use chlorine, so the water was very clean and fresh smelling. The pool was not just warm, it was nearly hot; its temperature ranged between 88 to 94 degrees most of the time. The best part was that nude swimming was permitted and usual there. From that point on I used the pool for exercise and play a couple of times a week. I had taken water aerobic classes a couple of times and liked the complete body work out it gave me so I bought some equipment and did water aerobics nearly every time I went. Often when I used the pool there was no one else there, but sometimes I did have company. I especially enjoyed it when it was nude female company. Although this fueled my fantasy life it never took the form of an actual sexual affair.

It was in the first week after Kathryn arrived home that the roofers were ready to replace the shingles on our roof. We had been planning this for months; it was arranged prior to discovering that Kathryn's cancer had returned. Kathryn and I talked about postponing the work for the three to five weeks it would take her to recover, but if we waited, the odds were good that it would start raining while the work was being done. In the end it was Kathryn who made the decision to go ahead and to put up with all of the noise during her recovery.

There were many times during this week that Kathryn asked me to take her out in the car, somewhere beautiful, to take a nap. I thought it was quite ironic. Years ago, when we first got together, Kathryn used to get upset with me when I would interrupt the flow of our day to stop and take a nap, but I was just too tired to go on and I knew I had to take one. Often this happened while we were out in the car so I would find a quiet place in the shade to stop for a twenty minute nap. Kathryn just had to put up with it. But in the last few years, she would notice when I was becoming tired and irritated, and she would ask me if I needed to take a nap.

A few years before I met Kathryn, I discovered that a short nap would completely refresh me. I discovered this while I was working for Decision Dynamics. I would get sleepy at my desk, and it became excruciatingly painful for me to try and remain awake. All I needed to do was relax enough to fall asleep, even for just a minute or two and I would wake up refreshed. I would close my door and slouch down at my desk and let myself snooze. I found that every time I woke up naturally after only ten to twenty minutes. It was then much easier to stay awake and work. I also found that if I took a longer nap, like when I was at home for example, that I woke up groggy and sleepier than I had been when I first lay down. So I learned to resist the temptation to go back to sleep once I initially woke up. This became a daily practice for me, some days I needed two naps. Later I learned that other people had coined the phrase "power nap" and that people like Albert Einstein used to take them too.

So now that we had all of this noise from this roofing that was going on, Kathryn wanted me to take her somewhere and nap with her in the car. It was also a way for us to get a break from Petra and my mother and to be alone together. This was a sweet time for us. Taking care of Kathryn brought out the best in me, and it brought out the best in her to allow me to do so. Kathryn used my strength to boost her own, and it boosted my strength to know that I was needed and being of assistance.

After my mother left, Kathryn and I began looking for an alternative treatment for cancer. We found a medical doctor in Bellevue who was using unapproved treatments and had subsequently lost his license to practice medicine. He continued to practice but was up front about the status of his license and that his techniques were not approved; we were to follow his advice only at our own discretion. We looked into some of the things he suggested but did not accept treatment or therapy from him.

When Kathryn's relatives came to visit her at the hospital, they brought a Penthouse magazine with them. In it was an article about using hydrazine sulfate, a component use in making jet fuel, to fight cancer. The article gave a specific example of how it helped cure someone of brain cancer. It was pretty convincing and we also found information on the internet about this treatment. We found a place to order this substance and Kathryn began taking it. However it did not take long before she rejected it because it did not feel right to her. Because it seemed to me that it was doing what it was reported to do, I thought Kathryn needed to give it more time and put up with the small unpleasant side affects. But she insisted that it felt wrong to her and she refused to continue taking it.

Many people came to us suggesting one thing after another. At first this was helpful, but soon it became a real pain. We tried so many different things with no real benefit that I got tired of hearing all of these amateur experts telling us about something they knew very little about. It was another good lesson for me to teach from my experience and not from the head knowledge I gained from reading or from my teachers.

Kathryn started receiving treatments a few times a week from Howard Simpson's naturopathic clinic and also went down south to Renton to another clinic a few times a week. They tried many things, enemas, hydrotherapy, intravenous chelated mineral and ozone and a few other things that I was not present to witness or just don't remember. A nurse at Howard's clinic taught me how to give Kathryn a hydrotherapy treatment, which I did five times a week every week from that point onward. We even brought the equipment with us whenever we traveled so she did not miss a day of treatment. One day a week, Kathryn received a hydrotherapy treatment from the clinic, and one day per week she had no treatments at all. This gave me two days off from this procedure every week.

For the hydrotherapy treatments I set the massage table up in our bedroom and played some nice soothing music. On the table I laid out a thick blanket, then a sheet. Kathryn lay down naked on top of the sheet, face down the first time, then this whole process was repeated as she lay face up on her back. I covered her torso with one dry towel. I then soaked two towels in boiling hot water. We found an old electric coffee maker, a large one, for this purpose. I took it apart to change the wiring and bypassed the thermostat which then allowed it to boil water continuously as long as it was plugged in. Before I rewired the coffee pot, it stopped heating the water once it came to a boil, and then it cooled down too quickly. Wearing thick rubber gloves I pulled the towels out of the boiling water and wrung them out. After one or two shakes in the air to cool them just a little bit, I laid them out on the dry towel that was on Kathryn's torso. I then wrapped the sheet and blanket around Kathryn and left her to bake for four to ten minutes. The nurse told us it was supposed to be for only four or five minutes, but as time went on Kathryn insisted on having the heat on her for longer and longer.

After the hot towels came the icy cold ones. I filled a plastic bucket with cold water and enough ice to so that there were some frozen bits still left at the end of the treatment. I soaked two towels in the freezing cold water, wrung them out as well as I could,[1] and placed them where the hot towels had been. Again I wrapped Kathryn up with the sheet and blanket. She relaxed this way for about ten minutes, just until she warmed up the cold towels.

The hot and cold treatment was given twice, once on her backside and again on her front side. The theory behind this was that the hot towels caused her blood to move to the surface and the cold towels caused the blood to move to the internal parts of her body. This was meant to flush all the cells of the body so that all toxins could be cleaned out naturally by her liver and skin.[2]

---

[1] My forearms became rock solid strong as a result of wringing these towels out nearly everyday.

[2] I am no expert in the whys and hows of this treatment. I am only reporting what I remember and experienced. Please do not interpret this as medical advice; however you may want to do more research yourself into such a treatment if it feels right to you.

Many of the times I gave Kathryn these treatments, I also sat down and gave her energy work at the same time. Kathryn was often correcting how I did it and was very aware of how clear my energy was whenever I put my hands on her. She forced me to pay much more attention to my thoughts and the effect they had on the energy I was sending to her. She also pointed out, with intense irritation, other little things like when I kicked the table as I moved around it or whenever I accidentally[1] brushed her face, tickling her, with my shirt tails. Even though Kathryn's comments annoyed me at first, it really helped me to get a feeling for what it was that I was doing with my energy.

Sometimes however, it was frustrating for me beyond my ability to keep it in. Often Kathryn would correct how I was preparing the hot and cold towels, when she did this, I thought she was being trivial, because on other days when I did exactly the same thing she had no complaints and even made good comments about the treatment. So there were a few times that we began arguing during her treatments. A couple of those times I was so mad that I imagined turning the whole table over with Kathryn on it. I never did such a thing, but just holding that sort of thinking is an indication of intense rage that needs to be sorted out. This is God-given creative energy being used in a destructive way. Those thoughts added to the energy soup that was our relationship. I knew this was not conducive to healing so I worked diligently to calm my energy and bring it back to a loving place. I wasn't always successful.

In hindsight, I realize just how helpful both the good and the bad experiences have been to me. It helped me to become aware of what I was doing with my thoughts and energy. It helped me gain control of my thinking to such a degree that I am now able to be in a place of peace, love, safety, wisdom, and harmony with all of life most of the time, even when the outside circumstances seemed to suck. The moments that I do lose my positive emotional state are brief. I allow pain and suffering to remind me to choose my thoughts consciously, and thus bring myself back into balance quickly. I have read the accounts of many enlightened Masters; all of them experienced some level of emotional excitement including anger. They just didn't make it real. Masters choose the mental and emotional state they want and skillfully move toward it.

---

[1] Accidentally is the same thing as absentmindedly...when giving someone a therapeutic treatment absolute awareness is essential. By paying attention, most of these annoyances can be avoided, and the therapist develops a habit of movement that improves the quality of the treatment.

Community

Meanwhile, our apprenticeship groups with Amoram continued to inspire us. Amoram began to talk about the necessity to build community. He began telling us that we needed to become self sufficient. Amoram talked about natural and social disasters due to the Y2K computer bug messing up everything from social security payments to grocery deliveries. At times he built a frightening picture of how things could be without preparation, and then told us not to worry because we would know what to do and where to be. Preparation and community was the primary topics of his lectures.

In my mind, I formed a theory and an image of Mother Earth and how she suffered under the great weight of a delusional humanity that both ignorantly and willfully destroys her every day. As a living being, she has the ability to correct the disease that is occurring in and on her body, and does so with natural disasters. There were many natural disasters occurring in Seattle, the USA, and all over the world at that point in time. Thus, I concluded that Mother Earth would keep it up until humanity learned or it washed enough of humanity away so that it was no longer a threat. It was a convincing theory, and one that motivated me to action.

As a group we began thinking seriously about buying land and forming a community and how the community would be structured. This caused us to get together more often and we began strengthening the community that we already had. I studied self-sufficient living, such as natural and hydroponic farming, greenhouses, composting, bio-gas creation, hydrogen and fuel cells, solar panels, wind and ocean power, cooking oil to diesel fuel conversion, straw bale home construction, waste water treatment, and many other related topics.

As we all know, the dreaded Y2K bug was a real fizzer. Nothing happened. Life continued on and we all had a good laugh at all of the silliness that happened around such predictions; there was a sigh of relief. So how did that affect my opinion of Amoram and his teachings? I have been with this questions many times. The answer continues to evolve for me.

I know that I learned many things as a result of my belief that some disaster was eminent. It was not just a casual learning; I gathered much technical material, performed experiments, asked questions of experts over the phone and through the internet. I even traveled to the

East Coast for a four day workshop on constructing "Living Machines"[1] for natural waste water treatment.

So I learned heaps during the time I was involved with this belief that a series of disasters were coming. On a deeper level I felt safer. I felt like I understood what it took to take care of myself if we lost the use of the modern conveniences that we now enjoy. What would happen if all petroleum being shipped to the USA stopped? That alone would be a national disaster. It could happen.[2] Thus, I felt like I was more in control of my own life with what I had learned.

I became aware of, and contemplated often, better ways for us to structure the systems that support our life here on this planet, thus I added that much more creative power to the ethers that surround us. Don't underestimate how much power is in the daydreams of a single individual. Creating eco-friendly communities in my mind has definitely had an effect on this planet. But it was not just me focusing on these issues, many others were doing the same; when you multiply this energy by each individual who has done so, then you have real power! The more of us that desire natural, self-sufficient systems, the quicker this will become a reality; this will raise the level of comfort and wealth for all who inhabit this planet. Now I am a well informed advocate of eco-friendly technologies; I can inspire and bring hope to those who worry about what humanity is going to do in the future. I know that we can have these technologies. We could have them now if the present population would pay more attention and push our governments for them. But we may have to wait until many of the old fools die off and enough of the newer generation become fed up with putting their head in the sand.[3]

Understanding who we are and how to use our power creatively for the good of all is one of the highest aspirations we can hold. Because I believed some sort of disaster was coming, I took actions that were a benefit to myself and to everyone on this planet. Did Amoram lie to us? Did he not know what was going to happen? Did the future change?[4] Is

---

[1] Visit http://gr8Wisdom.com/LivingMachine (proper capitalization is important when locating this website)

[2] So many things would shut down if we lost our foreign oil supply. Our ignorant way of being has caused us to ignore this for far too long. So much wealth, power, strength, and freedom would be gained not only for our country, but for the whole world too. Because what ever we develop here, we can be sure, if it is good, the rest of the world will follow suit. We must convert from oil, coal & nuclear to solar & hydrogen NOW. To become informed please visit http://gr8Wisdom.com/SolarHydrogen (proper capitalization is important when locating this website)

[3] For eco friendly sustainable technologies please visit http://gr8Wisdom.com/EcoFriendly (proper capitalization is important when locating this website)

[4] Kryon tells us it did. Visit http://gr8Wisdom.com/Books/Kryon (proper capitalization is important when locating this website)

Amoram just a figment of Brenda's imagination? The answer to these questions are not as important as knowing that one way or another, God uses anything He can to direct our hearts and minds in the service and for the benefit of All That Is. This is only one example of how this story of possible disasters changed one person. What did it do to the thousands of others who also believed such things might happen? How did that change the energy on the planet? How high was the awareness of humanity lifted as a result? We must be careful when we are quick to judge the ways in which God is teaching us, or how or in what form the messenger delivers the message. A lie may be precisely the way God gets us to move in the direction He wants us to move. Maybe the stories were true, maybe we were heading for disaster...we don't know; maybe we changed our future as a result of focusing on survival. I say maybe, but I know...the truth is a combination of all of this and so much more.

One beautiful autumn day, Kathryn and I drove to Joanne's home, left our car there, and then went on an outing in Joanne's new Dodge Caravan. Joanne loved it and went on and on proudly describing many of its wonderful features. Kathryn and I too fell in love with it...especially me. There was one feature in particular that really made me want one. It was its dual zone climate controls.

Kathryn and I were often fighting over the temperature in the car. We had a very difficult time finding a happy medium...oh, I thought I found the medium, but Kathryn would insist that it be at the extreme end that she favored. It was not even consistent between us, when she was too hot I would be too cold, when she was too cold I would be too hot. The fighting did not stop here...once we started fighting, Kathryn remained emotionally cold for many hours; this pushed other buttons for us. I would be trying to get some sort of acknowledgement from her that she loved me and was my friend, she would remain cold and distant. On an energetic level, my need for reassurance from Kathryn was like reaching into her solar plexus and grabbing what she was not freely giving. This caused her to be more irritated with me. Our dramas would grow too big once they got started, so I wanted to nip this one in the bud. I saw that we could end our hot-cold feuds once and for all.

On the way back to Joanne's house, she offered to let me drive her van home. With great enthusiasm I said, "Really? You bet!" I was very excited! After getting the grand tour of the controls, she released control of her beloved Caravan to me. I loved how it handled. Even though Joanne told me the van was easy to maneuver it was a delight to experience for myself just how easy it really was.

I had to test out the dual zone climate controls so I put full air conditioning on my side and hot air on for Kathryn who was sitting in the front passenger seat. It worked! It was too hot for Kathryn and she had to turn it down. It was too cold for me and I had to warm my side up. We each had our own controls and we both found a temperature that we liked. Now I really wanted one of these vans. I talked to Kathryn about trading my car in, but she said, "We can not afford it. Also we would lose too much money on the value of your car. It is only five years old and still in great condition. You should drive it a few years longer."

In November 1997, for Thanksgiving Day, Kathryn and I drove down to Portland to have a meal with her family. We met them at a restaurant. They had reserved two large tables and everyone showed up. Kathryn was happy and even I had a pretty good time. It was a little bit draining for Kathryn, but not nearly as bad as in the past. They all had more compassion for her knowing that the end could be near. They were treating her better, but mostly it was their energy that had shifted. That made it easier for Kathryn and me to spend time with them.

We had our dog Ali with us so we enjoyed a leisurely driving pace with many breaks along our route. We stopped at a rest stop on the way to Portland to let Ali out to run around. We found a park in Portland to go walking in for half an hour, and then on the way back to Seattle, we stopped at another rest stop. We listened to the second "Conversations With God" book[1] on audio cassette and to some beautiful music. We contemplated the wonderful life we have had together and shared some our best memories with each other. We commented on how much nicer Kathryn's family was to be around than before. Kathryn felt her suffering was worth it for this change alone. Even though they had inflicted deep wounds in her heart, she loved her family as deeply as she loved anyone. She would do anything for them.

It was dark and raining by the time we were nearing our house. I had just exited the freeway and was waiting at a red light; we were only three minutes from our house. When the light turned green I hesitated to look both ways as I usually do, and then I went. All of a sudden Kathryn screamed and I found myself hitting another vehicle, a king-cab pickup truck, which seemingly appeared out of nowhere. I hit the truck as it was crossing my path, coming from the direction of the passenger side. I hit the hind end of the back door, and the truck spun half way around. I slammed on the brakes and we came to a stop. The impact on us was not enough to deploy our air bags.

"I'm okay. Kathryn, are you okay?"

Kathryn replied, "Yes, I am fine...is the other driver okay?"

---

[1] I highly recommend the "Conversations With God" book series. Visit http://gr8Wisdom.com/Books/CWG (proper capitalization is important when locating this website)

"Let's go check...." we got out of the car and started walking toward the other car. I asked Kathryn, "What happened? That's not my fault, is it? The light was green for us, wasn't it?"

"Yes, you waited for it to become green. He came from my side at full speed...it did not look like he was planning on stopping at all."

The other driver, a young man around twenty, was getting out of the car as we approached. We could see that he had hit his head on the steering wheel. He had a small bump and scuff mark, but other than that, he looked to be uninjured. I asked, "Are you okay?"

The young man replied, "Yes...no...I'll be okay...my parents are going to kill me."

A voice came from behind us, "I saw it all." Kathryn and I turned to look. A middle aged man was approaching us, "I saw what happened, I was right behind you."

I asked, "Was the light green? For me...?"

"Yes, you even waited a couple of seconds before you went. He just came from the other side at full speed. There was nothing you could do. You are lucky he did not smash into your wife. Are you okay?" After a bit more conversation we got the witness's name and phone number and he left.

While we were inspecting the damage to the vehicles, a TV news reporter with a camera man showed up and started filming us. They happened to be in the area and came to interview us. They had hoped that one of us was drunk so they could fit it into a holiday drunk driving piece they were trying to do, but were having bad luck. It had been a slow night for them so something was better than nothing, our piece made it onto the news anyway.

The police showed up while we were being interviewed. So now we had a second interview. The young man told the police that it was his fault. The last time he looked, the light was green, but he got engrossed looking for a specific landmark; the light turned red; and he ran the light at full speed.

Kathryn had to visit the chiropractor about five times as a result of the accident, but overall she did not suffer much from it. I was fine. Our car was totaled. It could have been fixed, but the cost was more than buying that same car used. The young man's family had insurance which covered all of the damages.

Within days, we were paid out at the top blue book value for our car and now we needed a new one. Chalk up another one for the Universe and its endless way of providing us with our needs and desires. With all of our excuses gone, I began shopping around for a brand new Dodge

Caravan. I checked a few internet sites and called a few dealers. Then, armed with the pricing information I had gathered, Kathryn and I went to the dealer that had given me the best price over the phone. Later that evening, I drove Kathryn home in our brand new Dodge Caravan.

We thoroughly enjoyed this vehicle. The dual zone climate control did end much of our fighting, as I suspected it would. Within a few weeks I removed the two middle bucket seats so that there was a large space between the front row of seats and the back bench seat. This made it convenient for our dog Ali who could stand right behind us with her head resting on the padded shuttle between the driver's and front passenger's seat. This way she was not standing on the nice seats.

It was very handy in this configuration for our needs. Often I took Kathryn to her treatments and doctor's appointments. I could wait outside in the van; it was almost like kicking back in my own living room. Without those unused seats, it was spacious. I would either sit there and read or listen to music or inspirational programs. The bench seat folded back and made a fair sized bed. Often I just left it folded back since I took a nap every day at work; I kept a large blanket and a couple of pillows in the van at all times. There were many times that Kathryn called me at work and asked me if she could come, from home, and take a nap with me. Even if I had already taken one I would make the time for her, I had no idea how much longer I would have her around. Most of these times she would come to have lunch with me at the Microsoft cafeteria and then we would go out to the van for a nap.

Working a full time job and helping Kathryn with her healing process was not easy. It took up a lot of my time and energy. But no matter how difficult it became, somehow it was manageable. Sleep had always been precious to me; I was careful to get eight hours of sleep in every night that I could. Many months prior to this time, I started having sleepless nights. However, I didn't worry about how I would be able to make it through work and stay awake. I remembered how well I did when I was having those back pains earlier in the year; I was just fine the next day at work. I had been able to manage before and knew that I would manage in the morning too. While lying in bed, I would use the time to meditate and be creative with my mind. I noticed how wonderfully peaceful I felt when I was in this state, and even though I was not asleep, I was certainly not awake either.

A few times this restless period happened around five AM, I just decided to get up and go into work. When this happened, I was fine and it was easy to get my hours for the week in. I also noticed on the days when I stayed in bed, and then finally fell back to sleep, how miserable I was when seven thirty rolled around and I had to get up. Soon I got into the habit of getting up early, four thirty to five thirty AM, and going into work or beginning Kathryn's hydrotherapy treatment. I woke up to go to the toilet about that time and once I had finished I was usually pretty much awake; I would just start my day. So I was already in the habit of going into work early when I really needed those extra hours in my week to help Kathryn out. I had the time I needed to get everything done. I found it easy to get by on only five or six hours of sleep in a night, as long as I occasionally got an eight-hour night of sleep every once in a while. I have heard many people talk about having trouble sleeping, maybe it is time to go with the flow and find something useful to do with that time instead of calling it wrong or thinking that you are broken in some way.

Christmas 1997

It was an early December morning; I was giving Kathryn a hydrotherapy treatment; and we were talking about our plans for Christmas. We liked having people over to our house on Christmas day, and up until this point this is what we had in mind; already we had invited two people. Then Kathryn suggested, "I was thinking...we should go to San Diego to be with your family this year. We could...."

I interrupted Kathryn, "I would prefer to spend Christmas with our friends. I don't feel...."

Kathryn too cut me short and said, "You are not listening...let me finish. Let's find a nice place to stay and we can have a vacation in San Diego this time. Do you know anywhere nice to stay that is near your parent's house?"

Kathryn knew how to pique my interest. I responded, "Yes, that does sound good. Coronado is very nice. I think the Coronado Cays has a hotel, if not, Hotel Del Coronado is beautiful. That would work for me."

When my family came up here and stayed in a motel room the year before last, right after Kathryn's first surgery, it worked out so nice that Kathryn and I tried the same thing when we visited them last year at Christmas. Except that we stayed in a dingy motel room that my mother had picked out for us because it was cheap. The motel was in such an unpleasant environment that we spent as little time as possible in our room and most of our time at my parent's house. So it was not the best experience for us.

Every year on Christmas Eve we drove down to Portland and spent it with Kathryn's family, except for 1995, right after Kathryn's first surgery. A few times on Christmas morning we flew from Portland to San Diego, we did it that way in '96 and again this year too. This year we stayed for four nights in San Diego instead of three.

It turned out to be a very romantic experience for us. Even though Kathryn and I could not have intercourse, we still found ways to make love and enjoy. The hotel room was fantastic, it was great to have such a nice place to escape to once the family experience had become enough. We rented our own car this time and took a few trips around the greater San Diego area, traveling all the way up to Del Mar. We pretended like we were going to move down here and pointed out beautiful homes that we wanted to live in. We had much laughter and fun together. Even still, I could not help but wonder if it would be our last Christmas together. Then I would feel some guilt for thinking of her death instead of her healing. Because it looked like Kathryn was getting worse and not better, it was difficult to hold my mind on her healing, my mind gravitated to fearful thoughts of her death. So most of the time I tried not to think about her health in anyway, instead I found other things to focus on.

Super Pooper

Early in January of 1998 Kathryn called me at work to tell me about a dog that turned up at our house. Back in September we saw this same dog roaming the streets of our neighborhood. He was a big and scruffy looking black lab; we were a bit afraid he might be dangerous at first. But one day last fall, he finally came up to our house so I got to meet him. He turned out to be very friendly and sweet. He was just old and not being cared for very well. After giving him a big bowl of water to drink, which he quickly finished off, I got his owner's phone number from the nametag on his collar. When I called, a woman answered the phone. After making sure she was the owner of Truman I asked her if she was going to come and pick up her dog, she made many excuses and then said, "I'm very busy right now. I don't think I can."

"Lady, that's not how it works!" I said in reply, "Some people would just call the animal shelter and you would be slapped with a fine or lose your dog. You are lucky that I called you first. Now are you going to come and get your dog or not?"

"Okay, I'll be over soon. What is your address?" The tone in this woman's reply was like a child who was being forced to do her daily chores. I could not believe her casual attitude about it. For a moment I put on my robes of judgment, got out the gavel, slammed it down on the bench and declared that court was in session. I became very indignant about how she cared for her dog. In my mind she quickly became the scum of the earth and deserved to be eradicated from the planet forever.

It was not long before I remembered Amoram's words about judgment and reflecting and wondered what she was mirroring back to me. I could see in my own judgment that I had a great deal of inner pain and anger that needed some way to escape. This woman gave me a good excuse to vent and let my mind run rampant, or so it seemed. But my stomach was turning as a result of my thoughts. Anger was not the feeling I wanted to be going through my day with. She had no right to do this to me...or was this me doing this to myself? At the time, I was confused as to how this was but I was determined to take control of my mind back again.

I decided to go outside and play with the dogs. Our dog, Ali, was enjoying Truman's company and Truman was loving the human attention. I threw the ball for them; I had to hold Ali back some of the time so that Truman could get it. Truman was good at bringing it back and dropping it at my feet while Ali required a bit of coaxing to release the ball. While we were playing in the street, a car approached. The woman inside was looking around; I figured it was Truman's owner. We moved out of the street and stepped up on to the curb, and she passed us by. I thought it was strange; I could have sworn it was her, but she looked right at us and passed us by. She had not told me what she looked like or what kind of car she drove, it simply felt to me that this was her.

We continued to play ball and after a few minutes the same car came back from the direction it had gone. Again the woman driving looked directly at us and passed us by. Certain this was the woman, I began waving and shouting, "Is this your dog?" She just kept going…but then she stopped, got out of the car and shouted, "Truman is that you? Come! Come Truman Come!"

At first Truman looked up at me, like he was saying, "Do I have to?" It took a bit of shouting and calling but Truman finally began, with his massive tail tucked between his legs, walking slowly toward the woman and got into the back seat of the car. The woman said nothing to me, she just drove off.

After that incident, there were many days that we saw Truman walking around the neighborhood, but he did not come back to our house, not that fall at least. Now it was winter and there had even been some snow. We had not seen Truman for many months. Kathryn called me at work to tell me, "Truman came back; he is nothing but skin and bones. He was on his last legs, if I had not fed him he would have died any day, I am sure of it. I am not sending him back to that woman! There is no way she is getting him back. He does not even have a collar on. His neck looks like he has been tied up with a rope that was too tight for too long. His fur is all matted and dirty. Michael will you give him a bath when you come home?"

"What? Wait a minute…Kathryn! We can't take care of another animal right now! Or should I say, I CAN'T take care of another animal right now, because you know that is how it will be."

"Sweetheart, please calm down."

"No, you can't…."

"Michael please, don't do this. Right now we are keeping George until we can find a good home for him. I wouldn't force you to keep him…."

"Noooh. It won't work out that way. We will end…."

"He is not going back. He is staying here. Are you staying here?" Kathryn was more determined to take this course of action than I was.

George, did she say George? "What do you mean George? You haven't re-named him already have you?" I knew a losing battle when I was in one but I was not yet ready to give up this fight.

"Yes, Truman is not a good name for him. He is much too sweet for that. I have named him George."

"Kathryn, you can't keep him. We have to find him a good home...and quickly. I don't want to take care of another dog. Will you agree?"

"Yes, that is fine with me. He just cannot go back to those people. They are not taking care of him."

When I got home that evening I was shocked to see how skinny this large dog had become. Within two weeks he filled out and began looking healthy again. At this point in time I had been making homemade food for Ali. I started doing that because her body odors were getting too strong and her fur was looking rather shabby. In the past I had dogs and solved this problem with homemade dog food. Within two weeks of serving Ali my homemade dog food her fur was beautiful and smelled clean.[1] I had not given her a bath, I only changed her food. Many skin problems, balding rear ends,[2] and other such things can also be solved in this way. So I had to serve George the same homemade dog food, I couldn't feed him crap and give Ali the good stuff. Even if I wanted to, Kathryn would not let me do that. George ate half again as much more than Ali so this meant I had to make dog food much more frequently. Kathryn promised that she would help me make every batch. This was a promise that I knew she would not be able to keep nor would I even try to make her to keep it. When it came down to it, I knew her health would be more important than this silly issue.

Ali slept in our room with us; often Kathryn shared her side of the queen size bed with Ali.[3] Miss Kitty would be on Kathryn's pillow, Ali at her feet, and Kathryn scrunched up into the tightest place she could manage. I slept on the other half and did not let the animals encroach on my precious bed space. I was firm on this point; the animals quickly found the floor when they tried. Now that George was here, there was some discussion of how to manage with him in the bed too. But I think Kathryn realized that she was in danger of a full scale mutiny if she continued that conversation. Still he was a bed time pest...when he wasn't farting obnoxiously, he was coming over to my side of the bed and resting his head on the bed right next to my face, sometimes breathing

---

[1] Please visit http://gr8Wisdom.com/DogFood for a great homemade dog food recipe. (proper capitalization is important when locating this website)

[2] Balding rear ends are often caused by dry and unhealthy skin which causes the dog to bite and scratch more often.

[3] Ali was a small black lab, which means she was a medium sized dog. She took up considerable bed space.

into my face. How rude! I mean really! When I complained, Kathryn merely told me, "I love George so much because he reminds me of you."

Whenever I took the dogs walking, I had to take six or seven plastic bags with me. With Ali I got by with one or two. But with Super Pooper George, I needed four or five bags, all of the time. He would go into the bushes to do his business, often it was loose, often he would get it on the bush, and sometimes on himself. Because they were inside dogs I always wondered and worried. Even after inspection I would find it on his fur later, or worse, once we got home I'd find it in some unsuspecting spot on the carpet. I did not want poo on the carpet. As fanatically clean as Kathryn was, she had infinite patience for any dirtiness caused by the animals.

George had a thick tail and it was at the perfect level to wipe an end table clean, which he did on several inopportune occasions. When he stood in the hall and got excited it sounded like someone was banging on the front door with their fist. I did not like George. For me he meant more work and more I had to tolerate. He was the sweetest dog, even sweeter than Ali was. His heart was in the right place, but I still did not like him.

Nausea Returns

During January of 1998 Kathryn's ability to eat decreased and her nausea began to return. By the end of January she began vomiting again. On the third evening of this Kathryn gave up. She told me, "Michael, I am tired of fighting this; I am not going to eat anymore. I just can't...Please forgive me, but I just can't do this. Will you call Dr. Jones and ask him what's next, what will we do?"

What's next?!? I thought to myself, *You'll die if you don't eat, that's what's next!* I was a bit irritated from everything I was doing and all that had been going on. I hadn't heard her talk like this yet. This was the first time she sounded like she was giving up. I said to her, "Kathryn! You can't give up like that. You have to stay strong. Don't you think anything we are doing is working?"

"No, I just can't do this. I don't know what to think...I can't think, the pain and nausea are just too much. It never ends; it is always going on. Now I need something, some medicine. Please call Howard." I began to feel compassion for Kathryn and what she was going through. I felt silly for being upset with her. I wanted to help my dear friend now.

I called Howard Jones. I must have caught him out at a restaurant or bar; at least that is what the background noise left me thinking. After much conversation, with me energetically trying to get him to pull some sort of miracle out of his hat, Howard said in exasperation, "Michael, there is only so much we can do for Kathryn at this stage. I am amazed that she has lived this long. We can only keep her comfortable, without chemotherapy that is the best we can do. I will phone in a prescription to your pharmacy for more pain and nausea medicine."

"But how much do I give her?" I asked not understanding if it was different medicine or the same things.

"As much as she needs to stay comfortable. At this stage it's not going to do any more harm."

Kathryn and I were both left feeling unsatisfied with this conversation...poor Howard, he must have to face such difficult conversations all of the time. I did not know what we expected; somehow we were hoping Howard had become a god or something. Hadn't they invented a magic wand since the last time we talked to him? Hopelessness and despair was the mood of the moment. We held each other and cried. We discussed how long it would take for her to die. Kathryn expected it would only be a few more weeks. If only it could have been that easy.

On my way to the pharmacy I wanted to get stoned. It was impossible, actually not impossible, just irresponsible for me to try and get some pot at that moment, but I made my mind up that later, perhaps tomorrow, I definitely would do so. I stopped at the grocery store and got some wine and Ben and Jerry's Chunky Monkey ice cream, and then went to the Pharmacy for Kathryn's medications. Both stores were located in the same shopping complex.

Kathryn was lying in bed when I got home. She took her medications and we talked for a while. Kathryn apologized to me for putting me through this. She said many tender things to me. It was so senseless to talk about how sad this outcome was. So we reminisced about the good times we had. One of our favorite memories was the time when we had my car all loaded up with stuff from my Lake Oswego duplex apartment. The next day I was to depart for my first day of work in Bellevue. We got some ice cream and began eating it as we drove to Kathryn's house. We were talking and joking and became so hysterical with laughter that I had to pull the car over to settle down. Meanwhile ice-cream was melting and going everywhere. It was a very funny and memorable moment for us...although we remembered the moment and the laughter; we could not remember what we had been laughing about.

Kathryn reminded me how she once caught me literally jumping up and down with excitement when she arrived at my granny apartment from her home in Gresham. I didn't think she could see me; I was just happy to see her and was simply expressing myself naturally. She thanked me for all of the times I stayed with her in the hospital and for all of the times I drove down to Portland with her; she understood that I had plenty of other things to do. This was a bittersweet moment for us both. We were tired of fighting this disease, and we just accepted what was coming.

Soon the medications took effect, and Kathryn fell asleep. I went downstairs and had a few glasses of wine and watched a movie on TV. Again I remembered why I enjoyed wine so much. I was satisfied to save the rest of the bottle for another time.

For many months I had been thinking about how my life was going to be without Kathryn. Of course there was sadness, but I also knew that I would be fine. I thought of some of the fun things I could do that Kathryn would not want to do with me, like going to Britenbush Hot Springs for naked hot tubing. I would take a cruise. I would go out dancing again. I would travel to some other tropical location; perhaps move to the Caribbean or some other exotic tropical place...definitely I would stay much longer this time, perhaps years. I would get to make love to other women again; I do enjoy having variety—all such things I had already contemplated with joy.

But now I wondered and worried about the next few weeks or months. How long was it going to take for her to die? I noticed a desire to fast forward through this part. I did not want her to die quicker, but I did not want to suffer through watching Kathryn suffer either. If I thought too much about her being absent from my life, I suffered the loneliness. If I contemplated the adventures I was going to have, I suffered the anticipation of, "when can we get to that part?" If I thought about my immediate future, I suffered from watching Kathryn die.

The only thing I could do at the moment was be in the now moment; I suffered the least by being present right now; just being in my present moment and noticing what was going on and how I felt. It felt surreal to me, like, "How could this be happening?" Kathryn wasn't dead, she was right here. We were both able to look at each other and laugh and smile and hug and love…Actually, except for the puking part, the now moment was still very good. I lived in a warm and comfortable home, had plenty to eat, animals who loved me, and a wife who loved me. In that now moment, I had those things. In that now moment, I was fine.

In that now moment, I even enjoyed wine without going crazy with it. I liked the feeling of control I felt. I did not care what anyone, not even Kathryn thought of me drinking. I decided in a few days, if I still felt the same way I was going to tell her I was drinking and smoking pot and she just had to accept that. I didn't give it much more thought than that.

All this pain and suffering was happening in my life, and I was simply surfing through it. I was taking care of everything I needed to take care of. I was still sane. I had too much understanding to do something totally stupid or harmful. I was still feeling; definitely I was feeling very intensely, but I just kept my head about me while I observed what I was feeling. I thought about how far I had come as a person and in my spiritual awareness. I worried about how much further I still had to go; it seemed endless, like there was too much in me that still needed correcting. But even with that, the whole package, my life…I was fine. I was here. I was alive. And it was good to be alive.

The next day I did go out and score some pot. It was nice to have that back, I really enjoyed it. Within a few weeks, I also decided I was going to have a mistress. I felt young, strong, and healthy. I wanted passionate sex to be a part of my life again and I didn't want to wait until Kathryn died or became healthy again—either way that was too long to wait. I began surfing the internet, had a few exciting email and chat exchanges, and then I found someone who seemed ready, willing and able to meet up with me for a hot massage and perhaps more. I decided that I better tell Kathryn about these new behaviors that I had embraced before I got involved with this woman.

Kathryn did not know what hit her. She was in shock when she heard me tell her how I was going to be. She had power when she caught me in the act. But now it was different, she did not know how to respond. It seemed so obviously wrong to her, in her mind; she could not believe I was telling her I was going to do this, and she needed to accept it. We had to visit Amoram right away. Brenda had always said, "There are no channeling emergencies." Although Kathryn may have disagreed at this moment in time, Bren had no available appointments until the next day. So we had to wait. This was more difficult for Kathryn than it was for me.

Amoram was the same as always. Amoram acknowledged that I was clear about what I wanted to do and that I would do these things. He said he did not see that there had to be any great difficulties as a result. It was for Kathryn to decide how she wanted to be with it. I needed to be aware as I participated in these energies and come to understand how they were serving me. Amoram also told me that my dog would be helping me deal with the energy from the pot and to give it at least an hour after smoking before spending time with Kathryn. He suggested that Kathryn and I should sit down and talk about this more rationally and discuss what our boundaries would be and draw up a contract.

Amoram also maintained that Kathryn did not need to die from her cancer. This gave Kathryn more hope. At no time in the past or future did Amoram ever say Kathryn was going to die. He continuously told us she "could" become healthy again, that "she did not need to die." Although it gave me hope, I noted that he never said that she "would" survive this cancer. At times this just made me angry...I wanted to say, "Why don't you tell her, 'You don't need to die from this but you probably will.'"

Even with these frustrations, Amoram was a great calming force for us both. In Amoram's presence, we were much better able to give up our stance and see things from a new perspective, one filled with light and love and awareness of that which is beyond the physical. Whenever we took a difficult situation to Amoram, it was always met with the same detached clarity. There was not even an initial reaction that came from judgment. From start to finish, talking with Amoram was like talking to God.

When we went home, Kathryn and I took separate rooms in the house to contemplate. I came up with my plan, of the limits that I would place on my alcohol and marijuana consumption. I felt strong and secure that I was not doing anything wrong, that I was merely taking care of myself and my own needs. I still was not sure if Kathryn was going to throw me out or consent to living in peace with me around these issues. When we got together to talk Kathryn asked me as sweetly as can be, "Michael, I would like to apply for that position of mistress that you have open."

"What? Kathryn, what do you mean?"

"I can accept the pot and alcohol if you keep from going crazy with it, but I can't bear the thought of you being with another woman. I can still be your lover. Let me try. I can be exciting and adventurous like you want. I can go to the community pool and swim naked with you. Please let me try."

I was so touched by the tender way she asked me. Usually she was telling me how things were going to be. I always felt like I was the one who had to give in to her and her demands, even when they were silly and illogical. I hated the circumstances, but I loved the fact that she was actually considering my needs and was asking me rather than telling me how it was going to be. I replied, "Yes sweetheart, I will give you a chance to be my mistress. I will tell that other woman I am canceling my plans to meet up with her."

We talked for a while about the other boundaries. Kathryn wanted to be clear about what I meant and how much and how often I would get high. But she did not object to my plan. Kathryn was exhausted after this big day and lay down for a long nap. I took our dogs for a walk to a large wooded park that was near our house, and I celebrated my new found freedom by smoking a joint.

There was water running through the creek, a ten-foot drop created a small water fall with a beautiful sound. I enjoyed the play of sunlight that danced through the trees and the color of the tiny rocks that lined the creek bed. My dogs sniffed around and chased sticks while I relaxed in bliss on a moss covered log. It felt good to have more control of my own life once again, especially to choose what I felt was right or wrong for me. It was funny to me, because I was losing my wife and should be suffering, but right now I felt great. I knew it was not just because I was stoned, I knew I was quite capable of suffering while I was stoned. I knew I felt good because of how I was dealing with things in my mind. I also knew that the pot was intensifying my focus and how I felt. I did not need anyone telling me I was wrong or bad or not good enough. I thought, *I'll show them, even stoned I will be the best husband I can be; I will take care of my wife and live responsibly because that is how I am. No one will even know the difference.*

The next day Kathryn and I went to the community swimming pool. We were the only ones there, which made it much easier for Kathryn to swim naked. Much to my surprise and delight she did just that, took off her clothes and swam naked with me in the pool. Actually she put one of my aqua-aerobic bar-bells under each arm pit and used them to float as I swam and pushed her around the pool. Kathryn was quite thin, too thin; she was not at her most attractive weight. Yet, I loved her and I loved looking at her just the same; she was still beautiful to me. The water also helped by floating the sagging parts back to the right place; the view was very nice from underwater...good thing I had goggles. I enjoyed this adventuresome sexual play; it was just what I needed. Kathryn was happy that day; it was so easy with her willing participation. She came back to the pool and played with me five more times after that.

Kathryn found many ways to show her appreciation for me; she put more effort into giving me affection. It turned out that this was very satisfying to me. I easily forgot about trying to find a mistress.

Kathryn was still eating a little, actually drinking; she only drank things she could liquefy significantly. I was amazed at how well she was doing since she was getting very little nutrition each day. She still had energy to do things; in fact she was feeling better without all of the vomiting. For about three weeks, she rarely took any medication. She got tired easily so I would do as much as I could for her. I would drop her off right at the door of places we would visit such as stores, movie theaters, or restaurants. Anything that had to be carried I made sure I took them, Kathryn would try to get them herself, so I had to remember to beat her to it. That way she did not object to me taking them. But if she already had them, then she would object, "I can carry these."

At the end of March, I took a trip out to New Mexico with a friend to look at land as a possible place for a new home. While I was in the area I wanted to see Arizona too. So I rented a car and drove there at top speed. It was really cool because the roads were long and straight, they had very little traffic on them. Some of them had no speed limit, others had very high limits. It was thrilling to drive 140 mph and beyond. I found some properties to look at before coming, and made connections with the appropriate realtors. I drove around to nine properties that day and covered at least two hundred miles. That evening while I was out having dinner alone, I had a couple of glasses of wine. On the way back to my motel room I bought a small bottle of Cuervo Gold Tequila. I poured myself a large drink of the Tequila, but I did not think it was more than I could handle. In less than an hour my head was hanging miserably over the toilet bowl. It got to the point that even though it felt like I needed to puke up more, I couldn't. The room was spinning too fast, I felt horrible and just wanted to die. Since nothing would come up, I drank a lot of bottled water. As I suspected, the water did not stay down very long and puking it up did offer me some additional relief. I lay down in bed. At first I was too uncomfortable to sleep, but after about half an hour I fell fast asleep.

The next day I was surprised that I had such a strong reaction. There was still plenty of Tequila in the glass and bottle. I felt like shit. Even though I was sticking to our contract about my pot smoking and drinking, I had received enough resistance from Kathryn that it was just not worth the grief. After what happened the night before I wanted nothing more to do with the pot and alcohol. I called Kathryn and told her about what had happened and about my decision to give them all up. She was happy. Later I regretted that move, but still I stuck with my decision to quit. It was simply easier to go with the flow. I did not need the pot and alcohol that badly.

By the time April came around, Kathryn had forgotten that she gave up on life. She was back to talking about surviving her cancer. She continued with her various treatments, I was actually enjoying the time I spent taking her to her appointments. I enjoyed my quiet time waiting in the van. I could not help but think this could be the last day I'd have with her, so I wasn't going to waste this time. This attitude helped me to stay present with Kathryn and be of maximum service. We both enjoyed our time together. If I was hungry or tired, I found it difficult to be nice, but I found it easy to manage my physical comfort. I was able to sleep in the van while Kathryn was receiving a treatment. Nourishing snack food was easy to keep on hand. Most of the time, I made it my duty to be in service to Kathryn as often as I possibly could; this required me to take care of myself. I began to realize how important it was to maintain my own well-being, so that I actually had something to offer to Kathryn. It was no good to only go through the motions of helping her; we both suffered whenever I attempted this.

By the time May came around, I could not believe that Kathryn was still alive. She kept getting thinner, and she was still only drinking just a little bit of food. This was a bit disconcerting for me. I believed I could endure because I had convinced myself that this would only last a few months, but four months had passed since we gave up and thought the end was only weeks away. How much longer would I have to suffer watching Kathryn suffer? I needed an escape from all of this. I wanted to have some fun with Kathryn that did not involve taking her to a treatment. It took some effort but I finally convinced her to take a long weekend and go up to Vancouver BC. I had to bring up Bernie Segal's play therapy again, but it was worth it.

We stuck around the city, went to the movies and Stanly Park. Kathryn was able to walk around a little bit, very slowly, many times we stopped at an available park bench and just sat and enjoyed the beauty. We went to the aquarium; we found plenty to watch there while sitting down. At times Kathryn waited patiently for me while I had a look around. We found a peaceful rhythm in the time we spent together. Kathryn was aware of the limitations she was imposing on me and was being as flexible as she could. I was keeping in mind her condition and was as gentle as I could be. Although we never managed this to perfection, we marveled at how much better we were getting along than in some of our past.

We celebrated Kathryn's fiftieth birthday at the end of June in Cannon Beach, Oregon. Kathryn loved this place and had not been there in many years. Using the internet, we found a beautiful small hotel that was right on the beach near an outcropping of tall small rock islands, you can walk to them at low tide. Kathryn spent most of her time at the hotel, in the room or on the balcony overlooking the sea; she was not feeling up to doing anything more than this. I split my time between her and exploring the beach with its many rocky outcrops that made this place special.

That same weekend was the start of a well deserved summer vacation for me. Microsoft ended my contract. I was disappointed because I liked working for this group and they liked me. But I could not help but notice that God gave me time off right when the weather got really good. The days were long, and it rarely rained. Summer in Seattle is short but sweet. Again I went though the motions of looking for work but put no real intention into getting a job.

The timing for this break from work was good for another reason. Kathryn's health continued to decline. She had become nothing more than a walking skeleton. We took her into Dr. Jones. He had a special port surgically installed on Kathryn's chest for intravenous liquid food, glucose, saline solutions, and medications that might be needed later. We contracted with a hospice service provider; they sent a nurse to our house every few days with liquid nutrition bags and to check Kathryn's vital signs. They also showed me how to change the bags and take care of the port in Kathryn's chest.

For the next two months, my days consisted primarily of taking care of the animals and the house and spending time on the beautiful beach at Idlewood park. Often the dogs came with me. Sometimes Kathryn came too, but most of the time she stayed at home by herself.

Lessons in Energy

On one occasion I was giving Kathryn a full Reiki treatment; she was laid out on the massage table. I had been working on her for about five minutes when Kathryn commented, "That feels very nice; it is just what I need." By this time I had made the mistake of getting caught up in my ego too many times. Each time that happened, Kathryn would correct me. It almost got to the point where I did not want to work on her because of this. But as time went on I was grateful for the fantastic training I got at Master Kathryn's feet.

On this occasion, I held my focus on being a clear channel for the Holy Spirit to move through for about another ten minutes longer, until I got to Kathryn's abdomen. I knew this was where the cancer was. Fear came over me, but I did not realize it, I just became stupid and lost my focus. I began to imagine the energy flowing through me and into her like a raging white water river. I imagined this incredibly powerful force washing the cancer away. Clear clean white water flushing away the unwanted disease. I was just beginning to feel pleased with myself for coming up with such a great visualization when...

Within just a few seconds Kathryn said, "Whoa, that's way too fast...too intense! You have to slow that down. Please it hurts; it's making me nauseous!" Kathryn had a pained look on her face; she opened her eyes and began to sit up.

It took me a few moments to comprehend what was happening. I did not want to believe that I was doing harm, I wanted to help. Kathryn's pleas brought me back to a place of cooperation and openness, I silently asked the Holy Spirit, *Please work through me in exactly the right way that would best help Kathryn.*

Kathryn responded immediately, "That's much better. Thanks." She lay back down, and I continued giving her an energy treatment. I never even told her what I did, and she did not ask.

Being able to shift my energy on demand was a skill that I had to develop in order to support Kathryn as she was going through her most painful times with cancer. It seemed that Kathryn had to remind me when my mind was drifting into uncomfortable areas. There were also times where my intense passion for life could be very unpleasant for Kathryn, and she brought this to my attention as well.

Can you remember a time when you were uncomfortable in your body? For me this happens if I am tired or if I need something to eat. At those times, have you ever felt how your sense of irritation increases when someone else enters the room or comes near you? Kathryn had been in a state of intense irritation for many months now; I expect her cancer complications were beyond any irritation I had ever experienced. This amplified her sensitivity to my energy.

I would come home from some outside activity, and often I would be feeling full of life and enthusiasm. In great excitement I would go to say hello to Kathryn and to sit with her for a while. Just entering the room with my energy revved up to such a state was nearly enough to make her vomit. She often had to ask me to settle my energy down.

It was difficult not to take this personally. I would think, *I haven't done anything wrong. Why does she have to be like that? Can't she tell that it is her illness that is making her feel this way?* However, when I thought like this, it only made matters worse for Kathryn. She would grab the bowl and beg me, "Michael, please that is not helpful. Please change your energy or go somewhere else."

Eventually I would realize what I was doing and change my thinking to, *This is my beloved wife. She is suffering. It will be much easier for me to change my energy than it will be for her. What thoughts can I hold that will make this better?*

Kathryn replied, "That's it, now your energy feels much better." Yet I had only thought those things; I had not said anything out loud. I had not even found the new thing to focus on; there was only the questioning, the desired to find a loving place to focus. That turned out to be enough of a mental shift. When my mind was genuinely concerned for Kathryn's welfare she felt fine having me near her. But if I was excited, wanting to tell her about my afternoon, or if I was feeling guilt for not taking her with me, she was asking me to change my energy.[1]

---

[1] This is child's play to me now. I have since enjoyed many experiences of deliberately setting my mind and witnessing change in the outer world circumstances. I have been able to prevent harmful violent things from happening to me as a result. I am quickly able to gain the trust of people and animals. I have been able to take pain away from others. This is a topic I will cover in greater detail in my next book.

Dead Dogs Don't Lie

Kathryn never found a good home for George, she never even tried. Way back in January, about a week after we took George in, we started seeing missing dog posters scattered all around our neighborhood. After about a week a new lot of posters went up in the neighborhoods that were many blocks further away from our neighborhood. After another week we got a phone call from our veterinarian. When we first found George we brought him in to see this vet. They knew George was a stray that we had picked up and now the owners have shown up at his office asking if anyone brought Truman in. The vet told Truman's owners he did not know, but he would check with the other vets and staff.

The vet insisted that we give George back. Even though I did not like George, I still cared about his well-being. I told the vet, "Those people were not taking good care of George. He was nothing but skin and bone when he came to us, you saw that when we brought him in. He is just now starting to look healthy. Often he was allowed to roam freely throughout the neighborhood. George likes us and does not want to go back. We have let him free in our front yard and he does not go wandering. We leave the front door open; he could easily leave the house and go wandering. He stays here. Why do you suppose he went wandering for those people and not for us?"

The vet did not fight me, "Well I have not told them anything yet. I'll leave this one alone for now. But if there is any trouble, I am not promising what I will say or do."

We hoped this would be the end of this drama, but it was not. We noticed that the missing dog flyers were being refreshed when they became torn or someone[1] took them down. A couple of weeks later the vet called again, "The family came looking for Truman today. They really miss him, they even cried in my office. Now I am going to have to insist that you give Truman back to them. I am only calling to give you the chance to tell them before I do."

I thought about what Amoram said about the appearency of truth as I replied, "No, you have to trust us. Those people have some other agenda…it is like the dog is a possession and this is some sort of ego trip for them…they were not taking good care of this dog. We are certain of this. He loves being with us, and we are not going to send him back to be neglected again. We have discussed this many times and given it plenty of thought. We are certain we are doing right by this dog. If we have to,

---

[1] Kathryn or I.

we will send him to someone else, so there is no chance they will find him whatever you do. So please stop pressing us on this issue."

The vet was easily swayed; I could tell he did not want trouble. "This one is on your head. If the police come around I will have to tell them what I know. By not coming forward now, you are taking a big risk for yourself."

"I know I am taking a risk, but I think it is small one. The dog's welfare is more important to me and my wife. I won't ask anything else from you except that you keep client confidentiality."

We were concerned about the amount of effort George's old family was going through and began to doubt our perspective. Twice Kathryn tried to ask George verbally if he wanted to go back to his old home. Both times he turned his head and would not look at her. Whenever Kathryn spoke to George he would look at her and pay attention. But not these times, these times he actually turned his head away. We got quite a laugh; he looked so human when he did that.

Still we wanted to be sure. So we took two different walks with the purpose of leaving George near his old home. The first time we went down the street where George used to live, when we got about ten houses away we took him off of his leash, left him sitting there, and began to silently walk home. George followed us. The second time we went to the other end of the street, where it crossed with another major street. We left George only a few houses away from his old home and quickly began to walk away. Again George followed us home.

The vet called back a few more times and he talked to Kathryn. Kathryn explained to him how we tried these two ways to get George to decide where he wanted to live. The vet understood us and our conviction, but still he was stuck between two parties. In the end, Kathryn told the vet to talk to me. When he did he said, "We have to tell the family something. You have been telling me you are going to send George somewhere else, have you done that?"

I did not want to continue playing this game, "Look that is irrelevant. I have made our position clear on more than one occasion. We want no further phone calls about this. Please stop calling us."

"Okay, if you will do one thing. Call them and tell them you have their dog and that you are not giving it back. Then they will stop harassing me. They can tell I am hiding something, so they keep coming around."

"That is fine. I will have a friend call them and give them the message. I am happy to do that." Martha being a fiery Scorpio like me loved having the chance to leave a message for them. I don't know what she really said, but I am sure she let them have it in some clever yet tasteful way. That was the last we heard from the family. Slowly the missing pooch posters disappeared...we helped the process along.

All of that happened many months prior; now it was August. By this time George had grown on me, and I even liked him. The last few times I took Ali and George for a walk, George just sat down whenever he got tired and rested. So the last time I left George at home and only took Ali for a walk. Kathryn did not approve. She told me, "George sat by the window and whined the whole time you were gone. Didn't you notice when you came back...he was waiting at the door for you. You have to take him with you next time."

"But Kathryn, some thing is wrong with George. I don't think he is up to it anymore. I don't want to take him with us."

Kathryn insisted, "He will be okay. Look, he may not live much longer, why don't you just humor me and take George along with you. You can stop and wait for him when he needs to rest."

This was another losing battle that I did not fight very hard to win. Lately I had been giving in to Kathryn's demands with little or no fight. Her ideas were usually good, sometimes more work than necessary, but no harm came. It was just as easy to do what she wanted as it was to do what I wanted, if only I decided to do that. So I took George on a few more walks.

Eventually George could not walk home. Lucky for me his legs gave out just a few houses away from ours. After a long wait and many prods to get him up and going, I realized he was paralyzed and could not get up. So I lifted his hind end and pushed him along so that he walked on his front legs. After many hours of rest he was able to get up again and walk around the house. The next time I was getting ready to go for a walk George and Kathryn were waiting at the door. She insisted that I take George with me. At first I objected but then I agreed. George only made it to the end of the drive way and a few paces down the street before his legs gave out. I brought him back into the house holding his rear end up. I gave Kathryn an "I told you so" look and resumed my walk with Ali.

A few days later, we had to bring George to the vet. His back end seemed to be completely paralyzed; he was unable to walk at all. The vet told us he had a temporary solution, but the next time George got into this state would be a good time to put him down. The vet gave George an injection and in a short time George walked out the door and got into the van on his own four feet. Two days later George was paralyzed again. Kathryn could not bear the thought of having him euthanized; she wanted me to move him from place to place. I knew the time would come, so I waited for the appropriate moment to stage my mutiny. Later, when Ali needed to go outside to pee, Kathryn asked me to take George out too.

That was the moment I was waiting for, that is when I said, "If you want to hold his bottom up when he goes to the toilet, then you go ahead...knock yourself out. I am through." I walked out the front door and slammed it closed behind me. I began to walk down the drive way when I stopped. I thought to myself, *Where am I going? What can I do?* Then in a tone of voice low enough so that none of the neighbors would hear me I said out loud, "God why? Why do I have a wife that is nearly about to die and a dog who is dying too?!? Why...I just can't take this anymore."

Then I was quiet. This time I expected an answer and I was listening...*You said you wanted to be a healer, didn't you? What did you think being a healer was about? Being up on stage, being the one everyone looks up to? This is not what being a healer is about. You are being a healer now, in this situation, that is what is going on. Even if she dies, she will die in much more comfort and peace with you as a healer than without you. That is what this is all about; you are being a healer.*

I began to cry, "But my dog, I don't like him much but Kathryn does, and she wants me to keep him alive. I have to take him to the vet and have him put down today. Sometimes I want to have that done for Kathryn too...why does she have to suffer like this? How much more of this can she take? Tell her it is okay to go, I have."

Then I got the answer, *Don't worry, you know what to do. As a healer you are here to support her on her path, and this is it. One step at a time...you know what to do. You will be fine. Right now you are fine. Watch, in the next moment you will be fine too...See, I told you, still fine. It just keeps going on like that. Kathryn is fine too. This is nothing more than she can handle. She signed up for this. It's hard to imagine but she did.*

One step at a time, I was fine. By the time I went back into the house Kathryn had cooled down. "Michael, I am sorry. I know your plate is full. Are you sure there is nothing else you can do to help George?"

"Kathryn! You know the answer to that. Yes my plate is full, it is very full."

"Okay, then please take him to the vet and have him put down."

"Me, you are not going to come?" I paused for a moment waiting for an answer, and then I said, "You don't have to, I understand."

"Michael, I can't bear to watch him die. Please you go...and hold him."

I had my orders. I knew what to do. These days I was merely following orders, whether they were God's or Kathryn's; I had my orders. I always knew what to do when the time came. I knew I could walk through anything. I held George as he died in my arms. I cried. I went home and got on with my life.

A few days later, Kathryn said to me, "I wish they could just euthanize me too. Michael, I am tired. I am really tired. I don't know if I can fight this much longer."

"Kathryn don't…please don't fight this. Just let go and go with it. I don't want you to leave, but this is no way to live. It's harder for me to watch you suffer than it is to take your death. I will be okay."

"I am through fighting it. Whatever happens, I don't care anymore. Michael, when the time comes, I want to be able to take my own life if I need to. Will you help me?"

"Of course sweetheart…I understand. What do you have in mind?" I responded with intrigue.

"Is there a book or something that can tell me how to do this? I'd like to find the easiest way that we can." Kathryn tone was solemn and sincere.

"You're serious aren't you?" Although I understood why she wanted this, I was expecting a joke or something to be coming up soon. I was shocked that it was coming to this for her. I expected that she could easily just decide to leave her body and go; it seemed to me that this should be easy for her now. It was difficult for me to understand at that time, but now I know that this was her way of letting me know the end was near. I believe she was hanging around for me. Even though I had been telling her not to do that for me, she was doing it for herself. She loved me and wanted every last moment she could tolerate in her body to be with me. This is why she hung on so long.

Soon after this conversation finished, Kathryn took some more pain and anti-nausea pills and went upstairs to bed. She was serious about getting her a book on suicide. I thought about this for a while, and it made me crazy. I yelled out loud, "God, why are you doing this to my beloved wife?!? Why are you making me stand by and watch?!? I am so FUCKING PISSED OFF AT YOU. Get off your lazy ass and fix her NOW!!!" Kathryn was knocked out cold on her medication so I did not worry that she would hear me.

I got no reply. Just boiling blood, a churning stomach…I became a heap on the floor…curled up in a ball I cried longer and harder than I had cried in years. I can't ever remember crying that much.

It was the end of August and Kathryn had been vomiting nearly every day, many times a day, since the end of February. In those last few weeks it had been getting worse, more frequent, sometimes dry heaves. There was much more pain. Many times, in the middle of the night, when

I was sound asleep, I was awoken by the sound of a gold wedding ring hitting a stainless steel bowl, quickly that was followed by the sound of Kathryn heaving until the flow of putrid liquid was heard streaming into the metal bowl like it came from a hose.

The next sound was that of my feet running across the floor to dump a full bowl of vomit into the toilet and clean it up quickly. I never knew if the bowl would be needed again soon. Even if the bowl was not full, Kathryn did not want to hold the smelly thing under her nose any longer than she needed to. I had to keep it together every time this happened, which was way too frequent.

These sounds…these smells…have been etched in my mind for all time.

The End of Summer

September came, the weather was cooling down, the money was running out; it was time to get serious about finding a new job. I had applied for three jobs every week just to satisfy unemployment requirements. I had a head hunter supposedly looking for jobs for me. I got a few lame calls from him making excuses, but still no real prospects showed up. Two days after I truly decided to go back to work, I had a new job; I did nothing different to make this happen except decide that I was ready to go back to work.

I was hired to convert the 32-bit Windows database code into 64-bit code. I thought it sounded like it could be an interesting job when I applied, but I was not really thinking it through. My mind was preoccupied with thoughts about my how quickly my precious summer had disappeared, and how much I enjoyed lying in the sun at Idlewood Park. Once I began work, I discovered that the work was not interesting at all, indeed it was quite boring. Even still it was the perfect job for me at the perfect time. I did not need to use my brain much for this job. It was so repetitive that I could do it in my sleep. And it was the highest paying job of my career. But this was a time in my life, for the next five months, I needed a job I could do without thinking. Because my mind was somewhere else, it was not at Microsoft.

If you go back again through this book and look at every job related "coincidence" you will have to admit that there were a lot of "coincidences" lining up in my favor.[1] Was I simply lucky or is there a chance that the mental and spiritual work I was doing had been influencing all that happened? God takes care of everything, every little detail. Let go and let God…it is the best way.

I had been talking to Kathryn about hiring a live-in caretaker and housekeeper for her. She needed someone there while I was at work and in the evening I needed help, I wanted to get more sleep. Kathryn insisted, "We do not need this; we can't afford it." I told her, "Maybe you can't afford it but I sure can…you won't be here to pay the bills, I will." Then she said, "I refuse to allow anyone else to come here, especially not to live here in my home." I replied, "Kathryn, you don't have a choice. I will move out and leave you to take care of yourself if you keep going on like this." That got her attention; she fussed about a bit more, but she agreed.

---

[1] Many more job related miracles have occurred for me after the time period covered in this book as well.

I hired a temporary caretaker to cover my work hours from an agency and began advertising for a live-in caretaker. On her first day the temp asked Kathryn about her condition. Kathryn replied by telling her, "I am not doing very well right now. But very soon I expect to make a full recovery."[1]

It was Friday evening; I had just finished my fourth week at this new job; and the temp had just finished her third day and went home for the weekend. I had only spoken to a few live-in caretakers on the phone by this point. The last two evenings, Kathryn could not make it up the stairs. The night before that, I had to help her up. That was when we decided to bring a hospital bed and porta-potty home for the living room. Kathryn had the button for the doorbell to call me if she needed help. I went up to bed at ten thirty. At quarter till midnight I was woken from a very sound sleep by the ringing doorbell. When I got downstairs Kathryn was crying, she rarely cried, "Michael, I can't take the pain anymore. It is too much. Can't they just put me down like they did George? You have to do something."

I was calm and patient, I replied, "I don't know what to do, except give you some more pain pills."

"Yes, please give me two more." Kathryn sounded like she was begging me for them. She rarely took two of them at a time, and certainly not so soon after taking her last dose. She just took two pills right before I went to bed.

"Are you sure that is okay?"

"Yes, I want two more."

I quickly got her a glass of water and her pills. I sat with her and held her in my arms, hoping she would get comfortable and fall asleep. She did not. She tossed and turned. I got up and began giving her an energy treatment. Still she was in too much pain after forty five minutes had passed. I hated to call Howard at such a late hour, but I did not know what else to do. Howard instructed me to keep giving her more pills, two at a time, until she was able to get to sleep. He did not specify an upper limit to the number of pills I gave her. At first that shocked me but then I figured she was more likely to die from the cancer than a drug overdose.

It took four more pills before she settled down to sleep. While we were waiting for them to take effect, we talked. Kathryn was amazingly clear for the number of pills she had taken. She apologized many times for making me go through this. I kept trying to get her to talk about the funny things that had happened in our life, "Do you remember the time

---

[1] At the time she made that comment I thought Kathryn was crazy. But now I understand; she did make a full recovery.

you used your house alarm to announce to the world that you had a new boyfriend?"

Kathryn laughed, "I was mortified, my mother, Molly, and all of my neighbors found out I had someone sleeping over. It had only been a few months since I left James. Do you remember how Molly thought you were after me for my money?" Even in her pain I could feel the warmth of her heart opening up to be with me.

Kathryn was not comfortable in her hospital bed so she asked me to help her move to her recliner. After she fell asleep, I went and got my pillow and a blanket, and stretched out on the sofa next to Kathryn's recliner to sleep. Less than an hour later I heard noises and I woke up to see Kathryn falling over her portable toilet. She knocked it over and all of the urine spilt onto the carpet. *Damn, I should have emptied it right after she went.* I got her back into her recliner and asked, "What are you doing? Why didn't you call me to help you?"

Kathryn did not reply. She fell asleep immediately. Within two minutes she was trying to get up again. I was still trying to clean up the mess she had made when I first I heard her talking. What she was saying was clear and made sense, but she wasn't talking to me. She mentioned names of people I never met but knew from stories of her past, and some names I did not know. She talked about the house, some other house not this one. She talked about laundry, cooking and ironing. She had verbal fights with some of these people and with others she was nice and loving. She would carry on a conversation for a few minutes and then stop. I wished the tape recorder was handy so that I could have recorded her and played it back for her later. I thought it would have been interesting to try and make sense of it when she became sensible again.

Kathryn tried many times to get up out of her recliner. I discovered that it was impossible for her to do so while it was reclined; she had to bring the chair into a normal sitting position before she could get out of it. So I stretched out on the sofa in such a way that I could prop my feet up under the foot rest of her recliner to prevent it from going down. I tried to get some sleep. Every time she tried to get up it woke me up and my foot prevented her recliner from moving so she was stuck. After a short bit of fighting she would fall back to sleep or into a conversation with someone who I could not see. She seemed oblivious of me and had no idea that I was keeping her put in her recliner.

This went on for many hours. Finally around five in the morning, her fighting ceased and she fell asleep. Over the last two days her vomit had been slowly changing, the smell became more fowl each time she spewed. Now it no longer resembled vomit, it was diarrhea that was coming out of her mouth. The tumors were completely obstructing her bowels. She had gotten it all over the front of her night gown. Earlier I tried to change her clothing but it was impossible due to the way she was carrying on. Once she settled down to sleep I did not want to wake her. A dirty sleeping Kathryn was better than a painful or deluded one. We had two hospice nurses coming over at ten AM. I was hoping that they would be able to help me. I was at my wits end. I only had to make it five more hours before help arrived.

Lucky for me Kathryn stayed asleep. I woke up at nine thirty; four hours of sleep did me a lot of good. All I could think was, *I hope this is all over soon. Kathryn you have to be nearly ready to leave your body. Please God, let's get this over with.* In the daylight Kathryn and the living room looked much worse. I decided I had about thirty minutes before the hospice people arrived so I would use that time to clean up the mess. I kept a watchful eye on Kathryn while I cleaned; thankfully she remained asleep.

I was not able to change Kathryn's gown before the hospice nurses arrived, but they cheerfully offered to do so. Kathryn woke up while the nurses were cleaning her up. After Kathryn said a few coherent things, I asked her, "Do you remember what happened last night?"

"I remember being in a lot of pain and staying up late. I also remember some very weird dreams that involved, Jerry and Phyllis and…lots of people that I have not seen in twenty years or more."

"It was more than dreams, you were trying to get up from the chair and waving your arms and legs about like you were crazy. You were talking too, carrying on complete conversations, they almost made sense to me but I did not hear the other side of the conversation that you were hearing."

Kathryn was becoming exhausted again, "Where are you taking me?" she asked the hospice nurses. After they explained to her about the facility Kathryn asked me, "Michael, are you coming? Please don't waste any time here, just come with me."

"Of course sweetheart, I will come with you." Then I asked the hospice nurses, "Do I have time to take a shower before you leave?"

"Yes, it will take us another fifteen or twenty minutes to get everything ready. Go ahead, do what you need to do we will wait for you."

I took a shower. Earlier they had told me I could take our dog Ali with us to the hospice, so I got some food for her and a change of clothes for myself. I followed the ambulance to the Kirkland hospice center. It was a nice place, kind of like a cross between a hospital and a hotel. The grounds were very beautiful with gardens and fountains and walking paths. The room was big and spacious with plenty of room for family to sit comfortably.

After I filled out some paperwork, I went to Kathryn's room. She was already in her bed sleeping...or so I thought. But after some time went by, and the nurses had taken her vital signs a few times, and still she did not wake up...we all realized that she was in a coma. I remembered how Kathryn asked me to come with her to the hospice and I thought, *Was that the last conversation I would have with Kathryn? Was that the last time I would hear her voice? Somehow I imagined this happening differently...I thought I could talk to her right up until the time she died."*

I had so much more to say to her. "Kathryn, if you can hear me squeeze my hand." I waited for a response...I got none. "I am hoping that you can hear me. Please, don't die while I am away. I want to be present with you when you go. Ali is here with me. I will call our friends and have them come by to see you. I will do that soon...but first I want to talk to you. Oh, I hope you can hear me."

I choked up with tears. After I caught my breath I continued, "Kathryn, I love you. You have been the best thing that has happened in my life. If I could go back in time to when I met you, knowing what I know today, would I meet you or run away? Yes, of course I would...I would fall in love with you all over again, I would insist that you come and live with me as we have already done. Who else would go though this with you like this? I would not want to trust this job to anyone else. It had to be done right. I love you too much, too much to leave any chance you would not have been cared for properly. I know I signed up for this. I know you appreciated what I have done for you.,.just like I appreciate what you have done for me. It is huge. I am a totally different person because of your love. You brought my heart out like no one else was able to do. You have been my best friend and fucking bitch too. Sometimes I hated you. But it was only because it felt like you took your love away; I needed it so badly. I have loved you since the first dance you attended with me. I am going to miss you terribly...but please go now. Please, don't suffer anymore. Just be finished."

Walking to shut the door for a little privacy...I was crying and I could hardly see or breathe. After quite some time passed I continued, "I am very sorry for the ways I hurt you. I am sorry for the lies I have told you. That was not because I did not love or respect you, it was because I did not love and respect myself enough. I was afraid. You did not deserve it. Still you loved me anyway. This piece of shit for a husband...at least that's how I felt at times. I wish I could have been perfect for you. But I did the best I could; you must have seen it because you kept me around."

"You were so lovely, beauty inside and out. So thoughtful, so appreciative of me...so kind and so loving. Everybody loves you...everyone...except for maybe a few...but they don't count...We are all going to miss you."

After a long pause I got up, kissed Kathryn on the cheek. I whispered in her ear, "Please wait for me to be here with you when you go." I got up and took a short walk in the garden. I cleaned up after Ali. I was so grateful for Ali's company and her perfect behavior.

When I went back to the room the nurse recommend that we take Kathryn off of her nutrition bag. We decided only to make her comfortable but not to do anything to sustain her life or resuscitate her if she passed away. Kathryn and I had talked about this and she wanted it this way too. That is when I told the nurse about Kathryn's living will which I brought with me; the nurse took it and made a copy of it for their records. Then I called everyone I could think of. I asked them to come and say their goodbyes to Kathryn. I did not call her family; on our last visit to Portland Kathryn had said her good-byes to them as if it was the last time she would see them. Throughout Saturday and Sunday, people came and spent time holding Kathryn's hand and talking to her. She remained in a coma.

Late in the day on Sunday, coincidently after the last of the expected visitors had come and gone, a nurse told me that Kathryn would go sometime that night. The nurse had experienced death plenty of times and could see the signs in Kathryn's pulse, blood pressure, breathing, and the whole feeling of it.

On Sunday, I had been talking to Kathryn and with visitors, taking walks with Ali, napping and just hanging out. It was getting late, about ten thirty at night, when I began getting tired. I asked a nurse to help me move Kathryn over in her bed. Then I shut the door and got into bed with her. I asked Kathryn once again, "Please don't go while I am sleeping...wake me up some how. I want to be with you when you go." Then I went to sleep, pretty much instantly like I usually do.

When I began to awake, I felt peaceful for a few moments; then suddenly I fell into a panic when I realized where I was and what was about to, or may have already, happened. I looked at Kathryn...*was she still breathing?...no...no...a long time passed...oh, there she goes.* She took a slow shallow breath; it fell out of her quickly and easily. There was a very long pause before the next breath...she took four more breaths like that. The pause between them got just a little longer each time. The last pause was a long one. Kathryn's last breath had a certain faintness, a certain punctuation to it. She died. I was still barely awake. Perhaps, just one minute ago, I was sound asleep. I woke up, Kathryn took her last five breaths, and then she was gone.

Farwell Dear Friend

It took a surprisingly short time for Kathryn's body to turn a pale white color. Even the lips were the same pale white color as the rest of the skin. I did not expect that. Her body looked dead, Kathryn had looked like a skeleton by that point anyway, but now her body looked dead. There was no mistake about it. I spent eight to ten minutes with her dead body in private before I called the nurse. I just watched, felt, and prayed. A very strange sense of freedom came over me all mixed up with incredible grief and happiness. I watched her body. At one point, with the way the head hung, the body looked like Jesus on the cross. I was sorry to see my friend go. I was happy to be at the top of this mountain. It was all down hill from here.

I called in the nurse. After they confirmed that Kathryn was dead they called the mortuary. I called my parents. I called Kathryn's twin sister; Bridget informed the rest of her family.

My mother and father came out to be with me and helped me through this. They also gave me the news that my mother's breast cancer had returned after eight years of remission.[1] It was difficult to take that news in at that time. I could only handle my own completion with Kathryn.

As I contemplated how I would get along without Kathryn and how I would honor her in my life, I decided that I would take on the attributes I most admired in her.

I admired the way she listened to people, the way she genuinely cared about them, and how she remembered the relevant things that were happening in their lives. I admired how other people looked up to Kathryn...she was someone that other people wanted to spend time with. I loved how Kathryn would laugh uncontrollably; I loved it when she was happy. I admired how she did what she had to do without bitching about how much work she had to do or how much pain she was in. I admired how Kathryn knew, and that she knew that she knew. I wanted to be remembered for these qualities when I died. I wanted to have as big an impact on others as Kathryn had on me. I wanted to continue where Kathryn left off, giving unconditional love to the world. This woman anchored a lot of light on this planet...now it was my turn to take her torch and carry it on.

We held two funerals for Kathryn; one on the following Saturday in Bellevue Washington, and the other in Portland Oregon. I organized

---

[1] My mother died eight months later in May of 1999.

the one in Bellevue and her family organized the one in Oregon. They were both well attended.

After the second funeral, I was out walking my dog, Ali. I had been talking with Kathryn out loud, and of course I was not hearing a reply. Then I said out loud, "I have talked with you every day, but two, for the last seven years. How will I go on without talking with you? I want to hear you...at least I want to know that you hear me. Give me a sign, a shooting star...give me something...anything that will let me know that you hear me."

I looked up in the sky, out into space, and right then a shooting star streaked across the night sky. The words *Thank you, Kathryn; I love you!* burst forth from my heart, and I began to cry.

Kathryn replied, "I love you Michael; I always will." [1]

---

[1] April 20, 2005—God, Spirit, Kathryn talks to me through music all of the time. As an example, while proofreading this page and the next one, I got very emotional and began to cry, this went on for about five minutes. After I settled down, I began editing this section. While doing so I was contemplating how my connection with Kathryn is still alive. At that moment, for the first time in probably thirty minutes I heard the words of the music that had been playing. I knew it was Kathryn talking to me, using the only voice available to her in that moment...this is what she said, "If anyone should ever write my life story, for whatever reason there might be, oh you'll be there between each line of pain and glory, cause you're the best thing that ever happened to me." The song is, "Best Thing That Ever Happened to Me" by Gladys Knight and the Pips.

The End

[1] *"One thing in life is certain—and that is that it is constantly changing. The cycle of death and rebirth in each season are reminders that nothing ever truly dies but is rather transformed into the next cycle of reality. And so for you to accept being "deathly afraid of change" is for you to accept death without accepting the magic of what is to come next. I do have compassion for your pain! But in only accepting fear of the unknown and hiding from change, you are only able to see a small fraction of the picture. Perhaps by allowing yourself to step past the fear of change into the knowledge that you are safe in each moment, it will allow you to relax and expand instead of contract in fear.*

"In 1991, I left a very dysfunctional 16-year marriage, left my home of 12 years, family, and friends because I knew somehow that anything would be better than what I was living. And so I moved out of the state and began again. It was the scariest thing I have ever done and the single most miraculous thing that I could have done for myself. I won't tell you that it was all a bed of roses or that it was easy. But it has been filled with miracles beyond my wildest dreams. And it was the best year of my life. And each year since just gets better! Until we close doors that no longer serve us, we can't open the new doors that are waiting for us.

"I wish you many blessings on whatever adventures you choose. An ending is also a beginning. God bless you."

― *Kathryn*

---

[1] We live in a multidimensional Universe indeed. Kathryn wrote this note to a woman named Michelle. I have no idea who Michelle was, but I know it was also written for me, and for you. I came across this in February of 2005, while going through all of the apprenticeship group transcripts, journals, and automatic writings to find material for this book and to help me remember how it all happened.

Michelle is the feminine form of the name Michael. And certainly as I am writing this book, and pouring though all of this emotionally evoking material, I am utilizing the more feminine side of my being. In my world, in my reality, Kathryn just sent this to me...through the dimensions, to the time and place where I would be the most receptive to receive it, to let me know she is still with me. She also wrote this for you dear reader. All is in divine order and all is well. ― Namaste.

Opportunities for Further Studies

We hope you enjoyed the story, but more than that we hope that you are motivated to further your own growth along a spiritual path. We have provided many resources on our website to help you towards that end. Please come have a visit and even sign up for our newsletter.

The types of things you will find on http://gr8Wisdom.com are:

- Announcements of speaking engagements and workshops.

- Adventure travel combined with spiritual learning opportunities. For example kayak camping trips in tropical locations combined with campfire chats and personal one-on-one time with Michael.

- Teleclasses – Group and individual classes offered over the telephone so as to provide learning opportunities even when we are physically in different locations.

- Books, audio programs, and video recommendations.

- Eco-friendly technologies. Dear friends, it is up to us to lead future generations into a sustainable future.

- Sign up for our email list and newsletter. Receive time sensitive updates on what we are up to as well as interesting stories that further exemplify how we can improve our lives with proper awareness and spiritual practices.

Is this book a collectors item? This first edition of Unforgettable will have a very limited printing. Perhaps that will make this version of this book rare and valuable at some time in the future. Once we have a few reviews from well known people a new version will be printed containing review highlights on the back cover. Anything you can do to help this book receive a review by such a person would be greatly appreciated.

Kind Regards,
Michael Skowronski

Please send email regarding Unforgettable to:
Unforgettable@gr8Wisdom.com   No SPAM Please!

ISBN 1412092736

9 781412 092739